The Life and Diaries of

Field-Marshal

Sir Henry Wilson

Volume I

The Life and Diaries of Field-Marshal Sir Henry Wilson

Volume I

By C.E. Callwell

with a Preface by

Marshal Foch

Legacy Books Press
Military Classics

Published by Legacy Books Press
RPO Princess, Box 21031
445 Princess Street
Kingston, Ontario, K7L 5P5
Canada

www.legacybookspress.com

This edition first published in 2021 by Legacy Books Press
1

ISBN: 978-1-927537-59-6

First published as *Field-Marshal Sir Henry Wilson Bart., G.C.B., D.S.O.: His Life and Diaries, Volume I,* by Cassell and Company, Ltd. in 1927.

Printed and bound in the United States of America and the United Kingdom.

This book is typeset in a Times New Roman 11-point font.

Table of Contents

Publisher's Note

The original edition published in 1927 contained a number of images, all of which were of heavily reduced quality in the material used to create this new edition. While all reasonable efforts have been made to replace these image with higher quality versions of the originals, this has not been possible throughout. As such, for one image a replacement of similar context have been substituted in its place.

Translations have also been provided for a number of French, German, and Latin phrases and passages.

Author's Note

Henry Wilson kept a diary from the time of his joining the army in the year 1885, but the volumes prior to the year 1893 are missing. Subsequently to that date they provide a complete record of the Field-Marshal's career, and they therefore form the foundation of this biography.

Up to the time of his taking up the appointment of Assistant Adjutant-General at the War Office in 1903, these records of his do not — expressing the matter in general terms — furnish many passages of such striking interest as to suggest their being freely quoted, with the exception of those that narrate events during the months when he was serving as brigade-major of an infantry brigade during the South African War. But although his daily jottings during the campaign of the Natal Army in 1899-1900 are of value from the historical point of view, very full accounts of those operations are already in existence, and their details, furthermore, are not readily followed without the use of large scale maps such as could not conveniently be included in a work of this kind. It is from 1903 onwards that Sir Henry's diaries begin to assume a very real importance from the military, from the political and from the historical points of view. Then, after he became Director of Military Operations at the War Office in the year 1910 he was constantly coming into contact with leading men of this and of other countries, he was continuously engaged on labours of significance and concern to the State, and he subsequently played a leading part in great events of a stirring time. Inasmuch as he, almost daily, recorded the substance of weighty conversations or noted what passed at Cabinet meetings, or jotted down the main points of what took place at memorable conferences, besides representing his own opinions as regards individuals of prominence and as regards subjects of moment, those habitual entries of his — often very voluminous entries — serve in reality for effective footnotes to the annals of the epoch. And so, all those chapters of this work which tell the tale of the last dozen years of his life consist largely, and indeed mainly, of quotations from his diaries.

Outspoken in conversation and outspoken by nature. Sir Henry was no less outspoken on paper — so much so that it has been found expedient to omit some passages, even though of undoubted interest, and that it has been thought desirable to exclude some of the forcible expressions concerning individuals which find a place in these records of his. He had contemplated compiling his memoirs himself so soon as he should find the requisite leisure for embarking on such a task, and he had looked forward to making a commencement in the autumn of the very year in which he was struck down by the assassin's hand. That, as he methodically filled in the events and experiences of each succeeding day during all the later years of his life, he had such an undertaking constantly in mind is made evident by the elaboration which distinguishes the numerous entries that are concerned with events of public consequence of which he makes mention. But, however important might be the matters touched upon during any particular twenty-four hours, the register of events and discussions always also includes references to subjects of purely personal interest. References of that kind, it must be understood, have been excluded in the case of many of the quotations that appear in the following pages; nor has it been thought appropriate or necessary to signalize their excision by means of asterisks.

Preface

By Marshal Foch

Sir Henry Wilson occupied highly important positions on the British Imperial General Staff and he played a prominent rôle in influencing the policy of the British Empire. Notably was this the case during the progress of the War in the year 1914, when the struggle was soon to extend itself over the seas and to become a world-wide one. Hence the story of his life possesses an enthralling interest.

Well aware of the growing ambitions of the German Empire, he had already at an early date come to recognize that France and England must unite their forces if they were to be in a position to make head against the fighting power which Germany could place in the field. He was dominated with this ideal when he first entered into an understanding with me. In the course of intimate relations, I experienced in him an amplitude of prevision and a breadth of view that were most impressive, coupled as they were with a patriotism that was ever alive and with an unbounded love for his country. To the end of his days he was to remain one of my dearest friends. His foresight had, ever since the year 1908, been bringing us closer and closer together. That foresight on his part was to help us to see clearly and it was to attach us one to the other. It was to serve as guide to him when deciding upon the measures that the British General Staff must take. I can affirm without the slightest exaggeration that it was entirely due to his prevision, to his convictions at once shrewd and consistently maintained as to what was required, to his tenacity in insisting that preparations for a possible conflict must be made, that the British Army was enabled to disembark rapidly in France in August, 1914, and to take part with effect in the campaign.

With a character so ardent, so honourable, so frank, and above all so disinterested, it was easy to work in perfect agreement, and, even if one did not always wholly share his views about certain matters of fact or opinion, one remained none the less full of regard and affection for the man himself.

When the War came, he realized more fully than anyone else how imperative was the need for an absolute understanding between the commanders of the Allied armies. It was only by a complete union between forces, which were strange to each other and which differed widely in their organization, that an undertaking so formidable as a conflict with Germany, with her millions of organized and trained men, fitted out with the most perfect appliances and controlled by a General Staff fully competent to carry out plans which had been thoroughly studied, could be effectually grappled with. In his capacity of intermediary between the Allied head-quarters, what activity, what devotion, what intelligence and what solicitude did Sir Henry Wilson not display to ensure co-operation in the combinations, and to overcome divergences of view on the part of associated chiefs, divergences which were often due to the mentality of individuals but which the conditions of field service were apt gravely to accentuate.

I personally shall never forget how, during the progress of the Battle of Flanders from the second fortnight of October, 1914, to the violent attack on Ypres during the first fortnight of November, during the course of those Franco-British-Belgian operations, during the course of those improvised defensive measures carried out in an awkward terrain with insufficient means, during those days when disaster might at any moment have arisen to our coalition, he came night after might at 10 o'clock from British G.H.Q. at St. Omer to my head-quarters at Cassel. It was at those meetings that we informed each other of what had been occurring, and that we agreed upon the dispositions which must be put in effect to meet events that might occur on the morrow.

The story of his life lays bare the extent of the difficulties, powers and methods of a parliamentary government such as exists in the British Empire, when plunged into war. It exposes the repercussions which such a system of government is apt to exert upon the choice of theatres of operations, upon the decision as to what is to be the main objective, and even upon the actual handling of the armies. It shows how difficult of solution become the problems that arise in the case of a coalition, and it illustrates the effect which changes of government may exert when a war lasts for years and when it spreads out over the seas and over continents. It shows, moreover, when after victory has been attained it becomes a question of preparing the basis of a lasting peace, of establishing what are to be the conditions of the pact and of imposing those conditions upon the enemy, what gangs of labourers and their foremen come upon the scene — agents who are for the most part new to the subjects which they are called upon to deal with.

Whatever happened, Sir Henry Wilson, in his handling of these diverse matters, always remained a man capable, be those matters never so varied and so important, of approaching them in practical fashion, without allowing himself to be led astray by dreams or by the allurements of visionary projects. Typical representative of great English patriots, he was ever inspired by traditions of the past, but he at the same time saw his way clearly and took full account of the requirements of the present day.

Chapter I – Early Years

The Wilsons of Currygrane — Henry Wilson's childhood and schooldays — Failures to pass for Woolwich and Sandhurst — Joins the Longford Militia — Joins the Rifle Brigade in India — Severely wounded in Burma — Invalided home — Service at home — Passes for the Staff College.

The Wilsons of Currygrane trace their ancestry back to a certain John Wilson, who landed in the suite of William III at Carrickfergus in the year 1690, and who, on being awarded by the King a grant of land at Rashee in County Antrim, settled down there, not many miles from Belfast Lough. John Wilson's great-grandson, Hugh, towards the close of the eighteenth century, founded a business firm of shipowners in the rising city of Belfast, an undertaking which proved highly successful, and he was, in consequence, placed in a position to hand on a handsome fortune to either of his two sons.. Of these, the elder, William Wilson, abandoning the shipping trade, laid out much of his acquired wealth in the judicious purchase of land, and he thus became possessor of extensive estates in the counties of Dublin, of Westmeath and of Longford.

These estates were divided up between his four sons, and the Longford property passed in due course to the youngest of these, James G. Wilson, who afterwards became D.L., and who married Constance Grace Martha, daughter of J. F. Hughes, of The Grove, Stillorgan in County Dublin. For many years after their marriage

Mr. and Mrs. James Wilson lived partly at Currygrane, near Edgeworthstown in County Longford, and partly at a small place called Frescati at Blackrock near Dublin. They had a family of four sons and three daughters. The eldest son, James Mackay, succeeded his father on the latter's death in the year 1907, and the second son, Henry Hughes, who was born on May 5, 1864, is the subject of this biography.

There is little of special interest to record in respect to the very early days of the future Field-Marshal. One feature in the' educatio nal processes that he underwent as a child is, however, deserving of record here, for it was to prove of great value, not only to himself, but also to his country, in years that still lay far ahead. This was that Mr. and Mrs. Wilson secured the services of a succession of French governesses for their children and that Henry and his elder brother. Jemmy, had learnt to speak their governess's tongue fluently while they were still quite little fellows. Henry was from the outset particularly fond of French, and he was to enjoy many opportunities in later life of perfecting himself in the language colloquially; but it was undoubtedly due to this very early nursery and schoolroom training that he came to be able to speak it — when he chose — almost like his mother tongue.

He went to Marlborough at Easter in 1877; but although his reports might speak well of his general conduct and might pay tribute to his abilities, they could not give him credit for application, nor did they convey the impression that he was ever to win a high place in the scholastic sense as a Marlburian. So that when, early in 1880, his father learnt that a considerable temporary increase was to occur in the number of vacancies at Woolwich, the powers that be decided that Henry must try to take advantage of this unexpected opening. He was, therefore, withdrawn from the great Wiltshire school at the age of sixteen, and was placed under tutors at home to be prepared for the coming test. But although a succession of instructors of unimpeachable credentials used to journey out from Dublin to Blackrock and strive to cram knowledge into the army candidate, the results proved disappointing. For, during the course of the years 1880, 1881 and 1882 he failed on two occasions to pass for Woolwich and on three occasions to pass for Sandhurst — the last occasion, in the summer of 1882, being his final chance.

The competition for entrance into Sandhurst was at this time very keen; but, even allowing for this, it is somewhat surprising that a youth, who was in later years to exhibit brain power and intellectual resources so much above the common, should have suffered reverses in what would not, in academic circles, have been adjudged a very crucial test. His discouraging succession of failures can only, indeed, be attributed to a lack of application, a lack of application of which there was to be no indication when, a few years later, he had made up his mind to win his way into the Staff College as a first step towards rising high in his chosen profession. He used often to laugh over these early educational mishaps of his, when the time came for him to hold prominent appointments in the army that were largely concerned with the supervision of military studies.

Balked in his endeavours to obtain a commission by passing through either Woolwich or Sandhurst, it was decided that he must attain his goal by way of what used in those days to be called the back-door, i.e. through the militia. That same November (1882) he passed the qualifying test which allowed of his presenting himself at a competitive examination for direct commission in the regulars when he had undergone two militia trainings, and in December he was gazetted a lieutenant in the Longford Militia (6th Battalion Rifle Brigade).

Mr. James Wilson had decided to place his son in the hands of crammers but, to start with, sent him out to spend a few weeks at Algiers for a first experience of foreign parts, and then, after a first training with the Longford Militia, dispatched him to Darmstadt, to study under a Colonel Wilson and at the same time to improve his knowledge of the German tongue. Henry became acquainted there, thanks to introductions, with the members of the reigning house, and he spent many hours that should have been devoted to study in playing lawn-tennis with the young princesses. The two elder. Princess Victoria, who afterwards married Prince Louis of Battenburg, and Princess Elizabeth, who afterwards married the Grand Duke Serge, were just grown up at this time, while Princess Irene, who afterwards married Prince Henry of Prussia, was somewhat younger. With Princess Alix, then still quite a little girl,

Henry, who all his life long had a particular affection for children, made great friends; when next he met her thirty-four years later, as will be recorded in Chapter XVII, she was Empress of All the Russias.

The young militiaman, however, only spent a couple of months at Darmstadt, and he then returned to work under crammers in England during the winter of 1883-4. He underwent a second militia training, this time with the 5th Royal Munster Fusiliers, early in the summer, so as to secure the necessary certificate to enable him to go up for the competitive examination for direct commission in July. He presented himself for examination in London in due course, and on October 16 his name appeared fifty-eighth on the list of successful candidates. Few, suffering under no disability in respect of birth or fortune, or education, from amongst that select band who have reached the highest grade in the British Army, can have experienced greater difficulties in getting into that army at all than did the future Commandant of the Staff College and Chief of the Imperial General Staff. He was in the first instance gazetted to the 18th Royal Irish. But it was arranged that he should be transferred to the Rifle Brigade; this was notified in a *Gazette* that was dated November 26, 1884, and he shortly afterwards learnt that he had been posted to the 1st Battalion which was, at this time, quartered at Belgaum in India.

The future Field-Marshal sailed for India on February 12, 1885, in the old Indian trooper, H.M.S. *Malabar*, and he arrived at Belgaum about six weeks later. Brigadier-General the Hon. Sir H. Yarde-Buller, with whom he was much associated on the staff in years to come, joined the 1st Battalion at the same time, and the pair went through their recruits' drill together. Two of his brother subalterns of 1885, both of whom were to come to the front in the future, were General Sir J. Cowans, nearly four years his senior, and General Sir W. Congreve, who joined from Sandhurst shortly after him.

A comparatively small station in the Bombay Presidency, situated to the south of Poona, Belgaum proved to be an excellent sporting centre, and Wilson, who was already a good horseman, soon became an adept at polo, a pastime of which he was a devotee in later years when circumstances admitted of it; he, moreover, found many opportunities for enjoying the rough shooting which India so generally provides, while in the meantime entering keenly into his military duties. He soon became a prime favourite with officers and men, and Major H.A.N. Fyers, one of his brother subalterns at this time, writes of him that "he was then a tall, gaunt youth, with very long, bony arms and legs, a merry eye, and a most delightful laugh that carried you with him." Yarde-Buller, Fyers, and others of the Rifle Brigade who were in the 1st Battalion in those days, all agree that he kept a diary from the date of his joining, if not before; but any diaries of his that may have existed previous to the year 1893 cannot be found.

A year after his joining, he went on an expedition after big game with his friend Yarde-Buller, who writes of their experiences:

> We obtained two months' leave in April, 1886, and we went off together into Mysore in hopes of getting some tiger. We were, however, unfortunate in respect to locating any of these, so we turned our attention to bison instead; and we both were fairly successful in tracking and killing some. Henry bagged five or six of them, and he also shot a bear. It was towards the end of our leave that one day, when he was tracking a bison, he suddenly came face to face with a tiger and a tigress. He got the tiger, and he told me, when he returned to our modest little camp, that he nearly got a right and left. Anyone who has been after a tiger in the Indian jungle will allow that killing them, on finding oneself confronted with them quite unexpectedly in such country, is a fine performance.
>
> I recollect that most of us in the 1st Battalion very speedily came to look upon him as a man of quite exceptional brain power. I, personally, having been quite alone with him for two months in the jungle of Mysore, realized early that, concealed behind a somewhat boisterous manner and an unusually sunny disposition, there lay an unbounded ambition. This, added to a rare quickness of perception and to his natural gift of Irish eloquence, convinced me even in those very early days that he was a man who was destined to make his mark in the world.

Shortly after their return to Belgaum from this sporting excursion, the regiment received orders to proceed to Burma, where the dacoits were giving serious trouble and where harassing guerrilla warfare had been in progress for several months. The position was that, although Sir H. Prendergast had in the preceding year moved up the Irrawaddy to Mandalay, had dethroned and deported King Thebaw, and had disposed of the Burmese army, the settlement of this huge region as a sequel had been hedged about with all manner of difficulties. Its extensive jungles soon became infested with robber bands, its topography was but little known, and its climate proved to be such as to try sorely British, and even native, soldiers, when these came to be conducting operations in the field within its confines. Sir George White was now in command, and the considerable forces acting under his orders were for the most part split up into exiguous nomadic columns. These columns were engaged in avoiding — and in sometimes failing to avoid — ambuscades, and in seeking out bands of fugitive dacoits scattered over a wide area of country, which was largely overgrown with scrub and patches of forest, was intersected by watercourses, and was often found to be almost impassable owing to the swampy character of the soil.

On reaching Lower Burma the 1st Rifle Brigade were conveyed in steamers up the Irrawaddy to some distance below Mandalay. Then, no sooner were they disembarked, than one of the first responsibilities to confront the battalion staff was the formation of a detachment of mounted inf antry. Ponies were procured, volunteers were called for from the rank-and-file, and Captain H. L. Rokeby was, to start with, placed in command, with Lieutenants Burnett Ramsay and Wilson as his subalterns. Rokeby was, however, obliged to give up command owing to sickness, and the little improvised unit was then worked as two distinct detachments under Ramsay and Wilson respectively. Wilson was in his element while struggling with such, often comical, adversities as only determination and an unfailing gaiety could effectually overcome. His long legs proved a great convenience to him in a service which consisted largely of scrambling off, and on to, the backs of the very small chargers which Burma produces. In a short space of time, therefore, his little detachment could fairly claim to rank as a going concern, and was on the war-path in the vicinity of Mimbu, engaged on rounding up individual dacoits and dacoits in parties, when their presence was detected or reported.

His troop had more than one lively brush with the freebooters, and in March, 1887, it was increased to a strength of fifty riflemen. Its young commander met with occasional personal adventures of a hectic kind. On one occasion, for instance, he picked up a huge basket and found a dacoit reposing under it, who incontinently bolted. Had his diary been available, stories of other thrilling experiences encountered by him in these unconventional guerrilla operations would, no doubt, have been found set down in his own expressive phraseology. This, his first taste of active service, was, however, brought to an abrupt conclusion by an episode which for him very nearly ended fatally.

The policy encouraged by those in authority was that officers in charge of detachments should endeavour to capture dacoits alive, if that should prove possible. Wilson and some of his riflemen had one day tracked a couple of these cutthroats down, had fairly cornered them, and the bearing of the two brigands left their intentions in doubt. He made his men stand back; unarmed but for a bamboo walking-stick he advanced to take the pair himself, and he was about to do so when one of them suddenly slashed at his head with a previously concealed dah. Wilson partially parried the blow with the stick; but he was hit just over the eye, and the consequence was that a very serious injury was inflicted.[*] He did not report himself as wounded at first,[†] but when he did and he was examined by the doctor, he was promptly sent down country. The eye itself most fortunately was not damaged; but several small bones behind it had been chipped or broken; the wound proved most painful and difficult to heal at the time, and it was frequently to cause Wilson grave discomfort in future years. It moreover created a slight disfigurement, and this he carried with

[*] He constantly carried this stick afterwards, when in uniform. It was broken by a bullet at the battle of Colenso, and he had it mended with a silver band; he is shown holding it under his arm in the picture of him in Field-Marshal's uniform which was exhibited at the Royal Academy in 1921, which is in Lady Wilson's possession.

[†] It is noteworthy that his name does not appear as wounded in the Digest of Services of the 1st Rifle Brigade, although this includes a long list of casualties incurred during the campaign.

him for the remainder of his life.

In view of the severity of the injury he was granted sick leave to Calcutta, where an operation was performed, and from there he proceeded to Darjeeling; but he suffered much from the wound and from its effect on his eye, so that eventually he was brought before a medical board and this recommended his being sent home on sick leave. He sailed from Bombay for England and arrived at the Wilsons' place, Frescati, near Dublin, on November 22, after an absence of nearly three years from England. He had been recommended for the newly created Distinguished Service Order, but he was not awarded it; and at a later date he received the Burma medal and clasp for his services at the front.

He spent practically the whole of the following year on sick leave in Ireland, staying for most part of the time either at Frescati or at Currygrane, and he suffered a good deal of pain and inconvenience from his wound. He was now a member of the Royal St. George Yacht Club at Kingstown, and during the summer he was often out sailing in his father's yacht the Saraband. He kept some polo ponies and played much tennis. The Fitzwilliam Square Lawn-tennis week had recently become a most important social and sporting gathering in Dublin; he and his brother Jemmy were notable figures at it, and Sir W. Orpen in his "Stories of Old Ireland and Myself" makes due mention of the pair going up to it from Blackrock:

> I remember well (he writes) how, when they appeared on the platform of the little railway station in the morning to take the train to Dublin, a sort of hush spread over a little crowd waiting to be taken to the city for their daily tasks. Such perfect figures, such perfect clothes, spats to wonder at, boots to dream of. Sir Henry always with a rain-coat thrown over one shoulder, always with his yellow gloved hands clasped behind him. Him we called "Rake-faced Wilson" and his brother "Droop-eyed Wilson." Yes. Truly they were different from the little crowd; it was as if the Assyrian Princes mentioned in Ezekiel had arrived amongst us from the unknown world far beyond our ken. What a joyful creature Sir Henry was! His laugh ever made one laugh, though no one had any idea what he was laughing at. We kept our proper distance in those days.

Wilson had become practically engaged to Miss Cecil Mary Wray, daughter of Mr. George C. G. Wray, of Ardnamona, in County Donegal, whom he had known for some years, and during this prolonged period of leisure he started studying for the Staff College. Being still a subaltern in a somewhat expensive regiment, with no prospect of promotion for five or six years to come, he was stimulated in his desire to reach the haven of Camberley by the knowledge that the marriage which he hoped for would to some extent depend on his succeeding in securing admission. All this time he remained on the books of the 1st Battalion of his regiment, and, on his passing a medical board as fit for duty early in 1889, he joined the Rifle Brigade depot at Winchester as a preliminary to his proceeding back to the East. He was, however, very anxious to remain in the United Kingdom; he could fairly put forward a claim to stay at home on the grounds of the serious wound that he had been suffering from and that he was to some extent still suffering from, and so it was arranged that he should join the 2nd Battalion at Woolwich. The battalion moved on to Dover early in the autumn, where it had to be split up, two of the companies, D and H, finding themselves quartered in Fort Burgoyne, above the Castle, whereas head-quarters and the other companies occupied South Front Barracks on the farther side of the town. Wilson was one of the subalterns of D company, Cowans being the other; H company had Fyers as one of its subalterns, who writes of this time:

> We spent, I remember, a very peaceful and pleasant time there. Both Henry and Cowans were working hard for the Staff College. Henry was also engaged to be married, and I remember his once saying to me in one of his earnest moods: "For me two things are certain. The first is that I am going to pass into the Staff College, and the second is that I am going to marry Cecil Wray." When he had made up his mind to obtain a given thing he was the most unyielding man I ever met. Jack Cowans passed for the Staff College that year and joined it at the beginning of

1890.*

Although Henry was working very hard, he always allowed himself to relax when he joined our little mess. His unbounded high spirits, his keen sense of humour and his invariable geniality made him the life and soul of the party. His sympathetic ways, coupled with his ever ready wit and his brilliant conversation, endowed him with a charm that acted like a tonic on his messmates. People who did not know him were perhaps disposed on first acquaintance to set him down as a wild Irishman of equally wild spirits. I remember, for instance, one day on the musketry ranges a staff officer coming to watch us, who presently drew me aside to ask, "Who is that officer standing over there, and what is his rank?" "That is Mr. Wilson," said I, "a subaltern like myself." The staff officer gazed at him with a puzzled countenance for a moment or two and then turned away with the remark, "He seems a very comic fellow." Henry gloated over it when I told him, and he used to refer to the incident years afterwards.

But those who came to know him well soon realized that, underneath all this superficial gaiety and cheery chaff lay a deep and enduring purpose. He was determined to rise in his profession and, full of ambition as he was, he in reality concentrated all ms energies to achieve that end. Work under the circumstances came natural to him. He was fitted out with a wide imagination, and he possessed a good deal of what I should call the dramatic sense. He thought in armies, army corps and divisions, and he was full of admiration for Napoleon and his marshals. It was delightful to listen when, with rugged eloquence, he told us the story of some Napoleonic masterpiece of soldiership.

The battalion moved to Aldershot to form part of a flying column during the drill season of 1890, but they returned to Dover in August to embark for Belfast, there to be stationed. It was at this time commanded by Colonel (now Major-General Sir L. V.) Swaine, who had been Military Secretary to Lord Wolseley during

---

* The fact of Cowans going up for the examination in 1890 prevented Wilson's doing so; as only one officer could be admitted from the same battalion they would have been competing against each other.

the campaign of Tel-el-Kebir and the Nile Expedition, and who in later years proved an influential friend to Wilson.

In anticipation of the Staff College examination which was to be held in the coming month of May, Wilson spent the winter following, hard at work; and it was while quartered in the great Ulster city that an incident occurred which he used to relate in after years with the utmost gusto. A telegraph boy came up to him one day when he happened to be in the barrack square, and handed him one of the familiar orange-coloured envelopes. It was addressed "The Ugliest Officer in the Army, Victoria Barracks, Belfast." On opening the envelope, Wilson found it to contain a humorous message to him from Cowans; and he always declared that the boy, furnished with that precocious intelligence which is so commonly displayed by the city-bred young, had at once on meeting him. realized that he must be the warrior for whom the missive was intended. The boy had no doubt accosted some other officer or officers, who had guessed that Wilson was meant and had directed the youth accordingly.

The result of the examination was published on August 1 when his name appeared as No. 15 on the list— the order of passing and the marks obtained used to be announced in those days.. There was consequently nothing to prevent his marriage with Miss Wray taking place, and the wedding was celebrated at Christ Church, Kingstown, on October 3, 1891.

Chapter II – From 1892 to 1897

Wilson at the Staff College — First meeting with Lord Roberts — Posted to India, but saved from going by a Medical Board — At Aldershot for four months — Joins the Intelligence Department — Stirring times in 1896 — Appointed Brigade-Major at Aldershot — Army Manœuvres of 1898 — The trouble in South Africa — Mobilization for war.

In view of the two years' course at the Staff College, the Wilsons had leased a small house. Grove End, at Bagshot, about two miles from Camberley. The period between the conclusion of their honeymoon and the reopening of the college towards the end of January had admitted of their making themselves very comfortable in this, their first joint home. A modest residence. Grove End none the less had much to recommend it to a newly-married pair of restricted means. The house, if relatively small, offered a considerable amount of accommodation, and it stood in its own grounds of four acres, of which about three-quarters of an acre formed the garden, while the rest made a paddock. He and Mrs. Wilson became very fond of the place, they did much to improve its amenities, and they were glad to occupy it again for considerable periods several years after their first tenancy had come to an end.

They slatted with an establishment of three Irish servants, who remained with them for a long time and the most engaging of whom undoubtedly was one, Brown, who assumed office as groom, but who also served as a handy-man and gardener and who could be classed as a typical representative of the Emerald Isle. Brown was, in his horticultural capacity, aided by Alfie, the garden boy, and Wilson from the outset took an absorbing interest in the garden; there were few days that he did not spend at least a short time grubbing in the ground and planting and planning, devoting particular care to the vegetable portion. He and Brown were often at work together at such times, and the pleasaunce would resound with Wilson's peals of laughter at his countryman's quaint sayings. But when he tried lectures on the art of war on Brown the effort proved a failure, for, after his expatiating at length on certain of Napoleon's more dramatic achievements — the Bridge of Lodi, the wonder-stroke of Austerlitz, and so forth — all that he could exact from his hearer was a grudging admission that "them English is a clever people."

Mrs. Wilson proved herself to be a masterly administrator, furnished with quite exceptional gifts for setting a newly-acquired house in order. She was to be provided with ample opportunities for displaying her talents in the latter direction during the years to come, for the Wilsons, after leaving Grove End, were constantly changing their -residences until the time came for them to occupy "Staff College House" (the Commandant's abode) at Camberley. The young couple were by no means well off; only by skilful management were they able to make both ends meet, and the shifts and expedients to which they were put from time to time are illustrated by one of their earliest experiences when settling down. Neighbours had hastened to call on the bride, and before they had been many days in residence the new-comers were invited to a dinner party at a big house, near by but far enough off to make the question of how to get there and back in gala attire a question of moment. They had been given a pony-cart as a wedding present, and Wilson owned a pony; but there was no harness, and there were no funds to spare for harness. Country roads in winter time make bad walking in satin shoes. A fly was procurable, but a fly costs money. So Mrs. Wilson embarked in the trap, with Wilson in the shafts and Brown pushing behind, and they reached their destination without mishap. But when the festivity was drawing to its dose and the guests were preparing to take their departure, a sensation was caused by the solemn butler attached to the hosts' establishment appearing at the door and announcing in sepulchral tones: "Mr. Wilson's carriage — but there's no 'orse!"

The Staff College was at this time under charge of Brigadier-General (afterwards Lieutenant-General Sir G F.) Clery, and both the number of students and the establishment of the staff were considerably smaller than they have since become. Wilson began his course at the end of January (1892), and, while a student, was particularly closely associated with Captain H. S. (afterwards General Lord) Rawlinson, Captain (afterwards Major-General) Hubert Hamilton, and Captain (now Lieutenant-General Sir T. D. O.) Snow.

The course of studies at Camberley was by no means of the practical nature in those days that it has since become under the superintendence of a succession of progressive commandants, aided by carefully selected assistants. There, nevertheless, was much that was new to be learnt with regard to many of the subjects included in the curriculum, and Wilson thoroughly enjoyed the work from the start. He used generally to cycle over to the College from Grove End, although cycling at that time was still looked at askance, so that the machine had to be concealed within the precincts of the institution as though it were something unclean — as indeed it often was. Fellow students of his declare that his quickness of thought and readiness of wit were speedily recognized, but that at most times it was hard to tell whether he was chaffing or not, that he seemed to be at least as much interested with his stable and his garden and his home as he was with his military work, and yet that, when any really difficult problem arose, he invariably grappled with it eagerly and effectually.

Certain rearrangements took place in the staff of the College at the end of the year 1892 — one of them a change of great importance, for it led to the introduction of Major G. F. R. Henderson in the capacity of Professor of Military History and Tactics (the staff were still called "professors") into the institution. These were subjects that particularly appealed to Wilson, and it became a great pleasure to him to sit at the feet of so brilliant a lecturer and so profound a thinker on military subjects as was the author of "Stonewall Jackson." At the end of March he proceeded with a party to visit the battlefields of 1870, and one of them relates that Wilson's baggage somehow went astray and that he therefore tramped these scenes of bloodshed in a singular tail-coat, of obvious Irish extraction and fashioned out of a material of a violent texture, his long figure decked out in this garment (with his hands always clasped behind him under the tails) exciting no little astonishment amongst the peasants as they tilled their fields. He went on alone from Sedan to Brussels to view the field of Waterloo, returning from there direct to Bagshot. "I have had the *most* wonderful weather and have been most interested in all I have seen," is entered in his diary.

A few weeks after his return from this excursion an incident occurred which was greatly to influence the course of his mili tary career in the future. Going over one afternoon from Bagshot to watch a cricket match at the College, he was introduced there to Lord Roberts, who had recently returned to the United Kingdom on the expiration of his term as Commander-in-Chief in India, and who was staying at Camberley with Rawlinson, formerly his A.D.C. Next day, Wilson went over to Rawlinson's house with his paper on a scheme that had been set the "Senior Division" dealing with the defence of India, and an opportunity thereupon occurred for him to show his effort to Lord Roberts, who was greatly impressed with its vision and ability. This proved to be the beginning of a friendship between the young Rifleman and the great Anglo-Indian soldier, which went on growing in intimacy and mutual admiration up to the death of the veteran Field-Marshal at St. Omer twenty years later.

"We burgled a burglar this morning," appears in Wilson's diary on June 20, "thanks to Cecil and Paddy" (Mrs. Wilson and the dog). But on the next occasion the housebreaker was more successful, for the entry appears under date June 25: "We were burgled again last night to the tune of 15 or 16 lb. of meat. Too bad. Rode into Chertsey to tell police." Local bumbledom, however, failed to cope effectually with the situation, and the culprit remained at large. The garden at Grove End was in the meantime becoming a model of its kind under the watchful guidance of its temporary possessor, seconded by the strenuous ministrations of Alfie and of Brown; but on the date of the

Wilsons' departure for the summer vacation the field of hay still remained uncut and its prospects were becoming in the highest degree unpromising, shortly after their arrival at Currygrane their anxiety was, however, relieved by a note from Brown which ran: "God Almighty and me and Alfie has saved the hay."

General Clery was succeeded by Brigadier-General (afterwards Lieutenant-General Sir H. T.) Hildyard in the summer; Wilson was to serve on the staff under Clery in Natal in a few years later, and he was to be associated with Hildyard at the War Office subsequently. He was now near his promotion to the rank of captain in the Rifle Brigade, and he was somewhat exercised during this autumn on the subject of which of the four battalions he would find himself promoted into. The Duke of Connaught, Colonel-in-Chief of the Rifle Brigade, took up the appointment of G.O.C. at Aldershot during October, making Bagshot Park to some extent his headquarters at first, and he interested himself in the matter of Wilson's immediate future. This, however, still remained in doubt when the course at the College came to an end; but on calling at the War Office two days later, Wilson learnt that he was to be promoted at once and would fall to India. "This is a terrible upset," he wrote; "went and saw Military Secretary, who is afraid nothing can be done."

"An uncertain and uncomfortable month for me," Wilson wrote of January, 1894, in his diary; "daily expecting promotion and daily fearing orders for India. A finale of a Medical Board on the last day who, although I was much afraid of the reverse, have given me four months' leave." The finding on the part of the doctors did not actually suggest leave, but it amounted to a recommendation that he should not proceed abroad for four months — which in practice secured him against going out during the current trooping season. The doctors' instruction furthermore ensured his joining at Aldershot for the period during the drill season that officers, after finishing at the Staff College, spent (if at home) attached to branches of the service other than their own.

In the meantime, not having yet been gazetted captain, he still belonged to the 2nd Battalion, now stationed in Dublin. It was at this time commanded by Colonel (now General Sir N.G.) Lyttelton, with whom Wilson was to be much associated on the staff later on.

On the *Gazette* promoting him, he was posted to the 1st Battalion at Peshawar; but he remained on in Dublin, pending joining at Aldershot in April. At the beginning of that month he went with Rawlinson for a tour on the Continent, proceeding in the first place to Metz. They cycled round the battlefields, saw a big parade,* were taken round barracks by a staff officer, and dined with the 4th Bavarian Regiment. They afterwards visited Rheims, Epemay, and Chalons. On returning home Wilson settled down at Grove End, going over daily from Bagshot to Aldershot, where he was in the first instance attached to the 61st Field Battery.

During the succeeding four months he played a good deal of polo, having bought three untrained ponies and being very successful in breaking them in to stick and ball. On polo days Mrs. Wilson used to drive one of the ponies from Bagshot, with Brown in the back seat towing another one, while Wilson himself rode the third, the caravan moving at a sedate pace so as to save the animals for the more serious encounter to come. He left the 61st Battery after two months, and became attached to the 4th Dragoon Guards; but for the rest of his four months at Aldershot he was generally galloping for some general. In the middle of July, he, however, contrived to spend a few days on the northern coast of France in company with Captain a'Court (afterwards Lieutenant-Colonel Repington, the well-known writer on military subjects) of his regiment, who was at this time a staff captain in the Intelligence Department. The French were holding combined naval and military exercises, and Wilson helped his brother Rifleman to prepare a report on these. That accomplished, he spent ten days attached to the staff of a flying column which roamed the country around Aldershot, and which occupied itself in fighting other forces sent out from the camp from day to day.

Before the four months at Aldershot had expired he effected an

---

* In a letter to his wife, Wilson wrote of this parade; "To-day we spent all the morning on the great parade-ground, watching a large force at work. The precision or movement and power of marching is wonderful, and I am most certainly of opinion that 20,000 of our men in their present state would be no match at all for 20,000 of these men. They can beat us, and beat us with ease, in anything and everything that goes to make up good soldiers."

exchange into the 2nd Battalion; but within a few weeks of it he was offered the chance of going to the Intelligence Department to work for four or five months, on the understanding that at the end of that time he would succeed a'Court, who was due then to become D.A.A.G. and head of the French Section. He consequently began work at Queen Anne's Gate, where the Intelligence Department was then located, in November. The Director of Military Intelligence at this time was Major-General (afterwards General Sir E.F.) Chapman, and the head of the French Section was Major J.S.S. Barker. The Wilsons lived in London for the first two or three months, but early in 1895 they took a house, Selwood Place, near Staines, where there was a garden, and where there, moreover, were fields where horses and ponies could be exercised, and where hay could be grown.

Wilson greatly liked his work at Queen Anne's Gate at first, even if he found the long hours indoors somewhat irksome. Nor did the journey up and down from Staines cause him much inconvenience; unexpected instructions from his chief indeed caused him more, for on January 7, 1895, he records with concern in his diary that "the General sprung on me the fact that he wants me to 'pass' in the March German Exam, for Interpretership." This entry is followed three days later by "the General still wants me to go up for the Interpretership. It's a great nuisance, though complimentary as apparently he wants to send me off to Berlin." In this pass he arranged for lessons from a certain Herr Piper, who was to "pound German into" him, and there are frequent references to "pounder Piper" in the daily record dealing with the next few weeks. He presented himself for examination at the end of March; but the examiners would appear to have been dissatisfied and "pounder" Piper to have pounded in vain, because his pupil's name does not appear in the Army Lists of the time, nor subsequently, as a qualified German interpreter. He became a staff captain on June 24, which increased his emoluments substantially if it also added to some extent to his responsibilities.

A few days before this he had been dispatched to Paris in connexion with certain activities on the part of the French in the Borgu region. While there, besides discussing with the Embassy staff the political problems that were involved, he had a meeting with Colonel Monteil, the intrepid French explorer. He shortly afterwards became concerned in a somewhat delicate question that had arisen between the British and the Belgian Governments over the Congo Free State. He went to Brussels to see our Minister there in connexion with the matter, and at the same time to visit Baron Dhanis, recently arrived home after conducting an expedition from the Congo towards the Nile, in the course of which he had arrested the murderers of Emin Pasha. He was naturally gratified at finding himself engaged to some extent in these international controversies, and he, moreover, at this time came to be in the closest possible touch with Colonel (now the Rt. Hon. Sir F.D.) Lugard, who had recently returned to England from negotiating treaties successfully with a number of local chieftains in the Borgu region on behalf of the Royal Niger Company.

The sub-divisions into which the Intelligence Department at Queen Anne's Gate was at this time split up — and the same thing holds good with reference to the branch of the General Staff at the War Office which performs analogous duties to-day — had, each of them, different foreign countries told off to them, and they worked to some extent in watertight compartments. The "French" Section, although its labours were largely, if not indeed mainly, concerned with obtaining, registering, and collating information with regard to France and the French possessions beyond the seas, had also to do with certain other states, and notably with a great part of Africa. This brought Wilson into contact with the Foreign Office, and one result of this contact was that he came to be a close observer of foreign policies and of the handling of foreign affairs, and to preserve that interest after he had quitted Queen Anne's Gate. He moreover became, as will be seen in later chapters, a not over-indulgent critic of our Foreign Office and its ways. France and the French had always, even when he was still a child, attracted him; and the fact that he was particularly concerned with them during his period of service in the Intelligence Department undoubtedly strengthened that instinctive sympathy.

An event which aroused much attention in the army and in the country occurred a few days after Wilson's return from his mission to Belgium. The Duke of Cambridge on the last day of October resigned the position that he had occupied so long as Commander-in-Chief, and Lord Wolseley assumed that position in his stead — although with abridged powers. Wilson wrote in his diary:

> At four o'clock, all the H.Q. Staff assembled in the Military Secretary's room, and the old Duke of Cambridge came in and bid us good-bye. The poor old man broke down. He has been soldiering for 58 years and has been Commander-in-Chief for nearly 40.

The Duke's distinguished successor would appear to have lost no time in getting to work as titular head of the army, for on November 8 we find the following entry in Wilson's diary:

> Very busy day, and unsatisfactory, as the C. in C. asked about French high explosives, and Barker has gone away and I cannot find his "Gun" file.

Certain events that occurred immediately after this beyond the seas were to keep General Chapman's staff on the tiptoe of expectation and hard at work for several weeks to come. In the first place, an unpleasant dilemma arose in connexion with Venezuela. The rulers of that republic had for some months past been haggling with our Foreign Office over a section of the boundary between its territories and British Guiana. The United States now unexpectedly intervened and, invoking the Monroe Doctrine, President Cleveland sent a strongly worded message to Congress on one of the last days of 1895, based on the assumption that this boundary squabble was a question to which the doctrine applied. There was a panic on Wall Street. There were lurid head-lines in the Press on both sides of the Atlantic. But most people in this country, and Wilson among them, refused to take the matter very seriously, the more so as sober opinion in America looked askance at the President's somewhat aggressive action. The situation righted itself within a few days.

A mote serious difficulty arose when the Jameson Raid was followed by the German Emperor's famous message to President Kruger; but, although from that time forward the Intelligence Department always had the possibility of a conflict with the Boers in view, and collected much useful information concerning the supposititious theatre of war (information which the military authorities failed to make use of when the crisis came), the trouble for the moment blew over.

Then came the disaster to the Italian forces at Adowa, with its inconvenient repercussion on the Sudan; and in the situation that thereupon arose, Wilson's section at Queen Anne's Gate was particularly concerned. For the Dervishes at once threatened Kassala, which was then in Italian hands, and H.M. Government decided upon sanctioning operations on the Nile from about Wady Haifa — the Anglo-Egyptian outposts extended but little north of the Second Cataract at this time — by way of affording some assistance to Italy in her distress. "The last week has been very interesting to us on account of the Italians and Abyssinia," appears in Wilson's diary on March 7, 1896. And again, "Wolseley sent for me about Abyssinia," on the nth. Next day he wrote, "The Cabinet sat this morning and have determined to go to Dongola, which certainly ought to relieve Dervish pressure on Kassala, but is really almost too much, I think, unless they are ready with a programme for Khartum." "Busy about Egypt," appears in the diary on the 1 6th; "I think this proposed move to Dongola a mistake, but if that is cut down to a parade movement on Akasheh it will be of no use at all to the Italians." On the 20th he complains, "I am mightily disgusted at the way things are going in Egypt. My propositions for a short advance to Akasheh from Wady Haifa, with advances to Kokreb and Langeb from Suakin, are only being partially carried out." "Things both in Egypt and South Africa look very queer," he wrote on the 30th, "and I think the Government have botched the Egyptian business, with probable result of a big Expedition." On the following day he observes that "Egypt continues to give trouble, and Kitchener has done a foolish thing in weakening Suakin too much." (Troops were, as a matter of fact, promptly dispatched from India to replace the Egyptian units which Sir H. Kitchener had withdrawn from the Red Sea littoral for service up the Nile.) Wilson, in common with most British offices of that time (not excluding Lord Wolseley) was indisposed to trust the Egyptian army, having failed to realize what strides these troops had made during the past few years towards achieving genuine fighting efficiency.

Sir J. Ardagh succeeded General Chapman as Director of

Military Intelligence on April 1 of this year. He had taken part in earlier campaigns in the Nile Valley and was well acquainted with Egyptian conditions, conditions to which Wilson makes scarcely any references in his diary during the following few months. During those months, Kitchener advanced up the Nile with a force composed almost exclusively of units of the Egyptian army; he brought his campaign to a brilliant conclusion by the capture of Dongola on September 23, and from the time that the victorious advance up the Nile had commenced, some of the Dervish pressure which had caused the Italians such anxiety in the Kassala region had been drawn off. Wilson makes no reference to the Dongola campaign in his diary; but this omission may have been due to his having been somewhat seriously ill during the early summer and, in consequence, being a good deal absent from the office. He had, however, by the end of July recovered sufficiently to take part in some manœuvres on a small scale that took place at the beginning of August around Aldershot, in which he acted as D.A.A.G. to a division under command of General Kelly-Kenny.

It so happened that one of those frequently recurring differences of opinion between the Sublime Porte and the rest of Europe went near to creating an explosion in the month of October. Wilson's view of the imbroglio as expressed in his diary is particularly worth quoting, for it well illustrates his bent, even at this early stage of his career, for taking the long view in connexion with international problems of such a kind:

> Ardagh (he wrote) is drawing up a memo about our action with regard to Turkey, and he suggests each nation sending 2 ships of war off Constantinople. I think that this begs the question, as it presupposes unanimity amongst the Powers — the very element that is lacking. It seems to me that the only possible change that can be made will be made by England, Russia and France joining together "for this occasion only." I would throw open the Dardanelles to Russia and invite France to occupy Syria, on the understanding of our having a free hand in Egypt. Nothing is more certain to my mind than that the policy of trying to bottle up great nations is ridiculous, whereas the policy of encouraging all legitimate colonization should be our greatest safety.

The possibility of a serious struggle for the mastery in South Africa was all this time in the minds of military men. Wilson mentions in his diary having Lord Roberts to lunch with him on April 23, 1897, so as to meet a fellow staff officer of Wilson's in the Intelligence Department, Lieutenant-Colonel H. P. Northcote.* Northcote had recently returned from a visit to the Cape, whither he had been sent to collect information about a number of matters, and it would appear from the diary that Lord Roberts and the two staff officers had a particularly interesting discussion with regard to the situation in the sub-Continent and the military possibilities which this might bring to pass.

Wilson's time at Queen Anne's Gate was, however, now drawing to a close, for he was offered the brigade-majorship of the 3rd Brigade at Aldershot, falling vacant on September 1, which he accepted with pleasure. But, before the date came for him to take up his new duties, he had enjoyed the satisfaction of riding in the Queen's great procession through London to St. Paul's on the occasion of her Diamond Jubilee. He acted as D.A.A.G. of the second of the six sections into which the troops taking part in the procession were divided up, the route covering a total distance of six miles and the imposing cortege stretching four. "There was not a single hitch in the proceedings, and the whole thing went off magnificently," was his gratified verdict, and he shortly afterwards received the Jubilee Medal for his services. Of this award he observes philosophically in his diary:

> I am well pleased, tho' medals other than war medals are not to my fancy. Still, if they are going, I may as well have them as anybody else, and the occasion was historic.

A brigade-majorship at Aldershot was at this time justly looked upon as providing almost certain openings for good things to come on the staff of the army, and Wilson had every reason to be pleased at being selected for one of these coveted posts after having already enjoyed valuable experience on the staff of the War Office.

---

* He was killed at the combat on the Moddet River in 1899.

His brigade, the 3rd, moreover, was (Quartered in the North Camp, and was therefore somewhat isolated from the rest of the troops stationed in the great Hampshire cantonment, a circumstance which was generally held to be no disadvantage; it was under charge of Major-General W. O. Barnard. The brigade-major's house proved to be comfortable, and there was a garden for Wilson to interest himself in. The move thither from Selwood Place, after the painters had done their work, was rendered memorable by the variety of the live stock that shared in the pilgrimage, and Wilson always claimed to have been the first officer to join the staff at Aldershot with a cow and a calf.

The recovery of the Sudan from the Dervishes, for which the reoccupation of the Dongola Province in 1896 had laid the foundation, made considerable progress during this year. It was well known at home that an advance on Khartum was likely to take place in 1898, and on the last day of the year Wilson wrote in his diary: "Perhaps this day year I may be on active service in Egypt." His friend Sir Henry Rawlinson (Rawlinson had succeeded to his father's baronetcy in 1895), on giving up a brigade-major ship at Aldershot just at this time, promptly betook himself to the Nile on the chance of finding employment out there. "Bad luck to Rawly," was Wilson's comment, "he has the price of a ticket to Egypt." The entry appears on January 3, 1898, that he "drove to Farnham furniture hunting, and on the way called in on Snowball" (his fellow-student at the Staff College, Major Snow, who was brigade-major of the 1st Brigade). "As I walked into his office, his clerk came in also and brought him a wire ordering him to Egypt." Throughout the early months of the year he entertained hopes that he might somehow find his way out to the theatre of war, and these hopes rose to a high pitch when he learnt, towards the end of May, that Colonel Lyttelton was going out from the War Office to command a second British brigade that was being sent up the Nile. But the hopes were doomed to disappointment.

Very important manœuvres had been arranged to take place about Salisbury in the closing days of August, the Duke of Connaught ' commanding one force. Sir R. Buller commanding the other force, and Lord Wolseley acting as Director-in-Chief. The Duke's army consisted of three divisions, and Wilson acted as brigade-major of the 3rd Brigade, which was included in the 2nd Division. It did more marching than fighting during the exercises, and on September 7 he recorded in his diary:

> Reveille 3.30 a.m. The *longest, hottest, and most trying day of manœuvres*, commencing with a concentration in thick fog. I led the Division, and hit the place to 100 yards. An attack across the Avon. An awkward ford to cross. The Division was fairly done to a turn to-night.

Next day there was a great review on Beacon Hill, and that night Wilson entrained seven battalions between 8 p.m. and i a.m., and admits that he lay down very tired. "I am glad the manœuvres are over; I was badly fed and am short of sleep," he wrote in his diary on getting back to Aldershot; and the following entry appears in the same record on October 8:

> I was an actor in a very sad piece to-day. The Division paraded on Queen's Parade and marched past the Duke and Duchess and Princesses Daisy and Patsy. The latter three in tears. After parade the Duke shook hands with the C.O.s and Staffs. The bands took up position along the Farnborough Road and the cavalry, and at 12.30 p.m. the Duke and Duchess and Princesses Daisy and Patsy drove slowly down the line. I had the Brigade out to cheer at Cock Adwhir Wood. Very sad. All the four in the carriage were crying. They are an immense loss to us.

His Royal Highness was succeeded by Sir Redvers Buller. The Battle of Omdurman had been fought just as the Salisbury manœuvres were being brought to a close, and in the middle of November a large "Honours" *Gazette* was published, which put a number of Wilson's contemporaries well ahead of him in the army. This, to a man of ambition such as he was, could not fail to be trying, even if some of those advanced were his intimate friends.

The brigade marched over to Barossa Common near Camberley at the beginning of June, 1899, and remained in camp there for ten days engaged on brigade training. After dark one evening the troops were indulging in night operations, and an officer who was a student at the Staff College at the time, and who had proceeded after dinner to the scene of action to see what was to be seen, relates that when the affray was at its hottest, General

Barnard, who was short of stature, but of stocky build, contrived to tumble into a bog, in which he floundered almost waist-deep until hauled on to *terra firma* by his long-legged brigade-major. The whole countryside rang with Wilson's, stentorian laughter at his chiefs misadventure; but the victim of the contretemps was quite unable to see the joke. "We have had a pleasant to days under canvas without a drop of rain. General Barnard's last camp," summed up this outing in the brigade-major's diary.

From early in this year the prospects of a conflict in South Africa had been growing steadily. But a somewhat strained situation, as between the home Government and Mr. Kruger, had existed so long without matters coming to a head, mat soldiers in general were disinclined to anticipate that an appeal to arms was really at hand. Wilson in his diary mentions going up one morning to the War Office to try to find out what was in progress, and he wrote on his return:

> They are working away, cutting and drying a scheme for an Army Corps and a Cavalry Division for Kruger, and although I don't think the expedition will come off, undoubtedly things are shaky.

It had in the meantime been arranged that General Lyttelton was to succeed General Barnard, and Wilson was glad to learn that his old friend and brother-officer, Yarde-Buller, was to be the new A.D.C. The names of several officers who had been selected for special service in South Africa were announced a day or two later, and it came to be generally understood that, if an expeditionary force were to be dispatched to the Cape, the bulk of the staff and of the troops stationed at Aldershot would be included in the order of battle.

General Lyttelton arrived to take up command of the 3rd' Brigade on September 1, and for the first few days he stayed with the Wilsons at the brigade-major's house. Burglars were noticed about its precincts two days later, but a sentry who took a shot at them unfortunately missed the target. "Wonderful accounts in to-day's D.T. and Standard of our burglary last night," Wilson noted in the diary; "they said we were giving a dinner-party at which the Duke of Connaught was present and a large display of silver." But graver events were impending. All through September the tidings with regard to the dispute between the Cabinet and the Transvaal were growing more and more ominous, and by the end of the month orders with regard to placing the troops on war footing were being expected almost hourly. These arrived on October 7 and were to the effect that mobilization was to commence on the 9th and was to be completed by the 17th. The existing 3rd Brigade at Aldershot was to become the 4th, or "Light" Brigade, of the Expeditionary Force, and was to form part of the 2nd Division under General Clery; it was composed of the 2nd Royal Fusiliers, the 2nd Royal Scots Fusiliers, and the 1st Durham Light Infantry.

Mobilization of the brigade proceeded smoothly during the ensuing week, as the reservists poured in and the transport cadres filled up with horses. Orders were received on the 17th to the effect that the 4th Brigade staff would sail from Portsmouth on the 24th in the s.s. *Cephalonia,* that vessel also taking the Durham Light Infantry on board. And so, on the morning of the appointed day. General Lyttelton took his departure from the camp, accompanied by Wilson and Yarde-Buller, en route for the port of embarkation.

Chapter III – The South African War

Arrival in Natal — Spion Kop — Vaalkranz — The Relief of Ladysmith — Advance into the Transvaal — Wilson joins Army Headquarters at Pretoria — Return home with Lord Roberts.

Sailing from Portsmouth on the evening of October 24, 1899, the transport arrived at Cape Town on November 18. There orders were received for it to proceed on to Natal, where the situation had become somewhat critical, and the Cephalonia arrived off Durban on the evening of the 22nd and entered the harbour next morning. General Buffer's original plan of campaign had been that the Army Corps and the Cavalry Division should operate from Cape Colony against the Orange River Colony; the Indian contingent, together with the troops already in Natal before its arrival, was to secure that colony against serious invasion, Sir George White having gone out from England to take up the command. The 2nd Division under General Clery (of which the Light Brigade formed a part) was to have disembarked at Port Elizabeth, but everything had been thrown out of gear by the occurrences in Natal. In spite of discomfitures suffered at the start at Talana Hill and at Elandslaagte, the Boers had defeated Sir G. White in front of Ladysmith, had surrounded him there, and had penetrated southwards almost to Pietermaritzburg. This had led to General Clery, commanding the 2nd Division, being sent on to Natal to take charge of the forces in that colony outside of Ladysmith; and now General Lyttelton with his brigade, as well as other brigades, were being transferred to the same theatre of operations. The Army Corps as organized on mobilization had been broken up, and practically half of it had been diverted to Natal.

Another transport with the two remaining battalions of the 4th Brigade, the Royal Fusiliers and the Royal Scots Fusiliers on board, arrived in Durban harbour on the same day as the *Cephalonia*. The Boers who had advanced south of the Tugela were by this time trekking north, aware that large British reinforcements were assembling with the evident intention of moving to the relief of Ladysmith, so that the troops destined for this undertaking were enabled to push forward towards the Tugela practically unopposed. General Buller arrived on the 25th, to find that the situation had much improved and that the force under General Clery was free to concentrate for its effort to succour Sir G. White. A 5th Division, under General Warren, had been mobilized at home and was on the way out. The breaking up of the original Army Corps organization had not only carried with it the disruption of the original divisional organization, but had also led to a certain rearranging of battalions within some of the infantry brigades. The Light Brigade indeed came to be almost entirely reconstituted; to the Durhams were added the 1st Scottish Rifles, the 3rd King's Royal Rifle Corps, and the 1st Rifle Brigade (the battalion which Wilson had joined at Belgaum fifteen years before); Captain Cecil Wilson, Henry's younger brother, was adjutant of the K.R.R.C. The brigade, as reconstituted, arrived at Frere on December 8 and found the bulk of the relieving army already assembled.*

During the next day or two the force gradually moved forward to Chieveley, and on the 14th General Clery, who was still nominally in command, issued orders for forcing the passage of the river on the following morning. The Boers were known to be entrenched on the farther side of the formidable obstacle; but the exact position of most of the defence works, as also the strength of

---

* A sketch map illustrating the campaign on the Tugela will be found on page 47.

the enemy, remained in doubt. The plan contemplated a frontal attack by Hildyard's brigade at Colenso and a corresponding frontal attack by General Hart's brigade farther up stream to the left, while Lyttelton's brigade was to be in a position to support either of those in front line, with Barton's brigade on its right. The story of the disastrous fight of December 15 is a familiar one, but it may be retold in Wilson's words as recorded in his diary:

> We struck camp 2.30 a.m. and moved 4.30 a.m. At 5 a.m. the force was in position. A lovely cool morning which turned into a blazing day in the Tugela Valley. The Naval guns opened at 5.35 a.m. Hart moved for the drift at 5.45 a.m. At 6.15 enemy first opened on Hunt's batteries, knocking 10 guns out at once. Then opened on Hart who began retiring at 7. 1 5. We advanced with R.B. and D.L.I., and covered retirement from 7.40 to 12 noon. Hildyard attacked Colenso about 9 to 10 o'c. and fell back at 11.30. At 12 o'c. all rifle fire was over. Heavy guns went on till 4 o'c. A bad day's work, almost 1,000 casualties, of which 600 on our flank and 400 on right flank, and 10 guns. We fell back and camped at 3 p.m. on same ground as we had left at 4 a.m.

He wrote in a letter to his wife:

> We never got near the river, and although I was under fire for 5 hours, and sometimes brisk fire, I can only swear to having seen 5 Boers. It's quite marvellous. I doubt our having killed 100. More likely 50. And they remain complete masters of that side of the stream, and I don't see myself how we are going to cross it to get to Ladysmith.

On the following night part of the force moved back from about Chieveley to Frere, and General Buller arrived during the day; Wilson from him learnt that the 5th Division under General Warren had been ordered to Natal. It may be mentioned here that on the news of Colenso reaching home, following as it did on tidings of serious reverses at Magersfontein and at Stormberg, a 6th Division was mobilized. A pause of several days ensued in Natal, although Wilson made a reconnaissance with a troop of the Royals towards Springfield on the 21st. "Sir Redvers came up at tea-time and had a long talk," appears in the diary. "He told us that

Bobs had started to take over the Cape Command. Wonderful. This makes Sir Redvers C. in C. of Natal only." Two days later Wilson mentions having laid a plan before Colonel (now Lieutenant-General the Hon. Sir F.) Stopford (acting as Chief of the Staff) for seizing Potgieter's Drift, many miles above Colenso up the Tugela, with all the cavalry together with the Light Brigade carried on wagons. This project was seriously considered by Sir Redvers, who discussed it with Lyttelton and Wilson but who, after weighing the pros and cons, rejected it as too risky. He decided instead on a deliberate advance in force on Potgieter's Drift, and on casting the bulk of the Natal Army loose from the railway in so doing.

This movement began on January 10, 1900, most of the force proceeding some eight miles to Pretorius's Farm, although Lord Dundonald with his mounted brigade pushed on to Spearman's — heights short of, and overlooking the drift. On the following day, the Light Brigade was sent on ahead with some guns as a support to Dundonald, and it reached Spearman's early on the morning of the 12th. The mounted troops had in the meantime secured possession of the ferry-pont at the drift, the river being in flood. "From the top of this hill one has a magnificent view of the other side of the Tugela," appears in Wilson's diary of that day; "saw Boers working hard at entrenchments. They have a fine position, with one rather weak point in the centre." The enemy had been apprised of the British plan by the spectacle of the vast columns of troops and transport wending their way to Pretorius's Farm, and was already partially dug in when the Light Brigade reached Spearman's. The range of heights beyond the river extends from where there is a wide gap about ten miles west of Potgieter's, to another gap about four miles east of that drift, a gap which afterwards became the scene of the Vaalkrantz operations. The culminating point of the range is the Spion Kop hill, situated to the left front of Spearman's and Potgieter's Drift, and some hundreds of feet higher than the rest of the line of heights.

In view of the enemy's preparations. General Buller decided to move the bulk of his army farther to the left under Sir C. Warren, while the Light Brigade, with some mounted troops and artillery, was to remain at Spearman's under Lyttelton, with Wilson as staff officer. But progress was so deliberate that it was not till the 17th that Warren crossed the Tugela at Trichardt's Drift (about four miles from Potgieter's) and that the operations which terminated in the disaster of Spion Kop may be said to have begun. Lyttelton had, however, pushed two of the battalions and a howitzer battery across the river at Potgieter's on the previous evening to occupy aline of low kopjes within a loop made by the stream, and he had thus created a bridge-head. During the next few days this containing force strove to occupy the enemy's attention and to keep the Boers dispersed, while the main army away to the left was developing its attack upon that part of the range that lies to the east of Spion Kop.

On the evening of the 23rd Lyttelton learnt from Sir Redvers that Warren intended delivering a strong attack that night. The objective -was, as it turned out, Spion Kop, and it so happened that during the early hours of the morning of the 24th a thick fog shrouded the whole of that dominating eminence. When the fog lifted, however, about 8.30 a.m., Lyttelton and his staff at once detected considerable numbers of men in khaki crowning the summit of the mountain, whence, moreover, there came the sound of heavy firing. About an hour later a message came in from Warren asking for assistance to be given to these troops, and Lyttelton promptly set the Scottish Rifles and some of Béthune's M.I. in motion to comply with this request. He furthermore ordered the K.R.R.C. forward to take possession of a pair of lower peaks of the range, situated about a mile to the east of Spion Kop and (from the enemy's point of view) lying to that mountain's left rear. Realizing how important the possession of these twin peaks might be as a support to the troops on Spion Kop, Wilson was anxious to change the route of the Scottish Rifles and to send them to help the K.R.R.C.; but his proposal to that effect was not accepted. The K.R.R.C. nevertheless captured the twin peaks, and their presence there proved for a time of great value to the troops massed on the exposed summit of Spion Kop, who were under converging artillery fire, were losing heavily, and were hard put to it to beat off the determined attacks of ever-increasing bodies of Boer riflemen. But, as the day wore on. General Buller sent a message to Lyttelton taking strong exception to the detachment of the K.R.R.C., and the battalion was recalled late in the afternoon. Wilson wrote afterwards:

> Sir Redvers never approved of the attack made by the King's Royal Rifles. The position gained by the battalion would have been invaluable had the true bearing of its position on the left rear of the Boers on Spion Kop been realized by him at the time, and this has been abundantly proved since by Boer evidence.

During the night that followed there occurred the strange incident of both sides retreating from the scene of a desperate local struggle, of the swarm of officers and men belonging to many British units abandoning the very precarious hold that they had managed to maintain on part of Spion Kop since the morning, and of the Boers virtually taking to flight from the hill-top which was partially in their grip. But, on a few bolder spirits on the enemy's side discovering that their antagonists had retired, they promptly reoccupied the summit, and by doing so they rendered the discomfiture of General Warren's forces complete; these were withdrawn to the right bank of the Tugela during the succeeding three days, and on the 27th Wilson wrote tersely in his diary: "We stand where we did ten days ago, with a licking thrown in."

Buller now decided to make a fresh cast in this region, in spite of the handicap from which his forces were suffering as a consequence of their distance from the railhead. Having signally failed in the effort to turn — or to roll up — the right of the Boer defences laid out along the range of hills beyond the Tugela, he now adventured a stroke through the gap of Vaalkranz to which reference has already been made, and in this third essay of his to break through the enemy front the Light Brigade was chosen to play an especially prominent part.

The name Vaalkranz actually applied to a low, but well defined, spur that jutted out at the extreme western end of the range of hills beyond the river which Buller's forces had been more or less facing for the past ten days. The spur commanded the gap in a measure from its own side; but on the other side there rose lofty scrub-clad heights, known by the name Doomkop, which dominated it a good deal more effectually than did the Vaalkranz spur. The few days immediately following Warren's withdrawal across Trichardt's Drift had been occupied in quietly transferring the bulk of the troops from left to right, and on February 3 Buller assembled the divisional and brigade commanders and staff officers, and expounded to them the fresh plan of operations which he had devised. This was that the Light Brigade, supported by the fire of part of the artillery, was to cross the Tugela and to assail the Vaalkranz spur, with the 2nd Division and the nth Brigade in reserve ready to assist. In the meantime the 10th Brigade, which was acting as a containing force about Spearman's and Potgieter's Drift, and was holding the kopjes beyond that drift, was to make a demonstration with a large force of field artillery, so as to mystify the Boers and to deceive them as to the real point of attack. After demonstrating, the batteries would withdraw across the Tugela and move round nearer to Vaalkranz in support of the Light Brigade. "This being the only connected, thought-out plan we have tried," Wilson wrote in his diary that day, "may succeed."

"It's a hard nut to crack," he wrote on the 4th, "but not impossible, I think. I never heard the men so cheery as tonight. They are singing in masses." The combat opened soon after daylight on the following morning and at first all went well. By 11 a.m. a pontoon bridge had been thrown below the Vaalkranz spur, and the demonstration from about Potgieter's Drift was in full swing. By 4.30 p.m. the Light Brigade had captured the Vaalkranz spur, the demonstration at Potgieter's was at an end, and the batteries had been withdrawn across the stream and were taking their part in the real attack. But as the Light Brigade found the captured spur a very unpleasant place and a target for scattered Boer guns, it did not seem very clear to the staff of the brigade what was to happen now, and Wilson wrote in his diary next day:

> We had a very disagreeable night. At 5.30 a.m. the Boers opened a very sharp fire, which was practically kept up till 7 p.m. when darkness stopped it. At 4 p.m. they had a try at our extreme left flank, but were driven back after about 10 minutes. Hildyard relieved us at 9 p.m., our men having been under fire for 33 hours. Our loss was 16 officers and 253 killed and wounded. We were glad to get back, and Buller gave us each a horn of champagne, than which I never drank anything I liked so much.

While the Light Brigade had been clinging to their exposed position on the afternoon and evening of the 5th, the remainder of the force (other than the artillery) had been looking on. No attempt had been made to broaden the front of attack by thrusting other brigades across the river, so that by early on the 6th it was perfectly obvious that the venture had failed. Hildyard's Brigade (2nd) remained on Vaalkranz all day, and then Sir Redvers, realizing that no other course was possible, ordered a general retirement. This took place during the following night, and Wilson was now disposed to take a very pessimistic view of the situation, for he wrote in his diary:

> Poor Sir R.B., it must be bitter work for him, and they won't like it at home, but Buller is right. I am certain in my own mind that if we pushed on here we would probably have to lay down our arms. It's quite impossible |with 15,000 men to turn 8, 10, or 12,000 out of lines and lines of entrenchments. We should have at least 50,000.

Only some 3,000 out of the 15,000 men on the British side had, however, after all, been utilized during this abortive operation. Restricted efforts such as the capture of Spion Kop and V aalkranz simply played into the hands of a mobile enemy such as were the burgher forces, and, as the undertaking of February 5 was carried out, there never was the remotest prospect of its succeeding. The bulk of the troops who had been engaged in the campaign on the upper Tugela retired to Springfield on the 8th, and during a day's halt there General Lyttelton temporarily took over command of the 2nd Division in the room of General Clery, placed on the sick list. "It's a dreadful upset to me," Wilson wrote of this in his diary, "as I lose N. G. and have no idea who comes in his place. Altogether I am very lonesome this evening." It was arranged that Colonel Norcott of the Rifle Brigade should assume command of the Light Brigade in Lyttelton's place, and he retained control of it for some time.

Wilson wrote in a letter to his wife, from Chieveley, on the 12th:

> It's exactly two months to-morrow since we came here before, and in those two months we have lost heavily, fought heavily,

marched heavily, and are no nearer Ladysmith. And through no fault of the troops. But our entire failure is due to two causes. The first is that we have just a quarter of the proper number of troops, and the other is bad generalship. Not that Napoleon could have got through without more troops, but our losses have been much greater than they ought to have been owing to bad generalship, and this on the part of several generals, It is admitted by everyone that N. G. has done better than any other general, and I am not a little proud of this, as in some ways I may have helped him.

Sir Neville Lyttelton writes:

I did not really get to know Wilson until I went to Aldershot in September, 1899, to take over command of the North Camp brigade, of which he was brigade-major. My house was being repaired, so he put me up en garden, in his quarters for nearly a month, and, of course, that brought us into quite close contact. I soon realized what a capable staff officer he was in peace time, and the high opinion I formed of him at Aldershot was more than borne out in the much more trying experiences in the field in South Africa. I think that the most remarkable trait in his character was his unfailing cheerfulness in the arduous conditions that prevailed during the campaign in Natal. Nothing affected his spirits. He had a joke for everybody and everything, but he was far from being merely a *farceur*.* He was equally good at his duties in the camp and in the field. In fact "the little green tent on the hill," as my brigade headquarters were called, was almost the only cheerful spot in that gloomy seat of war.

When the unexpected return of General Clery from sick leave after the relief of Ladysmith deprived me of the command of the 2nd Division, I became G.O.C. 4th Division. I then tried hard to get Wilson transferred to me as A.A.G., but Buller thought he was too junior for the post; and so we parted and I saw no more of him in South Africa. Perhaps the most conspicuous service that he rendered in the field was the suggestion to me to send reinforcements to assist Thorneycroft in the very critical condition he was in on the right of Warren's line on Spion Kop. Warren himself told me that this had averted a second Majuba. Of course, the responsibility for this action was mine, but it was Wilson who first suggested it.

---

* "Prankster."

When Bullet's forces returned to the railway it was known that the situation at Ladysmith was growing critical, that there was much sickness, and that the garrison was already on very short rations and would before long run out of food. In the circumstances. Sir Redvers at once set a fresh plan of operations in motion. The Tugela immediately below Colenso makes a big loop northwards and the enemy was holding what roughly might be called the chord of this loop, their right resting on Hlangwane and their left on the Cingolo Mountain. But when the army moved out of Chieveley the actual line occupied by the burgher forces was imperfectly known, the ground to be traversed was partly overgrown with trees and scrub, the troops had to feel their way forwards before they gained full contact with the opposing array, and Wilson was by no means sanguine at the outset. Progress was indeed so slow at first that there was some justification for depression, for the five infantry brigades after four days only succeeded in advancing to some low heights about seven miles from Chieveley. But on the 17th the front was greatly extended and, pivoting on the left, the whole line was wheeled forward 45 degrees with the 2nd Division on the outer flank; four out of the five brigades were engaged, and Cingolo was captured. This success prepared for a much greater triumph on the morrow, for the troops were that night face to face with the real Boer position along a line of kopjes, of which the highest point was known as Monte Cristo, on which commanding height rested the enemy's extreme left. This position was attacked by the and Division and the 6th Brigade on the 18th, and the whole of it was captured with little loss. The enemy fled in disarray, several laagers were taken, and a certain amount of war material together with large supplies of food-stuffs fell into the victors' hands. "A real good day's work," Wilson wrote that evening exultantly, "and N.G. was much cheered. Dutch are on the run and we did damage."

The immediate result of this Monte Cristo success was that those Boers who remained on the right bank of the Tugela were at once placed in considerable danger. Their left had been completely turned, and if the British were now to advance rapidly it might well become difficult for the enemy to withdraw their transport, their impedimenta, and possibly even t heir guns, across the swollen river by the one ramshackle bridge that was available. But the British did not advance rapidly, and on the 19th the defeated burghers were allowed to retreat virtually unmolested, definitely abandoning their hold on the right bank of the Tugela below Colenso. Wilson wrote in his diary:

> To-day was practically wasted; there is no doubt the Dutch were on the run and we should have followed hot foot. These delays are miserable and lead to great loss of life, as the enemy can collect again and dig.

What he had foreseen came to pass. The enemy, given time to recover from the shock of Monte Cristo, dug hard on the farther side of the Tugela and set up formidable defences on lines of heights that had not previously been touched.

If the loop formed by the Tugela below Colenso formed from the British point of view a salient, the river about and above Colenso formed a loop which necessarily from the British point of view constituted a re-entrant. This re-entrant, moreover, consisted largely of low ground which was overlooked from Hlangwane and the salient out of which the troops had driven the enemy by their operations since marching out of Chieveley. Sir Redvers unfortunately decided to cross the river by a bridge to be thrown below Hlangwane, and the 2nd and 5th Divisions on the 21st descended from the high ground within the salient which they had cleared, into the low ground where they found themselves dominated by kopjes in the enemy's hands. These would have to be cleared before any advance could take place. There followed two most unsatisfactory days of confused fighting, in which little progress was made and in which heavy losses were incurred, and Wilson in his diary gives a vivid account of the trying experiences which his brigade underwent during these forty-eight hours. Much disorder occurred, and control was none too well maintained by those in high places. By the evening of the 24th it had become manifest that a mistake had been made, and steps were accordingly taken to repair the blunder. So the 6th and the nth Brigades, with most of the artillery, moved back on the following day into the commanding salient which they had quitted four days earlier. The

THE SOUTH AFRICAN WAR

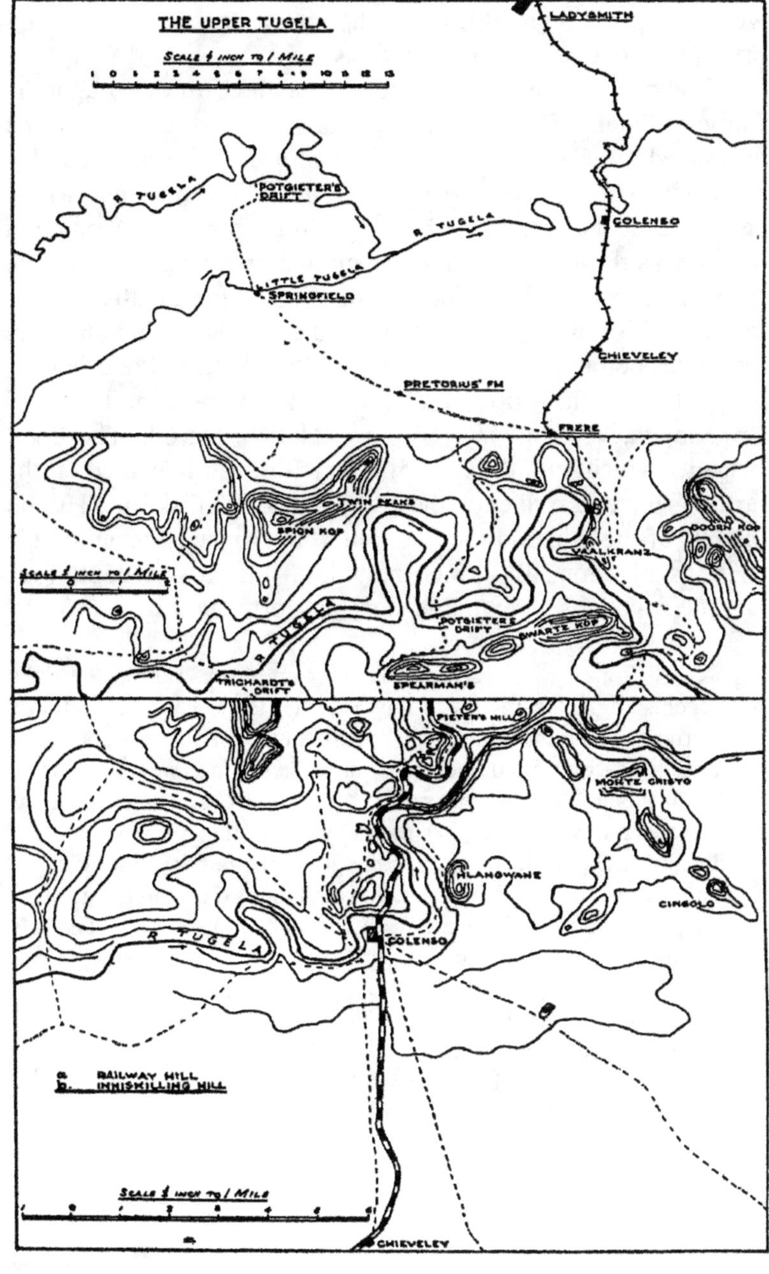

rest of Bullet's army remained where it was on the farther bank of the Tugela, and so his troops were astride the river on the 26th and were occupying a broad front, with most of their guns on ground offering them commanding positions.

That day was a day of preparation. On the 27th was fought the Battle of Pieter's Hill, which effectually decided the issue of the protracted Tugela campaign, for, as had been the case on the day of Monte Cristo, the troops attacked on a wide front which permitted of their numbers being given proper play. A pontoon bridge was thrown across the Tugela within a long reach of the river running in a deep ravine, and of this the 6th and nth Brigades made use. The 6th Brigade then moved down the ravine for about two miles before they deployed to the left to attack Pieter's Hill, which formed the extreme left of the Boer position. The 11th Brigade attacked Railway Hill on the left of the 6th. The Light Brigade (which with the 2nd, 5th, and 10th had remained on the farther bank of the river on the 25th) attacked Inniskilling Hill on the left of the nth, and the 2nd and 10th Brigades occupied the enemy's attention still farther to the left. Wilson's account of his brigade's work as given in his diary, is worth quoting:

> At 7 a.m. we received orders for an attack. Barton the right, Kitchener* in the middle, Light Bde. (R.B., D.L.I., half S.R., E. Surrey) against Inniskilling Hill. At 10 a.m. brisk fire was opened on both sides, some of our men being hit in the camp as we were forming up. Just before this Warren read a wire from Bobs saying Cronje had surrendered with all his men at 1.30 this morning. Our men cheered lustily. At 3 p.m. Kitchener having got to the railway cutting, Billy† and I were sitting with Warren, and the latter said we might go as far as the railway and wait there till Kitchener crowned his hill. The R.B. on the left and the S.R. on the right, being absolutely ready, moved off at once to the railway. It was dose on 5 o'c. before we moved on again and took Inniskiliing Hill. About 5.45, owing to repeated shouts for assistance from Railway Hill, confirmed, on a query of mine, by a flag from that hill, I sent across 4 coys, of E. Surrey and half S.R.

* Colonel W. Kitchener now commanded the 11th Brigade.

† Colonel Norcott.

> It turned out that these men were not wanted at all, and they returned to Inniskiliing Hill. At 8 p.m. with considerable difficulty, the night being pitch dark, I got half S.R. to relieve the R.B. on the point of the hill and got out rough outposts. At 8 p.m. the Boers ceased firing quite suddenly and the night was perfectly quiet.

Some of the mounted troops rode into Ladysmith on the following evening, and on March 1 Wilson accompanied his brigadier into the town which had been defended with such determination. That night he wrote in his diary:

> The relief is an accomplished fact. It all seems so curious. I was struck by how well most of the men looked. Rawly told me they could have held out for another month. It appears that they were practically not under rifle fire, and only under big gun fire which did little damage. They had considerable sickness, death rate last month 300. It's grand. London will go wild. Heavy rain to-night. Staff tents up. It's difficult to realize that Ladysmith is saved.

A long pause ensued after the relief of Ladysmith had been effected. The Light Brigade moved on to Sunday's River with the remainder of the 2nd Division, and it settled down under canvas on a plain at a short distance from that stream and on the near side of it. General Lyttelton remained in charge of the 2nd Division for the first few days, but General Clery then rejoined from the sick list, and Lyttelton was thereupon given command of a newly formed division, the 4th. Wilson was in hopes that he would accompany Lyttelton in the capacity either of A.A.G. or of D.A.A.G.; but to this arrangement Buller would not consent, and he therefore remained on at Sunday's River as brigade-major of the Light Brigade, now commanded by Brigadier-General C. D. Cooper. An unforeseen and disconcerting display of activity on the part of the Boers occurred on April 10, and of what took place Wilson gives the following pithy account in his diary for the day:

> I was just writing a letter at 7.25 a.m., when I heard a shell pass my tent. Then another, and another, and three pretty quick. The Boers had taken up a position on the other side of the river and were shelling us heartily. We struck camp, and we moved at midnight. An

> uncomfortable and tiresome day. We answered their shelling with 4.7 inch and 12-pdrs. The Durhams had three men wounded.

A month later the Natal Army moved north. Advancing on May 7, the 2nd Division arrived at Dundee on the 15th; it reached Newcastle three days later, and Wilson mentions in his diary that the troops got a great welcome from the townspeople when they tramped in in the evening, "Some of them, poor things, in crying delight." The Light Brigade pushed on again next day with the mounted troops as far as the Ingogo battle-field of 1881. This advanced force then halted for several days, to permit of supplies being brought up and while the rest of the Natal Army moved up to the front. The Boers had been busy fortifying Laing's Neck, and the hills on either side of that pass, and they had several long range guns in commanding positions. Buller was therefore confronted with the problem of how to force his way over the Drakensberg range, which forms a horse-shoe round the northern apex of Natal, and he decided to divide his army. The 2nd Division was told off to occupy the enemy's attention in front of Laing's Neck, while the 5th Division moved to the left to turn Laing's Neck on its western side. In anticipation of these dispositions the Light Brigade moved forward from the Ingogo to Mount Prospect immediately below Laing's Neck on May 28, reinforcing Lord Dundonald's mounted troops already there; and a day or two later Wilson enjoyed an interesting experience, owing to Buller having written to General Christian Botha (who was in command of the Boers on Laing's Neck) proposing a meeting. Wilson's story as told in the diary of June 2 reads as follows:

> The Boers sent in a flag of truce at 8.20 a.m. This was taken on to Gen. Clery at Ingogo. At 10 a.m. orders came to commence bombardment at noon. At 10.30 came orders postponing bombardment. At 11 a.m. orders came to say that the flag letter was to say that Gen. Christian Botha would meet General Buller halfway between outposts at noon. Buller left Newcastle quarter to 11 (20 miles), so I went out with a flag and Rennie* and an orderly 13th

* General Cooper's A.D.C.

Hussars and met Botha, 7 other Boers and 2 Kafirs, all, like us, unarmed.

Botha (a nice looking man about my age, who spoke English) that Buller would not be out till about 2 o'c. He elected to retire about 300 yards and wait. I retired about same distance and dismounted, keeping the orderly, and sending Rennie back to tell Buller I was out at the foot of the Neck. There we sat, Botha and his men, and I and my orderly for 2½ hours. It was a curious thing, this projected meeting of Buller and Botha, at the foot of Laing's Neck, right under Majuba and on English soil. I fear that Buller may get into trouble about this. At 2.10 p.m. Buller arrived, and I met him, riding at the head of the Boers, whom I had asked to ride forward to meet the general. Buller and Botha shook hands, then we all dismounted. The conference began. Buller told Botha the game was up, Roberts in Johannesburg, a large column coming up to Vrede, N.G. at Vryheid, and Delagoa Bay closed at last. Botha agreed that Boers were in a bad way. Buller suggested Boers going back to their farms with their rifles, but leaving guns here. Botha said he had no power, but would submit to his government. Armistice till Wednesday agreed upon. Meeting broke up 2.50 p.m. when each party returned to respective sides. It was very interesting and I was glad to have been out and present.

These unauthorized negotiations came to nothing, and two days later Sir Redvers started the operation by which the 5th Division, with the cavalry and artillery, after some fighting effectually turned Laing's Neck, by the west. The 2nd Division occupied it unopposed on the 12th and then led the advance into the Transvaal, and on to Standerton, which place was occupied on the 22nd. Then the Light Brigade, together with some mounted troops and artillery, moved on towards Heidelberg, which had already been secured by troops of the main army coming from Johannesburg, and it established connexion with these. "So, at last, the Natal Army and the Cape Army meet," Wilson wrote in his diary that night; "how long it has taken and how much it has all cost in lives and money!"

The Boers had, however, in the meantime been showing a good deal of most unwelcome activity about the line — so much so, that head-quarters and the bulk of the Light Brigade wandered about the country during the following days, seeing a few Boers from time to time and wearing out the transport, and Wilson's comments in his diary during the progress of this indeterminate pilgrimage were of a decidedly critical character. The following passages, for instance, are to be found on different days in its pages:

> What Buller can be thinking of, sending 2½ battalions fooling round with 400 cavalry it's impossible to imagine.
>
> We halted to-day to fill up our Supply Column to 7 days, and are off again to-morrow on another fool's errand. It annoys me beyond measure the way Buller sends the Bde. about, instead of using the 4,000 cavalry which he keeps in the mountains of Natal.
>
> This escorting a huge convoy of 200 bullock wagons round the country and being sniped all day is the most infernally idiotic thing that ever was done. It will prolong the war for months.

Head-quarters and part of the brigade, however, eventually moved off again in the direction of Heidelberg, and they finally marched into that place on July 27 and settled down for the time being. While halted there, Wilson paid a visit to Pretoria, and during a stay of three days he met all the head-quarters staff. He returned to Heidelberg, but was not destined to remain much longer with his brigade, for official orders came to hand on August 13 for him to join the headquarters staff, and he proceeded to Pretoria at once. On arrival he found himself called upon to take up the duties of D.A.Q.M.G., and while in Pretoria he lived in a house of which the other occupants were Major-General Sir W. (afterwards Field-Marshal Lord) Nicholson, Lord Stanley (now Lord Derby), and Rawlinson; Wilson saw a great deal of Nicholson during the ensuing weeks and they became close friends in consequence.

Lord Roberts, accompanied by some of the head-quarters staff, now proceeded eastwards to take personal charge of the important operations that were about to take place, and on August 27 he inflicted a severe defeat upon General Botha at Bergendal; the victory was followed up by the pursuit of some of the vanquished burgher commandos into the Lydenburg country, and of the rest of them in the direction of Komati Poort. It had become generally known that the Field-Marshal would very shortly be proceeding home to succeed Lord Wolseley as Commander-in-Chief, and it was also understood that he meant to take with him several members of his present head-quarters staff to aid him in the coming task in Pall Mall — Sir W. Nicholson, Lord Stanley and Rawlinson, among others.

Wilson learnt a few days after Lord Roberts's return from the front at the end of September, that he was to succeed (afterwards General Sir B.) Duff as the Chief's assistant military secretary. This meant that he would accompany the Field-Marshal to England, and that his arrival at home would moreover, almost certainly be followed by a period of some months' service in the War Office. Owing to the nature of its duties, he at once became closely associated with Lord Roberts, seeing the Chief and his family — Lady Roberts and the two daughters were in Pretoria — daily.

Considerable doubt, however, still prevailed as to when the Field-Marshal would actually start on his homeward journey. Incidents were occurring in various parts of the far-flung theatre of war which seemed to suggest that the struggle was not so nearly at its end as had been somewhat prematurely concluded. The home Government had not yet decided who was to assume command in South Africa on the Field-Marshal's departure, Lord Kitchener having been designated as Commander-in-Chief in India. But nobody at that stage foresaw that the contest was to last another year and a half, nor that numbers of comparatively junior officers were about to find rare opportunities for exercising independent commands in the field. Only when it became evident towards the end of October that the Boers were by no means done with, was it decided that Lord Kitchener was to remain on in the country in military control.

Just at the time when arrangements had at last been concluded for Lord Roberts to carry out a contemplated journey to Natal *en route* for home, the plans were thrown out of gear by the illness and death of Prince Christian Victor (who was one of the Chief's A.D.C.s), and then by Miss Aileen Roberts (now Lady Roberts) becoming indisposed. The party for England left Pretoria for Johannesburg on the 30th, but on arrival there Miss Aileen was pronounced by the doctors to be also suffering from enteric; all the plans were upset, and the Field-Marshal and his party were detained at Johannesburg for the whole of November. Wilson was busily engaged during this wait in connexion with the drawing up of lists of honours and rewards, a task in which he now acted as assistant to General Ian Hamilton, who was going home with Lord Roberts to become his military secretary in Pall Mall.

He had originally been brought up to Pretoria merely to act as *locum tenens** of an officer temporarily absent on special duty — had, in fact, to use the expression common in military circles, been given a "temporary job." The job had, however, spun itself out; it had become a long job, and the Commander-in-Chief's daughters used to chaff him about his protracted stay, and they came at last to call him "Long Job" — a sobriquet which, in view of his bent for applying nicknames to others, he accepted in a proper spirit. So it came about that not only the young ladies, but also some of the members of. Lord Roberts's personal staff, like Sir I. Hamilton and Rawlinson, acquired the habit of addressing him as "Long Job," and they continued to do so in later years.

Yet fresh temporary postponement was brought about after Miss Aileen had become convalescent owing to the Chief meeting with an accident while out riding; his horse fell with him, and he was much bruised and shaken. It was, however, at last definitely determined that they should leave Johannesburg for Natal on the 29th and embark at Durban, Lady Roberts and Miss Aileen starting at a later date direct by train for Cape Town and joining the remainder there. The party proceeded to Ladysmith, with stoppages at Dundee and at Elandslaagte. They visited Colenso and the scenes of fighting that had culminated at Pieter's Hill, they went round the Ladysmith defences, and they rode out to Spion Kop and Spearman's, Wilson on this last day acting as cicerone. On their arrival at Pietermaritzburg on December 4, there was a public reception, with speeches; on the following evening the party sailed from Durban on board the s.s. *Canada* of the Dominion Line, and on the 8th they reached Cape Town, where huge crowds were assembled in the streets to see and to greet the Field-Marshal with enthusiasm as he drove with his staff to Government House. There

* "Lieutenant."

followed a two days' stay, largely devoted to ceremonial observances, and then, on the evening of the 11th, the *Canada* steamed out of the harbour and out of Table Bay to the accompaniment of thundering salutes from the warships and of hearty cheers from the crews of the numerous ships lying in and off the port.

Lord Roberts and Sir A. Milner with some staff officers

Wilson had written more than once to the Duke of Connaught during the previous months, and shortly before leaving for Cape Town he had received a letter from His Royal Highness, the bulk of which can appropriately be quoted here:

> I am delighted to hear that you have got on to the Hd. Qr. Staff at Pretoria, which must be most interesting for you, and a complete change to your brigade-major's work in Sir Redvers Bullet's force. The poor Light Brigade will have been disgusted to have been put on the line of communications, but this work is a very important one and I am sure they will show how it ought to be carried out.
>
> I had hoped that, before now, I might have congratulated you on the end of the war, but, notwithstanding the flight of old Kruger, Steyn, Botha, and De Wet seem determined to carry on guerrilla

> warfare, which can do them no good and means the wasting of many lives and the laying waste of much country. I fear that harsh and drastic measures will have to be employed to put a stop to this sniping and these traps. I was much interested with what you wrote concerning your opinions of the lessons to be learnt from the war; we have always been bad at reconnaissance work, it has never been properly taught nor sufficiently insisted upon. I think the too highly civilized and cramped country at home has something to say to this, but more might have been done and must be done in future.

"The last day of the year and of the century," as Wilson wrote in his diary, found Lord Roberts and his staff on board the s.s. *Canada* in half a gale and a heavy sea, and they brought up off Cowes during the forenoon of January 2, 1901. Lord Roberts, with his military secretary and Lord Stanley, at once landed and proceeded to Osborne, where the Field-Marshal received the Garter from the Queen. On returning on board, much affected by the interview with his aged sovereign, he told his staff — so Wilson records in his diary — that Her Majesty was looking very old and that she appeared frail and tired. It had already been given out that he was to be advanced to an earldom in recognition of his great services. He was greeted at Paddington by the Prince and Princess of Wales, the Duke and Duchess of York, the Duke of Connaught, and a swarm of prominent people, and from the station the Field-Marshal ana his staff drove through excited and demonstrative crowds to Buckingham Palace. Wilson's second experience of active service in face of the enemy was thus brought to a close in a very blaze of triumph, after an absence from his native land of some fourteen months.

Chapter IV – From 1901 to 1906

At the War Office— Command of the 9th Provisional Battalion — Back at the War Office — The War Office Reconstitution Committee— The genesis of the General Staff— Lord Roberts and Wilson— The efforts of Wilson to establish the principle of an efficient General Staff— His success in the end — Appointed Commandant of the Staff College.

Safe home again, Wilson was obliged at once to settle down at the War Office to a continuance of the labours that he had been engaged on at Johannesburg and on board ship. Queen Victoria died three weeks after his return to England, and on February 2 he rode as one of the staff in the funeral procession during its progress from Victoria Station to Paddington. Lord Roberts's dispatches appeared in the Gazette a week later, and after their publication Wilson had to concentrate attention on the preparation of the long lists of honours and rewards to be granted for the first phase of the South African contest. He was present at an investiture held by King Edward at St. James's Palace on June 3, when he was handed the D.S.O., and on the 12th he received his South Africa medal and clasps from His Majesty's hands on the Horse Guards Parade. The five clasps that he was entitled to were for "Tugela Heights," "Relief of Ladysmith," "Laing's Neck," "Transvaal," and "Cape Colony."

Mr. Brodrick had some time before definitely launched his ambitious army corps scheme, and Wilson was therefore now called upon to assist Sir I. Hamilton in putting forward the names of generals and staff officers to fill the numerous fresh appointments contemplated. The tasks in connexion with South African honours and rewards were very nearly completed by the end of summer, and the Commander-in-Chief made no secret of his opinion that a comparatively junior officer, who had now been continuously on the staff from 1894 to 1901, had been quite long enough away from regimental duty. It looked, therefore, as if Wilson might soon find himself afloat and on the way to join a battalion of his regiment in South Africa; but he gained an unexpected reprieve owing to Sir I. Hamilton being suddenly asked for by Lord Kitchener for further service in that theatre of war, and to Lord Roberts being unable in the circumstances to dispense with the services of Sir Ian's assistant in the military secretariat. Wilson was promoted major in the Rifle Brigade on December 2, and on the following day was gazetted brevet lieutenant-colonel for services in South Africa. He wrote in his diary on December 31:

> During this year I have got a wonderful insight into the inner working of the War Office, and to my mind it is exceedingly unsatisfactory. The whole idea of governing the army by a civilian, whose whole training has been political expediency, and who knows less about the army than I do about the navy, is vicious in theory and hopeless in practice. Nor shall we ever do any good until it is the custom, and the right, of the C. in C. to state his case once or twice a year in the House of Lords. The country would then be in possession of the expert's view of the case and could judge as to its proper course of action.

All this time he was much at 47 Portland Place, where Lord Roberts was residing; he often would go up there with papers and would lunch there, and the Chief and he would afterwards either drive or walk down to Pall Mall to spend the afternoon in the office. But he had quite made up his mind that he would shortly be out with the Rifle Brigade in South Africa and participating in defensive operations, when the suggestion was made by one in authority in Pall Mall that he should be given command of a Provisional Battalion, and this was given effect to shortly afterwards by his appointment to the 9th of these units, then stationed at Colchester. Of this he took over the command on

February 24, 1902, and on joining he found the battalion to be made up of ten companies belonging to the Norfolk, the Suffolk, and the Bedford Regiments.

In spite of his appointment being merely a temporary one, seeing mat Provisional Battalions were bound to be disbanded as soon as the South African War (now obviously drawing to its close) should come to an end, Wilson from the outset took great interest in the work. Although just at first he found many matters in connexion with the unit that called for modification, he spent a year at its head as pleasantly for himself as it proved profitable to the battalion. This did not enjoy a very high reputation when he took it over, but he promptly set himself to the task of raising its tone and of increasing its efficiency. He could not, for instance, regard the presence of sheriffs' officers loitering in the vicinity of barracks in hopes of serving writs on some of his officers, with unqualified approval; so he let it be known that he would, if necessary, sanction the attendance of these representatives of the law at the orderly room to enable them to carry out their duties with effect and dispatch. The musketry of the battalion he found to be deplorably backward; but he took the matter in hand with enthusiasm, and within a very few months he had brought about a transformation by spending much time on the ranges and, by the force of personal example, exciting keenness amongst the rank and file. When it became known, early in the summer, that the 9th Battalion was entering for various inter-regimental musketry competitions, the Colchester garrison as a body were disposed to scoff; but the unit speedily won an enviable local reputation for itself in connexion with its shooting, and it even carried off cups that were open to the whole Eastern Command.

The only really noteworthy incidents, however, during Wilson's tenure of command were a special battalion parade on the occasion of news arriving of the Peace of Vereeniging, a ten days' course of military training at Clacton-on-Sea, a visit of the unit to London to line the streets on the occasion of Lord Kitchener's arrival from the Cape, a further brief stay in camp in Regent's Park at the time of King Edward's coronation, and, last but not least, the customary formal inspection at the hands of the general commanding. Sir W. Gatacre. The outing on the East Coast and the general's inspection both produced incidents that deserve to be recorded.

When the citizens of Clacton-on-Sea received tidings that the 9th Provisional Battalion from Colchester was proposing to make a descent on their township, alarm and despondency became rife in the streets and on the beach. So His Worship the Mayor, as in duty bound, set himself to avert the impending calamity, and that functionary made an official appeal to the battalion's commanding officer. He made representations to the effect that the amenities of the thriving health-resort of which he was the municipal head could not fail grievously to suffer, were a swarm of soldiery, whose reputation for sobriety had recently not been irreproachable even in their own garrison town, to be let loose on the place just when the bathing season was at its very zenith. Wilson was sympathetic. He, however, politely but firmly declined to cancel his arrangements, and Clacton-on-Sea, on hearing the news, feared the very worst.

The march from Colchester was one of about fifteen miles, and it took place on a particularly hot day. When about half the distance had been covered, Wilson called a halt for rest and refreshment. He then fell in the men and addressed them in a few well-chosen words, assuring them how convinced he felt that they would uphold the good name of the British Army while guests of a locality where that army was but little known. The effect was remarkable. During its stay by the sea, the behaviour of the battalion was exemplary; the band performed daily on the esplanade to crowds of enthusiastic holiday-makers; townspeople and visitors vied with each other in showing cordiality to the cheery and mannerly warriors planted down in their midst; and when the day came for the battalion to march back to Colchester, its departure aroused the keenest regret on all hands in Clacton-on-Sea.

One of the officers of the battalion, who properly belonged to the militia and who hailed from the Emerald Isle, was no master of the art of war nor even an effective exponent of the intricacies of infantry drill in the piping times of peace. In view of the ordeal that the unit was about to undergo, this officer had given rise to anxiety in the minds of the colonel and of the adjutant when the inspection was impending, and his commanding officer had personally impressed upon him exactly what he was to do and what he was to say in a given set of circumstances which, by tactful handling of General Gatacre, it was hoped to bring about. Inspection day arrived. At the proper stage of the proceedings and in pursuance of plan, Wilson rode along the line intimating what movement he was about to instruct the battalion to execute. Then — to the edification and amusement of General Gatacre — a penetrating "whisper from the Irish militia officer was heard all over the ground: “Kurmel, Kurrnel! What’ll I say when ye give the orrder?”

Wilson, moreover, spent a few days at Aldershot, at the end of July, in the capacity of commandant of the Public Schoolboys’ Camp, a duty that was most congenial and for the performance of which his personality particularly well fitted him. These camps were for several successive years about this time managed by officers of the Rifle Brigade, and, in the absence of a regularly constituted Junior Officers’ Training Corps (this only came into being some years later), they undoubtedly fulfilled a most useful purpose. Wilson made a great success of that of 1902.

It became known before the close of the year that the 9th Provisional Battalion would shortly be broken up, but although in some respects sorry to learn that his period as a commanding officer was nearing its end, Wilson knew that Lord Roberts had marked him down for a post in the newly formed Training Branch at the War Office. The battalion did not, however, actually cease to exist as an independent unit until February 11, although some of its companies had already before that date been handed over to a battalion returned from South Africa.

One result of experiences encountered in South Africa had been to impress upon the military authorities the imperative need of improving and modernizing the training and education of all ranks of the army for work in the field, at i d to no one was this more apparent than to the veteran Commander-in-Chief, Lord Roberts. Almost the first step taken by the Field-Marshal on the return of the bulk of the troops from South Africa was to establish a new department in the War Office under charge of General Hildyard, which more or less superseded the previously existing department of the Director of Military Education. This new department was, besides performing most of the duties that had hitherto been carried out by the department which it was replacing, also intended to deal comprehensively with questions connected with peace manœuvres, with staff tours, and with all matters connected with the practical training of the troops for active service. Hildyard was given Rawlinson (a full colonel in recognition of South African services) as his assistant with the grading of A.A.G., and Wilson was now brought in, with the grading of D.A.A.G. on the understanding that he would shortly be promoted to grade of A.A.G. He joined at the War Office on April 15, and on June 1 took over the work of A.A.G. from Colonel Delavoye, whose period of service had expired — it had, as a matter of fact, lasted seventeen years. He wrote in his diary:

> I took over from Delavoye, at 68 Victoria Street to-day and he went off, so I have to start a new office without any understudy or any knowledge of any sort. In the last 1 8 months I have been Private Secretary to the C. in C., then A.G.I., then C.O. 9th P.B., then D.A.A.G. Auxiliary Forces, and now A.A.G. for Education.

He speedily arranged that he should be shifted with his clerks from Victoria Street to Pall Mall, so as to be with Hildyard and Rawlinson and in a position to take a prominent part in dealing with questions of military training. He was, moreover, appointed secretary of the "Advisory Board," a body of officials who deal in a consultative capacity with all manner of questions affecting education in the military forces. He also found himself on a number of other committees, and he was freely consulted by Lord Roberts on all manner of subjects, notably in connexion with the answers that the Chief proposed to make when giving evidence before the Royal Commission on Militia and Volunteers which had been constituted. He also accompanied the Commander-in-Chief on inspection duty to Colchester and other places, and went with him to visit the cadets of the Royal Military College in camp on Salisbury Plain. "We came back attached to the cadets' special train," appears in the diary, "and at Woking where the Chief got out, the cadets gave him a great reception. Quite touching, the veteran and the boys."

Always a glutton for exercise, Wilson made it his practice to ride in the Row, or else to cycle in Regent's Park, or run and walk in Hyde Park, before breakfast every morning. On his way to the latter arena when about to engage in running and walking exercise accompanied by his dog "Paddles," he always carried the morning paper under his arm, and would snatch hasty glances at the more important items of news whenever he slowed down to a foot pace. He was wont to wear somewhat unconventional apparel on these occasions, and one day a boy, mistaking him for an itinerant vendor of press output, proffered a penny and demanded the paper, whereupon its possessor seized the penny in great delight and handed over his *Daily Mail*. He was much taken up during the summer with matters in connexion with the manœuvres on a large scale scheduled to take place in September, but the weather turned very wet during August, and it was for several days doubtful whether the whole project would not have to be abandoned — and thereby hangs a tale.

Hildyard, Rawlinson, and Wilson agreed, between them, that it would be impossible for the exercises to take place, and they had actually drawn up orders to that effect, when Lord Roberts, who was indisposed and confined to his bed, heard of what was afoot. He sent for them, carpeted them in his bedroom, insisted that the manœuvres could and should be carried out, and, from his bed and with no little warmth, denounced such pusillanimous deference to the vagaries of the climate as, he understood, had been contemplated. The presence of Hildyard, a general officer and one with whom the Field-Marshal had not in earlier days been brought into contact, would seem, moreover, to have to some extent embarrassed the patient in giving full vent to his feelings. For, when the dejected trio had gained the hall in safety and were about to effect their escape. Lady Edwina (from over the banisters) beckoned Rawlinson and Wilson back for the Chief to give the two former members of his personal staff a further dressing down, couched in less measured terms. Wilson used to delight in telling the story. Lord Roberts, moreover, proved to be right, for the weather mended just in time and the programme was carried out as originally elaborated.

The report of the Royal Commission appeared towards the end

of August, and its very outspoken findings aroused much public interest and were exhaustively studied by Wilson. He wrote in his diary on August 31:

> The papers continue the appalling story of our unpreparedness for war in 1899; the Report of this Commission must surely show up our rotten system of having our army run by politicians. I am going to draft a scheme trying to combine the Hartington proposals* for Chief of Staff with the Commission's proposals to turn us into an office like the Admiralty.

He perceived that reform must in the first place begin in the War Office itself, and that far greater attention must henceforward be paid to the question of preparation for war than had been the case in the past. He worked out several schemes, all of them based on the principle of a board analogous to the Board of Admiralty, and only differing from each other in points of detail. At the beginning of September he went down to stay with Lord Roberts at Englemere, the place which the Chief had purchased at Ascot. While there he showed his latest scheme of this kind to the Field-Marshal, who agreed with it in principle, and he then accompanied Lord Roberts to Belfast and found many opportunities for discussing it with the Chief on the journey thither and back. Lord Roberts enjoyed a thrilling reception when he drove through the streets of the city to receive its freedom at the Town Hall, and two days later he visited Lisburn accompanied by Wilson. They repaired to the local cathedral to see the memorial to John Nicholson, under whom Lord Roberts had fought at Delhi, and in a later chapter the story will be told of how, nineteen years afterwards, Wilson as a Field-Marshal revisited Lisburn for the purpose of unveiling another memorial to that illustrious fighter of Indian Mutiny days. On returning from the north of Ireland, he joined the Commander-in-Chief's camp at Marlborough for the manœuvres, and while there he visited his old school. The exercises lasted a week, and the operations ended very successfully

---

* The report of Royal Commission which had sat in 1889 under the presidency of Lord Hartington.

in a general engagement on the ideal battlefield provided by Lambourn Downs.

Mr. Arnold-Forster succeeded Mr. Brodrick as Secretary of State for War in October. Certain other changes took place at the same time as a consequence of one of those permutations of individuals which are such a feature of normal political life, and on Tuesday the 20th, we find Wilson, with an indignation that would not seem to have been wholly without warrant, writing in his diary:

> Bromley-Davenport, who only came in as Financial Secretary on Friday, opened his tenure of office by writing, "I don't agree" across the completed and approved papers of the War Office Journal scheme. How can good work be done with such fools?

Owing to both of them staying over one week-end at Englemere, Wilson was given an opportunity of getting into close touch with Mr. Arnold-Forster. The new Secretary of State had made a study of military questions and had written freely on the subject in the Press. But he had come to the War Office with certain preconceived opinions and theories on the subject of organization, terms of service and so forth, and he was by nature indisposed to change his mind after he had once made it up. He, moreover, was assuming the War portfolio at a particularly awkward moment, for the Cabinet was insisting that the Army Estimates must be cut down to a total of £29,000,000. Wilson's view was that this was impracticable unless about half of the auxiliary forces were disbanded, and he held that, if what was left of them were to be appropriately organized and trained, it would, taking our commanding naval position into account, be quite safe to leave the defence of the country entirely to them. "Arnold-Forster meanwhile writes enormously long minutes for the Cabinet as to what he proposes to do," appears in Wilson's diary on December 11, "but never shows them to the soldiers."

Rawlinson was transferred to the command of the Staff College at Camberley before the end of the year, and in view of the reorganization of the War Office that was about to be carried out, he was not replaced. For within a very few weeks of Mr. Arnold-Forster's appearance on the scene, the War Office Re-Constitution

Committee of three — Lord Esher, Sir J. Fisher and Sir G. Clarke — had been set up, and its activities were causing no small flutter in the dovecotes around Pall Mall. That the decisions arrived at by this very confident triumvirate — it was a case of decisions, as will be seen, not of recommendations — were upon the whole sound and appropriate, is generally admitted now. But the steps taken were taken so abruptly as to cause unnecessary confusion for the moment, the rather arrogant tone adopted by the committee was not unnaturally resented in the War Office and by the army, and several officers of unquestionable distinction and of considerable length of service were treated with a lack of consideration and of courtesy which might almost be stigmatized as brutality.

Wilson's diary throws an interesting light upon these vivacious days. He had been away for a short period of leave in Ireland in January, and on return stayed for some days with Lord Roberts in Portland Place. He wrote on February 3:

> I got here at 8 a.m., and the Chief came into my room while I was having a cup of tea and told me all sorts of gossip. Lyttelton, Douglas, Plumer, and Wolfe Murray replace Nick, K. K., Johnnie and Brackenbury.[*] This is a *sweeping* change. During the day I saw Nick, who is very sore, and I must say justly so, and Hildyard, who is to succeed Lyttelton in S. Africa.

On the 10th Wilson wrote:

> At the office I found matters getting worse and worse. The "Triumvirate" are appointing officers to billets here, there, and everywhere, quite regardless of anyone. Spencer Ewart[†] tells me that they had not drawn a single paper from his office and had not asked him a single question. The King has signed the Patent or Warrant, or whatever it is called, abolishing C. in C., A.G., etc., and when I went up to see the Chief before dinner I found that he knew nothing about it and had never been told. Douglas and Plumer have taken over.

---

[*] Generals Nicholson, Kelly-Kenny, Ian Hamilton, and Brackenbury.

[†] Then Assistant Military Secretary.

Next day he wrote:

Our days pass like nightmares. The Triumvirate are carrying on like madmen. This morning I was in Nick's room talking over things with him, and his opinion is that all these sudden changes lead straight to chaos, when in walked Jimmy Grierson* and said *Esher* had ordered him up from Salisbury to take over Nick's office. Nick himself had not been informed, nor had he been told to hand over, and he called me to witness that he gave over the keys of secret boxes, etc., to Grierson simply on the latter's word. This is most scandalous work. Gerald Ellison† lunched with me and I impressed on him with all my power that this bull-headed way of proceeding will absolutely ruin the scheme, which in itself has some excellent points.

An astonishing office memorandum was circulated to-day (I am having it framed), setting forth that, in future, correspondence will run, "I am commanded by the Army Council," and all letters other than routine are to be signed by the P.U.S. Routine letters to be signed by "Directors." But as there is no Army Council and as the title Director is quite unknown, we don't know what to do.

The next day's entry was:

This morning I was summoned before the Esher-Fisher-Clarke Committee, and Esher asked me if I would undertake the new office which dealt with Staff College, staff officers, their training and appointment, R.M.A., and R.M.C. and promotion exams. I said I would if I might have 3 D.A.A.G.'s and other officers. He said there would be no difficulty about that. Meanwhile I am to think the matter over and come before the Committee again to-morrow. Gerald tells me the Committee will go on their galloping career, kicking out and appointing, destroying and constructing at a pace and with a lack of knowledge which quite takes one's breath away.

In the meantime Wilson had been in consultation with the newly-appointed Directors of Military Operations and Military

---

* Afterwards Lieutenant-General Sir J. Grierson.

† Lieutenant-Colonel (now Lieutenant-General Sir G.) Ellison was Secretary of the Committee.

Training, he himself acting temporarily as Director of Staff Duties, owing to no appointment to that post having been made by the Esher Committee. They had agreed upon various points of detail and had been able to obtain the approval of the committee to their proposals, with the result that the organization of the General Staff at Head-quarters could be taken in hand without further delay, subject to the concurrence of the Army Council, which was now defini tely constituted. Sir Neville Lyttelton, who was to be Chief of the General Staff, was on his way home from South Africa; but all the preliminary steps were being taken in the meantime in his absence. Unconventional and open to criticism as had been the methods of the War Office Re-Constitution Committee, and precipitate as had been their procedure, the members of that body had shown themselves fully alive to the vital importance of ensuring the creating of a General Staff, and they are entitled to a share of the credit for its establishment on effective lines that took place within the succeeding three or four years.

During the previous months Wilson had played a considerable part in the compilation of the new *Cavalry Training*, based largely on the experiences of the South African War. Lord Roberts had taken a particular interest in the preparation of this work, which was to some extent based upon his conviction that under modem conditions shock tactics on the part of mounted troops would rarely prove practicable or effective, and that the trooper's principal weapon was his fire-arm! The book: was all ready for publication at the moment when the Army Council came into being, and one of the first decisions of that body was that its issue was to be deferred until April 1,

Wilson in conjunction with the Directors of Military Operations and of Military Training drew up the establishments for the General Staff at Head-quarters, and they had completed this task by the time that Sir Neville Lyttelton arrived to take up the duties of Chief of the General Staff, and that Major-General H. D. Hutchinson, of the Indian Army, was appointed Director of Staff Duties. Both of them accepted what had been proposed. But considerable difficulties arose with the Treasury over the increases that were being demanded, and the following entries from Wilson's diary bearing on the point may be quoted:

> The Treasury write to say that they won't entertain the idea of the cost of starting our General Staff. They write a most improper and truculent letter. Matters have now come to a pass when in my opinion the four Military Members must push back their chairs and resign unless they get what they want.
>
> I am much dissatisfied with the way things are going, and I feel sure that Treasury will beat us and that we shall be crippled in our General Staff; and I think we deserve it. We are a vacillating, ignorant crowd.

The Treasury, however, in the end gave way to a great extent in connexion with this question, and while the matter remained under discussion, Wilson went with Lord Roberts to Belgium, where they visited the battlefields of Ramillies, of Ligny, and of Waterloo. "Curiously enough, when we were on the top of the Lion Monument," appears in Wilson's diary, "we heard one of the guides comparing something the Chief had done in South Africa to something of Wellington's, which we could not catch."

Considerable stir arose after this on the military side of the War Office in connexion with Mr. Arnold-Forster's army reorganization scheme. The Secretary of State and the Military Members of the Army Council were in agreement that a reduction of expenditure could only be carried out satisfactorily by reducing the Auxiliary Forces and improving the organization of what was left of them. But to this the Cabinet would not consent; so Mr. Arnold-Forster eventually brought out a modified scheme, which the Military Members of the Army Council did not approve of and which found little favour in any quarter. This appears in Wilson's diary on July 21:

> What I have been anxious about all along is that the position of the Military Members should be clearly defined, and on June 22, I went to N. G., Douglas, and Plumer and strongly advised their drawing up a statement of their actual position and their exact wishes and thoughts. This was not done, and I feel sure the result will be serious. Because if Arnold-Forster's scheme of the abolition of the Militia, reduction of Volunteers by 80,000, and reduction of the Regulars by 14 battalions is hissed off the stage, the careers of the Military Members will be ruined at the same time.

He was, however, in need of a rest; in August he left London with Mrs. Wilson for a month's leave in Scandinavia, and on getting back he found the Staff Duties Directorate complete with its complement of eleven officers. "It's a wonderful change," he wrote, "from the time when I took over Delavoye's job last June year, when I was alone with a few clerks in Victoria Street." He set to work to make up for time lost by his absence, although he often felt sorely discouraged at the inertia that had constantly to be overcome by his own driving power before any progress could be made. He wrote in his diary on September 20:

> There are many things of great importance that I want to start, and I know so well that, if I don't do them, no one else will. I get very lonesome sometimes in regard to the future of the army and the War Office, and to-night is one of my despondent periods. It seems so hopeless to get anything through and to get anything started, and yet I cannot but admit that I have got much done in the last twelve months.

The staffs of commands and districts in the United Kingdom and overseas were being reorganized in view of the separation of the General Staff from the Administrative Staff, and Wilson had to fight hard, in view of somewhat halfhearted support on the part of those set over him, to prevent the General Staff being subordinated. His successful struggle over this question and over the position that the General Staff as a whole was to assume, is recorded in his diary for 1904 and 1905; and those who (like the writer) were serving in comparatively subordinate capacities on the General Staff at the War Office, and who were in close touch with him during this period, can testify to the resolution and the resource that he displayed in what was an extremely up-hill contest. But at the end of October his labours in this particular direction were for a brief period interrupted by the startling incident of the Russian Baltic Fleet firing on our fishing vessels on the Dogger Bank during its passage of the North Sea on its way to the Far East, an incident which for a few days created a very grave international situation.

He wrote in his diary on the 28th:

> We are balancing between peace and war, with a slight

inclination towards war, because it seems that Russia rather wants war. We are to-night in the most serious position we have been in since the Napoleonic Wars, because signs are not wanting that France is inclining towards Russia. So impressed was I to-day with the position, that I went to N. G. to discuss what final preparations we might make. He sent for Robertson and Hamilton Gordon* and we four talked over the situation. It is sufficiently and terrifyingly chaotic. We don't know whether Kitchener wants the 30,000 men he asked for in January on the outbreak of hostilities, and whether he will be satisfied with two divisions in the first four months. We know nothing about transports, remounts, ordnance, &c. Then, for home defence, we can man coast defences and can mobilize and call out the militia, but there is no scheme for brigading the militia, &c., no reserve of regular or auxiliary officers. &c. To-night I feel very much that to go to war with Russia would be serious, but to go to war with Russia and France would mean a life and death struggle, lasting possibly for years and costing an immense amount in lives and money.

During the succeeding few days many points were dealt with and many decisions were arrived at with regard to the various steps that were to be taken supposing that hostilities should actually break out in consequence of the outrage. The Dogger Bank incident may indeed be said to have acted as a blessing in disguise, for it brought home to the military personnel of the War Office as a whole the alarming lack of definite and detailed plans for dealing with probable, and with possible, national emergencies that prevailed at that time. The Russian blunder, moreover, gave a much needed fillip to the General Staff at Head-quarters, both in the sense of demonstrating its importance and of indicating the nature of its duties to the other branches of the War Office, and in the sense of awakening it to some extent to its own signal shortcomings at the time. The difficulties with the Tsar's government were, however, satisfactorily adjusted, so that within a fortnight of the trouble so suddenly arising, Wilson was able to resume consideration of the various problems of peace

---

* Representing the Directors of Military Operations and Military Training, who were both away.

organization with which he had previously been engaged.

He was promoted brevet colonel on December 2 and that day he wrote in his diary:

> It has taken me three years to go from captain to full colonel. This is most wonderfully quick, and places me very well for the future.

The position in the Army Council at this time was that the Military Members were making a stand against Mr. Arnold-Forster's scheme, that the War Minister was disposed to persist in his plans, but that the Cabinet also looked askance at the scheme. The field gun with which the artillery had been armed during the South African War was entirely out of date and a new weapon had been approved, but the proposed rate at which this effective gun was to be issued by no means satisfied the military authorities. Lord Roberts, however, took up the question, with the result that the period allowed for the issue of the new gun was reduced from 5 years to 2½ years.

Wilson was seeing Lord Roberts almost daily at this time, and on the last day of the year he mentions in his diary, that, during a talk that he had had with the Chief of the General Staff mat day. General Lyttelton had said that several people "not otherwise hostile" had been commenting on these frequent visits to the Field-Marshal. The question was to crop up again from time to time during the whole of Wilson's retention of his present appointment, and again later, and some reference to the subject will therefore not be out of place at this point. He was, in common with many others on the Head-quarters Staff, profoundly dissatisfied with the existing condition of the army and with the manner in which the War Office as a whole was carrying out its functions. Mr. Arnold-Forster's projects for reorganizing the military forces would, he believed, only make matters worse. The Esher Committee had laid great stress upon the creation of an efficient General Staff, and had set plans for accomplishing this in motion, but in spite of Wilson's persistent efforts to make a beginning little had been effected towards carrying the design any farther. Lord Roberts, member of the Committee of Imperial Defence as he was and holding a unique position as a military authority in the eyes of his countrymen, appeared to be the only hope. Wilson had been fully in the confidence of the Field-Marshal almost from the day when he had joined Army Head-quarters at Pretoria, and he had come to be an intimate friend, not only of the Field-Marshal himself, but also of the whole Roberts family. The Field-Marshal had, during the past four years, been in the habit of discussing all manner of military problems with him, and had to some extent leant upon him when in need of information. Even had he wished to do so, it would have been difficult for Wilson to break off these cordial and mutually acceptable relations with the greatest of living British soldiers, simply because Lord Roberts was no longer Commander-in-Chief and was now only an officially appointed and salaried member of the Committee of Imperial Defence.

Still, there is also something to be said on the other side. Wilson was an official in the War Office who was very much behind the scenes, and it was common knowledge that Lord Roberts was an opponent of the policy which that Department of State was supposed to' be following. As a member of the House of Lords, the Field-Marshal was entitled, should he think fit, to express disagreement in the Legislature with the attitude and the actions of the Army Council, and by doing so to embarrass Mr. Arnold-Forster and his colleagues, who were Wilson's military superiors. Even admitting that his procedure in this connexion was justified by the peculiar circumstances of the case, there can be no gainsaying that his attitude was irregular.

In the meantime he had accomplished one excellent piece of work. At the beginning of January, 1905, a large number of officers holding General Staff appointments at Headquarters and in districts and commands assembled at the Staff College for a conference which lasted over several days. The idea of holding such a conference was entirely Wilson's; all the arrangements, as well as the programme that was to be followed, had been worked out by him, and it was acknowledged by all who took part in the proceedings that the scheme had proved a success. It thenceforward became the practice to hold these conferences each year in January, and not the least of the benefits arising from such meetings was that General Staff officers were brought together and became acquainted with each other, and that a bond of sympathy and of mutual understanding was established amongst them as a body. But that the prospects of establishing a really effective General Staff, such as existed in Germany and in France, were not at the moment promising, is indicated by an entry in Wilson's diary a few days after the conference came to an end.

> The Military Members in the morning, and the Army Council in the afternoon, discussed the question of the General Staff, and by ruling that no brevets, no accelerated promotion, and no half-pay lieutenant-colonelcies were to be given, they gave the death blow to the whole idea. It's very disheartening, and although it doesn't matter to me personally, I feel very lonesome and angry to-night.

Only after much difficulty had it been found possible to induce the Military Members of the Council to agree to a suitable establishment being laid down for the General Staff. Now they set their faces against the General Staff being accorded any special privileges, or being accorded the position in the army that would enable it to make genuine preparation for war a consideration universally accepted as one of greater importance than were ordinary questions of military routine. But, with the knowledge that he possessed of military requirements and the ingenuity that he could bring to bear in devising expedients, Wilson combined a grit and determination that generally overcame obstacles, however formidable, in the end, and he refused to abandon the struggle. He kept — as he himself said — "pegging away."

A somewhat singular incident occurred on May 30. Wilson that day was handed a private letter from Mr. Arnold-Forster asking him for his views on the pressing question of the General Staff. He wrote in his diary that evening:

> This places me in a very curious position. Ought I to give A-F. my views about the General Staff behind N. G.'s back, and my opinions, moreover, are wholly at variance with N. G.'s? Ought I to

> tell N. G. that A-F. has written to me? Conk* tells me that the S. of S. told him that I ought to succeed Rawly at the Staff College. I am puzzled and will sit tight for a day or two.

He, however, decided after further consideration to prepare a memorandum for the Secretary of State, and this he sent in with a private letter a week later.

The objects to be kept in view in forming a General S taff, he pronounced to be: (a) To gather the ablest men in the army together, and by some system of advancement and promotion to make sure that the fortunes of the army are always in their hands; (b) By means of these men, to form a school of military thought which shall be abreast, or ahead, of that of any other army.

> It is impossible [he went on to say] to secure unity of policy and action without reasoned and well-ordered thought. At present every officer has his own opinion on every conceivable military subject, the net result being that there are as many opinions as there are officers. Hence the advice tendered to the S. of S. by his responsible military adviser is the individual advice and opinion of the officer concerned, and is not the carefully balanced opinion, after mature thought and deliberation, of a collective body of experts. Thus, continuity of thought and of action are wholly impossible, and in their place we find disjointed and unconnected plans, still-born for the most part and leading no where except indeed to chaos.

He insisted upon the Chief of the General Staff being given a great authority, on his having absolute power over all officers of the General Staff, and on his being relieved of routine work as the sole adviser of the Secretary of State on all matters of strategy and military operations. The General Staff must be composed of the pick of the officers who passed through the Staff College from year to year, and arrangements must exist for granting them accelerated promotion.

He heard no more of the matter for nearly three months; but at the end of August he was one day shown a minute, signed by

---

* Major Marker, then Mr. Amold-Forster's private secretary; he was one of the many rising officers killed in the Great War.

Arnold-Forster, which turned out to be a reproduction of his own memorandum. It caused no small stir in the War Office, everybody wondering who the real author was, and Lyttelton himself remarked that the more he studied the minute the more able he thought it. A considerable amount of correspondence took place on the file of papers that had thus been started by the Secretary of State. But finally, Arnold-Forster, on November 11, sent back the whole file to Lyttelton with a further minute, giving directions that the General Staff was to be proceeded with on the lines laid down in his original minute — that embodying Wilson's views. There followed another somewhat singular incident, which is recorded in Wilson's diary as follows:

November 21:

> Arnold-Forster sent for me and said he was tired of shilly-shallying and that he proposed to send his minute (my minute) about the General Staff to the Press to-night for publication to-morrow. He asked my opinion. I cordially agreed. He told me then to send it. When Hutch came back from lunch I told him this, and later Arnold-Forster sent for Hutch and repeated his orders. I wrote a couple of introductory lines to the minute, took it to C. 2., and told them to give it to the Press. This, I hope, will bring matters to a crisis. Arnold-Forster told me that all the Council — Arthur Balfour, French, Johnnie Hamilton and Kitchener — agreed to this minute, and added that it was rather funny for him and me, seeing that we wrote it.

November 22:

> Arnold-Forster's minute to C.G.S. is in all the papers this morning, and all have leaders on it, most of them being favourable. The Morning Post very hostile to Arnold-Forster personally. There is much chat about it in the office.

November 23:

> I found a message from N. G. who wanted to see me. I went to his room and found Hutch there. N. G. handed me a wire from Arnold-Forster to him in which "amazement" was expressed at his minute appearing in the Press, a proceeding which he considered was due to Hutch, as he (A-F.) had never wished for, nor sanctioned the

proceeding.

There had apparently been some very strange misunderstanding; but it has to be remembered that Mr. Arnold-Forster might possibly have produced a different version of the affair as a whole. Be that as it may, the publication of his very cogent and appropriate minute undoubtedly registered a distinct step in advance towards ensuring that a General Staff, composed of a personnel fully qualified for carrying out its very important duties, and organized in such a manner as to ensure that those duties would be effectively performed, would in due course be created. That Arnold-Forster himself, moreover, came to realize that the publication of the minute was advantageous is indicated by a letter written by him to Wilson, dated November 25, which ran as follows:

> I write a line to acknowledge with gratitude my indebtedness to you in respect to the form of my minute upon the duties of the General Staff. The only credit, if credit there be, which I desire to take for that portion of the minute to which you so largely contributed, is that I recognized immediately I saw the paper which you had prepared at my request, that the ideas I desired to express had been thought out with great clearness, and expressed with admirable force, and that I made the best use of such valuable assistance.
>
> I think the publication has done nothing but good, and I do not conceal from you that in my opinion its postponement for any long period might have jeopardized the success of a reform, which I believe to be conceived in the true interests of the Army, and which will now, I firmly believe, be carried to a successful, though it may be a long deferred, conclusion.

A few days later Mr. Balfour's Government resigned. Sir H. Campbell-Bannerman accepted office, and Mr. Haldane succeeded Mr. Arnold-Forster at the War Office; Sir W. Nicholson became Quartermaster-General with the tacit understanding that he would, in due course, succeed General Lyttelton. Wilson shortly afterwards proceeded to Switzerland to engage in winter sports,[*] and he made a practice of doing so in future years. On his return he found that further obstacles had to be overcome with regard to the General Staff. An Army Order embodying the principles which Mr. Arnold-Forster had laid down had been drafted before he left. But, in spite of his efforts, and of the consistent support given to its provisions by Sir W. Nicholson as an Army Councillor, months passed by before this order saw the light. It was, however, at last published on October 1, more than two and a half years after the Government had accepted the recommendations of the Esher Committee *en bloc*, the most important and novel of which had been that a General Staff must be set up.

While some credit for this tardy consummation of an urgently needed reform was undoubtedly due to the Esher Committee, some to Mr. Arnold-Forster, and some to Sir W. Nicholson for his helpful attitude from the time that he joined the Army Council, the main credit belongs to Wilson although he was still serving in a comparatively subordinate position in Pall Mall. By his initiative, by his comprehensive and prescient understanding of the question in all its bearings, and by his indomitable resolution in the struggle to achieve his object, he had not only devised a workable and an effective scheme, but he had also in the end overcome the resistance of hostile and unwilling members of the Army Council to its provisions, and he had made it a prominent feature in the accepted military organization of the country.

The comments in his diary on the attitude of the Government and of the Army Council at the juncture when, at the beginning of May, the Turks suddenly appropriated an old fort within the Egyptian confines at the head of the Gulf of Akaba, were the reverse of complimentary and deserve to be quoted. On different days he wrote:

> The ten days allowed to Turkey to withdraw her troops from

---

* This was his first experience of ski-ing and he very rapidly became an expert during his stay of three weeks at Adelboden. Putting skis on for the first time on January 29 he passed the severe test (up to the top of a hill, a height of 1,500 feet, and down again within 80 minutes), with 2½ minutes in hand on February 16.

Grove End

where she has crossed the border into the Sinai Peninsula will be up this week. It will be amusing to see what she does and what we do.

> The Cabinet now think that besides the Lane. Fusiliers and Worcestershires sent from Malta, and the Inniskillings and the R.H.A. battery from home, it will be necessary to send out the 1st Cav. Bde. and 1st Divn. from Aldershot. I hope this may be so and that the Sultan will stand fast, if for no other reason than to make our present beastly Government spend money, and to show them how they rely on the army when the pinch comes.
>
> Nick tells me that nothing has been settled about sending troops to Egypt. Apparently the idea now is that India shall send 6,000 men to guard the Canal and that we are to do nothing. I cannot understand that there are any plans if the Sultan remains obdurate and simply does nothing. The ten days are up to-morrow, and if the Sultan doesn't give in, the Fleet is to take Mytilene on Monday morning. If the Sultan still remains obdurate, I doubt if there are any further plans.
>
> The Sultan appears to have climbed down, which is 1,000 pities.

The Wilsons were now living at Grove End, and during the summer it was settled that Rawlinson was to give up command of the Staff College at the end of the year, Wilson had good reason for expecting that he would take Rawlinson's place; but that he was actually to get the appointment was not finally decided until the end of October, and he then learnt that he was to take over charge at Camberley on January 1. A pleasant and considerate mode of dealing with inferiors always made him very popular with such, and his parting on the last day of the year with the War Office messenger who had been mothering him and attending to his wants while in Pall Mall was, according to his own account, almost painful in its manifestations of mutual regard. "The officer who is taking my place is even uglier than I am," he remarked by way of easing the tension. "Oh, I hope not, sir," the messenger hastened to say, earnestly and with that ready tact that is so characteristic of the ex-soldier.

Wilson was delighted with the change from an office stool to the open-air life which he was about to enjoy at Camberley, and on December 31 the entry appears in his diary:

> I left the War Office to-day without a single regret, except that of

incomplete and unsatisfied endeavour to get a number of useful and necessary reforms carried out.

And yet he had accomplished much during the past three years — and this in spite of a torpor in certain influential quarters, and of an active opposition in others, that would have daunted any man less furnished with confidence and with fortitude than himself.

Chapter V – Commandant of the Staff College

Staff Tours — Visits to battlefields and to the French north-eastern frontier — Expansion of the College — Wilson and the students — Views on conscription — He makes friends with General Foch — Selected to become Director of Military Operations — Farewell to the College.

The appointment which, with the tank of brigadier-general, Wilson was now taking up, was one for the occupation of which he was peculiarly well fitted — and for the occupation of which he knew him self to be peculiarly well fitted. Presidency over the Staff College, it must be realized, called for additional qualifications besides the obviously requisite attributes of knowledge of the art of war, of acquaintance with military procedure in all its branches, and of that administrative capacity without which no important institution can be effectually and economically controlled. These qualifications Wilson possessed in full measure. But, for a soldier to have his name handed down as an ideally successful commandant of the great superior war-school at Camberley, he must furthermore be endowed with a fertile imagination, he must have cultivated a wide outlook upon public affairs, he must be urged on by an indomitable enthusiasm, and he must be equipped with that magnetic power of compelling the admiration and the affection of others which can best be summed up in the expression "personality." Wilson's record during the following three and a half years proves that assuredly he was not lacking in these latter virtues.

He assumed charge of an institution which was in a highly efficient state. His predecessor. Sir Henry Rawlinson, had introduced many valuable reforms during a three years' tenure of office at Camberley. The inefficiency of the staff work during the South African War had been one cause of its protracted duration and of the extent to which discomfiture had flayed a part in the proceedings of our troops, and Rawlinson had exerted himself to repair certain of the errors in the training of students at the College in the past, which had to some extent contributed to bring about the too numerous British failures on the veld. He had got together a highly efficient staff, and several of its members were to remain as assistants to Wilson for various terms. The College had also for the past three years been enjoying the cordial and discriminating support of the Directorate of Staff Duties at the War Office — and therefore of Wilson himself, who had been in the closest possible touch with its commandant throughout. Finally — and perhaps most important of all — the students were nowadays the pick of the officers of the army of their own standing, and they, therefore, furnished those set over them with almost perfect material for moulding into satisfactory shape.

The new commandant assumed his responsibilities on January 1, 1907, and his staff at this time consisted of seven officers, with the grading of D.A.A.G., viz. Colonel (now Lieutenant-General Sir J.P.) Du Cane, Colonel (now Major-General Sir G.) Aston, Lieutenant-Colonel (now Major-General Sir L.) Stopford, Lieutenant-Colonel (now Brigadier-general) F.L. Banon, Lieutenant-Colonel (now Lieutenant-General Sir W.) Braithwaite, Major the Hon. C. Sackville-West (the "Tit Willow" of Wilson's diaries), and Major (afterwards Lieutenant-General Sir G.) Harper, who is almost invariably spoken of as "Uncle" in the diaries. The number of students was 73. But, from the time that he took over charge of the establishment, Wilson made up his mind that he would obtain an increase in the strength of the staff, and he further resolved to press for an appreciable addition to the number of students. That he was successful in his efforts in this direction will be seen in later paragraphs.

A certain amount of monotony is inevitable in the labours of the commandant of an institution such as is the Staff College. The actual course consists in the main of lectures delivered to the students by the members of the staff, varied by an occasional address on the part of the commandant himself, and of a succession of staff tours. These latter are carried out for the most part in the country near Camberley, but some of them are pitched in more distant parts of England and Wales. There are always two batches of students, a "Senior" and a "Junior" division, undergoing the course simultaneously, and the commandant is kept busily occupied in supervising the training of both. Wilson's diaries for the years 1907-8-9-10 show that he enjoyed but little time to himself except during the vacations, and that even during these he was often busy upon military work of some kind or other that made serious inroads into such periods of supposed leisure.

The staff tours that took place in relatively distant regions naturally afforded novelty even to the commandant himself, for new areas of country were constantly being brought into requisition. The plan of holding joint naval and military staff tours had moreover been started in Rawlinson's time, largely as the result of a proposal on the subject by Aston, which was followed up by a dinner in Town at which they were joined by Wilson from the War Office, who gave all possible encouragement to the scheme, as representing the Staff Duties branch of the War Office. Tours of this nature were carried out in both the years 1907 and 1908, after a large party of naval officers had on each occasion spent a few days at the College, and of the first Sir L. Stopford writes:

> We arranged combined schemes with the War Course College at Portsmouth, then commanded by Captain (now Admiral Sir Edmund) Slade. I remember that one of these schemes was finally boiled down to a landing by night in Sandown Bay. The naval people had an obsolete old cruiser, the *Terpsichore*, attached to their college, and we embarked in this old derelict one fine afternoon at the proper hour to enable her to reach Sandown Bay at dusk. We waddled off round Spithead, and soldiers and sailors were standing in the waist, discussing our coming adventure, when suddenly a long figure appeared mounting the companion. It was Henry, dressed as usual in the "Kerry suit." He walked up to where we were standing with a preternaturally solemn face, and all that he said was, "Well, children,

are we safe?" Slade gave Henry one look and then fled for the bridge.

It was at a later date than this, but under somewhat similar circumstances, that, in an encounter with another very distinguished sailor, Wilson contrived at once to display his readiness of repartee and a very marked disinclination to let himself be brow-beaten. They were not previously acquainted and were meeting by appointment in the presence of a number of other officers of both services. The sailor was by disposition abrupt in his ways and a little inclined to bluster, and his greeting of Wilson was: "I've got a bone to pick with you, General." "Then I hope it's well devilled," rejoined Wilson, with his head cocked a little on one side in a way that he had, "because if it isn't I mayn't be prepared to eat it." The sailor's manner instantly became courteous to an extent verging on the deferential.

Each summer a staff tour was held in the Snowdon region to illustrate the peculiarities of hill warfare on the North-West Frontier of India. The work on these occasions was nearly all carried out on foot, scrambling up and down declivities and crowning hillocks; and Wilson always saw to it that staff, and students, and he himself, got plenty of exercise during the two or three days that the operations lasted. "To-day we went up Moel Siabod," appears in his diary under date June 30, 1909, " and although I stayed back at first, talking to Irby, I caught the others up and got on top first. I went up in 63 minutes, and I could have done it in 55 if I had not hung back." Moel Siabod, it may be observed, rises 2,880 feet above sea-level, and rears its crest some 2,200 feet, or so, above the Capel Curig hotel, so that the commandant's record shows him to have been an active man in good training. The numerous other tours that took place during Wilson's tenure as head of the Staff College were of great interest and value to the students, the commandant's lucid and vigorous summings-up at, what he always in his diary calls, the "Bow Wow" with which they closed, adding greatly to their instructional value. But there is no need to refer to them further here.

Another feature in the Staff College course, dating back to before the days when Wilson himself was a student at Camberley, was the practice of the Senior Division visiting the 1870 battlefields — Wilson's trip as a student has been mentioned in Chapter II. During his time as commandant these outings generally followed precedent, but he introduced what would appear to have been one distinct novelty. The scene of Von Bredow's historic charge at the Battle of Vionville — Mars-la-Tour was always studied in as practical fashion as circumstances admitted of, and that this was so will be realized from the account, given in his diary, of his last inspection of the historic ground:

> My 45th birthday. We did Vionville — Mars-la-Tour, lunching at the latter place and seeing a small field-day at Frescati on the way out. A beautiful day except for a high east wind. After lunch we went to look at the statue which, I think, the most beautiful of all those on the battlefields, and then we ran Von Bredow's charge, Moreton Gage as V. Bredow, and Henley and Hill Whitson as the two C.O.s.[*] I took the extreme left, and so had much the farthest to go, and yet was easily first; Perks[†] coming next. Not bad on my 45th birthday — 2 miles over plough and young seed.

This would not seem to have been the occasion on which the Senior Division happened to be accompanied by a German staff officer on the day when it visited the scene of the furious struggle of August 16, 1870. Whereas Wilson himself and his assistants and the students were on that occasion wearing the serviceable country clothes and the sturdy footgear which representatives of the Anglo-Saxon race usually assume when about to engage in a long day's work afield, the German staff officer was arrayed in the double-breasted frock-coat, the strapped-down overalls and the Wellington boots with spurs, that always had so striking an effect about the band-stand in a Rhineland garrison town in pre-war days. For this running business he was wholly unprepared. But he was not the one to draw back when he saw a band of British officers — and a general to boot — start on foot at a smart double to traverse the ground over which Von Bredow's troopers had galloped to their death a generation earlier. *Herr Kamerad* doubled too, and he

---

[*] Commanding officers of the 7th Cuirassiers and 16th Lancers, the two regiments which rode in the charge.

[†] Colonel Perceval, then in charge of the Senior Division.

actually stayed the course. But when he arrived at the winning-post — the spot where the French horse artillery battery had been in action when the brigade charged — he sat down, took off his boots and proved to demonstration that he was a genuine casualty.

On the last occasion, mentioned above, of Wilson's accompanying a Senior Division tour of this nature, the proceedings were brought to an abrupt conclusion owing to news of the death of King Edward reaching him at Metz, whereupon it was at once decided to abandon the rest of the expedition and to return to England. The party was very sensible of the courtesy displayed in the circumstances by the German general in command of the troops in Lorraine, who on hearing the tidings sent a letter, of which the following is a translation:

> General Command, XVI Army Corps. Metz, May 7, 1910.
> To the Royal British Brigade-General Wilson.
>
> The news of the death of His Majesty King Edward VII demands that I should express to you, General, and to all the English officers who have accompanied you to Lorraine, the sincere sympathy of the troops in Lorraine and myself in your sorrow at the loss of the Supreme Chief of the glorious British Army.
>
> The General in Command,
> W. N. Prittwitz,
> General of Infantry.

But Wilson also introduced another fresh feature into these excursions to the Continent, at least as regards his own share in th em. This was that he, on more than one occasion, paid visits to theatres of past warfare other than the campaign of 1870, as a corollary to his accompanying the students on their inspections of the familiar arenas of Woerth, of Spicheren, and around Metz. On these occasions he used to be accompanied by one or more of his staff. Thus in 1908 he made a tour of the battlefields of the 1866 campaign in Bohemia — Trautenau, Nachod and Sadowa — and then travelled on to Brunn to view the scene of Austerlitz. In 1909 he visited the principal battlefields of Napoleon's campaign of 1814 — La Rothiere, Montmirail, Vauchamps, and Champaubert. On another occasion, but this was when he was *en route* for his customary winter holiday in Switzerland, he visited the scene of the fighting on the Lisaine in 1870 — and at the right time of the year, as this had taken place in the snow.

But Wilson also turned to another account the trips to visit the battlefields situated around Metz and nearer to the old Franco-German frontier. Instead of proceeding thither by railway, he made it a practice to motor to and from Alsace-Lorraine, and thereby — altering his route on different occasions — to traverse much of the country that might conceivably become the theatre of war in the event of a fresh contest breaking out between the traditional foes. The German menace, it is true, was scarcely so ominous at this time as it came to be a very few years later, but the entente between this country and the French had already been established by King Edward. Moreover, just about the time that Wilson had assumed charge at Camberley, H.M. Government had sanctioned the making of guarded, semi-official approaches on the part of the Directorate of Military Operations to the Belgian General Staff on the subject of co-operation in conceivable eventualities. And Wilson himself held strongly that in case of a Continental struggle the British Empire ought to, and would be obliged to, stand side by side with France. Nor were his inspections of this territory confined to the occasions when he passed through it so as to be with successive Senior Divisions during the annual jaunt. At the beginning of the summer vacation in 1909, for instance, he spent ten days travelling, partly by bicycle and partly by rail, from Valenciennes to Belfort. On these tours he was almost invariably the senior in age of the party; but although long distances were covered by bicycle he was generally the one to suffer least from fatigue. In his letters to his wife he frequently reports that some companion has not proved a very seasoned wheelman and that this has retarded operations.

For the students at the College, or even for the bulk of the College staff, to have taken part in these excursions in the vicinity of the Franco-Belgian and Franco-German frontiers, would manifestly have been impossible. Even had the necessary funds been available for the purpose, the presence of large bodies of British officers, in regions where there were no battlefields of the past that might have accounted for their presence, would have attracted undesirable attention. Students and staff alike, nevertheless, benefited by the tourings of Wilson himself, with his chosen companions. For, fully convinced as he was that a European conflict was not only certain to come but that it was certain to come within a very few years, he made no concealment of that conviction in his intercourse with the contingents of officers successively under his control at Camberley. He laboured unceasingly to inspire them with the force of his own convictions on the subject.

Lord Esher wrote of him in "The Tragedy of Lord Kitchener":

> From the Surrey village where he taught the rudimentary principles of war, his pupils went forth imbued with the sense of its cataclysmic imminence. Below the ascending woods, where he so often stood, there lay, in lieu of cricket fields and polo grounds, the curving readies of the Meuse and the blood-stained flats of Flanders.... When others prattled of peace, he prepared their souls for war; not for an indefinite war, as men barricade their doors against imaginary thieves, but for a specific struggle with the German nation, the early stages of which he foresaw in detail with a soldier's prophetic insight.

Mr. Haldane, as Secretary of State, proved a good and useful friend to the Staff College; Wilson had met him one night when dining at Englemere. The War Minister paid a special visit to the College shortly afterwards for the purpose of discussing the details of what was required in respect to increase of establishment with its commandant; and a telegram from the War Office on March 31, 1908, informed Wilson that the increase which he had asked for was sanctioned. The upshot was that two A.A.G.S and one D.A.A.G. were added to the staff, and that the approved number of students was increased by twenty-two. Stopford and Braithwaite were advanced to the grade of A.A.G., while Lieutenant-Colonel (now Major-General Sir E.M.) Perceval, Major (now Lieutenant-General Sir G.) Barrow and Major Hon. G. Morris were brought in to fill the vacancies. Major (now Lieutenant-General Sir W.) Furse and Lieutenant-Colonel (now Major-General C.) Ross had taken the places of Colonels Aston and Du Cane at the beginning of the year.

One of the difficulties that Wilson, in common with

predecessors and successors, suffered from as commandant was that of becoming acquainted with the students individually. It is essential for the head of the institution to know the officers whom he is required to report upon at the end of their course, and it is, moreover, desirable that he should get to know them as soon as possible after they join at Camberley. The increase in the number of students which Wilson had secured made this task no easier for him during his last two years as commandant, and when an entirely new batch of some forty odd joined at the beginning of a year it took him some time even to tell one from the other or to remember their names. But he had found this a difficulty from the beginning — as the following story, as told by Sir W. Furse, suggests:

> Soon after becoming commandant he was over at Englemere, and Lord Bobs was asking him all about his new work. H. W. explained how he found it something of a problem to get to know the eighty students and the steps that he took to secure that end. "I get them into my office one by one," he said, "for a few minutes. I said to one of them this morning, 'Now tell me, is there anything about your *name* that will help me to remember your *face*?"
>
> "(Great perplexity on the fellow's face and no response.)
>
> "Well, then, is there anything about your *face* that will help me to remember your *name*?
>
> "(Greater perplexity — he evidently thought I was crazy)."
>
> The little Chief was much upset and begged H. W. to be more careful.

His keen sense of humour was highly appreciated by staff and students alike. The occasional flashes of this in the lectures that he delivered riveted the attention of his hearers upon what he had to impart, and made his disquisitions, even when these treated of comparatively speaking arid subjects, highly acceptable. A studious avoidance of assuming a didactic attitude on his part when discussing problems or when dealing with principles, was highly appreciated; and even when he made no concealment of his own views with regard to any particular subject, the junior officers with whom he had so largely to deal remarked how conscientious he was in also enunciating fully the arguments on the other side. His gift of always persuading any man with whom he discussed a question that he greatly valued that man's opinion, served him well in bringing what was best out of the students when debating points with them that had arisen during the progress of a staff tour, or that had been dealt with in the course of a lecture. "His influence on them," one of his staff at the College writes, " was extraordinary, which is not to be wondered at considering his remarkable personality." "He seemed to give out some of his personality to those he was with," writes another. Many stories are told of his quaint ways when grappling with some unexpected problem mat came to be referred to him at the College. The following anecdote may serve as an example:

> A Royal death had been followed by the issue of an order prescribing Court mourning for a given period, and it so befell that this order was issued shortly before an important staff tour was scheduled to take place away from Camberley. There was a certain student, one of those to take part in the tour, who hailed from north of the Tweed and who was credited by his comrades with a parsimonious bent. This officer took occasion to inquire personally of the commandant whether in the circumstances, it was imperative to take the field for the tout in sombre garb — as it happened, he possessed no dark coloured raiment suitable for the rough work which such exercises are wont to involve. With a portentous gravity the commandant uttered the one word "Surely."
>
> So the officer, in deep dejection, proceeded to fit himself out with a brand-new suit of clothes of funereal hue, and, arrayed in this, he repaired to the station where his Division were to entrain on the morning of the start from Camberley. But the very first figure that caught his eye on the platform was that of the commandant, decked out in his customary habiliment on such occasions (a creation in the loudest of loud checks) which was known to successive batches of Staff College students as the "Wilson tartan." And eye-witnesses whisper that there was a twinkle in the great man's eye, when the pair of them came face to face on the platform.

Owing to its vicinity to Englemere, Wilson saw a great deal of Lord Roberts during his term as the head of the Staff College, and he was in closest touch with the Field-Marshal at the time when the movement for compulsory service was definitely set on foot. Wilson's objections to Mr. Haldane's scheme were less due to the details of the scheme in itself, than they were to the fact that it made no provision for a great expansion of the military forces in case of war, an expansion such as could only be rendered possible by resort to obligatory training in some form or other. He particularly objected to the conversion of the militia into a Special Reserve, inasmuch as this transformation connoted the abolition of an existing power of unit expansion for war.

Lord Roberts made several speeches in the House of Lords during 1908 and 1909, criticizing the Territorial artillery, discussing the question of possible invasion, and pointing out the lack of any means of expanding the existing military forces in the event of a serious war; and he was much assisted in preparing these addresses by Wilson. That Wilson's views as to the need of compulsory service had come to be public property is, moreover, shown by the fact of his being attacked on the subject in a leading article in the *Westminster Gazette* in March, 1909. But this did not prevent his giving a lecture on "Is Conscription Necessary?" to the Senior Division at the College in the following November, at their request. He wrote of this in his diary on the 4th:

> My lecture yesterday has caused a tremendous lot of "chat," and has, I think, helped the Senior Division to some clear thinking. In answer to my invitation, quite a number of questions have come in.

A week later he gave a second lecture in which he answered these questions, and, as was only to be expected. Lord Roberts heard of these addresses before long. There appears in the diary for November:

> The Chief writes to say that he hears I gave two admirable lectures on conscription, and that he ought to have been present. He wants my notes *at once*. So characteristic!

And on the following day:

> I biked over to the Chief and told him of my lectures and left him my notes. He seems to be greatly struck with the picture. Curious if my lectures should do any good.

It was in the latter part of 1909, his third year at Camberley as commandant, that an idea came into Wilson's head which was to exert no small influence upon the history of his country, and also, incidentally, upon his own future career. This idea was that he should, after arrangements had been mutually made, pay a visit to General Foch, at that time Commandant of the *École Supérieure de Guerre in Paris*; this great military institution is, for practical purposes, the counterpart in France of our Staff College. Wilson's object was primarily to make himself acquainted with the methods employed and the nature of the course of study in force at this famous war school. But he also hoped that it might become possible for him to get into intimate relations with a French soldier who, already in those days, enjoyed a certain European reputation as a military writer and thinker on the art of war. In pursuance of this project. Colonel Fairholme, our Military Attaché in Paris, approached General Foch, who consented to Wilson's paying the proposed visit, but without manifesting any very special enthusiasm in connexion with the contemplated parley; and the story of this first meeting between Foch and Wilson is told in the latter's diary of December 2 and 3, 1909:

> Fairy and I arrived at *École Supérieure de Guerre* at 9.30 a.m. We were met by two staff officers (Captain Kochlin and another) and taken to the commandant's house. Beautiful house built by Louis XV. General Foch was increasingly nice as the day wore on. We went to 4 lectures and a conference, and then in the evening we had tea, and afterwards a couple of hours' talk; and I gave him a lot of our papers I had brought over. The teaching I saw to-day could scarcely be bettered. Very fine. There are 40 on the staff, for 180 students. Two years' course, each of 90, and this year they are keeping 15 for a third year.
>
> Another most satisfactory day at the *École Supérieure*, and a long talk with General Foch. His appreciation of the German move through Belgium is exactly the same as mine, the important line being between Verdun and Namur.

Wilson does not, however, in the above-quoted passage tell the foil story of this preliminary encounter of his with the future Commander-in-Chief of the Allied armies in France during their final triumph. When the hour for *dejeuner*[*] was at hand on the first day, Foch bade his visitors a pleasant farewell, under the delusion that he had done with them. Wilson, however, intimated that they were returning to the charge in the afternoon and requested information as to when work was to recommence. The same thing occurred in the evening. Foch imagined that now, at long last, his opposite number in England was satisfied; but he found that in this he was mistaken, for Wilson announced that he proposed to make his appearance at the *École Supérieure* afresh on the following morning. Foch had apparently already felt attracted by the personality of his visitor. This calm pertinacity would seem to have appealed to his sense of humour and to his appreciation of grit, and the result was that the discussion on the second day was conducted entirely without reserve and with advantage to all concerned. The meeting between the two commandants evidently, indeed, afforded satisfaction to both participants, for two months later Wilson was back again in Paris and paying a fresh visit to General Foch. He writes in his diary on January 14, 1910:

> I spent 3 hours this afternoon with General Foch at *École Supérieure de Guerre*. He was most open. Explained the whole working of the college again to me. How the staff is allotted — Infantry, Cavalry, Artillery, Strategy, and Tactics, Staff Duties — running through both years.
>
> Also told me much of the Russian unpreparedness, and we talked at great length of our combined action in Belgium. Most interesting. He asked me to come over for a staff tour in the summer, which I certainly will do. He is coming over to stay at the end of May.

It was probably on this occasion — although the incident may have occurred at a later date — that Wilson put the direct question to the commandant of the *École Supérieure de Guerre*: "What would you say was the smallest British military force that would be of any practical assistance to you in the event of a contest such as we have been considering?" "One single private soldier," responded Foch on the instant, "and we would take good care that

---

[*] "Lunch."

he was killed." What he evidently had in mind was the moral effect upon the French troops of knowing that England was standing by them, and the certainty that, even if only a single British soldier arrived, it would ensure others coming — the more so if the soldier fell.

Wilson was much impressed at the way in which tactical schemes were conducted at the French war school, the work being carried out at a rush, those in charge stimulating the students by "*Vite, vite*" and "*Allez, allez*";* and exercises carried out on this plan at the Staff College, when introduced by the commandant after his return to Camberley, came to be known as "*Allez, allez* operations." Foch was as good as his word with regard to paying the visit to England, and he arrived early in June. He spent some hours going over the Staff College, and on the morrow he and Wilson had a long day together, the details of which are recorded in the latter's diary on June 7:

> I took Furse in car and we met Gen. Foch and Huguet† at Farnborongh, and we went on to Long Hill. Saw a small field-day there, then round Lincolnshire Barracks, then lunch with Jimmy Grierson, then Supply Depot, then Field Stores, then back here. Then on to Englemere, tea there and the Chief and Foch made great friends, neither understanding a word the other said, then took the Frenchmen to the station and brought Furse and the wife home.

On the 8th, Wilson met Foch and Huguet at Andover and he motored them from there to Bulford Camp and to the Cavalry School at Netheravon, going on to stay the night at Salisbury. On the morrow they saw artillery practice at Lark Hill and rode round some Yeomanry camps, after which Foch and Huguet returned to London from Andover. Next day Wilson brought General Foch to the War Office and introduced him to Mr. Haldane, to the Adjutant-General, the Quartermaster-General, and the Director of

---

* "Quick, quick," and "go, go."

† Colonel Huguet, the French Military Attaché in London. His name will appear frequently in later chapters.

Military Operations, and after luncheon took him to the Royal United Service Institution. Sir A. Leatham, the Secretary of the R.U.S.I., relates that he was sitting peacefully in his office when the door was suddenly thrown open and Wilson walked in. "I've got a French general outside," said he, "General Foch, boss of their Staff College, whom I want to introduce you to. And mark my words, Leatham, this fellow's going to command the Allied armies when the big war comes on." Foch was then brought in and Wilson chaffed him about his future role of generalissimo of the Allied forces, after which they proceeded to inspect the museum and the rest of the building. With these Foch was evidently impressed, for he paid another visit later, and he then argued with Leatham over the famous Waterloo model by Captain Siborne, pronouncing it to be incorrect in some respects, but finally admitting that "for a model" there was not much wrong with it.*

Wilson's two visits to Paris, followed by Foch's visit to England, led to a warm friendship springing up between the two soldiers, a friendship that proved of great service to Wilson during the following four years when, as will be recorded later, he became Director of Military Operations at the War Office, a friendship that was to lead to the happiest results on many occasions during the progress of the Great War. But Wilson's visits to the *École Supérieure de Guerre* had, even before this, led to his securing a further addition to the establishment of staff and of students at Camberley. Sir W. Nicholson, who had succeeded Sir N. Lyttelton as Chief of the Imperial General Staff in 1908, had from the outset done all that was possible to support the Staff College. Mr. Haldane also interested himself in its development, and so, when Wilson reported what he had seen of the French war school, it was readily conceded that a further expansion of the institution must

---

* It was on the occasion of this first visit of his that the famous French soldier witnessed the march of the relieving guard on its way from Chelsea Barracks to Buckingham Palace. But what struck him most about the pageant was not the gallant bearing of the troops nor the martial music of the band at their head. "Mais pourquois les agents de police?" he demanded, noting the presence of the pair of stalwart constables who, in accordance with custom, stalked in front of the cortege.

take place without delay. This the Secretary of State announced when introducing the Army Estimates, and, thus it came about that, dating from April 1, 1910, the staff was increased by five officers, while five additional students were also sanctioned. The total additions to the strength of the College in the course of Wilson's tenure of office, therefore, amounted to eight staff officers and twenty-seven students, the staff, in fact, being more than doubled.

During the closing months of his time as commandant. Colonel Perceval and Colonel J.E. Gough, V.C. (who was killed in the winter of 1914-15, when chief General Staff Officer of the First Army) were his two senior assistants. Major (now Colonel) C.G. Stewart, Lieutenant-Colonel (now Lieutenant-General Sir R.) Whigham, and Major (now Major-General Sir A.) Hoskins were amongst the newcomers to join his staff, and experts of the Army Service Corps and of the Army Medical Department were introduced in the persons of Lieutenant-Colonel T.D. Foster and Lieutenant-Colonel W.M. Russell. For Wilson fully realized the importance of officers who hold the Staff College certificate being acquainted with the administrative side of staff duties. It had indeed appeared to him when he assumed charge that military administration had to some extent been neglected at the College of late years. Nor were the developments, carried out on his suggestion and under his superintendence, confined to questions of personnel. A number of improvements were carried out in the Staff College building itself, to some extent from his own designs, while he reigned as commandant. They serve to perpetuate his memory and to demonstrate the enthusiasm that he displayed for the institution of which he was the head.

He had not attended the General Staff conferences held at the College during the winter vacations in 1908 and 1909, spending these precious weeks of leisure in Switzerland. But he did so in 1910; and an incident that occurred while this one was in progress deserves to be recorded in view of its singularity. He tells the tale in his diary; —

> After dinner I went over with Nick to my room in the S.C., and here an extraordinary thing occurred.

> We found Edmonds* waiting for us with young Haldane (R. Scots), who had just arrived from the W.O., with information pointing to the fact that Germany was going to invade this country (south coast) next month. Nick, of course, at once wrote to the S. of S. and Admiralty, but I can't believe such a thing. With our *present* naval superiority the thing is absurd, unless the Admiralty are absolutely rotten. Nick, Kiggell, Braithwaite and I sat up till 1 a.m. discussing the matter.

No more would appear to have been heard of this strange story; Wilson, at all events, makes no further reference to it in his diary.

His first year as commandant, 1907, had been clouded by a sad event in the summer, just when the occupants of Staff College House had become thoroughly settled down in their new abode. Wilson and his wife had gone over to Ireland during the vacation to spend some time at Currygrane, where there was a family gathering. But while they were there Wilson's father, who had for some time past been in failing health, became suddenly worse and he died within a few hours on August 12. This necessarily prevented the Wilsons exercising their bent for hospitality at Camberley for some time to come. At a later date, however, they almost kept open house, having visitors constantly staying with them and entertaining freely. Only by very skilful management was this rendered possible; for they were not wealthy people, and the emoluments of the commandant were by no means excessive — they, however, increased by £200 a year in 1909.

Wilson's period in command at Camberley would in the ordinary course expire at the end of 1910, and his own wish at the time was to obtain command of a brigade — at Aldershot, if possible. So that, when Sir H. Smith-Dorrien, who was in command there, offered him the Bordon brigade, he accepted the offer joyfully, subject to Sir W. Nicholson approving the arrangement. He, however, speedily discovered that Sir William disapproved. The C.I.G.S. had decided that Wilson's services were needed as Director of Military Operations. The matter was

---

* Now Brigadier-General J. E. Edmonds; he was serving at the time in the Military Operations Directorate.

definitely settled during the month of June, and his disappointment is readily intelligible. Quite apart from his preference for an open-air life as compared to long days spent at the desk, he was at the time justified in believing that his prospects of professional advancement might suffer from a return to the War Office. The only opportunity that he had hitherto enjoyed of commanding troops had been when in charge of the 9th Provisional Battalion at Colchester, and this unit, in reality, meant little more than a glorified depot. The view is generally held by officers in our army — although they do not always act upon it when they come to be pulling the strings — that, to become fitted for high command, a soldier must have undergone an apprenticeship in commanding smaller bodies of troops. Wilson felt this himself. That his services to the army and to the country would be far more valuable in the post that he had been selected to occupy than they could possibly be while at the head of the Bordon brigade, he probably did not at the time realize himself. He could not then foresee that, as Director of Military Operations, he would within the space of four years invest the British Expeditionary Force with such vitality, and would so greatly develop the motive power needed for its effective employment as to permit of its being actually transferred from the United Kingdom to the Sambre well within three weeks of the order going forth for its mobilization to take place.

He was fortunate in one matter. He had, since the previous summer, been trying to arrange that the King should pay a visit to the Staff College. His Majesty had been unable to spare the time in 1909, but he found this to be possible on a date a very few days before Wilson was to bid the College good-bye; and of what then occurred the commandant gives the following account in his diary:

> We formed up in the Central Hall, and at 3.7 p.m. the King and Queen, the Duke and Duchess of Connaught and their staffs arrived. Cecil was in my room. We went there first. Then to the new Staff Room next door, where I presented the staff to the King. Then the big Library, where all the students were presented, the King shaking hands with each of them, then Henderson and Wilson Libraries, Mess Room, Ante-Room, and back to Central Hall, where all were gathered and the King told them how much interest he took in them. Quite successful.

He had received his orders to join at the War Office on August 1, and during July he was busy completing a number of matters that he already had in hand in connexion with the College, attending to confidential reports in view of his early departure, and, in the intervals, making arrangements for his own move to London. On one of the very last days. Lord Kitchener, who had recently returned from a tour of the Antipodes, following his vacation of the post of Commander-in-Chief in India, came over from Aldershot with Brigadier-General Robertson, then Sir H. Smith-Dorrien's chief General Staff officer, who was to succeed Wilson as commandant. Of this meeting with Lord Kitchener, Wilson writes in his diary:

> He attacked me about trying to form a "school of thought," but he got no change out of me, and he really talked a great deal of nonsense and imputed all sorts of things to us here which simply are not so.

Wilson was well aware that Kitchener had hoped to become Viceroy of India, and he regarded it as most unfortunate that Lord Morley should have vetoed this. He had also formed the opinion that Kitchener was in the right in his quarrel with Lord Curzon over the question of the military member on the Viceroy's Council, although Lord Roberts had entertained the opposite view. But this meeting of his with the victor of Omdurman would not appear to have conduced towards establishing cordial relations between them, and may even have contributed towards bringing about that mutual distrust, amounting almost to antipathy, which prevailed between the two men at the outset of the Great War.

The closing days at Camberley proved to be a sore trial to the commandant who was laying down his charge. "A big-hearted man, full of consideration for others and himself living up to a high standard," as one of his assistants describes him, he had achieved a rare popularity alike amongst the members of his staff and the students. Their determination to demonstrate by all means in their power how much they regretted his departure, gratifying as this was in itself, only served to make farewells all the more distressing. How much this was the case is made manifest by brief entries in his diary, certain of which may well be quoted here. On July 27, for instance:

> I gave my final and farewell address to the Juniors, and I was much touched by the way in which they stood up as I left the room. I have never seen them do that before.

On the 29th:

> The S.C. gave me a farewell dinner, 103 of us present, much the largest dinner ever given here. Stopford, Banon and Braithwaite came down from the W.O. I made my farewell speech, which apparently took them by storm, and I got the most extravagant praise from everyone. I am so glad it is over. It was a great ordeal.

On the 30th

> Everyone saying such nice things about my speech last night.

On August 1:

> To-night the staff and wives gave Cecil and me a dinner. There were 27 of us at dinner and I think we had the triumph of our lives. Such kindness, such thoughtfulness, such friendship, we can never forget. I was given a beautiful cigarette case, with all the initials of the staff. I can never forget, nor can Cecil, this night.

Of the scene on the occasion of the great farewell dinner in the College mess on the night of the 29th, one who was present wrote next day to Mrs. Wilson:

> I cannot yet trust myself to *speak* of Henry's farewell last night, so I write these few lines to tell you what a really beautiful speech he made. It was quite one of the best I have ever listened to and it impressed us all most deeply, and, more than that, touched us all so much that, when he sat down, we none of us liked to look at one another. There was a hush, and then they all got up and cheered him again and again. As you can imagine, it was all very trying. The most noticeable thing was how deeply attached all are to Henry, and can you wonder? What we all felt was that the College is parting with the

> greatest commandant it has ever known. When we left the dining-room there was none of the usual uproarious bear-fighting which takes place. We were, I think, too sad for that. The reception Henry got and the speech he made were indeed a fitting ending to his reign at the College, to whose welfare he devoted all that was best in him. Whatever the future may have in store for me, I can at least say that I was privileged to serve under him during his time as commandant.

"It has been a hard-worked three and a half years," Wilson summed his record up himself, "but upon the whole, I think, successful, though not nearly so much so as it ought to have been." No one who had been under him at the Staff College during those three and a half years would, however, have admitted that his success had been other than complete and unqualified.

Chapter VI – 1910 to 1911: Director of Military Operations

Wilson dissatisfied at the lack of practical preparations for war — The horse question and railway question — He meets Bethmann-Hollweg and von Tirpitz in Berlin — The Imperial Conference of 1911 — Agadir — Scare as to time required to mobilize the Expeditionary Force — The special meeting of the C.I.D. on August 23 — Conference with Generals Joffre and de Castelnau in Paris — He learns that some of the Cabinet disapprove of him — Progress made since August, 1910.

Immediately after formally taking over the duties of Director of Military Operations from his predecessor, General Spencer Ewart, Wilson proceeded to France in fulfilment of his agreement with General Foch to take part in a staff tour in that country. The proceedings were, however, interrupted just when they had got into full swing, by Foch being ordered back to Paris on his being chosen to attend the Russian manœuvres. Wilson, however, seized the opportunity, while returning through the capital, to go thoroughly into the work of Colonel Fairholme, our Military Attaché, and a note in his diary on August 5 is of interest as indicating his point of view:

> There is much that I will change here, and, I suppose, in the other Military Attachés. They appear to me to be dealing with details and with peace, and not with war.

In view of his taking up the appointment at the War Office, he had bought the lease of 36 Eaton Place, and he was soon settled down in this new residence and busy taking stock of the important department now under his charge. Colonel (now Major-General Sir J.) Adye, Colonel Count (now Major-General Lord Edward) Gleichen, Colonel (now Major-General Sir A.) Money and Lieutenant-Colonel F. M. Close were the heads of the four sections under him; but Adye's and Gleichen's terms were drawing to a close. His immediate chief was Sir W. Nicholson, with whom, at their first meeting he would, according to the following entry in his diary, dated August 8, appear to have enjoyed a heart-to-heart talk:

> Spent the day in the W.O. My first day really as D.M.O. I had a long talk with Nick and I told him what the Army thought of the Army Council. I am not sure that he liked my outspoken remarks, but I really can't help it.

Wilson, it may be observed, would occasionally adopt a tone when in conversation with official superiors that was frank to the verge of bluntness, and that in the military world would, in ordinary circumstances, be regarded as unconventional. As has been mentioned in Chapter IV, he had not forborne, while yet only a lieutenant-colonel and holding but a comparatively subordinate position in the War Office, to express his views without reserve to Military Members of the Army Council in connexion with their duties and with matters concerning the creation of the General Staff. But his ready wit, coupled with a bland ingenuousness of manner which he had cultivated successfully, was wont to gild the pill during such interviews and to aid those set in authority over him in swallowing what they might not have accepted at the hands of others of like standing. On one occasion, for instance, after he had been occupying the position of D.M.O. for some time, a question came up for discussion between the War Office and the Admiralty in which he was particularly interested, and in which he urged the C.I.G.S. to concern himself — but all to no purpose. He was trying in vain one afternoon to prevail upon Nicholson to take the matter up personally with the First Sea Lord, when that highly placed official at last observed, "If you are so anxious about it, why can't you go across and talk the business over with your opposite number, the Chief of the War Staff?" "That wouldn't be one bit of good, sir," rejoined Wilson: "Why not?" demanded Nicholson.

"Well, sir," replied Wilson, assuming his most submissive mien, "you see, it's this way. The Chief of the War Staff's just in exactly the same unfortunate position as myself. He's in an abject funk of his chief, and he therefore won't take the responsibility to settle, or even to discuss, one single thing." Nicholson laughed and remarked that in that case he supposed he would have to interview the First Sea Lord — and he did.

Wilson spent a few days with the Home Fleet at Cromarty, by invitation, during September, and he witnessed some of its gun practice. He was disposed to be rather critical in his comments on what he had observed, and on the occasion of the first day's practice he wrote:

> The first thing that happened was the ships started off to the wrong rendezvous. This was due to faulty orders and lost us an hour or more.

Then again, two days later:

> There was yet another hitch about the ships going out this morning. It seems to me these sailors want some practice in staff work.

On the last day he wrote in his diary:

> I think the chief points I noticed are: (*a*) Must have more rangefinders for close range. Only one now. (*b*) More turret and individual practice required, (*c*) The danger of thinking that actions can be won by playing at long bowls.

Wilson may possibly have modified his views as regards the last point after he had read the stories of Coronel, of the Falkland Islands and of Jutland. A few weeks later he went over to Paris to attend the wedding of Mlle. Foch, and on the following day he had a long and important interview with the bride's father. The following appears in his diary on October 13

> I went to *École Supérieure* at 8.50 a.m. by appointment, and had nearly two hours with Foch.

> He has just been to Russia as the Tsar's guest. He tells me that the Russian army is getting on, but very slowly; he tells me that the Russian secret service report that the Germans think the French army very fine; he says that he doesn't think Russia would actively interfere if Germany and France were to fight about Belgium, but Russia would do all her possible if war broke out through the Balkans; he tells me that the Emperor Bill has actually offered his army to Russia to quell internal disturbances, and always does all he can to get into Russia's good graces. This in order to pacify her if, and when, he moves west.
>
> He tells me that he believes Germany will absorb Belgium peacefully and throw the onus of war on France, and, in short, Foch is of opinion that, in the coming war in Belgium, France must trust to England and not to Russia, and that all our plans must be worked out in minutest detail so that we may be quite clear of the action and the line to take.
>
> He finished off by warning me that, for many reasons which he could not give, I was to remember that the year 1912 would be a dangerous year to live through.

A fortnight later an entry appears in Wilson's diary which is of signal significance, for it would seem to mark the point at which he definitely set himself the task of rendering possible the prompt employment of the Expeditionary Force on the Continent in the event of a European war.

> Long day in office (he wrote). I am very dissatisfied with the state of affairs in every respect. No rail arrangements for concentration and movements of either Expeditionary Force or Territorials. No proper arrangements for horse supply, no arrangements for safeguarding our arsenal at Woolwich. A lot of time spent in writing beautiful but useless minutes. I'll break all this somehow.

And he straightway set to work, always keeping particularly in view the problems that a co-operation with the French and Belgian military forces, in the event of these being opposed to those of Germany, would involve.

Some communications on this subject had taken place between the War Office and Colonel Huguet, with the cognizance of the Foreign Office so far back as 1905; but they had been carried out through an intermediary. In January, 1906, just at the juncture when Mr. Balfour's Government had been overthrown, the French Government through the medium of M. Cambon, the French Ambassador, drew the attention of Sir H. Campbell-Bannerman's Government to the German menace, and Mr. Haldane thereupon authorized our General Staff to discuss possible eventualities with the French and Belgian General Staffs, but on the clear understanding that this country was not to be committed in any way. General Grierson, then D.M.O., thereupon instructed our Military Attaché in Brussels to examine into the question of a possible dispatch of 100,000 British troops to Belgium, with the Belgian military authorities; and conversations also took place at this time between Grierson and certain of his assistants, on the one hand, and Huguet, on the other hand. These conversations were continued temporarily after General Ewart took Grierson's place in the latter part of 1906. But although plans were considered, and information of a military kind bearing on the subjects at issue was mutually exchanged, the discussions were always of an academic character. No action was taken on our side to render the carrying out of the plans a practicable proposition. The Algeciras Conference moreover created a *détente*, and the discussions subsequently to a great extent lapsed, although it was obvious to all who were acquainted with the political conditions in Europe, and who were aware of the formidable character of German military preparations, that a conflict in a theatre of war to the west of the Rhine was inevitable sooner or later.

This was the state of affairs when Wilson returned to the War Office in August, 1910, and when, on his investigating the question of the arrangements that existed for our army to take part in such a struggle, should it be called upon to do so, he speedily satisfied himself that there were, in fact, no arrangements at all. Certain schemes of a tentative character were to be found, docketed and put away in pigeon-holes; but not one single practical step had been taken to give effect to them, nor yet to make it possible to carry them out within the period of time that might reasonably be assumed to be available. The Expeditionary Force was now, it is true, a well-trained and a satisfactorily organized force in peace time; its war establishments were definitely laid down; and, in so far as the problem of raising its personnel from the peace to the war footing was concerned, this operation could be carrie d out within a very few days. But mobilization plans in respect to horses remained in a lamentably backward state, and no such thing as compiling a railway time-table for use of the troops on our side of the Channel had ever been attempted.

Wilson, even more than was the case amongst the general body of thinking British soldiers, felt convinced that a Franco-German struggle for the mastery must break out within a very few years, and that it might even break out within a very few months. He had debated with General Foch — already acknowledged to be one of the foremost authorities on the art of war in Europe — the course that such a contest might be expected to take. He had closely studied the strategical problems which would in all likelihood present themselves for solution whenever the emergency should arise. He had personally examined much of the ground that would presumably provide the arena for the embattled hosts. He was strongly of opinion that when the threatened conflict broke out, not only ought the Empire, on the grounds alike of honour and of policy, to fight side by side with France, but that in practice it would be compelled to do so. Therefore, no sooner had he convinced himself as to the inadequacy of the preparations then existing for meeting such a situation than he took prompt and eventually effectual steps to place these preparations on a proper footing, and his diary affords abundant evidence of his pertinacious activity in forcing the Quartermaster-General's department to take up the horse question and to get this absolutely vital matter settled. For instance:

> *October 28*. I got off my detailed queries to Q.M.G. in regard to horses for mobilization.
>
> *October 29*. Peter Granet came to see me about my paper asking information on the horse question on mobilization. He tells me he is quite unable to give the information I want, and that no one can tell where the horses are coming from nor when they will come. This is as I thought, but what a scandalous state of affairs! I'll push this to the end.
>
> *November 1*. I had a long talk with the D.S.T. about horse mobilization. He is taking my papers and will find out from Gs in C.

when they expect to be mobilized; but the fact is clear enough and is this — that at the end of 1910 no one knows how long it will take us to mobilize. A disgraceful state of affairs.

January 2. Ever since last August I have been trying to find out when the 4 Divisions (1, 2, 3, 5) of the Expeditionary Force will be ready to move, and up till now (5 months) have been quite unable to do so.

The other matter to which he devoted especial attention from a very early date subsequent to his becoming D.M.O. was that of railway organization in connexion with the supposititious movement of the Expeditionary Force to its ports of embarkation in the event of a European war. References to this question are frequent in the diary for the early part of 1911, or which the following may be quoted:

January 9. I told Nick he must support me in my endeavour to force Miles [the Quartermaster-General] to make detailed arrangements for railing the Expeditionary Force to ports of embarkation. At present absolutely nothing exists, which is scandalous.*

January 10. I had a long and serious talk with Nick, which resulted in my telling him that I would put my points re unpreparedness of the Exp. Force in writing. My chief points are:

I. Date of completed mobilization unknown.

II. No train arrangements to ports.

III. No staff arrangements at ports.

IV. No naval arrangements.

V. Emergency strengthening of fortresses by parts of 30 battalions.

VI. Emergency scheme for Aldershot to send troops to East Coast.

January 11. I drafted a serious minute to Sir Nick. It embodied what I told him yesterday. It will be typed and I will sign it to-morrow. I don't know what Nick will think of it. I have offered to take railway concentration and Admiralty arrangements off Q.M.G. and do them myself.

---

* Matters in connexion with railway transport were the business of the Q.M.G. Department.

January 20. Haldane asked me to lunch at 28 Q.A. Gate. No one else there. He wanted to discuss my minute. I told him exactly what I thought of the state of unpreparedness we were in, I said it was disgraceful and could be, and should be, remedied at once. He said that Nick had already been to him about the railways and that he (Haldane) had seen Grey, and Grey agreed we could go to the railway companies. This is good. I told him the horse question was in a disgraceful state. He said he was doing all he possibly could. I said it was no business of mine, but until it was put on a proper basis we could not mobilize. He asked me what else was required, and I enumerated the points I made in my minute to Nick, and I hope now we will get on with some practical work. I told him I wanted the loan of Freddie Kerr and Lubbock,* and he agreed. Later on I saw Nick and we settled to see Miles about this to-morrow.

On the whole I was satisfied and feel I have done a good day's work. I don't think Haldane is told the truth by the Council, and my impetuosity and determination to get something done, coupled with very plain speaking, carried the day. *Nous verrons*. This is only the beginning.

March 21. We had our first meeting about accelerating mobilization, and we settled that the whole of the infantry of the 6 divisions would embark on the 4th day, cavalry 7th day, artillery 9th day. We will work this out in detail and see what will have to be done.

But while dealing with the problems of accelerating the mobilization of the Expeditionary Force and initiating arrangements for railing it with the utmost rapidity to ports of embarkation in the event of its being required to take the field for war on the Continent, Wilson also had many other matters to attend to during the early months of his term as Director of Military Operations. He had been fortunate, shortly after joining at the War Office, in meeting at dinner two men. Lord Milner and Sir Arthur Nicolson,† with both of whom he was to be much associated in the future — especially with the latter during the succeeding four years; Sir A. Nicolson was at this time the Permanent Under-

---

* Lieutenant-Colonel F.W. Kerr and Major G. Lubbock, belonging to the Q.M.G. Department.

† Now Lord Camock.

Secretary of State at the Foreign Office. The D.M.O. and also his staff had always, for many years past, been in the habit of maintaining close, confidential relations with the Foreign Office—as was indeed demanded by the nature of their duties. While at the head of the Operations Directorate of the War Office, Wilson was in consequence frequently to hold discussions not merely with the Permanent Under-Secretary, but also with Sir Eyre Crowe, Sir W. Tyrrell and others amongst the more prominent of the officials assisting Sir E. Grey. He had written in his diary on November 17, shortly after making Sir Arthur's acquaintance:

> When walking to the War Office this morning, I overtook Sir A. Nicolson and went with him to his room in the F.O., and was much pleased with a long talk I had with him. He is fully alive to the fact that we have no army and can do little on the Continent, and he is quite prepared to help in remedying this.

On General Foch paying a visit to London some three weeks later, Wilson took him to see Nicolson, when they had a long talk; and Wilson on January 14 mentions having another conversation with Sir Arthur:

> He realizes as fully as I do the folly of having no army. He says our power of intervening on the Continent being almost nil, and Germany's position being enormously strong, she almost ignores us.

Wilson was now a member of the Committee of Imperial Defence; but his brief comments on the proceedings of that body do not suggest that he was very favourably impressed with the qualifications of the bulk of his fellow-members for deciding the questions laid before them.

He had introduced one of his old Staff College subordinates, Sackville-West, into his Directorate before this, and he had made arrangements that another. Harper, should join him shortly. He was seeing Lord Roberts frequently, and he was concerned to some extent in preparing that reply, drawn up under the aegis of the Field-Marshal, to Sir Ian Hamilton's book "Compulsory Service" with its preface by Mr. Haldane; he indeed drafted a chapter on "Balance of Power" for insertion. As had been the case when he was in the Staff Duties Directorate, his very friendly relations with the Field-Marshal gave rise to some criticisms — criticisms that were not wholly unnatural in view of his own official position, and of the attitude which the Field-Marshal maintained in the House of Lords when army subjects were under discussion. Wilson, however, was not to be deterred by this from keeping his former Chief acquainted with what was going forward at the War Office, -and from assisting him with advice and information in connexion with his campaign for National Service. A delightful passage in Wilson's diary on June 8 deserves to be quoted in this connexion:

> Went to see the little Chief at Bucklands after breakfast. I developed my ideas, already written to him on Sunday and Monday last, about our talking of peace, and every other nation talking of war, and how this would be the ruin of us. And at the end he chimed in with, "Very well, my dear boy, what we have to do is to change the whole mind of the nation. Now we must see about that at once." And he is 79!

Wilson had spent three weeks in Switzerland in February ski-ing, and on the way home had travelled with Mrs. Wilson by Munich and Nuremberg to Berlin. While there they dined with Sir E. Goschen at the Embassy, when the Ambassador, as Wilson records in his diary, introduced him:

> to Chancellor v. Hollweg, a big powerful man with strong face, about 55; also to Admiral v. Tirpitz, a big, fat, soft-looking man, without much power in face or figure. Interesting to see and talk to these two men.

He was much struck with the fact that at this banquet, at which some forty Germans were present, they all were able to speak English fluently. Von Tirpitz asked him if he was related to Admiral Sir A. K. Wilson, who was First Sea Lord at the time. He also met the French Military Attaché, Lieutenant-Colonel M. Pellé, who was afterwards to be General Joffre's Chief of the General Staff during most of the early part of the Great War. From Berlin they journeyed to Paris, and, while there, Wilson dined with General Foch to meet General Laffert de Ladibat, the Chief of the Staff, who also came by arrangement to call on him at his hotel next day:

> We had half an hour's talk on secret affairs. Quite satisfactory. The end of a very pleasant and interesting trip.

Wilson's old subordinate during part of the time that he was Commandant of the Staff College, Stopford, had recently taken up the appointment of Commandant of the Royal Military College, and at Stopford's request he went down to Sandhurst shortly after his return from the Continent to deliver a lecture to the cadets. Sir L. Stopford gives the following account of this address by the D.M.O., and of what led up to its being given:

> Happening to be in town one day, I went to the W.O. and walked into Henry's room, to ask him to come down to Sandhurst and lecture to the Senior Division. He consented, and I especially warned him to wear mess kit. The cadets, of course, did not know him, and they, moreover, always rather resented a lecture in the evening. Well, when the day came, Henry arrived in time for dinner, but he explained that Mrs. Wilson had, as usual, let his house, and he had been unable to lay his hands on his mess kit. So we arrived at the lecture room, he in evening dress with miniatures; and this is how he led off:
>
> "Before I begin my lecture I want to speak about three things. First of all about myself. Then about your commandant. Lastly about yourselves.
>
> "Now, as to myself. Seeing me dressed as I am, you would think I was either a conjuror or a waiter. I am neither the one nor the other, but my house being let I cannot find my uniform, so I have come in plain clothes.
>
> "Then as regards your commandant. I was quietly working in my room at the War Office lately when suddenly the door burst open and in walked your commandant. The *best* people always knock." (The G.C.s made such a row laughing that the remainder of his sentence could not be heard.)
>
> "Lastly, as regards yourselves. The more you listen to what I have to say the more I shall be honoured. But there is no reason why you should not sleep if you wish to, always provided that you do not fall off your seats and make a squishy noise on the floor. Snoring is strictly prohibited I"
>
> Needless to say he got the boys thoroughly on his side, and they listened with all their ears to a most interesting lecture upon frontiers.

At the end of May, 1911, he attended several meetings of the Imperial Conference which had assembled preparatory to the Coronation, and of the second and third of these he wrote in his diary:

> We had our second meeting of Imperial Conference, on defence. Asquith again in the chair. McKenna made a statement which was not at all bad, but it led to considerable difference of opinion, and Sir Joseph Ward, Premier of New Zealand, spoke up like a man. He said that unless we pursued a common policy the disintegration of the Empire was certain and that we were pursuing no policy, or at best as many policies as there were Dominions. Asquith adjourned the meeting at the end of Ward's speech, and we meet again at 11 a.m. to-morrow. It is difficult to imagine Asquith taking a strong straight line; and yet, if someone does not catch hold of us I think the Empire will go before long.
>
> We spent most of to-day continuing our discussions on the Impl. Conference, and my general feeling at the end of the day is this. The task of welding this Empire into one is the most difficult that any man was ever called upon to perform. Obvious, therefore, that we *must* get a great man such as Pitt, Bismarck, etc. I confess I see no sign of such a man in this country.

Neither the distinguished presence nor yet the silvery tongue for which alike Sir Wilfrid Laurier was justly famed would seem to have prevented Wilson from forming an unfavourable impression of that veteran statesman at this Conference. "If Wilfrid Laurier really represents Canadian opinion, then Canada is already gone. It's really tragical that all this should happen at Coronation time," he wrote. And he, moreover, expressed unbounded satisfaction, not unaccompanied by denunciatory epithets, when news arrived three months later of the result of the Canadian elections in which the Laurier Government was decisively defeated. "The most hopeful sign from an Imperial point of view that I have seen for a long time."

A few days later there came a bolt from the blue. The small German cruiser *Panther* appeared off Agadir on the coast of southern Morocco, which created a grave international situation, and one which was to last for several weeks. Wilson was in close touch during those weeks with Huguet, and also with Sir A. Nicolson, with whom he mentions in his diary having a long conversation on July 16:

> He told me of Metternich's visit yesterday week re Agadir, and of his curious half warning, half threat. Also we discussed every problem.

Three days later Wilson started for Paris, and there appears in his diary on the 19th:

> I had arranged to start with Huguet by the 2.20, but on arrival at the office I found Nick and Haldane had had a fright about something. They wanted to know all sorts of things, and in the end I laid out the forces of the Triple and the Dual Alliances on the frontier for them. No small thing to do in one day.

He wrote next day in Paris:

> I found Huguet waiting for me at the station on my arrival at 5.30 a.m. At 3 o'c., after much talk with Huguet, I met at the W.O. Gen. Dubail, Chief of Staff, Gen. Regnault, Sub-Chief of Staff, Colonel Hallouin, Chief of 3rd Bureau, Colonel Crepy, Chief of 4th Bureau. We worked till 5.30 in most satisfactory manner, and then Gen. Dubail, Huguet, and I called on the War Minister, M. Messimy, who was very pleasant and cordial, and we had another serious talk.

This appears on the following day:

> I lunched to-day with the War Minister, M. Messimy, at one of the cafes at the farther end of the Bois, in a private room. Quite charming. There were also there Gen. Dubail, Gen. Regnault, Colonel Hallouin, and also Huguet. We had much further talk. Caught the 4 p.m. train.

The question of the powers of the House of Lords had, at this time, reached an acute stage owing to the disinclination of that branch of the Legislature to pass the Veto Bill, which had been approved by the House of Commons. Wilson held strong views on the subject — largely due, no doubt, to his realization that, if the prerogatives of the Upper Chamber were to be abridged as was contemplated, the one guarantee that still existed against the establishment of Home Rule in Ireland would be gone. He wrote in his diary on July 23:

> We are entering on one of the most momentous weeks of our history. Before next Sunday the Agadir affair will have to be settled, and the final stage of the Veto Bill reached. I would side with France and would send a cruiser to Agadir. I would force Asquith to make Peers.

Mr. Lloyd George, Chancellor of the Exchequer, had on the 21st delivered a speech in the City, in the course of which he had plainly intimated that H.M. Government could not regard the attitude which Germany was assuming in Morocco with indifference. "No further news about Agadir," Wilson wrote, "every day Edward Grey procrastinates brings us nearer to a possible war" — from which it is to be inferred that in his opinion the Foreign Secretary ought to have conveyed some plain intimation to the German Government that the United Kingdom was prepared to support France by force of arms. The Militaiy Members of the Army Council were in the meantime beginning to realize that they were face to face with a crisis — as is shown by what Wilson wrote in the diary on the morrow:

> At mid-day I was sent for by C.I.G.S. in Q.M.G.'s room. Charlie Heath also present.* I was asked when the Expeditionary Force could be ready. I said I did not know, as the horse difficulty had not been solved. Neither Miles nor Heath could say either. We were told to get out a paper on the subject. During the afternoon I worked with Heath. We meet again at 10.30 a.m. I also saw Ewart about accelerating mobilization. We are unfortunately caught at a time when the proposals which I put forward for accelerating mobilization are not yet completed. We must do the best we can. Our rail and ship arrangements are worked out on my new tables; but the personnel

---

* Now Major-General Sir C. Heath, then the Director of Supply and Transport.

may not be ready. Meanwhile Macdonogh[*] came to me this evening and told me our Admiralty have lost the German Fleet and have asked me to find them. Macdonogh sent round the German ports. The whole thing is like a pantomime — or the Admiralty! I hear also that the Admiralty are short of coal because of the Cardiff strike.

Next day he wrote:

I was on committee with Miles, Heath, and others, to see how short we are in the Expeditionary Force. It comes out that we can only just make the Cavalry Division, four Divisions, and the Army Troops mobile. The 4th and 6th Divisions will have no horses, no A.S.C. personnel, no mechanical transport or mechanical transport drivers, and no medical units. Then we are 2,500 officers short, and so on. Still I insisted on sending the whole six divisions across. By the way, the German Fleet has been found (see yesterday)!

On the following day again appears:

Another day of semi-scare and scramble. I found some of our stores had no web equipment, and, still worse, that we could only fight our howitzers as four-gun batteries, and then only with half the proper amount of ammunition. Absolutely no medical arrangements made for the 4th and 6th Divisions.

The scandal grows, and I am keeping a diary so that I may write a minute on the whole situation. At about 5.30 news came from Brussels that the Belgians had stopped all leave and thought matters serious.

It is interesting to note our military position, as the exposure above pictured shows it to have been in the summer of 1911, when it is remembered how absolutely ready for active service the Expeditionary Force was — thanks almost entirely to Wilson's foresight and insistence — to be found when it came to be really called upon to take the field almost exactly three years later. The Agadir crisis did undoubtedly help him, because it accomplished something towards bringing realities home to those set in authority

---

[*] Now General Sir G. Macdonogh, then head of one of Wilson's sections.

over him at the War Office, and also to Mr. Asquith's Government. For, although there was a comparative lull for a few days during the opening days of August, the possibility of the country finding itself involved in a Continental conflict was to cause grave anxiety to His Majesty's Ministers for several weeks to come. On August 9, for instance, Wilson records in his diary being asked to lunch with Lord Haldane (he had been raised to the peerage), to meet Sir E. Grey and Sir Eyre Crowe.

> After lunch we discussed the present German-Morocco state of affairs. Grey began by asking me if I thought Germany was going to war with France and us. This was a question I ought to have asked him. However, I replied in the negative. He advanced the theory that Russia was a governing factor, which I shattered rather rudely by telling him that Russia in 28 days could only produce 36 divisions in Poland, which Germany could oppose by 27 and Austria by 36, and I said that Russian interference could scarcely relieve pressure from Paris, the Germans being able (in spite of Russia) to put 96 divisions against the French 66.
>
> After a long and, I believe, ineffectual talk, the chief points I made were three: First, that we *must* join the French. Second, that we must mobilize the same day as the French. Third, that we must send all six divisions. These were agreed to, but with no great heartiness. Eyre Crowe advanced the proposals to send Territorials. No officers, no transport, no mobility, no compulsion to go, no discipline, obsolete guns, no horses, etc.! Even Haldane said it wouldn't do. I was profoundly dissatisfied with the grasp of the situation possessed by Grey and Haldane

Consequent upon this illuminating discussion, Wilson was instructed by Lord Haldane to prepare a paper on a war between Germany and France, and this effort he followed up with another one putting forward the state of unpreparedness for undertaking hostility that the country was in. "This," he remarked cynically in his diary, "will not be so popular." On the day following there occurs this significant entry:

> Haldane sent for me early this morning. I found Nick in the room. Haldane said he had had a useful dinner last night of Asquith, McKenna, Grey and Churchill. He had told those ignorant men

> something of war, with the result that Asquith arranged for a small special meeting of the C.I.D. for to-morrow week. Haldane and Nick came down to my room and I showed them my map. This was a revelation. Later on, Winston Churchill also came over to my room, and Haldane came a second time, also Nick and Ottley.* Winston had put in a ridiculous and fantastic paper on a war on the French and German frontier, which I was able to demolish. I believe he is in close touch with Kitchener and French, neither of whom knows anything at all about the subject. Still, some good work was done this day.

The special meeting of the Committee of Imperial Defence, foreshadowed in the above extract from Wilson's diary, took place on August 23, and an outline story of what occurred can be given in Wilson's own words:,

> We had the emergency meeting of the C.I.D. to consider the problem of what we should do in the event of a war between France and Germany. Asquith (chair), Lloyd George, Haldane, C.I.G.S., self, Bethell,† Sir A. Wilson, McKenna, Winston Churchill, Sir Edward Grey, Sir John French. Asquith asked me to explain my proposals. I had all my big maps on the wall and I lectured for if hours. Everyone very nice. Much questioning, especially by Winston and Lloyd George.
>
> Then Sir A. Wilson developed his opposition plan, but he ran no chance in that audience.
>
> We sat from 11.30 till 6 p.m. About 7 p.m. I got a nice note from Haldane. It ran: "My dear General. You did admirably to-day. Lucid and real grip, your exposition made a real impression." This was nice, and I think good work was done in convincing the Ministers of the necessity of instant action.

This meeting was undoubtedly something of a triumph for Wilson. However ill-qualified most of the non-professional members of the audience who were listening to his elucidation of the strategical situation may have been for forming profitable opinions on the subject at issue, they were, all of them, practised

---

* Rear-Admiral Sir C. Ottley was Secretary of the C.I.D. at this time.

† Director of Naval Intelligence, now Admiral the Hon. Sir A. Bethell.

debaters and were accustomed to hear complicated questions perspicuously discussed. When reasoning with politicians, soldiers are usually at a serious disadvantage owing to lack of practice in expressing themselves clearly and concisely. But on this occasion the Prime Minister, and those of his Cabinet colleagues who were present, found themselves hearkening to a general who not only had the matter that he was dealing with at his fingers' ends, but who was also capable of presenting his thesis with a precision and lucidity that left nothing to be desired; and on no one present did Wilson's exposition make a greater impression than it did upon Mr. Churchill. Nor was that impression in Churchill's case a mere passing emotion, for in the first volume of "The World Crisis," written some ten years or so later, he makes special mention of this C.I.D. meeting of August, 23, 1911. We read:

> General Wilson, as Director of Military Operations, stated the view of the General Staff. Standing by his enormous map, specially transported for the purpose, he unfolded, with what proved afterwards to be extreme accuracy, the German plan for attacking France in the event of a war between Germany and Austria on the one band, and France and Russia on the other hand. It was briefly as follows: [Mr. Churchill gives details.]
>
> The number of divisions available on both sides and on all fronts when mobilization was completed, were estimated as follows:–
>
> French, 85
> German, 110
>
> It was asserted that, if the six British divisions were sent to take position on the extreme French left, immediately war was declared, the chances of repulsing the Germans in the first shock of battle were favourable. Every French soldier would fight with double confidence if he knew he was not fighting alone. Upon the strength of Russia, Wilson spoke with great foresight, and the account that he gave of the slow mobilization of the Russian army swept away many illusions. It seemed incredible that Germany should be contented to have scarcely a score of divisions to make head against the might of Russia. We shall see presently that the loyalty of Russia and the Tsar found the means, by prodigious sacrifices, to call back to the east vital portions of the German army at the supreme moment. Such action could not have been foreseen then, and most people have forgotten it now.
>
> There was, of course, considerable discussion and much

questioning before we adjourned at two o'clock. When we began at three it was time for the Admiralty, and the First Sea Lord, Sir Arthur Wilson, with another map expounded his views of the policy we should pursue in the event of our being involved in such a war. He did not reveal the Admiralty war plans. These he kept locked away in his own brain, but he indicated that they embodied the principle of a close blockade of the enemy's ports. It was very soon apparent that a profound difference existed between the War Office and the Admiralty view. In the main, the Admiralty thought that we should confine our effort to the sea; that if our small army were sent to the Continent it would be swallowed up among the immense hosts conflicting there, whereas, if kept in ships or ready to embark for counter-strokes on the German coast, it would draw off more than its own weight of numbers from the German fighting line. This view, which was violently combated by the General, did not commend itself to the bulk of those present, and on many points of detail connected with the landings of these troops the military and naval authorities were found in complete discord. The serious disagreement between the military and naval staffs in such critical times on fundamental issues were the immediate cause of my going to the Admiralty. After the council had separated, Mr. Haldane intimated to the Prime Minister that he would not continue responsible for the War Office unless a Board of Admiralty was called into being which would work in full harmony with the War Office plans, and would begin the organization of a proper Naval War Staff.

Churchill was at this time Home Secretary, and was not therefore — except in his capacity of Cabinet Minister — concerned in plans for war. But he had taken part in, or been present during, several campaigns, and he had written masterly accounts of two of them. Problems arising in the prosecution of war by sea and by land had an irresistible attraction for him, and Lord Grey mentions in his "Twenty-Five Years" that his then colleague at the Home Office remained in London at a time when most Ministers were away on holiday, was following the anxieties of the Foreign Office during this Agadir crisis with interest, and was, moreover, seeing much of Wilson. That this was so is also made plain in Wilson's diary. He wrote on August 28:

After lunch Winston Churchill came to my room and discussed

the present situation, which according to him has become critical. He remained nearly three hours with me. Jack Seely* also in and much frightened. I was rather pleased with Winston. He asked me to write him a letter, which he could show to Asquith and Lloyd George, of my opinion on: Policy; Value of Antwerp; Confining Germans south of Meuse; Strength of Russia. I will do this to-morrow. Winston also showed me a letter he had received from Lloyd George, who is also frightened.

And next day:

I wrote Winston Churchill a long letter to-day on the points he raised during our conversation yesterday. I also sent Nick a copy. I hope Winston sends on my letter to Asquith and Lloyd George, as I wrote freely on policy and strategy going hand in hand. Not much news to-day. A dispatch from Fairholme, M.A. Paris, describing an interview he had had with General Joffre, the new Chief of the Staff in Pans. In the main Joffre seems to agree with me.

Wilson remained in close communication with Churchill. He mentions in his diary spending more than an hour with the Home Secretary on August 31, and being with him again on September 4; on this latter occasion Churchill read out two letters from Mr. Lloyd George which seemed to Wilson "quite good." That evening, as it happened, he received a letter by the late post from one of his officers, who was in Bavaria.

He wrote in his diary:

I thought it of such importance as describing the present warlike temper of the German people, that, knowing that Winston and Grey were dining at the Café Royal, I telephoned to Winston and asked him if he and Grey would come back here to my house. They arrived soon after 11 p.m. and stayed until 12.15 a.m. We discussed matters in the most open manner, and I was especially anxious to enforce the necessity of a policy, the particular policy which I advocated being an offensive and defensive alliance of England, France, Belgium, Denmark, and Russia. In the end Grey said that, if the present crisis passed without war, he would most undoubtedly consider my

---

* Colonel Seely was at this time Under Secretary of State for War.

proposal.

I insisted on the enormous importance to us soldiers of an actively friendly Belgium, showing Grey and Winston my maps with the French and the German troops laid out on them, which interested them greatly. I don't think our talk to-night has done any harm, and I think it has done good.

He wrote next day:

I had a long talk with Winston Churchill this morning. He told me Grey was much impressed with our conversation last night and was thinking most seriously over it. This is all to the good. Meanwhile Winston professes to be in entire agreement with my views, and in this he is apparently joined by Lloyd George, another of whose letters he read me. Winston wants me to write a paper for him and the Cabinet embracing the whole problem. I will do so to-morrow if I can; but I am busy from morning to night pushing things for the Expeditionary Force.

On September 9 we have the entry:

Huguet spent an hour with me in the office. I impressed upon him the value of Belgian active support. He went straight back and told Cambon, who is going to Paris to-morrow and will lay this before the Ministers.

Huguet came to No. 36 to see me again at 5 o'c., and we worked from 5.30 to 8 o'c. I showed him my maps with German and French troops on them. He was immensely struck at all the work and knowledge this meant. He told me where the French G.S. want us to go, and what their plans are. This is the first time I have been told. He told me also that if I had gone to the manœuvres, M. Messimy was himself going to have invested me with the collar of the Legion of Honour.

Wilson mentions having a long interview, on September 1 x, with Sir A. Nicolson, who had just returned from Balmoral, where Lord Kitchener had also been staying preparatory to going out to Egypt as High Commissioner. The following three extracts from the diary are of interest, in view of what has already been mentioned on page 100 and of the relations that were to arise between Lord Kitchener and Wilson at a later date:

> Nicolson told me that Kitchener had said our army was not ready, was badly trained and rotten, that England would be shouting for him to take command, and much more in this manner.
>
> I had a long talk with Lloyd George, who was passing through London on his way up to Balmoral. I impressed on him the value of a friendly Belgium, the absolute necessity for our mobilizing the same day as the French, and of our sending the whole six divisions. I think he agreed to all this. He was quite in favour of a war now. I asked him if he would give us conscription, and he said that, although he was entirely in favour of a ballot, yet he dare not say so until war broke out, which I told him was too late. He told me Lord K. had told him that the French army was rotten, and ours was not much better.
>
> Winston telephoned me this morning (September 14) to say K. had seen him and told him the Germans were putting off the war until the autumn and winter, when the Russians could not move. This, of course, is the exact opposite to the truth. The best months for Russian movement are September to March.

Towards the middle of September the situation as between France and Germany became decidedly easier as a result of the smooth progress of negotiations between their respective Governments. These had as their basis an understanding that France was to make some cession or cessions of territory elsewhere, to serve as a compensation for being given a free hand by Germany in Morocco. The matter was not finally settled until November 4, when two separate treaties were signed. But it became from day to day more apparent during the autumn that the prospects of war were for the moment at an end. Wilson was in need of a rest and change of air and scene, and he therefore prepared himself for something in the nature of a "busman's holiday" — a visit to the French north-eastern frontier. He, however, received a message from Huguet from Paris asking him to proceed thither for a meeting with the General Staff to be held on the 29th, and he consequently crossed the Channel and arrived in the French capital on the 28th. He wrote that evening:

> Huguet met me at the Nord and we spent an hour before dinner walking up and down the Tuileries Gardens, discussing our meeting

of to-morrow. Huguet tells me the General Staff here think I have overrated German numbers and dates of concentration. So best. Also they want to do away with our advanced base at Amiens and place it at one of the ports. I see no grave objections. Foch is sure of war in the spring. He only reckons value of Russians at 4 or 5 German corps. Anxious about Belgium and Holland, easy about Italy.

He wrote next day:

Huguet and I went to the W.O. at 10 a.m. Gen. Joffre, the new C. in C., Gen. de Castelnau, G of Staff to Joffre, Gen. Dubail, Chief of Gen. Staff at the W.O., Col. Vignol, 2nd Bureau, Col. Hallouin, 3rd Bureau, Col. Crepy, 4th Bureau, and Huguet were there.

They were most cordial and open. They showed me papers and maps, copies of which they are giving me, showing the concentration areas of their northern armies. Intensely interesting. Then they showed me papers and maps, copies of which they are giving me, showing in detail the area of concentration for all our Expeditionary Force. We had a long discussion. Afterwards we went through many other matters. They also showed me a map, and are giving me a copy, showing 15 through roads in lower Belgium. They told me of a *Kriegspiel*[*] held by the Great General Staff in Berlin in 1905, a copy of which, with v. Moltke's remarks, was in their possession. In fact, by 12.30 I was in possession of the whole of their plan of campaign for their northern armies, and also for ours.

I never spent a more interesting morning. Some of their calculations are different to mine. [Here follow details.] The French divisions available against Germany rise to 72-75, instead of 66 which I had allotted.

I formed a good opinion of Joffre, a fine, manly, imperturbable soldier with much character and determination, and I formed a high opinion of de Castelnau. A clever and very intelligent man. Castelnau and Joffre entirely approved of my proposal to fortify Boulogne and said a survey and a plan would be at once drawn up.

Huguet and I dined with Foch at the Cercle Militaire, and de Castelnau also dined. After dinner we four retired to a private room and with maps we had an exhaustive talk on the whole problem, which was most satisfactory. Castelnau and Foch know their business thoroughly, and it is a real pleasure to discuss matters with them.

---

[*] "War game."

> Altogether, I am greatly pleased with the result of my visit, and greatly pleased also with Messimy's changes, whereby Joffre and Castelnau have been appointed, as well as the generals and superior officers of the different armies.
>
> Italy appears to have gone to war with Turkey and to have occupied Tripoli and Benghazi. Extraordinary piratical business.

After a few days, back in the War Office, Wilson started with Major Farquhar, one of his assistants (he was killed while in command of Princess Patricia's Canadian Regiment towards the end of 1914), for Brussels; and on the day following, "having missed the train owing to a cursed Spaniard squabbling with the booking-clerk," they arrived at Dinant. From this starting-point Wilson made a tour of the Franco-Belgian frontier, paying especial attention to the stretch of country between the Sambre and the Moselle, cycling backwards and forwards across the border-line so as to familiarize himself with such roads as he had not yet inspected. Then, after turning southward along the Lorraine frontier, he rode across the field of Mars-la-Tour, and in his record of that day in the diary a remarkable entry appears. He had always, on his tours of the Metz battlefields when commandant at the Staff College, been much struck with one particular memorial that had been erected near the village of Mars-la-Tour close to what was then the Franco-German frontier, invariably making mention of it when setting down his account of talcing the students over the scene of that desperate encounter. On this occasion he wrote:

> We paid my usual visit to the statue of "France," looking as beautiful as ever, so I laid at her feet a small bit of map I have been carrying, showing the areas of concentration of the British forces on her territory.

While he was at Verdun next day, the general commanding the 39th Division came to call on him and asked him to lunch on the morrow at Toul, There he was taken over Fort St. Michel, the governor of the fortress having obtained special permission for this by telegram from Paris; he was much impressed with the formidable nature of the fort, as also of this great French place of arms in general. On returning to London at the end of October, he learnt with no small satisfaction that Mr. Churchill had become First Lord of the Admiralty; for his efforts to arrive at a clear understanding with regard to the transport of Expeditionary Force across the Channel had up to the present made very slow progress. Then, a few days later, the following entry appears in his diary:

> Great excitement because Hardinge [Viceroy of India] has wired to Crewe saying he had heard of my plans and work for bringing troops from India to help in Europe. Uncle, Tit Willow, and I think that there is some game going on against me, because I am so powerful.

That Harper, Sackville-West, and he, himself, were right as regards the latter matter, was made apparent at an interview which he had with the C.I.G.S. a week later. Sir W. Nicholson, during their conversation, informed him that the peace party in the Cabinet were, as Wilson expresses it, "calling" for his "head."

He wrote in his diary:

> They think I forced the pace during the crisis and they quote all my teaching at the S.C. as evidence of my villainy. Old Nick, who told me as little as he could, seems all up for fighting. I told Nick I did not care for them personally, though I was quite ready to go if he wished. He said there was no question of that at present. It will be interesting to see what happens.

The next day's entry runs:

> Haldane sent for me this morning, I found old Nick in his room. Haldane told me there was no question of my being asked to leave the W.O. On the contrary he twice told me how "amazingly" well I had done, and how I had impressed his colleagues at the meeting of August 23. The fact was, he told me, that there was a serious difference in the Cabinet Asquith, Haldane, Lloyd George, Grey, and Winston on one side, agreeing with my lecture of Aug. 23, whilst Morley, Crewe, Harcourt, McKenna, and some of the small fry were mad that they were not present on Aug. 23 (McKenna, of course, was, and got kicked out for his pains), and were opposed to all idea of war, and especially angry With me, Morley and others quoting my teaching at the S,G and so forth. The Government fear that there may

> be a split, but Haldane told me he had informed Asquith that if there was a change of policy he would go. They will stop my going to Paris, I think, but not much else.

It would appear from Lord Grey's "Twenty-Five Years" that several of his colleagues were entirely unaware that conversations between our General Staff and those of France and Belgium had been sanctioned six years earlier, and had been in progress long before the Agadir crisis arose, and that members of the outer ring of the Cabinet were disposed to resent their having been kept in the dark. But in so far as Wilson's intention and prospects were concerned, the dissatisfaction of the "wasters" (as he, somewhat unkindly, calls them in his diary) made no difference whatsoever.

He entered in the diary on November 21:

> I had an hour with Winston Churchill this afternoon. He was most nice. Told me many things, and, in fact, was most open. He will play in with us all he can, and I feel sure will do a great deal of good in the Admiralty.

He wrote a week later:

> There is a sort of somnolence in the office which annoys me, so I am preparing another bomb to see if I can wake things up. Grey's speech [his statement of British policy in the House on the previous evening] was good. It will annoy the Germans and the Radicals, which is good. Winston has moved out the 1st, 2nd, and 4th Sea Lords, and put in Bridgeman, Prince Louis of Battenberg, and Pakenham. This is a fairly comprehensive and clean sweep.

It had been arranged that Sir J. French was to succeed Sir W. Nicholson as C.I.G.S. in the coming spring, and on December 29 Wilson launched the bomb which he referred to in the passage quoted above. He wrote in his diary that day:

> I sent in my final appeal to Nick to help me to get ready for war; if he does not take action on this I will not do anything more until he goes away, and then I will begin on French.

Although almost in despair at the lethargy with which he had to contend, he had, nevertheless, accomplished much during the seventeen months that had elapsed since his taking up Ills present appointment. Thanks to his initiative and to his persistence, the mobilization of the military forces in respect to horses had almost become practicable within a reasonable time. The preparation of railway time-tables to be brought into play should the Expeditionary Force be required to hasten to ports of embarkation at the outset of a European War, had been taken in hand. To the Prime Minister and to his more influential colleagues the vital importance of a definite understanding with France and with Belgium in anticipation of probable eventualities, had been — at least to some extent — brought home. That understanding moreover had, in a military sense, been satisfactorily established with the French General Staff, and Wilson had set cordial personal relations on foot with those prominent officers of the Republic on the farther side of the Channel, who would presumably control the operations of French armies in the European struggle which could not much longer be delayed. No one realized better than the Director of Military Operations himself that his task was still far from completed. But he had made a fine beginning.

Chapter VII – 1912: Director of Military Operations

The Admiralty begin examining the question of transporting the Expeditionary Force across Channel — Sir J. French C.I.G.S. vice Nicholson — Reduction of our naval strength in the Mediterranean — Wilson meets Bonar Law and Balfour — At the French Manœuvres — Wilson visits Russia and Galicia — Start of the Balkan War — A plan for ensuring Compulsory Service.

"I am very uneasy about the outlook in Europe," appears in Wilson's diary under date of January 3, 1912, "and our state of inefficiency and unpreparedness. I have done everything I can to wake Nick and the War Office up. There is nothing more I can do except sit and look on at the drift. But it's very discouraging." He found little cause for dissatisfaction, on the other hand, with the attitude that was now being taken up by the Admiralty in respect to the problem of transporting the Expeditionary Force across the Channel as a matter of principle, should such a movement become desirable or necessary. Mr. Churchill's advent had, in fact, entirely altered the point of view hitherto maintained by that department with regard to the question in which the D.M.O. was so specially interested, and he wrote in the diary on January 8:

> At 6 o'c. Winston Churchill sent for me and I had an hour with him. He, at all events, is alive to the German danger. Bridgeman and

> Troubridge* also came in and we discussed the whole situation. Winston brought out his new scheme of War Staff to-day.

On the 17th he wrote:

> I dined to-night at the Arch House with Bridgeman and Troubridge. We had a long and intimate talk about things, and I am greatly pleased with their outlook and their most kindly feeling to me personally. They agree with all my proposals. I showed them my maps of the French and German concentration on the frontier and explained the situation. The most satisfactory evening I have spent for years.

Next day the entry appears:

> At last I forced Nick and Miles to send to the Admiralty the letter we drafted months ago about ferrying us across to France. I was able to do this owing to my dinner last night.

The result of so satisfactory an understanding having been established with Churchill and his principal professional assistants, was that a question of vital importance in connexion with planting the Expeditionary Force down in the area that had been provisionally decided upon between Wilson and the French General Staff as the best for its concentration, could now be taken up in detail by the Admiralty. The selection of ports of embarkation and of disembarkation was a matter in which both Admiralty and the War Office were concerned. But the problem of assembling the transports was necessarily one for the naval authorities alone. The question as to what amount of tonnage might be calculated as certain to be available at any moment would have to be worked out. Many points of detail in connexion with the carrying out of embarkations and disembarkations would also have to be discussed between naval and military authorities., And the task was rendered all the more difficult owing to the imperative

---

* Sir F. Bridgeman, the First Sea Lord, and Rear-Admiral E. C. Troubridge, Chief of the Naval Staff.

need of absolute secrecy being maintained with regard to what was in progress. Good will on the part of the sailors, and their acceptance of the principle that this transportation of troops across the Narrow Seas at the very outset of a probable naval campaign was of fundamental strategical importance, were essential from the military point of view, and this good will had now been assured. But two years were, nevertheless, to elapse before the problem was in reality grappled with in earnest on the western side of Whitehall.

Mr. Churchill and his advisers were in the meantime growing very uneasy about the continual German naval expansion, and this matter had no doubt been freely discussed by them with Wilson in the course of the conversations that have been referred to previously. That he shared their anxiety is indeed indicated by the account that he gives in his diary of a conversation at the Foreign Office on January 11:

> I had a long talk with Sir Arthur Nicolson this morning. He is very anxious about the future, and, curiously enough, he, too, believes the Germans would attack our ships in a time of profound peace. [The "too" suggests that the sailors had spoken of this.] I cannot bring myself to agree to this, but I feel now that it is a contingency that we ought not to put aside. It puts us at a desperate disadvantage. Nicolson quite agrees with me that if the Germans seriously increase their building programme we should ask for an explanation.

At the beginning of February he proceeded abroad for his customary holiday in Switzerland; but he spent a forenoon with Generals Joffre and de Castelnau on the way through Paris, and in the afternoon he called on M. Millerand, the new War Minister. He broke his journey eastwards at Chaumont so as to spend the night at General Foch's quarters — Foch commanded the division there — and he had a long talk with this intimate friend of his, arriving in Switzerland on the 5th. "I never saw so many 'frights' as there are in this hotel" (which shall be nameless) he complained, on arrival, in his diary; "old Girton girls I should think." On the way back to England, with Sackville-West, at the end of the holiday he visited what he calls "The Appendix" — the singular, decanter-shaped patch of Dutch territory that separates the north-eastern comer of Belgium from German territory — and they then moved on to Stavelot and Malmedy to see how the railway that was in construction across the German-Belgian frontier between those places was progressing.

Colonel Seely had now to answer for Lord Haldane in the House of Commons, and the apologist found himself in an uncomfortable position with regard to a subject that was raised in debate early in the session. Wilson wrote in his diary on March 13:

> Jack Seely made another ridiculous speech last night, and waved an envelope in his hand, which, he said, proved we could send a force of 150,000 men, complete in all details, in a few days. When I asked to see this preposterous letter, I found it contained a copy of "War Establishments."

He wrote next day:

> Jack Seely made me lunch with him and he wants me to get him out of the mess he got into by his speech the night before last. Now that he is in a mess, I will pin him down to the 6 divisions as Expeditionary Force.

That day, March 14, was Sir W. Nicholson's last day at the War Office as C.I.G.S. and Sir J. French took up that position on the morrow. The new holder of the appointment took an early opportunity to inform his three Directors, Sir A. Murray, Wilson, and General Kiggell, that he intended to get the army ready for war; and he, moreover, speedily showed that in this he was in earnest. For Wilson had in the previous September, at the time of the Agadir crisis, written a long appreciation of the European situation. This had hitherto lain dormant in the archives of the C.I.G.S. But it was now printed by the C.I.D., and the new C.I.G.S. lost no time in taking a copy of the document to Lord Haldane one afternoon, when, according to Wilson's diary, "old Haldane nearly had a fit and was terrified out of his life. What a funny old thing it is. These politicians will not look facts in the face." A few days later "Haldane saw Sir John and me about my appreciation. He talked rubbish for about half an hour, and we could not get any good out of him." A few days later again, the diary mentions that "Haldane is inclined to fight Johnnie French over a demand for ammunition which we three Directors put forward. We will knock him."

In the meantime a serious question had arisen in connexion with the Mediterranean. The Lords of the Admiralty had come to the conclusion that certain battleships must be withdrawn from these waters and added to the squadrons at home, in view of the growing potentialities of the German navy and in order to secure at least some sort of superiority in capital ships over the aggregate that our rivals had at command in and about the North Sea. One result of the contemplated weakening of our naval strength in southern European waters would be that the Empire would no longer enjoy command of the sea between Gibraltar and the Suez Canal, and Wilson was much concerned when he heard of what was intended. "Busy getting out paper to show what the naval withdrawal from the Mediterranean means," he wrote in the diary on May 3. Three days later comes the entry:

> Haldane sent for me this morning to discuss the question of our naval retirement from the Mediterranean. I advocated an alliance with France for the specific case of German aggression, but he is opposed to it because he sees it would probably mean conscription. He, however, agrees with me that it is high time that the F.O. (or Cabinet) laid down a policy, and our coming withdrawal from the Mediterranean heightens him — and no wonder. The decision to do this was come to by Winston and the Admiralty without permission of the F.O. or Cabinet, and without discussion by the C.I.D.

On the 7th:

> Another long talk with Haldane. He showed me a letter he had received from Winston in which Winston specifically said that he cannot guarantee the North Sea without the Mediterranean squadron, and that if the Mediterranean is still to be kept he will want another 3 millions a year. Haldane, who is more fussed than I ever have seen him, inclines to more ships. I incline to more soldiers.

On the 8th:

> Haldane had another long talk with Sir John and me. Sir John

was excellent and stuck to his point (and my point) of the necessity of an alliance with France. The alternative, in Haldane's mind, and a preferable alternative, is more money on the navy. I prefer soldiers, and think we have ships enough. About 5 o'c. I had a talk with Eyre Crowe. He sent me over a copy of his paper on the Mediterranean problem. This paper is the result of a meeting we had in Troubridge's room of Troubridge, Eyre Crowe, and self, at which I said the F.O. must write a policy paper first. Crowe also insists on the necessity of an alliance. Grey seems to be coming to believe this, but says such a step would break up the Cabinet. So best.

This appears in the diary on June 12:

I had a long talk with Troubridge to-night. He tells me it is now proposed to add 2 battleships to the 4 cruisers in the Mediterranean, and some small craft to Malta and Alexandria, but in no sense could it be said we had regained command. This is serious news. He told me also that he had gathered that this Government won't have an alliance with France. Altogether a serious outlook.

This appears on the 26th:

Sir John, Seely* and I had half an hour about the Mediterranean. The politicians are bamboozling Sir John, and Seely wanted to outface me hat we had not lost the command. But I would not have it at any price. At 5 o'c. I went to the Admiralty and had an hour with Troubridge. It is just as I thought. By drawing the 8 Mediterranean battleships to the north we can just pull the fight with Germany. We have (or will have next year) 25 Dreadnoughts in the North Sea. The Germans likewise 25. Our 8 from the Mediterranean (poor class) will make 33, and 8 with nucleus crews quite unfit to fight. Germany also has another 4 fully equipped. Then, owing to McKenna, we are 11,000 seamen short.

The net result is that we can just hold our own in the North Sea (33 against 29),† and the Mediterranean is gone. This is a most

* Lord Haldane had gone to the Woolsack and Colonel Seely was now Secretary of State.

† 29 should apparently be 25. See also page 137.

> parlous condition of affairs. McKenna has written a paper traversing all that Troubridge and Winston have said; but I saw Troubridge's papers, which are excellent and conclusive.

Wilson was already acquainted with a number of the more prominent members of the Unionist Party, having met some of them at Englemere and others on various occasions elsewhere. But he had never, up to the present, come into contact with Mr. Bonar Law, the leader, and he was anxious to do so. This was arranged for him by Sir Charles Hunter, an old brother-officer who had left the Rifle Brigade many years before and who was now in Parliament. He tells the story of their first meeting as follows in his diary for June 27:

> This afternoon I met Bonar Law by appointment at Charlie Hunter's, and I had if hours talk with him on Mediterranean, North Sea and frontier problems. I was very much pleased with his quiet, unostentatious manner and his exceedingly logical and practical mind. His questions were all to the point and his deductions sound and straight. He gives me the impression of being thoroughly honest and upright, anxious and determined to do all in his power to save the country. He was more than nice and flattering, and he said he would see me again within the next fortnight.

The two met again at Englemere in November, and Wilson mentions a long talk taking place between them on that occasion at Lord Roberts's house. Bonar Law was evidently much impressed with what he had learnt at these interviews, for, on December 3, Wilson received a note from him which led to a particularly interesting meeting on the following day. Of this Wilson writes in his diary:

> Went to Pembroke Lodge at 12 o'clock this morning, where I met Arthur Balfour and, of course, my host, Bonar Law. We discussed military and European matters for 3 hours.
>
> Balfour had written a paper on his "beliefs," which Bonar Law sent me last night. This was practically devoted to home defence and formed the basis of our conversation. I used the usual arguments, said that I could not understand the meaning of home defence, that it meant defeat, that I could not understand what the voluntary effort

had to say to war, that we apparently spent 50 millions on an army that solved no problem, and so forth. Before half an hour Balfour agreed that his paper was no use at all, and at the end of 3 hours he and Bonar Law, with whom I have already had long talks, agreed with me. It was something of a triumph. Both he and B.L. were most nice and flattering.*

What Wilson refers to as a C.I.D. meeting of great importance had taken place on July 4 with reference to the Mediterranean and North Sea questions, and of its proceedings he |writes in his diary:

There was a long duel between Winston and McKenna, the latter trying to make out that Winston's dispositions and withdrawal from the Mediterranean were quite wrong, and Winston more than held his own. Harcourt said he wanted to know Kitchener's opinion. French chimed in and said that he did not know what K. had to say to it and that he (French) would gladly state the General Staff opinion. Asquith agreed. After a long talk — we sat from 11.30 to 5.30 — Asquith read out what *he* said was the sense of the meeting.

1. That the necessary margin must be kept in the North Sea, i.e. 33 of our capital ships to 25 Germans. 2. That at the same time we must keep a fleet in the Mediterranean equal to the strongest Power there, exclusive of France.

This was so much better than what I had thought would be the outcome that I was quite pleased, though not quite satisfied. Winston said towards the close of the proceedings that, if the Committee did not agree to his 33 to 25, he would feel it his duty to rouse the country on the matter. This was a direct threat and, I think, clinched the matter.

The following entry appears in the diary next day:

---

* I have a vivid recollection of meeting Henry in Kensington Gardens — it must have been very shortly after this — and of his giving me one of his racy descriptions of this parley. A good many people happened to be strolling about, but Henry on such occasions was wont to scorn the sotto voce of an official burdened with secrets, I could see out of the tail of my eye the passers-by turn and stare as they heard such expressions as: "You should have seen old Balfour's face," and "I tell you, I had Bonar Law in fits,"— interspersed with guffaws of the heartiest enjoyment.— C.E.C.

> This afternoon I met Lord Charles Beresford at Charlie Hunter's house by appointment. I was pleased and greatly amused at his chat. He was very sound on the Navy and the Mediterranean. Sir J. Maxwell* came to see me before dinner. He is off to Egypt to-morrow. He showed me a copy of letter he had written to Lord K. urging him to come out in favour of compulsion and saying he was the only man the country believed in.

At a meeting of the C.I.D. which took place a week later five Canadian Ministers were present, for whose benefit Sir E. Grey explained our foreign policy, while Mr. Churchill explained our naval policy and finished up by putting forward the suggestion that Canada should give three Dreadnoughts, "The outstanding feature of the meeting," Wilson wrote indignantly in his diary, "was the way in which Grey entirely and absolutely ignored the military problem. I happened to meet Winston about 6.30 on the Horse Guards Parade and told him what I thought of this. He quite agreed." The D.M.O. was in the meantime leaving no stone unturned in his efforts to make the dangerous condition into which the naval and military situation was being allowed to drift known to prominent public men. He describes in his diary a meeting that he had with Mr. Walter Long on July 14 in pursuance of this object, as follows:

> I breakfasted and spent 3½ hours with Walter Long at 65 Eaton Square. I discussed the whole situation with him and advised him to go to Asquith and suggest a Round Table conference. I pointed out that the hands of the Conservatives are very clean in this matter, that they have never made a party business of it, and that, in fact, the whole of the County Associations are run by them. This being so, they can claim as a right to be posted in the matter and to have the views of sailors and soldiers put before them. If Asquith refused I would go to the country. Long listened very attentively, and I think was inclined to agree.

A few days later he saw Troubridge at the Admiralty and asked whether the War Office could, or could not, count on being able to

---

* Lieutenant-General Sir J. Maxwell was commanding in Egypt.

reinforce Malta and Egypt in time of war, and to send troops through the Mediterranean to and from India, and the answer was in each case in the negative. Thereupon he wrote a long minute to the C.I.G.S. pointing out that the military problem ought to be reconsidered thoroughly, inasmuch as the loss of command of the sea (except in respect to the North Sea) had entirely changed the aspect of affairs. Early in September he proceeded to France to be present at the Autumn Manœuvres that were to be held south of the Loire in Poitou; and he was accompanied by Macdonogh and Farquhar. Wilson and his companions were treated with special honour during their stay with the French army, and on arriving at Loudun they found themselves members of General Joffre's mess, with de Castelnau and four junior French officers. He was upon the whole very favourably impressed with what he saw on this occasion, although critical in regard to certain matters. Some of his comments are therefore worth quoting:

> We rode all the morning with the 7th Cavalry Division and a brigade of Chasseurs. The cavalry was *very* ill handled, as they would not dismount. Curious these Frenchmen being so obstinate about the "*arme blanche*."* The Chasseurs brigade were wonderful. They were marching and moving for twelve hours, then attacked, and were still attacking for seven more hours, altogether 19 hours on the go.
>
> Saw some of the 9th Divn. entraining. Very well done. They did not know which station they could use till after the fight was over, yet all was working like clockwork.
>
> Saw the best part of a Cav. Divn. almost surrounded by Colonial Bde and Chasseurs Bde, who had marched 52 k. and ran hard at the end of it. They certainly are wonderful marchers. Cavalry men and horses excellent, but handling is all "*arme blanche*" So useless.
>
> The outstanding things about these manœuvres are: (*a*) The ease with which these Frenchmen move, feed, and fight large masses of men; (*b*) The marching of the infantry.

The following entries to be found in Wilson's diary on September 14 and 15 respectively, are also of interest:

---

* "Cold steel."

> We then went to the Minister of War's (M. Millerand) lunch at Montcouteur. The Minister made a speech and proposed the health of the Russian and English missions. Grand Duke Nicholas replied for Russia and I for England. I think I got through all right, but it was a little trying speaking in French. Was afterwards presented to the Grand Duke and to a great number of French generals, who complimented me.
>
> We rode out to go right along the 15 k. of entrenched position on the right bank of the R. Viene. After crossing on to the island we saw a large crowd, and we were sent for by M. Millerand, who presented me with the Commander, and Macdonogh and Fanny with the Officer of the Legion of Honour. We put them on in a barn and were as proud as peacocks.

From Paris Wilson proceeded straight to Berlin, and from there on to Warsaw, where he was met by Major (now Major-General Sir W. A.) Knox, our Military Attaché in Russia, and where he called on the Governor. Continuing the journey to St. Petersburg he there put up at the Embassy with Sir G. Buchanan, and he also called on the Chief of the Staff, General Jilinski. Wilson then travelled with Knox to Moscow, with which city he was much impressed. He wrote in the diary:

> We went off at once and spent 2 or 3 hours in the Kremlin, a wonderful old citadel about 300 years old, well placed above the Moskova stream, about 70 yards broad. Saw the churches where Napoleon put his kitchens, his horses, his staff, etc. Where he went himself. After lunch we went to the "Hauteurs des Moineaux" about 6 miles out, the hill on the road from Borodino from which Napoleon first saw Moscow. It was a lovely evening and the setting sun behind us shone on the Kremlin and other churches. The R. Moskova, which flows into the Volga, was immediately below us.

Then they moved on to Kiev, where news came to hand that Bulgaria, Serbia, Greece, and Turkey were all mob ilizing, and that the outlook in the Balkans had become very warlike. After a two days' stay they proceeded to Lemberg, and from there on to Cracow and to Vienna, where Knox took train back for Russia. Wilson wrote in his diary there:

> We (Knox and I) had a long talk this morning, going over all the country we have seen, and discussing the whole frontier question thoroughly. I am delighted to have taken this trip; the problem is now alive to me and my opinion is more worth having.

He had intended to visit Constantinople; but the situation in the Balkans had become so critical that he felt obliged to proceed homewards, although he went round by Venice. ("What a wonderful town. I have never imagined such a place, even after seeing Stockholm.") While passing through Paris he found time for a long talk with General de Castelnau, and he got back to 36 Eaton Place on October 12, after having been absent from the office for nearly six weeks.

He wrote in the diary on the 18th:

> Had 2 hours with Winston this evening. He is gravelled for want of a staff and superior leaders. He wants to borrow a couple of my boys. He said that, if only he could have the General Staff that I have, he would have the finest navy in the World. He is right.

Next day he wrote:

> Dispatches in from Brussels and St. Petersburg show that Belgium and Russia and France all mistrust us. And all owing to Grey sitting on the fence and trying to be friends with everyone. He will end by being enemy with everyone. I will write a strong minute to Seely on the subject of a friendly and a hostile Belgium.

On the 22nd the entry appears:

> I had a long talk with Seely. I gave him my minute, written on Bridges'* dispatch of his conversation with Michel, the Belgian War Minister. I pointed out the difference to us and the French of a friendly Belgium, which I put at 12 to 16 divisions. He took my minute away to show Grey.

---

* Major (now Major-General Sir Tom) Bridges was our Military Attaché in Brussels at this time.

Meanwhile the Balkan War had broken out and the Turkish forces were finding themselves quite unable to check the advance of the Bulgarian, Serbian, and Greek armies during the opening exchanges. On intelligence arriving of the complete defeat of the Ottoman troops at Lule Burgas and of their hurried retreat to the Chatalja lines, Wilson wrote in his diary:

> This is very serious. Exactly a month after mobilization was ordered. It must be a warning for men like Haldane, with their 6 months' preparation after the declaration of war.

Convinced as he was of the need of introducing compulsory service, he was much gratified on finding that the necessity for this was coming to be more generally recognized. He wrote in his diary on November 5:

> Dined to-night at the Carlton with Sir John, who had Troubridge, Seely, Winston, and Lloyd George. Talked till 12 a.m. Lloyd George and Winston both in favour of conscription, but said it could only be done by agreement with the other side. I did not tell them of my talk with Bonar Law last Saturday week, but I will tell him of this dinner. L.G. told me that at the Round Table Conference after the King's death the Radicals proposed conscription, but Balfour would not have it. Seely also is coming to heel, and it really was amusing to hear Sir John and myself pounding in the fact that unless we got conscription we were dead men. And all this in front of Seely.

On the 8th the entry occurs:

> At 12 o'c. this morning Seely sent for me. Sir John was already in the room. Seely proceeded to say the state of Europe was critical owing to Serbia wanting a port on the Adriatic, Russia backing her and Austria equally determined to stop it. I don't know how much to believe, though the dispatches to-night confirm this; also one from Lowther stating that if the Bulgars come into C-ple there will be a massacre. Altogether Europe is restless. I was going to Englemere this evening, but was afraid. Seely sent for me again at 6.30 p.m. and asked if France would go to war about the Balkans. I said the French would side with Russia, chiefly because of the balance of power, and also because it was impossible to allow the Turks to disappear out of

Europe. There is no doubt that Albania presents a difficult problem, and it's quite possible that Russia has already come to some agreement with the Balkan Powers.

Wilson was present on November 12 at a meeting of the Military Members of the Army Council, at which the names of the officers who were to hold commands and were to occupy the chief staff appointments in the Expeditionary Force in the event of war, were discussed and settled. He himself was nominated D.M.O. under Grierson, who was to be Sir J. French's Chief of the General Staff. He wrote in his diary that evening:

> At this meeting Jack Cowans* told us the Admiralty now said they could not ship us in time. This is disgraceful, and I fairly let myself go. I said one of three things must be done. Either the Admiralty must ship us, or we must make the arrangements ourselves, or I would go to Paris and say we were not coming; but I refused to allow my name to be a guarantee unless we could carry out my promise.

However, better counsels had evidently prevailed on the other side of Whitehall, as on the 29th the entry occurs:

> The Admiralty come to their senses about shipping us over.

Wilson had in the meantime, with the approval of Seely and of Grey, gone over to Paris and had a meeting with General de Castelnau and some of his staff, to discuss what action ought to be taken supposing Belgium to be hostile in a Continental war. De Castelnau explained his proposals, with which Wilson agreed.

During the closing weeks of this year Wilson had come to the conclusion that the most promising method of compelling the Government to resort to a form of conscription was to demonstrate the inefficiency of the Territorial Forces to the nation, as a first step, and then to induce Mr. Asquith's Government to approach the Opposition with a proposal to introduce obligation to render

---

* Cowans had been appointed Quartermaster-General at the beginning of June.

military service as a measure agreed upon between the two political parties. He was present at more than one meeting with Lord Milner, Mr. (now Lord) Lee, Mr. F. Oliver, and others, at which this mode of proceeding was debated, and he on several occasions makes reference to the subject in his diary. Wilson had also been affording willing assistance to Lord Roberts in the preparation of the speeches which the veteran Field-Marshal had been delivering to large and highly sympathetic audiences at various places in the country during this autumn. On November 23, for instance, he wrote in his diary:

> Lord Bobs slept here last night after his speech about the Territorials. It has staggered Seely and his crowd; they have all sorts of fantastic plans to bolster up the Terriers, and I am terrified they may get Sir John to allow his name to be used. I spoke openly to him about this at a meeting he held of David,* Kiggell and myself.

The Director of Military Operations, who was seeing Sir A. Nicolson at the Foreign Office almost daily, was in the meantime becoming much preoccupied concerning the unsatisfactory position of affairs in Europe. Although the Turks had repulsed a Bulgarian attack on the Chatalja lines with loss, and although Constantinople appeared to be no longer in peril, the campaign in Macedonia, farther to the west, had gone definitely against them. The Serbian and Greek armies, between them, had so completely gained the upper hand, that Ottoman power of resistance was by this time practically confined to the two strongholds of Yanina and Scutari. Austria Hungary was watching events with undisguised jealousy, unwilling that Serbia should gain a port on the Adriatic. Russia appeared disposed to back the Serbian claims, while, on the other hand, determined that King Ferdinand of Bulgaria should not establish his seat of government on the Golden Horn. "The fact is," as Wilson wrote in his diary, "all Europe is on a hair trigger, and all are ready except England, who seems as careless and reckless as she is ignorant." His summary written on the last day of the year

---

* Brigadier-General (afterwards Lieutenant-General Sir David) Henderson, who was now Director of Military Training.

contains the following sombre passage:

> The news to-night is not good. Rumania is threatening to mobilize, and Russia is requesting Austria to demobilize or she will strengthen her Polish corps. The year opened in gloom and closes in deeper gloom. The Peace Conference of the Balkan States is sitting in St. James's Palace, but it looks like breaking up, and the Great Powers are grouped in veiled hostility. It seems possible, though I think not by any means certain, that we shall have a European war this next year. And in spite of all I have written and worked during the whole year, we are not ready. It is disgusting and scandalous.

Chapter VIII – 1913: Director of Military Operations

Meeting with Joffre, de Castelnau, and Foch — The Irish question — Colonel Seely's statement as to General Staff views on invasion — Wilson proceeds to the Near East — Anxiety about the army and Ulster — Lectures in various places.

Early in January Wilson started for his usual trip to Switzerland, and on the way out he had a talk with General de Castelnau, in Paris. The French Chief of the Staff expressed himself as anxious about the coming spring, seeing that Germany was making great preparations in her dockyards and arsenals and was recasting her concentration arrangements, and also in view of her assets in dirigible airships and their possible moral effect. Wilson asked him how many army corps this country ought to be able to place in the field, and he agreed that eight to ten would be sufficient — Wilson having the possibility of compulsory service in his mind when raising the question. He returned home via Paris, and on February 14 had another meeting with the French there, of which he writes in his diary:

> At 10 o'c. I went to see Gen. de Castelnau, who had sent his A.D.C. for me. Huguet came also. I spent 2 hours with him and Gen. Joffre, and was then presented to the new Minister of War, M. Etienne. The third I have known (Messimy, Millerand, Etienne).
>
> My talk with Castelnau and Joffre was about Repington's recent

articles in *The Times*, where he claims that our Navy is worth 500,000 bayonets to the French at the decisive point. I had written to Fred Oliver that our Navy was not worth 500 bayonets. Castelnau and Joffre did not value it at one bayonet I Except from the moral point. It was realized by these men what a serious statement this was, coming at this particular moment, and it was agreed that it should be thoroughly exposed in the French Press. We went into the whole question. I can't help thinking that time is on the side of the Entente.

After lunch Huguet and I came down here (Bourges) where Huguet has a charming house, and we dined with Foch, who has just come here to command the VIIIth Corps. Foch is exactly of the same opinion as regards a'Court's egregious articles as are Castelnau and Joffre, and we talked till midnight.

In connexion with this and other visits that Wilson paid to high French military authorities during these years preceding the Great War, it ought to be mentioned that representatives of the French General Staff, other than General Foch, would from time to time make their appearance in London and would, shepherded by Huguet, wend their way to the War Office to see the D.M.O. Wilson used to tell of one particular "little Frenchman, with button-boots and a dicky tie," who turned up after this fashion and with whom he enjoyed a lively discussion, one of his huge maps of the Franco-Belgian frontier spread out on the table before them. In the course of the debate the little Frenchman, on finding that their views were not absolutely at one concerning some point, became so excited and gesticulatory that the dicky tie became unhinged and shot out with a flop on to the map. But he snatched the object up, clamped it back in its place, and proceeded with his argument quite undisturbed by the incident. That little Frenchman with the button boots and the dicky tie was in a few years to prove himself one of the outstanding figures in the mighty conflict when it came.

The third Home Rule Bill had been passed through the House of Commons after stormy debates in the previous year; but the measure had, as usual, been thrown out in the House of Lords. It was, however, generally recognized that the Bill would be reintroduced in the current year in the Lower Chamber and would be accepted, would again be rejected by the Upper Chamber, and that this same sequence of events would recur in the coming year.

In view of the curb that had been placed upon the powers of the Lords by the Veto Bill of 1911, the general expectation was that an acute political and national crisis would consequently arise in 1914. In no quarter had this been more clearly foreseen than in the North of Ireland, and the loyalists of Ulster had, therefore, with characteristic prescience, administrative capacity, and resolution, already taken steps to meet the situation which Mr. Asquith's Government apparently intended to force upon them. They were, moreover, in some of these steps receiving effective support from sympathizers — many of them men of acknowledged light and leading — in other parts of the United Kingdom. In view of his ancestry and of his associations, Wilson, Irishman and Imperialist, could not but be a warm supporter of the loyalist cause, and of the loyalist cause in Ulster in particular; and he had viewed the proceedings of the Cabinet in connexion with Home Rule with a growing indignation for a long time past. The first reference in his diaries to the preparations being made in the North of Ireland for, if necessary, resisting separation from Great Britain, however, appears on March 13 of this year:

> Jemmy arrived, having come over on deputation to Bonar Law. He told me of the plans for the North, of the 25,000 armed men to act as citadel, and the 100,000 men to act as constables. Of the arrangements for the banks, railways, etc., election, provisional government, and so on. As far as I could judge, all very sensible.

Wilson's resentment at the attitude and the actions of the Government in connexion with the Irish question undoubtedly tended to make him even more hostile to their policy in regard to foreign affairs, and to their attitude in respect to offence and defence problems, than he would otherwise have been. This also, no doubt, accounts in some measure for the very strong expressions that he uses from time to time in his diaries during these years in connexion with certain members of the Cabinet and with their proceedings, quite apart from Irish matters.

Lord Wolseley died in the south of France on March 25, his body was brought home for interment, and lay in state at the War Office for two days. The military funeral of the illustrious Field-

Marshal took place on March 31, and, in view of that other impressive, sombre pageant that was to take place nine years afterwards in London — to be recorded later — Wilson's references to the stately ceremony in Wren's cathedral possess an interest of poignant significance:

> I went to Lord Wolseley's funeral in St. Paul's. A magnificent service in a glorious place. A curious fog and darkness which added to the weird effect. The cathedral packed with people, and immense crowds along the whole line from the W.O. to St. Paul's. A wonderful sight.
>
> Very pathetic to see Frances Wolseley kneeling alone when the coffin was lowered into the crypt. The final drums and Dead March, and "Last Post" up in the top gallery, was extraordinarily impressive.

A sub-committee of the C.I.D., especially set up to consider what scale of attack ought to be prepared for when deciding upon the military forces necessary for home defence, was, in the meantime, holding its sittings. The matter was brought into public prominence by an incident that occurred in the House of Commons on April 11, and Wilson's reference to this singular episode in ms diary on the morrow, as also his further references to it on later days, are of considerable interest. Some of his expressions are, however, so forcible that they have been omitted.

> Seely made an amazing speech last night on Sandys's Bill for compulsory service. He said the General Staff said we could deal with 70,000 men if the Expeditionary Force had gone abroad. Bonar Law twice challenged this statement, and Seely twice repeated it. He also said the General Staff were against compulsory service, and this after the paper Kiggell and I drew up, and Sir John signed on Thursday, specifically saying we were in favour of it.
>
> *April 15.* I saw Sir John about Seely's speech last Friday. I told him we three Directors were quite prepared to resign, and I told him we were sick of this class of work, and that the officers at the W.O. and in the Army were looking to him to redress matters. He told me I might tell Bonar Law to-morrow, when I am lunching with him, that he (Sir John) would resign unless Seely climbed down.
>
> *April 16.* Saw Sir John this morning. We showed him Hansard's report of Seely's answer to Bonar Law.

I lunched with Bonar Law at his house. Arthur Balfour also there. I told B. L. that we (General Staff) were clear Seely must recant this Friday statement. We then discussed the Sub-Committee on invasion, which A.B. is on, and I told A.B. that in my opinion it was impossible to examine the problem of invasion apart from the general problem of war. We discussed for two hours, and Arthur Balfour and Bonar Law were more than nice to me.

Later I had a talk again with Sir John and impressed upon him that we must resign unless Seely contradicted his Friday statement. He entirely agreed and Seely is to do it this afternoon. We shall see.

April 17. Seely did read out what Sir John said he must, but he then went on with prevarications. I told Sir John what I thought; hut he is not inclined to take further action.

April 20. I drafted a speech for Sir John for the Chamber of Commerce next Thursday, and I took it up to the Marlborough Club, where I lunched with him. He was very nice, and agreed with much that I had written, but he told me he had been made a Field-Marshal, which, human nature being what is it, a little crippled him and made him anxious not to be more nasty to Seely than he could help. This is very natural.

Although there had been an armistice lasting for some weeks during the winter, hostilities had been resumed in the Balkans during these early months of the year. But Scutari at last, after a prolonged defence, surrendered to the Montenegrins on April 22, and this brought the struggle with Turkey to a close. Yanina had fallen to the Greeks on March 5, and Adrianople had been taken by combined Bulgarian and Serb forces on the 25th of that month. The situation, as between Austria-Hungary and Russia, which, as we have seen, had been somewhat strained at the end of 1912, had gradually improved — thanks to no small extent to a Conference of Ambassadors which had been intermittently sitting in London under the presidency of Sir Edward Grey since December. But the occupation of Scutari by the Montenegrins now created fresh trouble lasting for a few days, inasmuch as the Government of the Dual Monarchy was resolved that this ancient stronghold should not remain in possession of the victors.

Wilson wrote in the diary on April 26:

Sir Arthur Nicolson sent for me this morning; he is disturbed at the outlook. Austria certainly seems to be getting impatient, and he read me the instructions |which Bercholdt had telegraphed to the Austrian Ambassador, but which he did not carry out. The instruction was very clear. Either the Ambassadors would agree to collective military action, or Austria would act alone. The Ambassadors apparently could not agree to joint military action, and could only agree to the blockade extending to Durazzo. There the matter lies to-day. I told Sir Arthur we were examining how many Austrian troops it would take to knock out Montenegro, and said it looked like 80,000 to 100,000 men.

The King of Montenegro, however, on realizing that Austria-Hungary was determined, and was prepared, if need be, to take strong measures, submitted with as good a grace as was practicable, and Wilson was consequently able to write in his diary on May 9:

Now that Montenegro is leaving Scutari, the European outlook is for the moment quiet.

He went over to Paris in the middle of June, where he met Foch and Huguet (who had especially come up from Bourges to meet him), and where he spent two hours with de Castelnau. A few days later he met Mr. Austen Chamberlain and Doctor Jameson at Mr. Oliver's house, Checkendon Court, near Reading. "Much talk with Austen Chamberlain," he wrote in his diary, "which interested me. As Chancellor he was on the C.I.D. in the late Government." "Balkan news looks bad," he noted a few days afterwards, "as the Allies are fighting regular and bitter like man and wife" — this refers to the sudden outbreak of hostilities between the Bulgarians on the one hand and the Serbs and Greeks on the other hand, hostilities which terminated within a month in the overthrow of King Ferdinand's forces and the loss of practically all that Bulgaria had won at the expense of the Ottoman Empire earlier in the year.

It should be mentioned that some important changes took place on the General Staff at the War Office just at this time. General Robertson replacing General Henderson as Director of Military Training, and Brigadier-General (now General Sir F.J.) Davies succeeding Kiggell, who took Robertson's place at the Staff

At the French Manœuvres
From left to right: unknown officer, Col. Vie de la Panouse, Lord Brooke, Brig.-Gen Wilson

College. Wilson accompanied Sir J. French and General Grierson to the French manœuvres about Chalons early in August; Sir John, on this occasion, was treated with great honour, taking the salute of the 40th Division at the march past and formally inspecting the Cavalry Division. Afterwards, in company with Harper, Wilson motored about the frontier near Mezières and thence on to Trèves; they afterwards proceeded to Aix-la-Chapelle, seeing something of the German strategic railways in the Eiffel country, and from there they ran through the Ardennes to Namur to complete their tour. Wilson was, however, only back in England for three weeks, for he then returned to France to attend the manœuvres of the XXth Corps, which Foch now commanded; Russian officers were also present at these exercises and he wrote on September 13:

> To-night we had dinner at 7 o'c., and the town band played for us and gave us the Russian hymn and "God save the King." When we walked home a large crowd cheered us the whole way, shouting "Vive la Russie," "Vive l'Angleterre." Quite spontaneous.

Immediately after returning home the D.M.O. attended our

own manœuvres in the Midlands, at which General de Castelnau and several other French officers were present, with whom he spent the time. Then, early in October, he started for the Near East with Sir C. Hunter, proceeding via the Iron Gates to Constanza and thence by sea to Constantinople. He has much that is noteworthy to say in his diary during the week that they spent on the Golden Horn, of which the following extracts must, however, suffice:

> *October 9*. Charlie and I, with guide, to Stambul. We saw the first train from Sofia arrive since the war began a year ago. We saw San Sofia, a wonderful dome, all dome in fact. We saw at midday the callers from the minarets calling the Faithful to prayers. We saw the old Roman remains, we walked through the caves of the bazaar and went hither and thither in Stambul. Still the enormous crowds of Turks, old and young, which puzzles me. A wonderful mixture of people east and west.
>
> Fairholme, staying here, and Fitzmaurice dined — a most interesting man, who is 1st Dragoman here and who knows the Turk better than any European alive. He has grave doubts as to the future existence of Turkey. The substitution of party government for the Padishah and Islam may, probably will, be fatal to the country. Our steam back up the Bosporus at midnight was beautiful. Our loss of prestige out here is appalling.
>
> *October 10*. I have heard more, learnt more, and understand more of the Eastern Question now, than I have done in the 3 years as D.M.O. And, overshadowing everything else, and coming from every side, is our loss of prestige.
>
> *October 11*. Fitzmaurice, Charlie, and I went to the Sublime Porte and called on Talaat Pasha, the most powerful man of the Committee of Union and Progress. This was most successful, and he passed us on to Djemal Pasha, comdg. VIth Corps and Governor of Constantinople. Talaat is a stout, modernized Turk, who a short time ago was a telegraph clerk. I did not like the look of him. An oily schemer without principles or, I should say, backbone. Djemal Pasha is a nice looking, bearded soldier and man of action. He has given me a "passe partout" and attached one of his A.D.C.s to me until we leave the country.
>
> After lunch Fitzmaurice drove us out to the old Constantine walls (about 400 A.D.) which stretch across the Stambul peninsula from Golden Horn to Marmora. They are wonderful.
>
> *October 12*. Malet, the new ambassador, arrives next week. I fear

he comes here with that awful thing "an open mind."

October 13. Charlie and I up at 3 a.m. and met Yunni Bey (Djemal's A.D.C.) at the station at 4 a.m. We reached Hadhum Keui, at 8.45, this side of the Chatalja lines. There we met Hakki Pasha, the commander of the lines, who had horses and an escort for us, and we rode almost the length of the lines, including the central Bulgar position from which they launched their big attack against Chasseur Hill. From the Bulgar position the panorama of the lines is superb. I don't know that I have ever seen a stronger position than Chatalja. It could be made untakable by assault or by siege, provided, in the latter case, the Turks had command of the sea.

October 14. At 6 p.m. Djemal Pasha came to call on me at the hotel. He opened his heart, or pretended to. He asked why England was hesitating to help by lending two men of affairs like Milner, and a number of officers to command the gendarmerie in Anatolia. He understood England was afraid of offending Russia. What business was it of Russia? He would prefer going to hell in his own way than to Paradise under the tutelage of Russia. The Young Turks were honestly anxious to improve matters in Armenia, and could do so best under English direction. Their eyes were turned neither to India nor to Egypt, whereas Russia was looking to India. The Young Turks would dispose of the Greeks and would then turn their eyes to the Danube. He (Djemal) always thought that Hakki Pasha's diplomacy of trying to be friends with Germany and Austria, in the hope that these would prevent Bulgaria and Serbia from falling on Turkey, was wrong, and this had now been proved. Hakki was now anxious to be friends with England and France.

A strong Turkey in Asia would be good for England, a movement of Russia into Turkey in Asia would be fatal for England owing to India. He repeatedly expressed his wish for the assistance of England in men who would administer, execute, and command. The Turks could not now change their military teachers (Germans), but in all else, in finance, administration, navy, and reforms they wished to be under English guidance.

Leaving Constantinople at 4 a.m. on the 15 th, Wilson and Hunter arrived early in the afternoon at Lule Burgas and drove over the battle-field, of which Wilson gives a detailed description in his diary. They went on by train during the night to Adrianople, where the governor and commander of the IXth Corps placed two cars and his A.D.C. at their disposal. That day they motored round part of the defences, and on the morrow they motored to Kirk Kilisse and back. Wilson notes in his diary:

> We saw many villages, chiefly Mohammedan, which the Bulgars had. burnt to the ground. They destroyed some 600 houses in Kirk Kilissis, We met whole villages of people on the trek: men, women, and children and herds and household goods. Very curious to see the poor things with nowhere to go. We met a division on the march from Adrianople to Chorlu. It was little better than a rabble, and all the Turkish soldiers I have seen are in rags.

He wrote next day:

> We spent the morning on the southern and western face of the fortress being shown *everything*.
>
> I have been immensely interested in Turkey. We have talked to all sorts of people. I have seen every serious field of battle in Thrace, and been right round the fortress of Adrianople; and two things stand out clearly: (*a*) The fighting was neither heavy, frequent, nor good; (*b*) The Turkish army is not a serious modern army. Other things there are also: no roads, only single railways and very few of them, and, in fact, no sign of adaptation to western thought and methods. The army is ill-commanded, ill-officered and in rags. I cannot think Turkey in Europe will survive another shaking.

At Sofia, their nest stopping-place, Wilson was much impressed with the progressiveness of the Bulgarians, as contrasted with the Turks, and with the buildings, the streets, and the general cleanliness of the city. "The more I see, the more I am astonished," he wrote in his diary. They spent a day at Belgrade, and then proceeded home via Paris, where Wilson saw de Castelnau and told him of the trip. Ten days later, on November 4, he was gazetted major-general, at the age of forty-eight and a half, and after twenty-eight years' service. He had risen from the rank of captain to that of major-general in twelve years — an unusually rapid rate of promotion in peace time. On that same day there appears an entry in his diary of an ominous nature, which must therefore be quoted:

> Sir John had a long talk with me about Ulster. He is evidently

nervous that we are coming to civil war, and his attitude appears to be that he will obey the King's orders. He wanted to know what I would do. I told him that I could not fire on the North at the dictation of Redmond, and this is what the whole thing means. England qua England is opposed to Home Rule, and England must agree to it before it is carried out. I was much struck by his seriousness. I cannot bring myself to believe that Asquith will be so mad as to employ force. It will split the army and the colonies, as well as the country and the Empire.

Next day he delivered a lecture on "Frontiers" at the University of London. He had been delivering addresses on this subject at a number of places during this and the previous year, saying much the same thing on each occasion although suiting his treatment of the subject to the different audiences, composed as they were, sometimes of schoolboys, sometimes of cadets, and sometimes of officers or of mature civilians. On this particular occasion Colonel Seely would seem, in view of an entry that appears in the diary, to have taken umbrage at views that had been expressed by the lecturer.

Seely sent for me and tried to check me for my lecture yesterday, but I wasn't for it. We then discussed the evidence that I was to give at the C.I.D., on the 12th, and I told him I had refused to give evidence unless I had a problem, and as no one could, or would, set me a problem I was drawing up two for the C.I.D. This I did during the day, i.e.:–

Problem H. A duel between England and Germany.

Problem W. Triple Entente versus Triple Alliance.

I sent them to Hankey to-night, to be submitted to Asquith to-morrow. I told Sir John I had been thinking over Ulster, and that I thought he ought to put in writing the fact that he could not be responsible for the whole of the army. This Ulster business is getting serious.

Of a visit which he paid Mr. Bonar Law, on November 9, he wrote in his diary:

I told him that there was much talk in the army, and that if we were ordered to coerce Ulster there would be wholesale defections;

It had been suggested to him that 40 pc. of officers and men would leave the army. Personally I put the pc. much lower, but still very serious. I then told him of Cecil's idea that Carson should pledge the Ulster troops to fight for England if she was at war. I pointed out that a move like this would render the employment of troops against Ulster more impossible than ever. He was much pleased with the suggestion and at once tried to get Carson on the telephone. He was, however, away for the day. Bonar Law will see him to-morrow.

I then told B. L. of my coming evidence before the C.I.D; Invasion Committee, and how I proposed to tackle the subject with my problems. He entirely agreed. We then discussed the Linlithgow and Reading elections. Asquith was going to approach B. L. with a proposal to exclude the 4 Northern Counties. This, of course, wrecks the present Bill, and puts B. L. into an awkward position, as Ulster won't agree; and then Asquith can exclaim intolerance.

On the other hand, Asquith is in a much tighter place, because Johnnie Redmond and Devlin can't agree to the exclusion of Ulster. The thing to do, therefore, is to make Redmond wreck the proposal. This, and much more talk of a confidential nature made my morning very interesting. B. L. realizes what a difficult place he is in with tariff reform and food taxes. But on the whole his prospects are much more rosy than Asquith's.

He wrote in the diary on the 12th:

I gave my evidence before the Invasion Committee of the C.I.D. Asquith led off by being rather rude to me, but he and the others soon saw that I was not going to stand any nonsense, and later on Asquith was as nice as he could be, and at the end was most complimentary. I went through my three Problems* and 6 answers and expressed clear and definite opinions on all of them. Jimmy Grierson told me I terrified Harcourt and Crewe with my picture of the size of foreign armies.

This appears in the diary next day:

---

* He had only mentioned two on the 6th. The third may have been that which actually presented itself nine months later, viz: the Triple Entente versus the two Central Powers.

> This evening about 6 o'c. I went in to see Macready.* He told me he was being sent over to Ireland on Sunday, ostensibly to see after the riots, etc., in Dublin, in reality to watch the North. He told me the Cabinet have settled not to try to employ troops, as they realize at last the temper of Ulster and tie army. They are afraid of a Jameson raid on some depot. I told him there was not the least danger, and that on the contrary the North was probably going to offer her army to England if in difficulties. We discussed other points, but the really important thing is that the Govt, at last realize that they cannot employ the army in this work.

On the 14th Wilson wrote:

> Charlie Hunter and I dined with Milner at Brooks'. Milner was emphatic in support of Ulster and said that the Unionists of England would soon have to pass from words to deeds. One of the first declarations to be made would be that, if any officers resigned, they would be reinstated when the Conservatives came into power. I was glad to hear all this.

Next day there is the entry:

> The Edward Sclaters to lunch. He is one of the "Five" who are running Ulster. He was most interesting. I warned him of such pitfalls as seizing depots where there are arms, and any action hostile to the army, which was now becoming most sympathetic to the Ulster movement. Also the advisability of constantly repeating the fact that the whole Ulster army would come over and help England if she was in trouble.

The Director of Military Operations was in great request as a lecturer about this time. The reputation which he had earned for delivering singularly lucid and informative addresses, that were wont to be enlivened by the employment of highly original metaphors and by the introduction of anecdotes as pungent as they were apt, had spread far and wide. Within the space of a single month he appeared at the Royal Military College, at Newcastle

---

* Sir N. Macready was at this time Director of Personal Services in the War Office.

(where he gave two lectures, one to the boys of the Royal Grammar School and the other to the local "War and Peace Circle"), at the War College, at Portsmouth, at Lichfield and at Tidworth. On these occasions he generally chose for his subject, either the strategical aspects of the late Balkan Wars, or else the military questions involved in the configuration and in the extent of the various European frontiers. His address to the "War and Peace Circle" at Newcastle was admirably adapted to meet the case of an audience which was somewhat disposed to regard anything connected with problems of national defence as "militarism." Wilson on that occasion confined himself to facts and he studiously eschewed the expression of opinions. But those facts were so deftly marshalled and were set out so dearly that they effectually brought home to his Tyneside listeners the perils to which their country stood exposed. The lecture aroused the utmost interest locally, and it exerted a noteworthy influence in a community of decidedly Radical tendencies — so much so, indeed, that some of those well acquainted with the Newcastle of 1914 attribute, to some extent at least, the almost exceptionally patriotic attitude of its citizens during the Great War to the effect of Wilson's visit of a few months before.

His liking for young people in general was such that he was always at his happiest when speaking to an assemblage of schoolboys or of cadets, and his lecture at Sandhurst on this occasion was one of his most remarkable efforts in this direction. It took place as usual in the evening, after dinner, and as they were walking together up to the hall, the commandant. General Stopford, begged that something might be said of a nature to encourage the lads, and that would help to bring home to them how much would depend upon them when they went out into the army as commissioned officers. The Senior Division, who were about to pass finally out of the College were to form the audience.

The rows of seats in the lecture-hall form a semi-circle, raised in tiers one above the other, and the cadets were gathered thick on these in their red mess-uniform. Wilson mat evening was very grave and very earnest. He knew that war was inevitable before long. He may even have felt a presentiment that most members of this youthful audience towering face to face with him would be in the field within a year, a presentiment that only too many of them would already, ere twelve months were out, have fallen by the way. The cadets sat motionless, intent, drinking in each word, every eye fixed upon the long, somewhat gaunt figure standing over against them. He, on this occasion, dealt with frontiers, and he laid a very special stress upon the Franco-German border-line, its strategical features and their significance — which he had never before done at Sandhurst. Then, in bringing his lecture to a close, he spoke of the Empire and of its future, and he went on to refer to those pessimists who were ever declaring that we had become a decadent race. "I myself," he exclaimed, raising his voice in ringing peroration, "am not a pessimist. I am an optimist, because," and he shot his arm out to point at the rows of cadets facing him in rapt attention, "I see before me the future of the British Army." There followed a momentary silence. The audience seemed to take a long breath. Then the cadets sprang to their feet and burst into a tempest of cheering. They cheered him again and again, and would hardly let him go. The incident made an extraordinary impression not only on the cadets, but also on the many officers of the College staff in the room, as these noted the effect which Wilson's words and his striking personality had exerted amongst the youths who were about to go out into the world and to take up command of British soldiers.

Although particularly concerned owing to the menacing conditions that were arising in Ireland, the D.M.O. was also growing more and more anxious about the general military situation; and that this was the case is made plain by his diary under date November 25, which runs as follows:

> Wherever I look, to China, to India, to Egypt, to S. Africa, to Morocco, to Europe, everything is restless and unsettled, and everyone except ourselves is getting ready for war. This frightens me. Our Territorials are falling down — witness the Deputations of County Associations who are going to wait on Asquith to-morrow; our regulars are falling down — witness our recruiting returns; our Special Reserve is a thing *pour rire*.* And we are doing nothing.

---

* "For a laugh."

As regards the Ulster question he was much pleased with two points that had been brought to his notice. The first was that in the event of actual hostilities, England would be obliged to give the North of Ireland belligerent rights, just as the Federals had to the Confederates in the American Civil War. The other was a suggestion that all Unionists now in the Territorial Army should resign. Lord Halsbury, however, held that England would not be obliged to grant belligerent rights. Wilson was disappointed at a ruling which could not be ignored, as he had hoped that this aspect of the question might have deterred the Prime Minister from proceeding to extremes — Mr. Asquith had announced that he meant to employ the army if necessary. He wrote in his diary on December 2:

> I lunched with Fred Oliver. I impressed on him the irreparable damage which the present state of affairs is doing to the army, and the necessity of ending the disgraceful state we are in. He was fully seized. There is no time to be lost. Already all ranks are talking in a hostile manner of being employed against the north of Ireland. This questioning of orders is something quite new, and yet very natural in the circumstances in our army, and is a real and pressing danger. Something must be done to end the present tension — and quickly.

The following entity appears in the diary on the last day of the year:

> Enormous preparations everywhere for war, except with us, and great and universal unrest, interior and exterior, in all parts of the world. Ulster rapidly becoming the sole and governing and immediate factor in the national life.

Chapter IX – 1914: Director of Military Operations

Wilson's task almost completed — The Ulster question, risk of the army being involved — The Curragh incident — Wilson takes the matter in hand — Political crisis — Resignation of Colonel Seely, the C.I.G.S. and the Adjutant-General — The European crisis — The scheme for transferring the Expeditionary Force to its war concentration area in France — The work just finished in time — 7 Draycott Place becomes the mobilization centre of Unionist pressure on the Government — August 4. War.

Nearly three and a half years of the four years which Wilson's appointment as Director of Military Operations was supposed to last, had expired by the beginning of 1914, and the question of his future was beginning to exercise his mind. There had already been some discussion as to his period being extended, and on January 10 Sir J. French definitely asked him if he would accept prolongation, on the understanding that he would then in all likelihood succeed to the command of the 4th Division, which would fall vacant early in 1915. He did not desire the extension, but he expresses himself in his diary as satisfied with the proposed arrangement. In this he makes no reference to one circumstance which no doubt influenced him in his wish to leave the War Office at the end of the four years' normal term.

Completing arrangements for, in certain eventualities, transferring the Expeditionary Force from its peace stations in the United Kingdom to the concentration area in France, which Wilson had provisionally decided upon in concert with the French General Staff, had been proceeding steadily during 1912 and 1913. The whole scheme was very nearly consummated at the beginning of

1914, and Wilson could count upon its being absolutely ready before the end of the coming July, when his period as D.M.O. would in ordinary circumstances expire. Further detailed information with regard to the scheme will, however, be reserved until the end of this chapter, which carries the story of Wilson's career up to the date of the rejection of the British ultimatum by Germany on the night of August 4. In the opening days of 1914 the Irish question and problem of Ulster was the subject especially engaging Wilson's attention, and what caused him particular anxiety was the obvious inability of men of affairs in general to comprehend the gravity of the situation, or to appreciate the dangers to the army which a further development of that situation was likely to bring about. The very fact that no plan of any kind for utilizing the troops in the event of a crisis in Ulster existed, that no plan had ever indeed been thought of at the War Office — or apparently by the Government[*] — served to show how completely the Cabinet failed to realize that it was face to face with a dilemma of its own creation.

On January 7 the entry appears in the diary:

> Robertson, Joey,[†] and I had a long and serious talk about Ulster, and whether we could not do something to keep the army out of it. We agreed to find out the feeling in Commands at the conference next week at Camberley.

Towards the end of January Wilson started for his usual holiday abroad, and almost immediately after getting back to England he paid a short visit to Belfast. While there he visited the old home of his family, Rashee, now in ruins; he delivered a lecture on the Balkans to the troops in the Victoria Barracks; he also paid a visit to the Ulster Union Offices, and he wrote in the diary:

---

[*] That there must be a plan seems to have occurred to Ministers for the first time two days before the "Curragh incident" so suddenly precipitated events three months later.

[†] General F.J. Davies, the D.S.D.

> The arrangements of the Ulster Army are well advanced and there is no doubt of the discipline and spirit of men and officers.- I must come over later and see the troops at work. Many remarkable stories of Carson's power were told me.

A C.I.D. meeting took place on the day after his return to the War Office at which the proceedings would not appear to have been of an edifying nature. His description of what occurred was:

> Usual rubbish talked, but especially about the Channel Tunnel; I gave my opinion as being that, if we are going to take part in European wars the more tunnels we have the better, if not, then the fewer we have the better.
>
> After the meeting [he continues] Seely sent for me to ask what I thought of the Ulster situation. I told him exactly what I thought, which was that the Government are done. That they have bumped up against 100,000 men who are in deadly earnest, and that, as neither the Cabinet nor Englishmen are ever in earnest about anything, Ulster was certain to win. Seely said he had always told the Cabinet that they could not coerce Ulster.

Although, the situation in Ireland was obviously critical, and although the Government were in serious difficulties in view of the certainty that the Home Rule Bill, as it stood, would be rejected for the third time by the House of Lords and would then automatically become law, the view generally prevailed during the first half of March, that the Cabinet would not dare to use the army to force separation from the United Kingdom upon Ulster. The Army Annual Bill was to come before the House of Lords very shortly, and, as there was an idea that a proposal might be made to amend it, Wilson paid a visit to Mr. Bonar Law at his residence with the object of discussing this project — one which had not at first appealed to him. He wrote in his diary:

> We had an hour's talk, and he entirely persuaded me to his side. The proposal is for the Lords to bring in an amendment to the effect that the army shall not be used against Ulster without the will of the people expressed at a General Election. This gets over my difficulty. Bonar Law told me that the only alternative to this is to go on in the ordinary way, in which case the Bill will be passed as it stands,

Carson will set up his provisional government, and civil war is inevitable. We discussed it all backwards and forwards, the handle it will give against the Lords, the possibility of no army remaining after April 30, the effect abroad; and I am convinced that Bonar Law is right. Desperate measures are required to save a desperate situation.

I made one suggestion to Bonar Law, which he approved. I said that before the Lords touch the Army Annual Act he (B. L.) should get up in the House of Commons and ask Asquith the point-blank question, "Are you going to use the army to coerce Ulster or are you not?" As Asquith is sure to return an evasive answer, Bonar Law must anticipate by saying, "There are three ways of answering the question, i.e. Yes — No — No answer. In the event of No answer, the inference will be Yes"; and Bonar Law should say that, if Asquith gives an evasive answer, it will be counted by him and his party and the country as meaning Yes.

Wilson mote in the diary on the 18th:

Sir John sent for me after luncheon to talk about Ulster. He told me he had been discussing affairs all the morning at a meeting of Crewe, Seely, Winston, Birrell, Sir John, Ewart, Paget and Macready. It appears they are contemplating scattering troops all over Ulster, as though it was a Pontypool coal strike. Sir John pointed out that this was opposed to all true strategy, etc., but was told that the political situation necessitated this dispersion. He said that, as far as he could see, the Government were determined to see this thing through. He did not say when troops were to be sent. He asked whether the General Staff had done anything, and I replied that if we took it over it would fall to Robertson as Home Defence.

I then told him that in my opinion if the Government wanted to crush the North, they would have to mobilize the whole army, and that, even so, I had great doubts whether they could do it, as there would be serious work for troops in the rest of Ireland and also in the large towns of England, and that the Continent would not look on unmoved. Furthermore, there would be a large proportion of officers and men who would refuse to coerce Ulster.

He seemed surprised at all this. I told him the whole thing was a nightmare to me, and that I could not believe that the Government were so mad as to start this war. After I left him I began to think that I ought to have spoken more about his personal position as C.I. G.S. and his responsibility. I will see him to-morrow.

> Later on Amery came to see me, and he is greatly impressed with the gravity of the situation. He also favours amending the Army Annual Act. Later I dined with Charlie Hunter, where were Milner, Doctor "Jim," and Carson. A long and most interesting talk. Carson says his speech to-morrow on the Vote of Censure will be his last in the House of Commons till after the Ulster question is settled. They all agree the Lords must amend the Army Annual Act.

Wilson saw Sir J. French again on the following afternoon (19th), Sir W. Robertson being present. The D.M.O. repeated what he had said on the previous day about the gravity of the military problem which any attempt by the army to coerce Ulster would create, and about the disastrous effect which such an undertaking must have upon the army itself. "Sir John," he remarked in his diary, "I think, agreed with very little that I said." It would appear, however, that at this meeting the question arose between Wilson and Robertson as to which of them was responsible for carrying out the operations, supposing that military actions were to take place. Sir William makes a brief reference to the matter in his "From Private to Field-Marshal" which deserves to be quoted here:

> The responsibility for operations outside the United Kingdom rested with the Director of Military Operations; that for operations inside, but only as against oversea attack, rested with me, the Director of Military Training; and the Adjutant-General dealt with the use of troops in aid of the civil power. The case of Ulster did not fall within any of these three spheres, and not wishing to have anything to do with it, each of us agreed that it was not his business. In the end it was settled that, if troops had to be employed, the duty would come under the heading of Home Defence, and the arrangements would accordingly fall upon me.
>
> I then asked a few further questions: "Are we supposed to be going to war with Ulster: that is, will the troops be on active service? If we are not going to war, what are we going to do, as the case obviously is not one of suppressing civil disorder, because there is no disorder at present? If we are going to war, is mobilization to be ordered, and what ammunition, supplies, and transport are the troops to take? What instructions are to be given to the General in command regarding the nature and object of his mission?"

Wilson also told the C.I.G.S. that the Government must give Irish officers the option of not going over to coerce Ulster, and the C.I.G.S. promised to put this and other points to the Cabinet on the morrow. On the evening of the 20th he was unexpectedly summoned from the War Office to Eaton Place to see General J. E. Gough on a matter of urgent importance. Gough had heard from his brother Hubert at the Curragh. Hubert, commanding the cavalry brigade there, had been ordered either to undertake operations against Ulster or to be dismissed the service, had been given two hours to make up his mind, and had accepted dismissal. John Gough was proposing to send in his papers at once, but was persuaded by the D.M.O. to hold his hand. That night the D.M.O. heard by telephone that the whole of the officers of the 16th Lancers, Hubert Gough's old regiment and now under him at the Curragh, had resigned. "We must steady ourselves a bit," he remarked in his diary at the end of an exciting day. He wrote next day (Saturday):

> Hubert Gough and some 50 officers of the Curragh Camp have resigned because, as far as I can make out, they were asked to operate against Ulster. I was at Bonar Law's at 9.30 a.m. and told him how serious everything was, and how on my present information I thought it would, be imperative to back Hubert. I had several interviews during the day with Sir John. Robertson backed me like a man. Joey was away. I told Sir John there was still time to stop the breakaway of the officers if he made Asquith take instant action, but it must be done at once or the General Staff would break away next. Sir John not yet "seized" with the gravity of the situation. After much coming and going of Sir John to Seely, the latter asked what the army would agree to, and I was asked to put it in writing.
>
> This I did in the form of a promise on the part of the Government not to employ the army to coerce Ulster to accept the Home Rule Bill, and the reinstatement of Hubert and all his officers. Sir John took this paper to Seely, and I gathered that it was not agreeable to Asquith and his crowd.
>
> At 7 o'c. I went to Seely. He opened the talk by thanking me for the way I have behaved during a trying two years, because he knew my sympathies were with Ulster, and so forth, and he consequently wished to thank me as S. of S. I replied that no thanks were required as I had only done what I considered right. We then had ¾ hour about

> the present crisis. I told him the same story as I had told French — no officers on the General Staff at the War Office, the regiments depleted of officers, a hostile Europe, our friends leaving us because we have failed them and our enemies realizing that we had lost our army. Seely remained untouched. At ½ to 8 Bonar Law came to see me at No. 36 and we talked over the events of the day. I am more than ever determined to resign, but I cannot think of a really good way of doing it.

The diary next day reads:

> Went to Sloane Square to see Hubert and Johnnie Gough. I got from Hubert a written account of what happened on Friday last. Arthur Paget put to the Brigadiers (Hubert and Cuthbert) the alternative for them and their officers of undertaking "active operations against Ulster" or "dismissal with loss of pension." Officers belonging to Ulster would "disappear" and be reinstated after the operations were over in their proper seniority. On this Hubert and 56 out of 60 Curragh officers elected for dismissal.
>
> All this is a perfect God-send for me, because I can now write and say that I understand these alternatives were put before these officers, and, if and when they are put before me, I will give the same answer. Therefore I am in the same boat as Hubert and demand same treatment. Great coming and going here all day of a number of fellows all wanting to know what they are to do. I explained new situation. Bonar Law came round here to see me, and wanted me to go and dine at Lansdowne House to meet Balfour and Austen. I thought wiser not. I gave Bonar Law my copy of Hubert's report of what A.P. said, and told him he might use it.

Wilson saw Bonar Law next morning (Monday the 23rd) and told him how the situation was developing. Hubert Gough had been to breakfast at No. 36, and they had agreed that any proposals that should be made must be made in writing, and must state that Gough would not be called upon to employ his troops to coerce Ulster to accept the Home Rule Bill. Gough saw the Adjutant-General and the S. of S. during the forenoon, and the latter agreed to put in writing that the Government would only ask troops to aid the civil power in maintaining law and order. To this Wilson objected absolutely, because, as he pointed out, as soon as the

Home Rule Bill became law the coercion of Ulster would automatically come under the head of aiding the civil power. So Gough and he between them drafted a Tetter asking the question whether, in the event of the Bill passing, troops would be liable to be called upon to coerce Ulster in the name of law and order. As a result they received a draft, initialled by Col. Seely, Sir J. French, and Sir J. Ewart, which appeared reasonable, although the last paragraph was unintelligible to Wilson, seeing that it spoke of not using troops to suppress "political opposition." So they wrote a short note saying that this final paragraph was not wholly understood, but that they read it as meaning that the military would not be employed to coerce Ulster to accept the Bill, and asking if Gough might so inform his officers. This Gough took to the C.I.G.S., who wrote underneath that he also read the final paragraph in that sense, the colonels of the 5th and 16th Lancers and the Adjutant-General being in the room at the time. Gough and the colonels in consequence returned to Ireland that night. Wilson, however, felt sure that the Government would disapprove of Sir J. French having agreed to the view that the final paragraph in the document constituted a definite promise. This appears in the diary on the 24th:

> Robertson went in to Sir John to try to tell him this, but only got his head snapped off, which amused me. However, he found out that Sir John has not yet told Seely of the little addition he made to the letter to Hubert last night. Bonar Law rang me up in the morning and we discussed the day's work. I told him how Hubert went back, and on what guarantees. He also told me he was putting up Arthur Lee to ask Seely some questions this afternoon. Arthur Lee also rang me up and talked about the situation, which I explained. No further developments during the morning.
>
> After lunch Ollivant[*] came to see me and told me an amazing story. He said as a fact (and I believe him) that Winston had drafted orders to the 3rd Battle Squadron and 2 Flotillas to go to Lamlash under Lewis Bayley, and from there to make a regular Jameson raid on some Ulster stronghold. This was frustrated by our action in the

[*] The late Lieutenant-Colonel A. H. Ollivant, a General Staff officer who had been especially lent by Wilson to the First Lord during the past two years.

army. I at once gave this information to Robertson.

After this, Gwynne, the editor of the Morning Post, came to see me, and he told me that one of the Cabinet had been to see him and tell him he knew nothing of all this work with the army, was very much annoyed, and thought that Sir John ought to be "outed" for giving such misleading information. Later on I saw Sir John. I told him that I thought he would be kicked out by the Government when they found out what he had written for Hubert, and that in that case the army would go solid with him.

That afternoon the Opposition failed to get any answer out of either the Prime Minister or the S. of S. for War, serving to clear up the extraordinary situation that had arisen, and of which the public were being kept almost fully informed by the Press. But the document which Gough had been given and which he had carried off with him to Ireland was published in a White Paper. There were violent scenes in the House next day, and Mr. Asquith repudiated the last two paragraphs of the White Paper, intimating that Colonel Seely alone was responsible for the document. Colonel Seely, very properly, resigned; but his resignation was refused by the Prime Minister, and he would not appear to have insisted on its acceptance at the moment. Wilson wrote in his diary that night:

I wired Hubert at midnight to stand like a rock. This is vital. Any false move now on our part would be fatal. So long as we hold the paper we got on Monday, we can afford to sit tight.

Strong speeches had been delivered in the House by Sir E. Grey and Mr. Churchill, the political atmosphere was in a highly charged condition, and Wilson wrote in his diary next day:

Talk with Bonar Law and Milner after breakfast. It seems to me Johnny French must resign, but the rest of us must stand fast unless the Government take action against Hubert. Wired him again to keep absolutely quiet. Sir John sent for us three Directors at 1 o'c. and told us he had resigned, but that Seely would not accept. Directly after, all C.s in C. and Divisional Commanders came into the C.I.G.S.'s room and told him the army was unanimous in its determination not to fight Ulster. This is superb. At 3 o'c. Johnnie sent for me to talk things over. He told me the Cabinet are all opposed to his going and were trying to find some way out of it. I told him that he and Ewart must stick to their resignations, unless they were put in a position to justify their remaining on in the eyes of officers.

While we were talking Ewart came in, and I repeated all I had said with emphasis, and made Ewart read Grey's speech of last night. While this was going on, and I was gaining ground, Haldane sent for Sir John. On Sir John's return he sent for me again and told me that Haldane had said that he had consulted the Prime Minister and that they had agreed on Sir John's writing to Hubert and telling him privately that the pronouncement made by Haldane last Monday held the field. Haldane had said, "No orders were issued, no orders are likely to be issued, and no orders will be issued, for the coercion of Ulster."

Accordingly we drafted a letter (Ewart being present) to Hubert to tell him this, and Sir John went off with the draft to show it to Asquith and Haldane before sending it off.

Next day (Friday, 27th) the diary records:

Sir John was 2½ hours with Cabinet before lunch and 1 hour after lunch. He stood firm on Haldane's speech of last Monday. Asquith was to have made a statement at 11 o'clock last night, then 12 o'clock to-day, and in the end got up at 5 o'clock and said nothing except to read ridiculous Army Order which has been brought out. Sir John was charming to me and thanked me, etc. He showed me the letter on which he stood, drawn up by Haldane in his own house and signed by Haldane and Sir John. After some platitudes, it said that Sir John took his stand on Haldane's speech of last Monday, and that Asquith should make this clear.

On the 28th Wilson wrote in the diary:

I saw this morning the text of Asquith's statement last night. There is absolutely nothing in it which in the faintest degree changes the situation.

Sir John sent for me and told me how he stood. He told me of the two Cabinet meetings at which he was present yesterday, and of how he remained firm in his determination to adhere to Haldane's speech of last Monday. His resignation (and, of course, Ewart's) remain temporarily in abeyance. He asked me my advice as to whether he should resign or not, and told me that Jack Cowans and Von Donop* had both been to him begging him not to go.

I told him in my opinion that he ought to go, and I pointed out that the Army Council were completely out of touch with the army, and that we could not afford to be stupid again and must, therefore, make sure of what the army was saying. I told him that before he came to a Goal decision one way or another I should like to consult the officers of the Staff College, a place which represented the opinion of the whole army, To this he agreed and I drove down to Arborfield, where the Staff College were having their point-to-point. I consulted with... These consulted again with their friends and then reported. The result was perfectly unanimous opinion that he must resign.

Next day there is the entry:

I telephoned to Sir John at 9 a.m. and told him the result of my mission to the Staff College yesterday. Charlie Hunter came in to say that Milner had said to him yesterday: "They talk a lot about Gough, but the man who saved the Empire is Henry Wilson." This, of course, is much too flattering. I lunched at Bonar Law's house, only Carson there. We talked about the situation in all its bearings. Carson told me of Macready's state visit to him, and of his return visit, of the visits of all officers of the *Pathfinder* to him, and of the petty officers, of the friendship between the Navy and the Ulster boys, and of the signalling practice that goes on between the two, and of how excellent the Ulster men are.

At 5 o'c. I went up to Sir John at 94 Lancaster Gate. I was much upset to find he was still havering. He had been for hours with Haldane who had produced another letter to square the circle again. I read this letter carefully several times. It is from Sir John to Asquith. It sets out that Sir John had conceived that, by giving Hubert the assurance, he was only carrying out the instructions of the Government, that the idea of any solders dictating to the Government was just as distasteful to him and to every soldier as to the Cabinet, and that they never have done so. Hubert simply wanted to have the situation clearly defined. Then followed a paragraph to which I took grave exception, and which Sir John cut out in consequence — it said that Asquith's statement on Friday last had satisfied Sir John and, he

---

* The remaining two Military Members of the Army Council.

thought, all others. It wound up by saying that he believed it was the Government intention not to coerce public opinion in Ulster, nor to initiate any movement which would result in active operations there, and that the whole incident might be considered as closed. So no action would be taken against Hubert and the letter which he held.

The idea then is that Asquith should read this letter out to the House of Commons to-morrow, and that then Sir John and Ewart should withdraw their resignations. Provided this is done, and the obnoxious paragraph is cut out, I should be inclined to agree.

Gwynne is to see Sir John at 7 p.m. At 9 p.m. I rang up Gwynne and he told me Sir John was resigning. He said that he saw Sir John and saw the letter, and even with the obnoxious paragraph cut out, he objected *in toto*. On this Sir John told him he might announce that he had resigned. This is splendid.

The result was that Colonel Seely also resigned, and that Mr. Asquith became Secretary of State for War. General Ewart resigned as well as the C.I.G.S., having seen throughout that this was the proper course, but being in a difficulty owing to Sir John's hesitation. So ended what has come to be known as the "Pogrom." The Government maintained that they had no intention of coercing Ulster, that the whole trouble arose owing to Sir A. Paget misunderstanding his instructions, and that the ordering of the Fleet to Lamlash had no sinister intent. But, be that as it may, Wilson's handling of an awkward and threatening situation had put an end to all possibility of the army being used against the loyal North of Ireland.

Sir Charles Douglas became C.I.G.S., Sir H. Sclater succeeded Ewart as Adjutant-General, and affairs at the War Office speedily resumed their normal course. The situation with regard to Ulster, however, remained in a very unsatisfactory state, as there appeared to be strong likelihood of civil war breaking out so soon as the Home Rule Bill was passed by the House of Co mm ons, and Wilson watched its developments with the utmost anxiety. He wrote in his diary on April 4:

I went to see Milner, and had an hour with him. Impressed on him the vital importance of making the Government explain what orders they gave Arthur Paget. The disclosure of these orders will absolutely abolish the cry of "the people versus the army" and will

> ruin Winston, Lloyd George, Birrell, Seely and (I think) Asquith; hence his determination not to let it out. Monty Browning came to lunch. He is RearAdmiral of 3rd Battle Squadron and was, under Lewis Bayley, lying off Galicia when the order came for the squadron to go to Lamlash. Delay of 18 hours due to the wire (not wireless) going to the *King Edward*, though addressed to Senior Naval Officer, *Britannia*. Weather so rough that *Britannia* could not send for it till following (Saturday) morning. Orders cancelled Saturday afternoon. It appears that Winston tumbled to the situation, i.e. the army refusing to act, quicker than Seely, who on Saturday, up to 8 p.m., was telling me he would court-martial officers, etc.

On the 8th the entry appears:

> Douglas sent for me early to show me an immense long dispatch and intelligence report from Paget. I noticed that it was not till 5.30 on the 21st (Saturday) that Paget heard that the detachment sent to Carrickfergus had arrived safely. Winston said the movement of the 3rd Battle Squadron to Lamlash had been countermanded because all detachments had reached their positions without opposition. As a matter of fact, the order to the 3rd Battle Squadron to "break off" was issued when they were abreast the Scillies on Saturday afternoon, and therefore, before Winston could have known about Carrickfergus.

Wilson crossed over to France a few days later for the express purpose of seeing General de Castelnau, and of explaining to him exaedy what had occurred at the Curragh in connexion with Ulster; for the singular situation that had arisen in Ireland was naturally attracting a great deal of attention in France and, indeed, all over the continent. The Government were kept continuously on their defence in Parliament in connexion with the question for some weeks; but the Opposition experienced the utmost difficulty in eliciting from those in authority what orders had been issued concerning the contemplated coercion of Ulster.

Little progress could in the meantime be made with regard to a number of matters of importance at the War Office, owing to the obviously provisional character of the Prime Minister's retention of the post of Secretary of State. Wilson, for instance, wrote in the diary on Wednesday, the 22nd:

> Not much news in office, Asquith sent word to say he would not be in War Office till next week, so all our superior work is at a standstill. He has done practically nothing since he has been S. of S., and he has not seen Douglas since last Friday.

There would therefore appear to be very serious disadvantages to the public service when the duties of First Minister of the Crown and of War Minister are combined in one person. If he was revolted by such a state of things, the D.M.O. was to some extent comforted by the appearance of a White Paper which clearly indicated that the "Pogroms" (as he designated the Cabinet) had, without any requisition from the Lord Mayor of Belfast or any magistrate, and without any civil disturbance having taken place, superseded the civil power by military power in appointing General Macready as Governor of Belfast and in granting that officer jurisdiction over the police. He wrote in the diary on the 25th:

> Bonar Law telephoned wanting to see me, and I went at once. He told me of the mobilization of the Ulster men last night and of the way they got in 25,000 rifles (the evening papers say 70,000). We discussed the White Paper. I pointed out the deficiencies — i.e. Paget's meeting at 2 p.m. on 20th, and at Curragh on 21st; also that Gough's letter and Sir John's endorsement to the paragraphs were missing; also no paper of what Seely or Winston said to Paget; also no hours of dispatch or receipt put on any of the letters or telegrams, a most important matter. And I also impressed upon him the importance of the military power having been put over the civil power in Belfast.

Wilson saw Mr. Asquith on May 6, for the first time since Colonel Seely's resignation, when there was a discussion between the C.I.G.S., Sir W. Robertson, Wilson, and the War Minister as to the Invasion Committee's report and the Exp editionary Force. Mr. Asquith settled that the present arrangements as to the latter, viz: that in the event of its proceeding to France five divisions would go at once, the 4th Division being held back for the moment, should not be interfered with. "This is good," Wilson (who had let 36 Eaton Place and was now living at 7 Draycott Place as a temporary measure) wrote in the diary. He attended a staff tour directed by General de Castelnau at the end of May, and on the conclusion of this exercise he remarked in his diary:

> I was rather struck by the inefficiency of cable and wireless telegraphy, also by the serious want of intercommunication between army, army corps and divisions. We are bad at this also, but I think we are better than what I saw here.

"I have seen some quite new things and novel ideas; these Frenchmen really are the mischief for imagining things," he had written to Mrs. Wilson from the house of "an awful-looking cut-throat" in the theatre of operations.

All through June the situation with respect to Ireland remained critical, and at the end of the month Wilson prepared a paper, which was signed by the Military Members of the Army Council. After observing that they had not been taken into the confidence of the Government, the paper intimated that they wished to point out how, with India, Egypt, and Europe in their existing state, and with 200,000 to 300,000 men drilling and arming in Ireland, the military forces of the nation were liable at any moment to be called upon to perform duties which they would be quite incapable of carrying out. The document was not received with favour by the Prime Minister. "Douglas told me this morning," the D.M.O. noted in the diary on July 10, "that Asquith is furious with the Military Members for sending him in my paper drawing attention to the military aspect of civil war."

On the 3rd he had written:

> I went to see Lord Milner. He told me that unless Asquith agreed to the Lords' amendment, and he does not think that there is a chance of it as Redmond won't allow it, Carson will set up a Provisional Government and will take over such Government offices as he can without bloodshed. This will bring matters to a head. Milner, who is giving the whole of the time to the Ulster business, is entirely in favour of this action. He is altogether against Ulster waiting any longer to suit Asquith's convenience, and is urgently in favour of a strong forward policy. He says that, of course, the Ulster Government will at first be a "ragged thing," but there are good men behind it and

it will presently get into working order. It is undoubtedly a tremendous step to take, but I agree with Milner. Milner wanted to know what the army would do. I told him th at so much depended on the way the picture was put to us. I thought that if Carson and his Government were sitting in the City Hall, and we were ordered down to close the hall, we would not go.

Later I talked the situation over with Douglas and Sclater, without, of course, saying anything about Milner. I was pleased with the result. They have no intention at all of moving, except in the ordinary way of quelling riots.

On July 20, 1914, the King summoned a conference about Ireland to sit at Buckingham Palace, and on the 25th the first entry referring to the European crisis that had arisen as a sequel to the assassination of the Archduke Franz Ferdinand, appears in Wilson's diary. He had seen Sir A. Nicolson in the morning and had been shown a dispatch from St. Petersburg indicating that Russia would not tolerate an attack upon Serbia by Austria-Hungary, and that the Russian Foreign Minister and the French Ambassador had asked Sir G. Buchanan what part England proposed to play. But, before recording Wilson's actions and impressions during the ten days that followed, it will be convenient to revert to the subject of the arrangements that had been in progress during the past four years, partly under his own immediate superintendence and partly at his instigation, for mobilizing the Expeditionary Force as a complete entity, and for transferring it within a minimum space of time from its peace stations to the war concentration area in France that had been determined upon in concert with the French General Staff.

The difficulty with regard to immediate provision of the necessary horses on mobilization, which had caused him so much anxiety when he had looked into the matter in 1910, had been overcome at a comparatively early stage of his efforts to secure promptitude and efficiency. But the drawing-up of the railway time-tables had only been completed recently and this had been a work of no small difficulty. Quite apart from the uncertainty which was caused by the lack of any definite policy on the part of H.M. Government — an uncertainty which made the basis of the whole scheme a matter of conjecture — it had been necessary throughout to perform the work with the utmost secrecy. The fact that Wilson and some of his staff were in communication with the French had to be kept concealed. The whole of the clerical labour — the typing and duplication of the time-tables, and so forth — was in the hands of about half a dozen officers, who alone in all the War Office knew of what was in progress. Maintaining profound secrecy, and limiting the time that the operation would take as a whole, were the dominating factors in the transaction throughout. Time-tables had, moreover, to be prepared not only for the British side of the Channel, but. also for the farther side; and as the normal French troop-train held more than the normal English troop-train, special calculations were necessary when dealing with the farther side. The work was in the hands of one particular section of the Military Operations Directorate, M.O.I. (under charge since 1911 of Colonel Harper), which, to ensure secrecy, had become the one channel of communication with the French and the central co-ordinating authority in connexion with all arrangements for the move of the Expeditionary Force.

A staff tour was held at Amiens in the latter part of June, 1914, which was attended by British officers belonging to M.O.I., and d uring the course of this the railway movement, as planned, was thoroughly tested. The French railway staff officers occupied their war stations, and the steps that would have to be taken in the event of various mishaps, such as might occur, were practised. The great features of the scheme as a whole were its elasticity and its adaptability to conditions that could not be foreseen. That it possessed these qualities when actually put to the test was abundantly proved by its not breaking down in spite of the delay that took place at the outset in dispatching the Expeditionary Force, by no confusion arising in spite of two of the divisions being retained in England, and by its standing the strain imposed upon it by the retreat from Mons and by the change of the main base of the British troops from Havre at St.. Nazaire.

But the scheme as a whole had to do with the sea as well as with the land, and the elaboration of this portion of it had been attended by delays which were very nearly fatal. Wilson had, as we have seen, received little or no encouragement from the Admiralty until Mr. Churchill became First Lord in 1911. But, although from that time forward the principle that the naval authorities must be prepared to transport the Expeditionary Force across the Channel was accepted on the farther side of Whitehall, he had found it very difficult to get the problem grappled with in real determined fashion by the sailors, and to induce them to elaborate a definite and detailed programme of transportation movements. At last, however, at the beginning of 1914, an Admiralty Committee had been set up under the chairmanship of Vice-Admiral Sir E. Slade, with Colonel (now Lieutenant-General Sir R.) Stuart-Wortley representing the War Office. This Committee had gone thoroughly into the question, and had drawn up a detailed programme which became part of the scheme as a whole. Ports of embarkation and disembarkation were definitely decided upon. Berthing at the wharves had then to he settled, plans of ports had to be prepared ready for issue, and officers for embarking and disembarking purposes had to be told off. All this took time, and some of the necessary printing was actually only carried out under high pressure during the night of August 4 after the declaration of war. But, in spite of this, the naval portion of the scheme was actually put in force on the following day, and it worked without a hitch, just as did the railway arrangements on both sides of the Channel.

Beyond occasional complaints that all was not ready during the course of his four years as Director of Military Operations, Wilson makes practically no mention in his diary of this "W.F." Scheme (as it was officially called). That he does not do so may be taken as an indication of how secret its preparation was kept. It was due to his ardent spirit, his wide vision, his tireless energy and his indomitable perseverance that the undertaking was set on foot, and that it was brought to maturity by able assistants working under his orders and by representatives of the Senior Service inspired by his own enthusiasm and prescience, in time for the great emergency of August, 1914. During the critical days when the question of a European war was trembling in the balance, during those hours of almost agonized doubt as to what action H.M. Government would decide upon in the grave international situation that had so suddenly arisen, the author and virtual creator of the scheme had at least the satisfaction of knowing that it was practically complete and could be put in execution the moment that the word was given.

The story of the train of events preceding the British ultimatum to Germany of August 4 has been often told. Here it will suffice to record Wilson's views and activities and experiences (as recorded by himself) during the days of uncertainty that immediately preceded the participation of the British Empire in the mighty conflict. Just at first — as will be seen from what he set down in his diary — he was disposed to think that the trouble would blow over after all. He wrote on July 26:

> Went to see Sir A. Nicolson and found a lot more dispatches, all warlike. Austria, Russia, and Serbia seem to be going to mobilize, but, so far, no news of Germany moving. Until she moves there is no certainty of war. The Serbians have agreed to almost all the Austrian terms, making it difficult to Austria and Germany to have a European war. My own opinion is that if Germany does not mobilize to-day there will be no war. Saw Sunny Jim[*] and told him all the gossip.

On the 27th:

> A lot of dispatches in all day, but no sign of Germany mobilizing, so I think there will not be any war. Meanwhile, after some fuss about gun-running at Howth yesterday, 2 companies K.O.S.B.s were mobbed in the streets of Dublin and fired on the mob, killing 3 and wounding 40. This is a further upset for this Government. Panouse[†] told me this afternoon that the Austrian Ambassador in Paris had told the French Foreign Minister that the Austrians would move to-morrow.

Next day the entry appears:

> Went to the Foreign Office and had a long talk with Arthur Nicolson, which was interrupted by Asquith walking in. I presume now the Austrians will take Belgrade. There may then be a pause, but further advance will mean a mobilization in Russia, and then impossible to say what will follow.

---

[*] Sir C. Douglas.

[†] General Vicomte de la Panouse, the French Military Attaché.

On the 28th he wrote:

The Russians have ordered the mobilization of 16 Corps. The Austrians are mobilizing 12 Corps. The Germans and French remain quiet. At 3 p.m. a note came to Douglas from Asquith ordering the "Precautionary Period." This we did. I don't know why we are doing it, because there is nothing moving in Germany. We shall see. Anyhow it is more like business than I expected of this Government.

This appears on the 30th:

The news is all bad to-day and war seems inevitable. Sazonov and the German Ambassador fell out last night, and the German went to Sazonov's house at 2 a.m. this morning in tears and said all was over. The Germans asked us to guarantee neutrality. Grey answered, "Wait and see." Nicolson, whom I saw several times, expects German mobilization to-morrow. I confess it looks like it. Panouse to-night brought me a paper which Cambon gave Grey this afternoon, showing German preparations.

No news when I called for my usual visit to Arthur Nicolson at 9 a.m. Later (11 a.m.) the Cabinet met. Later we began to suspect that the Cabinet was going to run away. [So begins Wilson's record of Friday the 31st.]

Later, 5 p.m., Eyre Crowe came to see me and told me that Germany had given Russia 12 hours to demobilize. Russia's answer was an order for "General Mobilization." Germany was going to order mobilization to-night, followed by France; and we were doing nothing. Later Johnnie Baird* came in. I told him of the state of affairs and got him to write to Bonar Law, who had gone to Wargrave, begging him to come up and see Asquith to-night.

Later I saw Panouse and advised him to get Cambon to go to Grey to-night and say that, if we did not join, he would break off relations and go to Paris. An awful day.

No C.I.D. has been held, no military opinion has been asked for by this Cabinet, who are deciding on a question of war. Douglas was unable to get Asquith to agree to stop training of units which happen to be a long way from their mobilization centres. Sclater tells me this dispersion would delay us three days. Asquith said he would ask the

---

* Sir J. Baird, M.P., now Lord Stonehaven.

Cabinet to-morrow.

Kept fully acquainted by the Foreign Office with the rapid progress of events abroad, Wilson, on the 31st was, as appears from his diary, seriously disturbed. 7 Draycott Place in consequence became for the moment the centre of a movement of vital importance for awakening the leaders of the Unionist Party to a sense of their responsibilities in this national crisis, and for assembling them in London with a view to their bringing pressure upon the Government to support France in the struggle that had now become inevitable. For Germany had this day sent an ultimatum to Paris demanding to know, within 18 hours, what would be the French attitude in the event of a Russo-German war. In an article that was published in 1918 in the *National Review*, recording the inner history of this hectic juncture, Mr. L. Maxse relates how, late on the 31st, he got into communication with Wilson over the telephone, to ask how matters were proceeding. Wilson's reply was: "We are in the soup." He intimated that the situation was in the highest degree unsatisfactory, and he asked Maxse to come to breakfast at Draycott Place on the following morning.

On Saturday, August 1, Sir A. Nicolson sent for Wilson at 7 a.m., and showed him a dispatch, received over night, indicating that the Germans were about to assume the offensive on both frontiers. The pair thereupon proceeded to Lord Haldane's house, where Sir E. Grey was staying; but Grey was in bed and Nicolson would not in the circumstances go in and see him. On getting back to Draycott Place for breakfast, Wilson found Lady Aileen Roberts, Lady Sybil Grey, Rawlinson, and Maxse at his house. They held a consultation and Wilson was able to give the party all the latest news. Maxse writes:

> As there was no time to lose we then and there constituted ourselves into an informal "Pogrom," as it was called, under the inspiration of the General, whose service at this juncture is fully known on the other side of the Channel, though unknown here.

They got into touch with Mt. Amery, Mr. George Lloyd (now

Lord Lloyd), Mr. Wickham Steed, Lord Lovat — "whose passionate and single-minded zeal makes him invaluable in a tiger hunt" — and others, with the object of bringing the pressure of the Unionist leaders to bear upon the Government. The leaders were for the most part away from town for the weekend, which presented a difficulty, but Lord Edmund Talbot fortunately remained, and steps were taken to get into touch with the absent leaders. Then, having started the ball rolling, Wilson proceeded in the first place to the Foreign Office, and from there on to the War Office. He records in his diary:

> At 11.30 a.m. Asquith wrote to C.I.G.S. saying training was not to be suspended, and "putting on record" the fact that the Government had never promised the French an Expeditionary Force. Percy* to lunch, he arranged to send George Lloyd and Charlie Beresford for Bonar Law to Wargrave. I went to the French Embassy, 3 p.m., to discuss with Panouse what it would mean if Germans were restricted to German-French frontiers. M. Cambon came in to see me. He was very bitter, though personally charming. Ollivant in to see me, 4 p.m., and report that Winston wanted him to lecture Lloyd George on the European military situation. Saw Crowe 7 p.m. — very pessimistic, all countries mobilizing except us.

In the meantime Lord Lansdowne had been telegraphed to requesting him to come up to town from Bowood, Amery had gone down to Broadstairs to bring up Mr. A. Chamberlain, and at about 10 p.m. Lloyd arrived at 7 Draycott Place, famished but triumphant, having succeeded in bringing Bonar Law up from Wargrave. Then, at 11 p.m., Wilson and Lloyd went together to Lansdowne House, where they found Lord Lansdowne, the Duke of Devonshire, Mr. Bonar Law, and Lord Edmund Talbot assembled, and, as a result of an hour's talk, it was arranged over the telephone that a meeting should take place with Mr. Asquith next day. So, at noon on the. 2nd, Bonar Law's famous letter, drafted after consultation with Lord Lansdowne and Mr. Chamberlain, was sent to Downing Street. The result is well

---

* Now the Duke of Northumberland.

known, although the consequences of the receipt of the letter were not at first apparent inasmuch as the Government took no immediate action. Of Wilson's share in these dramatic proceedings Mr. Maxse writes in the article already quoted:

> Speaking as one knowing what he did in the opening days of that sultry August, I remain lost in admiration of his wonderful nerve and verve and unrelaxing grip of a formidable situation.

Wilson himself, although to some extent reassured, still remained seriously perturbed — as appears from the entries in his diary concerning the events of that day:

> Leo Maxse and Amery to breakfast, and much telephoning to Bonar Law, Austen, and others. Panouse in at 10 a.m. Office all day. Two Cabinet meetings with quite indecisive results. I believe that a note has been sent to the French to say that, although we were not going to take part in the war, we would not allow the Germans to descend on the French coast. Was ever anything heard like this? What is the difference between the French coast and the French frontier? The German light troops were over the frontier to-day, and some fighting took place. Crowds outside the Palace 10 p.m. cheering. We have got permission to send troops back to peace quarters.

Events now moved quickly, as is made apparent by the brief entries made in Wilson's diary on Monday, August 3:

> Usual 9 a.m. visit to Nicolson, no decision yet to mobilize. Saw Sir John, who now thinks of going to Antwerp — but we can't cross the North Sea, mouth of Scheldt is Dutch, and no arrangements made for transportation, so quite hopeless. At 1.9 p.m. Moggridge [the private secretary of the C.I.G.S.] came to my room to show me order for mobilization. Great crowds in streets and opposite Buckingham Palace. Saw M. Cambon in Arthur Nicolson's room. He held out both hands to me. So. different from day before yesterday.

But although mobilization had been decided upon, the order was only issued next morning, the 4th, whereas the French order for mobilization had been issued at 3.40 p.m. on the 1st — a difference of between two and three days. The arrangements made between the D.M.O. and the French General Staff had always assumed a simultaneous mobilization of the two military forces.*

Wilson went to the French Embassy early on the 4th to discuss the question as to what changes of plans would he necessary owing to our delay in mobilizing. He, also, had long discussions with Sir J. French and Sir A. Murray with regard to the Expeditionary Force. He, moreover, had interviews during the day with Lord Milner, Mr. Amery, Sir J. Baird, Mr. Maxse, Lord Lovat, and other prominent Conservatives. These were busy making arrangements to bring the full force of Conservative opinion to bear upon the Government so as to ensure an immediate utilization of the Expeditionary Force. It was on this day apparently that an old friend of his who came upon the D.M.O. in a passage in the Admiralty building found him in tears at the delay in deciding to employ that force! He was, however, pleased to learn that Lord Kitchener was about to replace Lord Haldane as Secretary of State for War, the latter having only been appointed to that office on the previous day in substitution for Mr. Asquith. "Grey's delay and hesitation in giving orders is sinful," Wilson wound up his diary for the day. Such procrastination as there had been in taking up a firm stand had, however, been the fault of the Cabinet as a whole. Several members of that body had at first been opposed to making the quarrel ours, and three of them had resigned when the right decision was at length taken. At 11 o'clock that night the country was at war.

---

* In response to a telegram from Wilson, I had come up to town from the country on the Saturday, and had learnt from him that I was to take his place in the event of mobilization. He was profoundly disturbed that day at the attitude which the Government appeared to be assuming. On this day (Monday) he was in a very different mood, haying no longer any fear that we were going to abandon France, but impatient at no orders yet having been given by the Government with regard to the Expeditionary Force. — C. E. C.

Chapter X – 1914: The First Month of War

The Great War Council in Downing Street — Lord Kitchener and Wilson — G.H.Q. proceeds to France — Meetings with General Joffre and General Lanrezac — The Retreat from Mons — The night before Le Cateau — Wilson's bracing influence at G.H.Q. — The B.E.F. across the Marne — The order to advance.

A decision had been arrived at some weeks before the emergency actually arose to the effect that the Expeditionary Force was, in the event of war, to be commanded by Sir John French, and that he would have Sir A. Murray as Chief of the General Staff, Sir W. Robertson as Quartermaster-General, Sir N. Macready as Adjutant-General, and Wilson as Sub-Chief of the General Staff. Rooms had been taken at the Hotel Metropole; General Head-quarters of the Expeditionary Force were constituted there on August j, and the various officers who had been detailed in advance for service therewith joined promptly from their peace stations. Colonel Harper and Colonel Macdonogh had been selected for the appointments respectively of head of the Operations Branch and head of the Intelligence Branch of the Force.

Wilson was sent for by Lord Haldane that morning — Haldane was still Secretary of State — and he found the military members of the Army Council assembled in the room. The D.M.O. at once informed the Secretary of State that, on the strength of Mr. Asquith's ruling given on May 6 (mentioned on p. 175), he had informed the French that our Government would, if it decided to go to war, send five divisions across the Channel. He urged that the divisions should be dispatched as soon as possible. After this, as he records in his diary, he spent an hour and a half in consultation with Sir John and Haig, when the latter made the suggestion that troops ought not to cross the water for two or three months, during which period "the immense resources of the Empire" could be developed. But Wilson pointed out that there were no resources for a long war, the view being very generally entertained in military, as in other, circles, at this time that the contest upon which the nation was embarking would be a brief one. Such a delay would, moreover, have been in contravention of the unofficial understanding that existed — largely owing to Wilson's own labours — between the British and French General Staffs.

Then, at 4 p.m., the great War Council summoned by the Prime Minister assembled at 10 Downing Street. At this gathering were present Mr. Asquith, Sir E. Grey, Mr. Churchill, Lord Haldane, Lord Roberts, Lord Kitchener, Prince Louis of Battenberg, Sir J. French, Sir I. Hamilton, Sir J. Cowans, Sir S. Von Donop, Sir D. Haig, Sir J. Grierson, Sir A. Murray, Colonel Hankey, Colonel St. G. Gorton, and Wilson. Accounts of this historic meeting have been given by Lord French in his "1914," by Mr. Churchill in "The World Crisis," and by Lord Grey in his "Twenty-Five Years." They all agree with each other fairly well, although Lord Grey makes a special point of Lord Haldane's strong insistence on the principle that the whole of the Expeditionary Force ought to be sent across the Channel. Wilson also furnishes a crisp record of the proceedings in his diary for this critical day, and it reads as follows:

> Asquith said he had summoned the great soldiers at the earliest possible moment. Then a lot of platitudes on the situation and strategy generally. Sir John stated what he had arranged to do; he said that probably Maubeuge was no longer available for concentration, and then plumped for going at once and deciding later where to go to — but then he dragged in the ridiculous proposal of going to Antwerp.
>
> Churchill said the Dover Straits now completely sealed. Jimmy Grierson spoke up for decisive numbers at the decisive point. Sir John urged we should go over at once, and decide destination later. I mentioned the flexibility of French railway system for switching. Haig

asked questions and this led to our discussing strategy like idiots.

Johnnie Hamilton plumped for going to Amiens as soon as possible. Then desultory strategy (some thinking that Liége was in Holland) and idiocy. Lord Kitchener plumped for Amiens, but wanted to get in closer touch with French; suggested that they should send over an officer. Sir John urged we should order the transports to be fitted at once. Decision taken to order transports for all 6 divisions at once.

Question then arose what strength the E.F. should be. Winston in favour of sending 6 divisions, as naval situation most favourable owing to our having had time to prepare. Lord Bobs agreed. Decision was taken that we should prepare at once for all 6 divisions. Lord Kitchener said one division should be ordered from India to Egypt. All agreed. Slight discussion on Colonial and Ulster contingents, but no decision reached.

An historic meeting of men, mostly entirely ignorant of their subject.

Lord Kitchener assumed charge at the War Office on the following morning, and that evening another War Council met at 10 Downing Street. Wilson pointed out at this gathering that the Expeditionary Force would not be able to fight a general action, in which the whole of the Expeditionary Force could take part, for twenty days. The decision arrived at was that for the present only four divisions, the 1st, 2nd, 3rd, and 5th, and the Cavalry Division were to embark, but that a fifth (the 4th) should embark later; embarkation was to begin on Sunday the 9th. Owing to an unreasonable scare as to a contemplated hostile landing on the east coast. Lord Kitchener had that day decided that a brigade of the 6th Division stationed at Lichfield should move to Edinburgh, and that two brigades of the 4th Division should proceed respectively to Cromer and to York; he, moreover, seriously contemplated sending brigades from Aldershot to the east coast. This latter project, when Wilson heard of it, excited his violent indignation, seeing that an excursion of this kind, if actually undertaken, would throw the whole of the scheduled arrangements for moving the Expeditionary Force to its ports of embarkation out of gear. The suggestion that had been made by Lord Kitchener on the previous day to the effect that the French should be asked to send over a specially accredited

Général de Brigade A. Huguet

officer, had led to immediate communications taking place through the French Embassy at Albert Gate, and General Huguet arrived in London during the course of this afternoon. He had, however, left France so hurriedly that he had not had time to obtain any special instructions, nor yet to obtain the most recent information as to the dispositions and intentions of the French military authorities.

The following very noteworthy entry appears in Wilson's diary next day, Friday, the 7th:

> Long talk with Huguet, who then returned by special train and boat to France to see Joffre and to return here on Wednesday morning. Lord Kitchener sent for me 1.45 p.m. and was angry because I had let Huguet go, and angrier still because I had told Huguet everything about our starting on Sunday. I answered back, as I have no intention of being bullied by him, especially when he talks such nonsense as he did to-day. He is bringing the 6th Division to England* and sending troops from Aldershot to Grimsby, thus hopelessly messing up our plans.

This was an unfortunate interview, and it had unfortunate consequences. Some slight antagonism had already existed between the two men even before this, an antagonism dating back to the discussion that had taken place between them at the Staff College, which has been mentioned in Chapter V. This parley in the Secretary of State's room at a very critical juncture unquestionably served to accentuate that antagonism. Wilson had good grounds for feeling irritated by what passed, in view of the proposed diversion of Aldershot troops, and also of Lord Kitchener's apparent inability to realize how seriously such a diversion would affect the carefully elaborated plans for getting the two Aldershot divisions and two others to France, considering that the operation was actually to commence on the 9th, only two days off. Still it must be allowed that, even on his own showing, Wilson adopted a tone towards his superior which any superior would be justified in resenting, and which to a man of Lord Kitchener's record and temperament was bound to give serious offence. The

---

* The bulk of the 6th Division was stationed in Ireland.

Secretary of State would, moreover, seem to have had some justification for feeling annoyance, if it was the case that Huguet had been sent back to France without his knowledge; for he may well have wished to hold further discussion with this emissary who had been sent over to London by our Allies in obedience to his own suggestion. But that he should have objected to Huguet being made aware that the Expeditionary Force was to begin pouring across the Channel two days later is more difficult to understand. Secrecy was of great, indeed of vital, importance. But to conceal the date of the movement from General Joffre and his head-quarters staff would have been to carry secrecy to almost preposterous lengths.*

It was not the altercation in itself that mattered, but its sequel. During the first six to eight months of the war, the relations between Lord Kitchener and Wilson remained unfriendly. Although not holding a predominant position at G.H.Q. in theory, Wilson, in virtue of the confidence that Sir J. French reposed in his knowledge and judgment, held almost a predominant position in practice. Had the terms that he stood on with the Secretary of State been less antipathetic, he might well have proved as successful in smoothing over the difficulties and misunderstandings that arose between Sir J. French and Lord Kitchener, as he was in smoothing over the difficulties and misunderstandings that arose between Sir J. French and high French military authorities. Wilson's counsel, moreover, asked for from time to time and freely given, could hardly have failed to be of assistance to the Secretary of State in the tremendous task that had been imposed upon him by the will of the Nation, and it might have helped to avert certain mistakes and misapprehensions on Kitchener's part that were to prejudice the

---

* An interview took place between Lord Kitchener and Mr. Churchill at the Admiralty about 3 p.m, on the 6th, with regard to the scare of an imminent German descent on the east coast; at this, representatives of the Admiralty and of the War Office (including myself) were present. In view of Mr. Churchill's assurances, all idea of danger passed away. The meeting possibly did not take place till the 7th but I am almost certain it was on the 6th. I believe that at the hour when Wilson had this interview with Lord Kitchener the project of sending Aldershot troops to Grimsby, if ever seriously entertained, had been abandoned; but Wilson probably did not know this. – C.E.C.

national cause.

There is no longer question but that Lord Kitchener formed a far more correct opinion of the situation as between the Entente and the Central Powers as a whole, than did Wilson or, apparently, anybody else on the staff of G.H.Q. From the moment of his assuming office in Whitehall he realized that the United Kingdom must accomplish a prodigious effort of military expansion, and he based his entire policy on this conviction. He entertained no illusions as to the potentialities of the British Expeditionary Force, as constituted, in a struggle in which the whole manhood of the other belligerents could be thrown into the scale. He perceived that, even when supported by divisions of regulars to be formed of troops called home from India and elsewhere, Sir John French's little army would be totally incapable of exercising a decisive influence in the contest about to commence— and he perceived it, moreover, before that little army had quitted the shores of the United Kingdom. His methods may in some respects have been open to criticism, his failure to insist upon the application of compulsory service at a moment when he had the whole country at his back was most unfortunate, his strategical conceptions may been have imperfect, but his grasp of the problem in its widest sense assuredly was little at fault. The views — narrow and erroneous, as they were — which prevailed at G.H.Q. during the first six months of the war on the subject of Lord Kitchener's plans for multiplying the British fighting forces, would perhaps have been formed in any case. But Wilson's influence with Sir J. French's entourage was strong. A believer in compulsion, he consistently and effectively ridiculed the Secretary of State's designs and intentions. G.H.Q. followed his lead. It is conceivable that his attitude with regard to those designs and intentions might have been less outspokenly hostile had he felt less out of tune with their author.

The intention at the outset had been to call the forces under the three subordinate commanders, Haig, Grierson and Pulteney, "Armies"; but on the 11th this nomenclature was very sensibly altered to "Army Corps," and from an entry in Wilson's diary on that day this change would appear to have been made on his proposition. The troops had in the meantime begun to cross the

Channel on the 9th, and all was going smoothly and in accordance with the details of the "W.F." scheme. The following entry appears in the diary on the 12th:

> Saw Huguet and 1 French officers (just arrived) at the French Embassy at 8 a.m. They had just come over from Joffre's head-quarters. They told me all the French and German dispositions. Later, at 10 a.m., I returned and took the 3 officers to Sir John's house, where was also Archie Murray. Then we went into the whole situation, and Sir John plumped for concentration in our old area.
>
> At 3 o'clock we six. Sir John, Archie, self, and 3 Frenchmen, met in Lord K.'s room in the War Office. There we wrangled with K. for 3 hours. K. wanted to go to Amiens, and he was incapable of understanding the delays and difficulties of making such a change, nor the cowardice of it, nor the fact that either in French victory or defeat we would be equally useless. He still thinks the Germans are coming north of the Meuse in great force, and will swamp us before we concentrate. In the end he agreed to a small and perfectly useless alteration, just enough to give trouble and add confusion. Then Kitchener and Sir John went to Asquith, who also agreed, not knowing anything at all about it.
>
> Lord K. declared that at a Cabinet meeting on August 6, it was decided that the Army was not to concentrate under Maubeuge, but was to concentrate at Amiens, and that he, K., had told Huguet this and everyone else.

One noteworthy point emerges from this. Thanks, no doubt, rather to his gift of divination than to any meticulous calculations on his part based on knowledge of times and distances, Lord Kitchener had come to the conclusion that the Germans intended to carry out the wide sweep in formidable force through Belgium north of the Meuse, which they were actually concentrating their forces to accomplish at the very time when the meeting with the French officers in the War Office was taking place. For that wide sweep, determined upon by Count von Schlieffen several years before, the French were wholly unprepared. It resulted in the entire left wing of the far-flung allied host being hustled back, more or less in disarray, to the River Marne within three weeks.

Arrangements had been made for Sir J. French, with part of his General Head-quarters, to cross the Channel on the 14th, and

Wilson had, therefore, many farewells to make on the previous day. Lord Roberts came up from Ascot on purpose to see him. He also makes mention in his diary of crossing Whitehall from the War Office that afternoon to take leave of the First Lord of the Admiralty:

> I went to say good-bye to Winston. I told him that we had often differed and had never been afraid to cross swords, but that he had behaved like a hero at Downing Street on the 5th, and I wished to shake hands with him and to bid him good-bye. He began to tell me he was sure I would "lead to victory," and then he completely broke down and cried, so that he could not finish the sentence. I never liked him so much.

A party consisting of Sir J. French, Sir A. Murray, Sir W. Robertson, Major Hereward Wake, Wilson, and some others, left London for France on the following afternoon, and they spent that night at Amiens. Reaching Paris next day at noon, they met the French War Minister and a number of highly placed French officers at the War Office, and on the morrow they proceeded on by car to General Joffre's *Grand Quartier Général* (G.Q.G.), which was located at Vitry St. François. Here they were warmly welcomed and were made acquainted with the existing situation in so far as it was known. From Vitry the party drove on to Rheims, where they passed the night. Next morning, the 17th, they drove to Rethel, where Sir John and his staff met General Lanrezac and a number of French staff officers. Lanrezac was in command of the Fifth French Army, on the left of which the British Expeditionary Force was to form up, and the meeting did not pass off altogether satisfactorily, neither of the two distinguished commanders apparently forming a high opinion of the other.[*]* Wilson, however,

---

[*] Lanrezac knew no English, and Sir John's French was not of a kind readily intelligible to a Frenchman; the discussion was therefore carried out mainly through Wilson, acting as an interpreter. An officer who was present mentions that, during the course of the colloquy, information was conveyed from the French side to the effect that Germans were reported as having arrived on the right bank of the Meuse at Huy (mid-way between Liége and Namur). Sir John wanted to know what they were doing there, and what they were likely to do. Would they

mentions in his diary being shown plans and reports by Lanrezac. That afternoon the party arrived at Le Cateau and established General Head-quarters in that little town, as had been contemplated from the outset. They found that the concentration of the 1st, 2nd, 3rd, and 5th Divisions, as also of the Cavalry Division under General Allenby, was proceeding smoothly and in accordance with the schedule drawn up in advance under Wilson's direction in the War Office. He wrote in his diary that evening:

> We hear of Castelnau and Pau's successes in Alsace which I don't so much like, as I think it means that the Germans ate transferring corps from Alsace to Belgium. I don't like to write details of French movements.

And the next day:

> I am inclined to think now that we shall have 15 German corps in Belgium, of which 4 to 6 will be north of the river Meuse.

He wrote to Mrs. Wilson that same day:

> The Germans appear to be massing more and more troops up on the north side, so after all, our prophecies look as though they were going to come true. The French are quiet and confident and I am sure my estimate is right and that they will put up a magnificent fight. We are getting on all right and all the plans of the last four years are working smoothly and quietly, but it is criminal and sinful to keep 2 splendid divisions back in England, when they are so badly wanted here.

This appears in the diary on the 19th:

---

cross the river? He misunderstood the answer and asked again, whereupon Lanrezac, who was somewhat excitable and was growing a little impatient, ejaculated, "Pourquoi sont-ils arrives? Mats pour pécher dans la rivière!" "What does he say, what does he say?" demanded Sir John of Wilson. "He says they're going to cross the river, sir," replied Wilson, and the conference ended with the usual compliments and bowings and hand-shaking.

At 7.30 a.m. I went to Sir John's house, and he and Murray showed me an Appreciation, received last night from Joffre, and their proposed answer. I found that, in my opinion, they had entirely misread Joffre's purpose, not knowing French well, and as a result had written quite beside the point. They allowed me to draft the answer, which Sir John signed.

Joffre suggested either heavy masses north of the river, which I put at 4 to 6 corps, or small forces there, which I put at 1 to 2 corps. In the first case the Ist, IIIrd, and XVIIIth Corps will cross the Sambre and help us to deal with them. In the latter case those three corps will cross the Meuse between Namur and Givet and will help the Third and Fourth Armies whilst we deal with the troops north of the river.

In the afternoon a colonel of Chasseurs, who passed through here yesterday leaving Joffre's letter, and went on to the King of the Belgians at Louvain, came in to see me. He reports that the Belgians got pushed back yesterday. He says he thinks that Joffre leans to the belief of a large turning movement in the north, but that the staff incline to the belief that the main attack will be towards Mezières and Verdun. Personally, I incline to the big turning movement — which is German, but would suit us.

Wilson wrote in the diary next day:

Much information in this morning, all pointing to an immense German movement over the Meuse.

To-night we think we have determined that the enemy has 3 cavalry divisions and 6 corps over the river. The more the better, as it will weaken their centre.

On the 21st Wilson wrote home:

To-day we start our forward march, and the whole line from here to Verdun set out. It is at once a glorious and an awful thought, and by this day week the greatest action that thc world has ever heard of will have been fought. I am full of confidence, but nothing is certain in war. I would be happier if those people at home had let us bring out our 6 divisions; but, as it is, we must do the best we can with 4. The fifth won't be here till this day week, which I fear will be too late for the first dash. Our line of battle will be 90 miles long, the same 90 miles I have so often been over, and thought over, and written about.

It all seems so curious. I was up all last night (except for a couple of hours) but to-night I hope to get some sleep.

This also appears in his diary for this day:

> During the afternoon many reports of Germans advancing in masses from north and east, also that Namur was going to fall. I can't believe this. We find ourselves to-night executing a somewhat confused march in presence of the enemy, and passing our cavalry after to-morrow's march from out left to our right — a clumsy and confusing movement. I shall be glad when it is over and when we get thoroughly well linked with the XVIIIth Corps (Mas Latrie).

The XVIIIth French corps was that on the left of the Fifth Army, and the importance of the Ist Corps on the right of the B.E.F. (as the Expeditionary Force was now generally spoken offsetting into closest touch with it before the great clash of arms should take place, was obvious. The British cavalry was in contact with the enemy mounted troops on the 22nd, and some fighting took place between them. The evacuation of Namur was begun, and the Fifth Army was attacked by the enemy in great force at Charleroi and to the east of it, its right being gradually outflanked and its Xth Corps forced back. Sir John and Wilson had started at an early hour for General Lanrezac's head-quarters; but they learnt on the way that he had gone up to the front, so they turned back. _ News of the reverse to the Xth Corps reached G.H.Q. during the afternoon, and at 11 p.m. messages arrived from Lanrezac confirming this, intimating that he was going to take his stand farther back, and asking Sir John to assume the offensive.

Wilson wrote in his diary:

> Sir John, Archie, and I consulted. At midnight Sir John told Huguet that he could not advance without knowing what was in his front, but that he would stand where he was — i.e. south of Binche — Mons— Corny, until he got reports from his aeroplanes, and would then decide his action. He asked that the two Reserve Divisions should come up on his right, as the French Corps of cavalry had fallen back behind the Meuse (instead of coming up on our right as agreed upon) and had left a gap between us and the XVIIIth Corps.
>
> There is no doubt, we are a little in the air; but Maubeuge on our

right rear relieves from anxiety. How roughly the Xth Corps has been handled we don't know, but rather badly, we gather. When they fell back they lost touch with Namur. Reports to-day said Namur would fell to-morrow, but I can't believe it. Altogether the day has not been satisfactory, although nothing serious has happened. I wish I could have got Sir John to go and see Lanrezac. It is of great importance they should understand each other. I got Haig to see Mas Latrie, which was good.

Next day, the 23rd, the B.E.F. was attacked about Mons, but upon the whole our troops held their ground satisfactorily in face of superior forces. The French Fifth Army, on the other hand, gave way along the whole of its front, Namur was occupied by the Germans, and a general withdrawal of the French between the Sambre and the Moselle set in. The full gravity of the situation was not, however, realized at G.H.Q., news of the overthrow and retreat of Lanrezac's troops arriving slowly; and that this was so is made clear by Wilson's diary. He wrote:

During the afternoon I made a careful calculation, and I came to the conclusion that we only had one corps and one cavalry division (possibly two corps) opposite to us. I persuaded Murray and Sir John that this was so, with result that I was allowed to draft orders for an attack to-morrow by Cavalry Division, 19th Bgde., and IInd Corps, to N.E., pivoted on Mons. Just as these were completed (8 p.m.) a wire came from Joffre to say we had 2½ corps opposite us. This stopped our attack, and at 11 p.m. news came that the Fifth Army was falling back still farther. Between 11 p.m. and 3 a.m. we drafted orders and made arrangements for retirement to the line Maubeuge—Valenciennes. It has been a day of sharp fighting and severe disappointment. If the Cabinet had sent 6 divisions instead of 4, this retreat would have been an advance and defeat would have been a victory.

The absence of the 4th and 6th Divisions was undoubtedly unfortunate. But the Expeditionary Force on the night of the 23rd had six divisions facing it, and others were approaching. Owing to the retirement of the French Fifth Army that of Sir J. French was already becoming isolated. An attack delivered in the circumstances even by six British divisions might, therefore, unless it proved completely successful, have led to very awkward consequences, seeing that, in view of the French retirement all along the line, the British forces would have been obliged to fall back eventually in any case, separated from their Allies. Even as it was, the retirement of the B.E.F. was only carried out on the 24th with considerable difficulty and at the cost of appreciable loss. The leading troops of the 4th Division under General Snow, however, began arriving at the front this day, and they moved up, as they detrained, so as to be on the extreme left of the B.E.F. (as facing the enemy), outside of the IInd Corps, with the Cavalry Division under General Allenby still farther out on that flank. Snow wrote in his diary that day:

> On my arrival at Le Cateau the situation was explained to me by my dear old friend Henry Wilson, who was Sub-Chief of the Staff, in that half-chaffing, half-serious way which was peculiar to him. It was a graphic description of the whole situation. Coming in that way, and from a man who was the greatest optimist I have ever met, it was not quite so overwhelming as it might have been if unfolded by others: but in all conscience it was bad enough.

This appears in Wilson's diary:

> Lanrezac sent in written offer to attack if we would attack. The tiling is ridiculous and is done to save his face. Had he offered two days ago, instead of withdrawing from the Sambre and then getting defeated, it might have been successful.

On the next day, the 25th, G.H.Q. was withdrawn from Le Cateau to St. Quentin. The troops retreated and were much harassed on the way by the pursuing enemy, the anxieties of Sir J. French and his staff being increased by the fact that the Ist Corps on the right, under Haig, had become separated by the Forest of Mormal from the IInd Corps, which was now under General Smith-Dorrien, that general having filled the vacancy caused by Sir J. Grierson's sudden death. The 4th Division was assembling, such of its troops as had reached the front were ready for action, and Snow mentions receiving about 6 p.m., a private letter from Wilson, beginning "Dear Snowball" and ending "Yours, Henry" in which were set forth very briefly and concisely the situation, in so far as it was known, and the nature of the task which the 4th Division was likely to have to perform. In fact, but for the unconventional beginning and ending, the communication amounted to an order pure and simple, and no formal order on the subject was received. The Chief Staff Officer of the division was somewhat scandalized — but Snow understood. Wilson mentions in his diary that French and Murray wanted to halt on the following day, but that he insisted that if a halt were called it would mean disaster. He persuaded them to continue felling back, and, in view of what occurred on the 26th, his diary dealing with that day is of peculiar interest. It reads as follows:

> All night [he is referring to the night of 25-26] ominous rumours of attack on Haig at Landrecies, and separation of the Ist and IInd Corps. At 2 a.m. message from Smith-Dorrien to say that, in spite of orders to retire he, haying consulted Allenby, had determined to remain on the Le Cateau position, I took this at once to Sir John, who did not quite grasp what it involved. He would not wake up Murray, and, in spite of all I could say about separation of Ist and IInd Corps, the weakness in guns of 3rd, 5th, and 4th Divisions, since the 4th Division guns are not up yet, he agreed to S-D.'s proposal. This will lead to disaster, or ought to;
>
> Heavy action going on all day at Le Cateau, and, of course, no assistance from Ist Corps, which itself had sharp fighting at Landrecies last night, and is obviously unable to help owing to the Forest of Mormal and to confusion of having same billets as two French Reserve Divisions.

Wilson would seem to have made a mistake in his diary as to the hour when Smith-Dorrien's message arrived at St. Quentin. It was only sent off by car from Le Cateau at 3.30 a.m. and it appears to have reached G.H.Q. about 5 a.m. Colonel C. Deedes, who was then a junior staff officer at G.H.Q., gives an interesting account of what followed shortly afterwards. He writes:

> At about 6.30 a.m. a further message was received that Sir Horace wished to speak to the C. in C. or the C.G.S. on the telephone.

> Sir A. Murray was *hors de combat*,* so H. W. went to the telephone, and took me with him to write notes. The only line available between St. Quentin and Bertry (Sir Horace's H.Q.) was by the railway telephone, and we accordingly went off to the station in H. W.'s car. H. W. had no time to put on his leggings and drove off with about six inches of bare leg showing above the top of his ankle boots. He was quite calm, although he thought that "Smith-Doreen" was in the devil of a hole. When he spoke to Sir Horace, who had asked about help from the Ist Corps, he said that "troops fighting Douglas Haig cannot fight you," and that he personally felt more nervous about the outer flank of the IInd Corps.

Sir Horace mentions this conversation with Wilson over the telephone in his book:

> Henry Wilson asked what I thought of chance of success, and I replied that I was fully confident and hopeful of giving the enemy a smashing blow and slipping away before he could recover. He replied, "Good luck to you. Yours is the first cheerful voice I have heard these three days." With these pleasing words in my ears, which I shall never forget, I returned to my head-quarters.

The first volume of the official "Military Operations, France and Belgium, 1914," sets the question as to the wisdom of Smith-Dorrien's decision to stand and fight, in spite of having received orders from G.H.Q. to continue the retreat, finally at rest. The official account says:

> With both flanks more or less in the air, they had turned upon an enemy of at least twice their strength, had struck him hard, and had withdrawn except on the right front of the 5th Division, practically without interference, with neither flank enveloped, having suffered losses severe, but considering the circumstances, by no means extravagant.

Thanks mainly to the work of the und Corps, aided by the 4th Division and the Cavalry Division, on this critical day, the

---

* "Out of action."

Expeditionary Force was enabled to continue its retreat on the 27th without being seriously molested by the hosts of Von Kluck. G.H.Q., now at Noyon, was visited this day by an officer sent with a message by General Joffre, and Wilson seized the opportunity to transmit to the French Commander-in-Chief a clear expression of his own views.

> I told him how useless the present plans were. Another corps (the VIIth) sent to Amiens will simply be caught by the Germans. I told him to get all five corps up here from Alsace, and then we could advance again.

Since the retreat from Mons had begun, Wilson had been performing invaluable service at G.H.Q., not only in carrying out his staff duties under great difficulties, but also in heartening those with whom he was closely associated at a time of grave anxiety. No more convincing evidence of the severity of the labours imposed upon him during these days of stress could be produced than is afforded by the extreme brevity of the entries in his diary, and by the curtailment of his letters to his wife to a mere sentence or two — for that was not his way when there were stirring events to record. Of the encouragement which his demeanour conveyed to those associated with him on the General Staff, his assistants write with enthusiasm. "H. W.'s inimitable way of saying, 'Well, and where are we now?' on entering the O.(*a*) room during the retreat," one member of G.H.Q. writes, "was a tonic which invariably brightened the prevailing gloom. His insistence that '*battre en retraite*'[*] was an operation of war fully recognized by all the Great Captains, also had its encouraging effect at a trying period." "His cheerfulness and moral courage," writes another, "were in rather marked contrast to the attitude of certain other members of G.H.Q.". And Sir N. Macready, in his "Annals of an Active Life," strikes the same note when giving his own personal experiences of the great retreat. He records:

> At Noyon I was eye-witness of a scene so characteristic of my old

---

[*] "Retreat."

friend, Henry Wilson, that it is worth relating. A long, dark room — a schoolroom, I think — had been commandeered as the Head-quarters office, each of us having a table or two round the walls. Murray, who for the last five days had been severely taxed night and day with a crushing weight of anxiety and practically no sleep, was sitting at a table looking over messages from the front, when he suddenly dropped forward in a dead feint. Our Head-quarters medical officer, Cummins, with some staff officers, earned him to a bench and applied restoratives, while Henry Wilson walked slowly up and down the long room, with that comical, whimsical expression on his face, habitual to him, clapping his hands softly together to keep time, as he chanted in a low tone, "We shall never get there, we shall never get there." As he passed me I said, "Where Henri?" And he chanted on, "To the sea, to the sea, to the sea." It was just the way to keep up everybody's spirits, some of the younger members of the staff not always remembering the golden rule of appearing cheerful under any and every turn of circumstances.

And Macready adds:

However dark the situation might be, Henry Wilson never lost his cheery optimism or failed to wring a smile from the most serious-minded pessimist by his quaint quips on persons and things, his admiration and affection for our good friends the French, whose language he spoke fluently, being another tie between us.

Lord Esher also wrote of Wilson during these dark days in his "The Tragedy of Lord Kitchener":

During the retreat from Mons all the resources of courage, good sense, stinging wit, and uproarious Irish mirth of which he was possessed had been placed torrentially at the service of the army and its Chief, In his vicinity no heart quailed, and before his caustic glee in battle men's tired spirits revived. When the climax of disaster came, authority seemed naturally to slip into his hands. His comrades, French and English, recall with affectionate admiration how at St. Quentin, when fatigue, depression, and an encircling foe had brought strong men to the point of collapse, a gaunt figure, scantily clothed, laughed through the silent hours, absorbing every military point, urging the French peasantry to be helpful and the English soldiers to stand firm. Even here, his prescience never failed. In that darkest

> hour, he is recorded to have said, "The Germans are over hasty. They urge the pursuit too fast. The whole thing is overdone. They are bound to make a big mistake. And then your hour will have come." Already he had divined the Battle of the Marne.

It was not that, during the dark days of the close of August, 1914, Wilson did not most fully realize the gravity of the position in which the Expeditionary Force was placed, nor the severity of the discomfiture which the Allies had suffered between Lille and Verdun. "I am afraid we are in for a disaster. Personally, quite well. Not a moment," he had written to Mrs. Wilson on the 26th. He could not but feel bitter disappointment at the French failure to stay the hostile advance, and be disillusioned by the now obvious fact that General Joffre had been out-manoeuvred and that the plans of the French General Staff had deplorably miscarried.* But in spite of misgivings and mortification, in spite of nights without sleep and of days spent in incessant labour, he maintained an unruffled demeanour and displayed that calmness in adversity that stamps the born leader of men.

By the night of the 28th, the Expeditionary Force had put the River Oise, with its two canals, between itself and the enemy and it consequently was able to continue its retreat without further serious disturbance. Next day Wilson proceeded to Joffre's headquarters at Vitry le Francois, but he found that Joffre had gone to see Lanrezac attempt a counter-attack with me Fifth French Army. He wrote in his diary that day:

> I had 2½ hours with Belin and Berthelot. I spoke strongly about the madness of Lanrezac attacking with 4 corps, because they would be met by 7 corps. I spoke of the danger of eccentric movements like the VIIth Corps detraining west of Péronne, of scattered Reserve Divisions, of the absolute necessity of bringing up corps from Alsace, and of gaining time. Of the urgent need of stopping Lanrezac from doing more than a demonstration. We had a long, at one time hot, discussion; but I stuck to my points and in the end I got my way. They agreed to the wisdom of my proposals and said Lanrezac would be

* One cause of this was that the French General Staff had underestimated the numbers with which the Germans would start the war.

stopped from going beyond St. Quentin.

Meanwhile Joffre had gone to Compiègne. On my way home after my long talk with Belin and Berthelot I was met 10 k. outside Rheims by an officer who told me Joffre wished to see me in Rheims on his way back to Vitry. I met him at the Lion d'Or at 7.30 p.m. under the electric light of the archway. I had a long talk with him, recapitulating what I had said to Belin, and begging him not to commit Lanrezac irretrievably. He was tired but he insisted on the fact that Lanrezac must go "*au bout*."* I urged him to bring corps from Alsace. I don't know if my day's work has been any use, but I think Lanrezac will be withdrawn.

On this day part of the Fifth French Army had in reality delivered a very effective counter-attack upon the pursuing Germans (an action generally spoken of as the Battle of Guise), and, whether it was due to Wilson's representations or not, that Army continued its retirement on the morrow. The B.E.F. had, thanks to Le Cateau and to its rapid retirement during the past three days, virtually eluded the enemy, although the cavalry covering the movement remained fully in touch with the hostile mounted patrols. While Wilson was looking for Joffre at Vitry le Francis, the French Commander-in-Chief had, according to the diary, paid a visit to Sir John at Compiègne to propose that the B.E.F. should assume the offensive. But Sir John did not, as he explains in his "1914," consider that his troops were in a condition to undertake any such operation at the moment. He maintained that they must continue their retreat, although he undertook to keep the gap between the Fifth French Army and the Sixth French Army, which was now being formed on the left of the B.E.F., filled up. On this day it was also decided at G.H.Q. that, as communications with the base at Havre were now threatened, a new base must be established. So St. Nazaire and Nantes near the mouth of the Loire were fixed upon, and the necessary steps for making this transfer were undertaken within the few days immediately following. The transfer, however, of necessity gave rise to considerable delay in the arrival of armament and equipment at the front that were

---

* "At the end."

urgently needed to make good the losses which had been suffered since the opening exchanges at Mons.

Wilson wrote home from Compiègne on the 30th:

> We are still here, gradually -withdrawing our troops to the west under cover of the R. Oise. No fighting for us to-day, and if we get ten days of quiet we shall be able to get out of the really great confusion we are now in. We have men of every battalion and battery scattered all over the place, columns of ammunition, sappers, ambulances, parks, etc., mixed up in the most bewildering way. Still quite impossible to say who has been killed, who wounded, who missing, though a preliminary list goes home to-day, I hope. We are still waiting for the 6 th Division, and what on earth keeps the Cabinet from sending it here passes all understanding.

The retirement was continued on August 31 and September 1, the Expeditionary Force always lying one day's march farther back than the Fifth French Army on its right, and the French Sixth Army on its left. Wilson wrote in his diary:

> A ridiculous position, as it is neither one thing nor the other, and it makes two French flanks ragged and insecure.

On the 1st Sir J. French had his meeting with Lord Kitchener in Paris, of which so much has since been heard but as to which Wilson has nothing to say in his daily record.

This appears in the diary on the 2nd:

> The corps got down near the river [Marne] and it was a quiet day on the whole. Sir John saw G.O.C.s of Corps at 2. 30. He had taken a cursory glance at a wrong position. Suddenly changing plans and position, I had to get out orders for flank march to-night In time available quite hopeless. Have gravest fears for to-morrow if attacked in force.

Wilson wrote on the 3rd:

> We moved across the Marne to-day in very hot weather on the order I had to get out at a moment's notice last night Sir John agreeing to a counter-stroke with the Ist Corps from the right, instead

of by the IIIrd Corps from the left which he had proposed; We got over without being pushed, providentially. The enemy fastened on the Fifth Armv, and especially XVIIIth Corps, and gave them rough handling. Joffre writes to Sir John and tells him of his new proposals for delaying action and gaining time. So my visit to Vitry bore fruit.

Next day, the 4th, the Germans were observed to be crossing the British front from west to east, and that day, Wilson, who at once realized what an opportunity the move of the enemy was likely to furnish, went to see General Franchet d'Esperey who had succeeded Lanrezac. It was agreed between them that the Fifth Army should fall back next day so as to bring it back into line with the British troops, and that these should make a half wheel to the east, with a view to the Sixth Army under General Maunoury, composed of troops that had been transported round, via Paris, from the extreme right in Lorraine, coming up on their left. Maunoury's army and the B.E.F. would then be in a position to strike at the outer flank of Von Kluck's forces which, it was now definitely established, were moving south-eastwards. Wilson wrote in his diary:

> The above scheme seemed a good one and I was all in favour of it, in fact it was, I think, my idea. When I got back here I found that Sir John had already ordered a retirement, having this morning specifically stated to the Governor of Paris that he would remain on the Marne unless turned out, and also that he would co-operate with the Fifth or Sixth Armies, or both. It is simply heart-breaking.

This appears in the diary next day:

> This morning at 3 a.m. Huguet brought me Joffre's orders for the attack to-morrow of the Fifth and Sixth Armies and Foch's army and asking us to join. I spent a miserable night, because we have already had one day's retirement and because I thought Sir John would go on retiring. However, I went to see him at 7 a.m., and he has agreed to retrace his steps and join in the offensive movement of the Fifth and Sixth Armies. This is good. General Maunoury came to see us at 9 a.m. He moves up the right bank of the Ourcq at 9 a.m. to-morrow.
>
> At 2 p.m. General Joffre arrived. He at once made it dear that the whole French armies are going to attack to-morrow. He begged Sir

> John to co-operate with all his might. "The lives of all French people, the soil of France, and the future of Europe" depended on the coming battle. Sir John agreed to co-operate and advance alongside the Sixth Army. We got out orders at once for a movement to the east with a view of attacking the enemy to-morrow.

When it was proposed, on this 5th day of September, as thus indicated by Wilson in his diary, to transform the movement of retirement, which had been proceeding almost uninterruptedly for nearly a fortnight, into one of sudden, resolute advance, the situation as a whole in the theatre of war in France and Belgium still appeared ominous from the Allies' point of view. In so far as the British Expeditionary Force was concerned, the main base on which it depended for its supplies and munitions and reinforcements had, under the pressure of dire events, been shifted in haste from Havre to St. Nazaire at the mouth of the Loire, and Boulogne had perforce been closed as a port of disembarkation. The historic stronghold of Namur, upon which a considerable reliance had been placed by French and British alike, had yielded to forces hitherto unexpected, without any serious attempt having been made by the Belgian garrison to defend its works. Abandoning Paris in some precipitation, the French Government had betaken itself to a place of greater security, but that was admittedly remote, Bordeaux. The opening phase of the campaign had, in fact, unquestionably proved a sore and disconcerting discomfiture for the Allies. Those sanguine anticipations of embarking upon a determined offensive so soon as their preliminary concentration should be an accomplished fact, which the French General Staff had cherished for years, had broken down completely during the initial stage of the great adventure.

The early exchanges had made manifest that the centre of gravity of the Franco-British hosts had from the outset been improperly disposed for meeting the hostile offensive. The consequences of the serious miscalculation as to the enemy's strength and intentions on the part of the French High Command had indeed been deplorable. For, surging forward almost unchecked but for the combats of Le Cateau and Guise, the German armies had already, within a fortnight of the first serious clash between the rival hosts, made themselves masters of French soil so far forward as a line running westwards approximately from the vicinity of Verdun to within a few miles of Paris. Still, if the portents had appeared for a time to be in the highest degree threatening, and if the designs of the enemy even yet remained subject of grave doubt. General Joffre had now interpreted them aright. He was giving the correct impulse to a great forward movement of the Allies, to be carried out in the right direction and at the right moment.

Chapter XI – 1914: The Last Four Months

The Battle of the Marne — The Aisne — The move to Flanders — The First Battle of Ypres — Lord Roberts's death at St. Omer — The December offensive — Appointment of Wilson to be C.G.S. of the B.E.F. vetoed at Home.

The general advance of the left and centre of the Allied forces which General Joffre had ordained began, in accordance with plan, on September 6, with the British contingent insinuated between the French Sixth Army under Maunoury and the French Fifth Army under Franchet d'Esperey, with the French Ninth Army on Franchet d'Esperey's right. All went well. Sir J. French's troops indeed met with little resistance, and by midday it was clear that the enemy in their immediate front was retiring. The Sixth, Fifth and Ninth French Armies, all three, had a less easy task, but they were all equally successful in driving back the German forces in front of them in confusion.

Wilson wrote in his diary that evening:

> Sir John and Archie, who were out motoring, have pulled the IIIrd Corps up facing north on the Grand Morin River, instead of facing east and north-east. This, of course, caused some unnecessary marching to-day, and will do to-morrow to get them facing right for a forward move. I believe that the Germans are in retreat, although I think that they may give us some shrewd knocks in the process. It is only three days ago that I had to fight all I could to prevent retiring

behind the Seine for 3 weeks' rest.

The advance continued on the 7th and 8th, and on both days the French Sixth and Fifth Armies met with a good deal of opposition, while the B.E.F. had little fighting to do. It reached the Maine on the 9th, crossed that river on the morrow and, continuing its forward movement, arrived on the Aisne on the 12th. In obedience to a request to that effect from Joffre s head-quarters, now established at Châtillon-sur-Seine, Wilson proceeded thither by car on the following day, and a prolonged discussion took place. The French General Staff had come to the mistaken conclusion that the German hosts were splitting in two, their First and Second Armies, respectively under Von Kluck and Von Bülow (which had been facing Maunoury, French, and Franchet d'Esperey) retiring in a northerly and north-easterly direction, while their forces farther to the east were retreating eastwards. The decision come to at Châtillon was therefore, that the Allies' left wing should continue the pursuit northwards and north-eastwards, that the Allies' right wing should try and cut off the enemy forces retreating eastwards, and that Foch's Ninth Army in the centre should be prepared to strike in either direction. French G.Q.G. had in reality exaggerated the greatness of the success gained by the Allies in their effective counterstroke, and this is made very apparent by an entry made in Wilson's diary after the meeting at Châtillon:

> Beithelot asked me when I thought we should cross into Germany, and I replied that unless we made some serious blunder we ought to be at Elsenborn in 4 weeks. He thought 3 weeks. I told him of my proposal, should they stand on the Namur — Meuse — Thionville line, to attack everywhere, but to force the line through the impossible country south of Givet. They agreed, after much argument, and allotted the task to Foch. They were all perfectly charming to me, and far too complimentary. What a different interview to that of August 30th! I am glad to think that, as a result of that interview, Lanrezac's army was saved, and that all the corps in Alsace, except one, have been withdrawn and are now with either Foch in the middle, or with Maunoury on our left. And this has been the cause of all our success.

But the somewhat sanguine forecasts upon which these plans were based soon proved to be wholly unwarranted by the facts of the situation. The Allies on the 15th found themselves checked at all points, although the British, it is true, gained a footing on the farther bank of the Aisne after severe fighting. The 6th Division arrived from home on the 15th and 16th, and it was at once utilized in the hopes of overcoming the stubborn resistance of the enemy forces confronting Sir J. French's forces. Wilson was at first inclined to assume that the B.E.F. was only opposed by a strong rear-guard, and under that impression he wrote to his wife on the 15th:

> If we drive in the force in front of us we won't have any more trouble till we get to the Meuse. We find great difficulty in getting our casualties replaced, and we have had considerable loss again yesterday. K.'s "shadow armies," for shadow campaigns, at unknown and distant dates, prevent a lot of good officers, N.C.O.S and men from coming out. It is a scandalous thing. Under no circumstances can these mobs now being raised, without officers and N.C.O.s, without guns, rifles, or uniforms, without rifle-ranges or training grounds, without supply or transport services, without *moral* or tradition, knowledge or experience, under no circumstances could these mobs take the field for 2 years. Then what is the use of them? What we want, and *what we must have* is for out little force out here to be kept to full strength with the very best of everything. Nothing else is any good.

Two days later he wrote:

> His (Lord Kitchener's) ridiculous and preposterous army of 25 Corps is the laughing-stock of every soldier in Europe. It took the Germans 40 years of incessant work to make an army of 25 Corps with the aid of conscription; it will take us to all eternity to do the same by voluntary effort.

It, however, became more and more apparent from day to day during the nest week that the Allies had been brought to a complete standstill, and that the somewhat precipitate retirement of the Germans a few days earlier had merely been of a temporary nature. No progress whatever could be made on the Aisne. Continuous heavy fighting, day after day, produced little result other than heavy losses to the Allies — the side which was acting on the offensive against well-prepared positions held by an enemy enjoying the advantage in respect to artillery. Joffre, therefore, decided to reinforce his extreme left, with the idea of outflanking the Germans in the country north of the Aisne; and he placed General de Castelnau in command of the troops assembling in that quarter. But, after some initial successes, de Castelnau found himself unable to make much further impression, and, as was already the case on the Aisne, the operations of the Allies against the enemy's extreme right came virtually to a standstill.

G.H.Q. was now at Fère-en-Tardenois, and on the 24th Wilson motored over to de Castelnau's head-quarters near Amiens to see how events were proceeding. On the way back he, as he wrote in his diary, hit upon the idea of transferring the B.E.F. from its present position on the Aisne, with me French forces on either flank, to an entirely new position on the extreme left, outside of de Castelnau. So placed, it would in all probability be able to utilize Boulogne to some extent as a subsidiary base.* On getting back to G.H.Q. he, according to the diary, "told Sir John — said it was his idea and let the proposal mature." He wrote in his diary next day:

> All day passed and Sir John came to no decision. Before dinner he told me he had given up all idea of going on the left, because the Indian Division could not be here till the end of October. He said he would not go on the left with 3 Corps and 2 Cavalry Divisions, because he would be afraid after his Mons and Le Cateau experiences. I pointed out that the German corps of to-day were very different indeed to their corps of a month ago, and that they no longer were an avalanche. After considerable argument I nearly got him round to my way of thinking. Later, at dinner, he aired the idea of going on the left to Huguet who was dining, and Huguet, of course, backed it up for all he was worth.

Mr. Churchill arrived on a visit next day and his appearance excited some apprehension. "I am nervous about this," Wilson

---

* Havre had again been made the main base of the B.E.F.

remarks in his diary, "and what Sir John will be got to say." Moreover, on the 27th there occurs the blunt entry, "Saw Winston for 5 minutes, but he talked such nonsense about the 'shadow' forces that I got to grips at once." Churchill's impressions gained on the occasion of this meeting with Sir J. French and his staff, as they are set down in the first volume of "The World Crisis," are, however, well worth quoting here, for they serve to show the complete divergence of view in respect to fundamentals which existed at this time between Lord Kitchener and his colleagues on the one side, and the officers composing General Headquarters of the Expeditionary Force on the other side. He writes:

> But I could not share the universal optimism of the Staff. It was fully believed and loudly declared on every side that, if all available reinforcements in officers were sent to the army without delay, the war would be finished by Christmas. Fierce were the reproaches that the War Office were withholding vitally needed officers, instructors and material for the purpose of training vast armies that would never be ready in time. I combated their views to the best of my ability, being fully convinced of Kitchener's commanding foresight and wisdom in resisting the temptation to meet the famine of the moment by devouring the seed-corn of the future. I repeated the memorable words he had used to the Cabinet that, "The British Empire must participate in the land war on the greatest scale, and that in no other way could victory be won." Taking a complete survey, I consider that this prudent withholding from the army in the field, in the face of every appeal and demand, the key-men who alone could make new armies, was the greatest of the services which Lord Kitchener rendered to the nation at this time, and it was a service which no one of less authority than he could have performed.

General Joffre was at first most unwilling to fall in with the proposal that the British force should be shifted to the extreme left of the line. "The fact is, and I think there are some grounds for it, that the French are dissatisfied with us. It is very unfortunate," Wilson wrote in his diary, and in the end it was arranged that he should go and discuss the matter with the French Commander-in-Chief. So he motored over to G.Q.G. on the 29th, arriving late, after Joffre had gone to bed; but he saw Belin and Berthelot that night and found that they were strongly opposed to the plan. He gives the following account in his diary of the much more encouraging meeting next day:

> I met Joffre, Bella, and Berthelot (Huguet also present) at 9 a.m. We discussed till 10.30. Very different atmosphere from last night. Joffre took command. He agreed to all points of my note except th at the removal of our forces must be done "*au fur et à mesure.*"* Luckily I had put this case to Sir John last evening before coming here, and he had agreed to this procedure.
>
> Joffre said he thought the Germans had sensibly weakened in front of the XVIIIth Corps, of us, and of the right of the Sixth Army. He, therefore, proposed we should make a push and see what was in front of us. When we know result we can act accordingly. If we can get on, so best; if not, then he is quite ready we should begin to move across to the left, and suggests that the cavalry and the IIIrd Corps should go first, followed by others as he could get corps to replace. Joffre quite agrees to importance of our getting on the left as soon as we can. He was quite charming to me.
>
> I got here 2 p.m., saw Sir John, and he agreed to withdraw the 2nd Cavalry Division (Gough) IInd Corps and 19th Brigade, without reinforcements. He wrote this to Joffre. A real good day's work.

The transfer of the British Expeditionary Force from the Aisne front to the extreme left of the Allied line began, as proposed above, on the night of October 1. News arrived next day that Antwerp was in grave danger; so Wilson proceeded to G.Q.G. on the 2nd to arrange that the relief of Sir John's troops on the Aisne should be expedited as far as possible. On the following day he learnt that Lord Kitchener was contemplating the dispatch of the newly formed 7th Division† from England to Antwerp instead of sending it to reinforce the B.E.F., and on the 4th this news was

---

* "As we go along."

† Although there had never been any idea of a 7th Division being actually included in the Expeditionary Force as contemplated before the War, plans for the constitution of such a division had been in existence, the troops being to some extent drawn from foreign garrisons. Lord Kitchener was, however, forming four additional divisions of regulars, the 8th, 27th, 28th, and 29th, entirely out of regular units brought home from India and other foreign stations.

confirmed, with the addition that the newly formed 3rd Cavalry Division was likewise to proceed to Belgium, the whole under command of Rawlinson. Wilson was much concerned at this; but he hoped that these troops would not, at the worst, reach the fortress and find themselves invested within the girdle of works. He wrote home on the 4th:

> Our news from Antwerp makes us think it is going to fall in a few days. The Belgian Field Army of 6 Divisions — where are they? There are Winston's Marines which have given us much amusement. There is that splendid Territorial Army of ours, which Haldane and Johnnie Hamilton have for years said could put up a superb fight. Then why should Antwerp fall?

"I still think," he had written the day before, "that the war will be over in February or March."

G.H.Q. moved on October 8 from Fère-en-Tardenois, where it had been stationed since immediately after the opening of the operations on the Aisne, to Abbeville. The party visited de Castelnau at his head-quarters on the way. General Foch had recently been placed in command of the French troops that were moving up in the direction of the extreme left of the line, simultaneously with the B.E.F., and he was met at Doullens, a little town which was to gain historic importance in March, 1918. "Here a guard of honour and bugle," Wilson wrote in his diary, "and Foch kissed me twice in front of the whole crowd! Foch absolutely full of fight." Wilson, moreover, expressed himself as greatly struck with the way that the harvest, as the country was viewed from the road, had been saved by the old men, the women and the children.

Nearly half of the B.E.F. had arrived in the northern region by this time, and some portions of it were already on the move forward from about Abbeville in the direction of Lille. Reports from various sources, however, indicated that the Germans had become aware of the extension to the left of the Allies' line which was in progress, and that they were making preparations to forestall, or in any case to meet, this. Antwerp had been evacuated by the Belgians on the 7th, and the Germans were in complete possession of the great place of arms by the 10th. "So K. and

Winston have so arranged their childish strategy," Wilson wrote in his diary, "that they have lost 2,000 Marines and some guns, and have not saved Antwerp." Nor were matters proceeding altogether smoothly at G.H.Q. — as appears from the following entry in his diary under date the 10th:

> Sir John, Murray, and I out to see Smith-Dorrien at Hesdin, then General de Maud'huy at St. Pol. Sir John wrote a wire to Joffre this morning to say that if the Ist Corps was not relieved at once he would withdraw it to the left bank of the Aisne. [The Ist Corps was still in its old position facing the Germans on the farther bank of the Aisne.] Luckily a wire from Joffre saying he hoped to entrain Ist Corps close to the front came in before the other went off, so it was not sent. Similarly, at our interview with Maud'huy at St. Pol, Maud'huy asked urgently for help at Béthune. Sir John said he would not march before 9 a.m. When we got back here at 5 p.m. Foch turned up and simply said what he wanted done, and when.
>
> This morning Archie spoke to me about his position as C. of S. He said it was becoming very difficult. He asked for my opinion as to whether he should resign. I replied that, for the moment, I thought there ought to be no change, that I knew of no one who could take his place with greater success, and that I thought we ought to tide over the present and watch developments. This was agreed to.

G.H.Q. moved north from Abbeville to St. Omer on the 1 3th. Indications from the front had by this time proved that the enemy was pushing troops into Flanders and massing forces in this quarter almost, if not quite, as fast as were the Allies, although the 7th Division and the 3rd Cavalry Division under Rawlinson were now approaching Ypres from the Bruges direction to join the rest of the Expeditionary Force. Wilson was, however, growing impatient at the comparatively slow advance of the IInd and IIIrd Corps eastwards, and that day he wrote in his diary, "We must push, push, push, as we have nothing in front of us, and if we have, we shall have 3 or 4 Corps in line against us."* He was much distressed to hear on the 14th that his old friend, Hubert Hamilton,

---

* The IInd and IIIrd Corps were in fact confronted by the VIIth, XIIIth, and XIXth German Corps, as well as by a Cavalry Corps.

who was commanding the 3rd Division, had been killed, and he grew more and more dissatisfied at the lack of thrust that appeared to be displaying itself just when thrust seemed particularly wanted. But the enemy was gathering thick, and by the 17th the B.E.F., so far from acting on the offensive, was already being heavily counter-attacked. On the 19th he wrote to his wife:

> Our news to-night is not so good, though there is nothing to be anxious about. But the Germans are crowding up against us, and I am afraid that, from the fact that we have not pushed as hard as we ought during the last week (for various reasons), we are now going to find the boot on the other leg. We shall know more to-morrow. I still think the campaign will be over in the spring, that is to say if the Russians do moderately well, and I know of no reason why they shouldn't.

In his diary of that day he expresses himself as much disappointed:

> Owing to nothing but absolute incompetence and want of regimental officers, we have lost the finest opportunity of the war and are now being thrown on the defensive. *Maddening* and perhaps disastrous.

His account of experiences and events as jotted down daily at this time and during the weeks immediately following is of considerable military importance. It throws light upon a number of varying phases of the critical struggle which was developing about the Lys and the Yser, and which lasted up to the end of what has come generally to be known as the First Battle of Ypres. But the story, as it is unfolded in the diary, cannot be properly followed without a large scale map, it would have to be amplified by material to be drawn from other sources to render it readily intelligible, and the details are in reality rather of professional than of general interest. Only some of the more striking passages of the diary will therefore be quoted, and even these cannot in many cases appear in full owing to their containing forcible criticisms which ought not to be published so soon after the event.

Wilson was seeing Foch almost daily, as was indeed necessary, owing to the extent to which the French and British troops were becoming intermingled in the hustle on the part of the Allies to bring into action the forces that were being hurried up from the south, so as to make head against the growing strength of the hostile array. He was experiencing considerable difficulty in persuading Sir John to fall in with Foch's plans and arrangements. He was, indeed, having a difficult role to play in maintaining those cordial relations with the French that were demanded in the interests of the Allies by the difficulties and dangers of an awkward situation. On the 20th, for instance, after having discussed certain intended movements with Foch and having arrived at a satisfactory understanding as to what ought to be done, we find him writing in his diary:

> It is a tonic to have a talk with Foch. I brought all this back to Sir John who said he would not take orders from a junior, etc., but he accepted the inevitable. He still clings to the Ist Corps going to Bruges, but I don't mind this, as Bruges for all practical purposes is as far as Berlin, and to-morrow's fighting will settle that.

Next day he wrote:

> General Joffre came to see Sir John. He explained the same story that Foch told me, with the addition that the whole of the IXth Corps goes to Ypres. All went satisfactorily until Sir John asked for facilities to make a great entrenched camp at Boulogne to take the whole E.F. Joffre's face instantly became quite square and he replied that such a thing could not be allowed for a moment. He would make some works to safeguard against a coup-de-main, but an entrenched camp he would not allow. Sir John was checkmated straight away and said I was to discuss the matter with General Joffre. So that nightmare is over. Huguet had gone to meet Joffre and had carefully prepared the. ground.
>
> We were very heavily attacked right along the line and had to give ground everywhere. Owing to Sir John's eccentric movement of the Ist Corps north of Ypres towards Bruges, we are on a front of 35 miles. This must be contracted; as we cannot leave our point of junction with the French at La Bassée, we must draw south.

The troops which had been sent from England to Zeebrugge under Rawlinson in the hope of saving Antwerp were now in touch with the rest of the B.E.F. and had come under Sir J. French's orders. The first of the two divisions which had been dispatched to France from India, the Lahore Division, had also joined just at this time. The second, the Meerut Division, arrived at the front on the 29th. But, welcome as were these reinforcements. Sir J. French's army was suffering such heavy losses in the continuous fighting in which it became involved as soon as it moved forward towards the Lys, that it could only act on the defensive in face of the desperate efforts that were being made by the hostile hosts to gain the upper hand. The Germans were generally acting on the offensive after the first few days, and their commanders were now bent on gaining possession of the Channel ports. On more than one occasion, and notably on October 31, when, owing to the enemy capturing Gheluvelt in front of Ypres, the British line was for a brief space broken, it looked as if the Allies were to suffer defeat. The situation remained so critical and strained that large additional bodies of French troops were hurried up from the south to bear a hand, and their arrival tended to make the opposing sides about equal in strength. But this concentration of Allied forces had the result that British and French divisions became intermingled along the front to a most inconvenient extent. Owing to Murray's temporary absence in England from October 26 to the 29, Wilson was acting as C.G.S. during some of the most critical days of this prolonged contest, and the following extracts from his diary and from letters of his to Mrs. Wilson serve to indicate how great were his anxieties:

> *Diary, October 22*. During the night the 19th Brigade dosed up its left, and made a gap of 3 miles between its right and the left of the IInd Corps. I wired 3 a.m. to IIIrd Corps to say this must be dosed. In early morning all messages showed we were going to be heavily attacked along our line and along whole Belgian line.
>
> *Diary, October 25*. At midnight Smith-Dorrien came in to report that he was afraid his corps might go during the night. Sir John rather short with him, and I think fails to realize what it would mean. The only reserves we have are some 4.7 guns at Hazebrouck, and I ordered these to Smith-Dorrien at once.
>
> *Letter, October 26*. Another anxious 24 hours, as last rught after midnight we got afraid our right was going to come back, which

would have been almost a disaster. However, the measures taken proved sufficient for the moment, and another 24 hours ought to see the great danger over, as the Meerut Division will begin to arrive to-morrow and after that I shall be comparatively happy. The Russian news is good, and I still think we shall finish in the spring; but this German army is a superb fighting machine. I get daily a greater admiration for the French soldier. He is a marvel.

Letter, October 28. Things are going better, and the anxious times about the IInd Corps are passing, as most of the Meerut Division is now in rear of it. So I hope to get a real good sleep to-night. No news from the Belgians since the early morning, when we heard some French reinforcements were coming up, and they may save the situation.

Letter, October 31. All yesterday we were heavily attacked on our left hand and had to fall back. This morning the attack recommenced with increased violence, and as I write the fire is very heavy. All last night again I was at work collecting reserves for to-day's fight, and Foch, who came to see me at 1 a.m. this morning, only left me at 2.30 a.m., and then lent Sir John 8 battalions and 6 batteries.

Diary, November 1. At 5 a.m. message from Allenby to say cavalry was heavily attacked all night and was being driven in. By 11 a.m. Allenby was retiring on Kernel. Lord K. called me up on telephone from British Consulate at Dunkirk and asked for situation. I told him. He was upset and asked if he could do anything. I replied, "For the moment — no— but send us more troops." He telephoned to War Office to send 5 more battalions of Terriers. Foch has now taken over the cavalry line by the 3 2nd Division, and he has the equivalent of another division coming up to-night, and if the 1st and 7th Divisions (both stone-cold) can hold on, I believe Foch will save the situation. He is a fine fellow. The German Emperor was down opposite to us to-day, no doubt thinking he was going to see Ypres taken. But he won't

Letter, November 2. I am spending a good deal of time these days with Foch up on this curious hill on the way between Ypres and St. Omer. We have got our troops so much mixed up with his that no order can be issued to either without the other's approval, etc. I think we are going to beat this attack with the aid the French have given us. It has been a stiff business.

Letter, November 4. Fighting goes on, but not so bitter, and we still hold our own though hard put to it.

Letter, November 6. Our news to-day is that the French are being

> violently attacked and are giving ground. I was out this afternoon, and I have to go and see Foch again. The Germans have got up another corps, and in spite of 230 guns they are pushing the gallant little Frenchman back. We are being attacked everywhere also, but not with any ferocity so we are holding our ground all right.
>
> *Letter, November 11.* We are having heavy fighting again to-day and the Germans are pushing us back in rather an awkward manner, but I hope we shall readjust to-morrow when some 12,000 good French infantry will be reinforcing us.
>
> *Letter, November 13.* A good deal of reinforcements (French) have come to us now, so I think our position ought to be secure, though the state of the mixture of troops is fearful.

During this period of peril at G.H.Q., the question of Wilson succeeding Sir A. Murray had come up for consideration, as matters were not proceeding altogether smoothly at St. Omer; hut a decision was for the moment postponed. It, moreover, appears from Wilson's diary that an even more important substitution than this had been mooted, for he mentions Foch coming to see him on November 5, to tell him that Lord Kitchener, when at Dunkirk on the 1st, had proposed to the French President and to General Joffre to remove Sir J. French and to replace him by Sir I. Hamilton, but that Joffre had at once said he could not agree as he had worked cordially and well with French. M. Poincaré had backed Joffre up. On Wilson asking, Foch said he thought that Sir John ought to be told, and Wilson thereupon conveyed the intelligence to his Chief. In his diary next day he wrote:

> Sir John and I went to Cassel at 3 p.m. when Sir John thanked Foch personally and in the warmest terms for his comradeship and loyalty. They shook hands on it. Sir John told Foch he proposed to go and see Joffre and to thank him also. We discussed some minor matter and the two parted great friends.

As the situation had become fairly satisfactory and the enemy attacks were dying away, Lord Roberts arrived at St. Omer on the 11th, with Lady Aileen, to stay with Sir John. Major Hereward Wake had been Lord Roberts's A.D.C. in South Africa and, as a member of G.H.Q., was on the spot to accompany him; while

Major Lewin, his son-in-law, had also specially come to St. Omer from his battery. The Indian troops were visited on the following day, and on that evening Lord Roberts and his daughter dined at Wilson's cheery mess. Next day, accompanied by Wilson and Lewin, they proceeded to Cassel to pay a visit to General Foch, with whom the Field-Marshal exchanged graceful compliments and who produced maps on which the course of the recent fighting was made clear. The party then went on to Bailleul to see more of the Indian troops, Wilson, however, remaining with Foch as Sir John was coming out for a discussion. Lord Roberts unfortunately contracted a chill during this day, which happened to be very wet and stormy, and when Wilson went to Sir John's house late at night to inquire, he learnt that the doctor took a serious view of his patient's condition as pneumonia was developing. By next morning the case had become grave, the doctors who were called in agreed that there could be little hope in view of the Field-Marshal's great age, and Lewin crossed the Channel in the afternoon to convey the painful news to Lady Roberts at Englemere. Wilson wrote in his diary that night (November 14th):

> The little Chief got steadily worse. I was in and out all day with Aileen, and. took her for a little walk at 4 o'clock. At 7.43 p.m. Hereward sent for me. When I got there the Chief was dying. Aileen, Hereward, and I, with 3 doctors and 3 nurses were with him to the end. He died at 8 p.m. in absolute peace and quiet. The story of his life is thus completed as he would have wished himself, dying in the middle of the soldiers he loved so well and within the sound of the guns.

He wrote next day:

> I saw Aileen and Here ward off at 7.30 a.m. for Calais, and I feel easier in my mind. I went round and saw the little man, lying so gracefully in his bed.
>
> Went out to see Foch at 11 a.m. Long strategical talk, in which we were agreed that Germany has still one chance, and one chance only, namely to shorten her front on this frontier sufficiently to allow her to transfer 20 to 30 corps to Russia, thrash the Russians, and then come back to us. To do this she must retire to the line Liége — Metz,

or possibly even to the Rhine. Any middle course would be fatal to her.

Saw Sir John at 2 o'clock. He told me that he wished me to take the little Chief home and to represent the "Army in the Field" at the funeral. I am proud, glad, and sorry.

On the morning of the 17th a procession was formed and, to the skirl of Highlander pipes wailing a lament, the coffin was borne on a gun-carriage to the little Town Hall in the main square, where a funeral service was held. The French Army was represented by Generals Foch and Maud'huy and by a picked detachment of the 22nd Dragoons. The Indian princes who were attached to the Indian Corps were all present, and, when the motor-hearse started on its thirty miles journey from the Town Hall to the sea, the veteran Maharajah Sir Pertab Singh took his place on it, to act as a personal guard over the remains of his old chief and friend. M. Christian Mallet writes:

After the ceremony, which we did not see, twenty-one guns thundered out, fired by batteries posted behind the square. An immense rainbow, as sharply defined as if drawn with a stroke of the brush, cut the sky with a perfect and uninterrupted semi-circle. Symbol of peace, it came to earth directly behind the batteries, and the flash of the guns showed up against its iridescent screen.*

At Boulogne the garrison turned out and marched past the coffin, which was then conveyed to Dover by the Onward, and was left there for the night, to be moved to Ascot in the morning, while Wilson went on up to town. He visited the War Office next day, where he saw Lord Kitchener and others, and on the 19th he was one of the Insignia Bearers in the procession at the stately funeral of the great Field-Marshal in St. Paul's. He expresses himself in his diary as much impressed by the beautiful service, arranged on the same lines as that held on the occasion of Lord Wolseley's burial, which he had attended three years before. He spent one more day in England and recrossed the Channel en route for the front on the

---

* "Impressions and Experiences of a French Trooper, 1914— 15."

21st.

On his return to G.H.Q. at St. Omer he found that great interest was being taken in the reports coming to hand at G.H.Q., as also at French G.Q.G. and indeed all along the Western front, of the steady advance of the Russian hosts both in Poland and in Galicia, where they had gained very substantial successes. Extravagant hopes were indeed being founded on what was to turn out to be merely an ephemeral tri ump h. The French military authorities were indisposed to believe the tales of shortage of munitions from which the Tsar's troops must ere long be suffering, that were reaching the War Office in London from British military representatives in the eastern theatre of war. G.H. Q., assuming that the French must be well informed, accepted their view on the subject, and the delusion was to prevail for some months to come.

H.M. the King arrived for his first visit to his troops on the 29th. He decorated several of the senior French officers on this occasion. Foch was given the G.C.B., and Wilson makes some references in his diary to His Majesty's stay. He, for instance, wrote on December 2:

> Huguet told me this morning that when, yesterday, Joffre met the President at the station here, and they motored to Merville to see the King, the President made Joffre go in his motor, and the President and Viviani (Prime Minister) sat at the back and Joffre had to sit on the little seat in front!

On the 4th there is the entry:

> Dined with the King. Also Prince of Wales...and Stamfordham. Had little talk with the King, but much with Stamfordham, who said amongst other things, that I was more responsible for England joining the war than any other man. I think this is true. After dinner Sir John showed me a long wire just come from Buchanan (Petrograd), saying the Russians would come to a standstill if we did not prevent more Germans going over.

Next day Wilson wrote:

> Sir John and I went over to Cassel at 10 a.m. to see Foch and

read Buchanan's wire to him. He was not the least upset, but said that, of course, we must attack, and that in any case he was going to do so. He had already sent his plans to Joffre for an attack north of Arras, at Warneton, Messines, Wytschaete, and Hollebeke, and at Nieuport. Sir John agreed to take over the line of the XXIst Corps, south of the Indians, so as to release that corps.

Mr. Churchill had come over on another visit to Sir J. French, and during a conversation with Wilson asked him to help in bringing Lord Kitchener and Sir John together. Lord French has told the story in his "1914" of how he had wished, from the time that the B.E.F. moved north from its position on the Aisne, that his army should be on the extreme left of the Allies' line, close to the coast, so that it should be in a position to work in co-operation with the British fleet. He has further related how he had discussed the project with Churchill on the occasion of that statesman's former visit, and of how they now discussed it again on the occasion of this second visit of the First Lord, who returned to England promising to arrange everything with the Prime Minister and Lora Kitchener. But just at this very time Foch, besides pressing for the relief of his XXIst Corps, as had been arranged on the 5th, asked Sir John to deliver an attack on Messines on the 11th, the day on which the French were going to attack at Arras and at Nieuport. To this, after raising many objections. Sir John agreed, although he showed himself disposed to go back on his promise to relieve the XXIst Corps. Wilson, who was no believer in the idea of offensive operations along the seashore, expresses himself strongly in his diary on the subject of Sir John's attitude, and on December 10 the entry appears:

Sir John sent for me at 10 a.m. It appears that he had advanced the theory to Winston of going on the left of the line, so as to have ground for his cavalry and the support of the fleet. Winston fell in with this scheme and went hot-foot to London, and he, K., Grey and Asquith put their heads together and sent off a kind of demand for this movement to the French Government. Meanwhile, Sir John had got committed to the Messines attack and to relieving some of the XXIst trenches, so he has got himself into a tight place and sent for me. Later on I went out to Foch and explained situation, and said that Sir

John would not say anything about moving until after the pending attacks. Foch understood. Huguet came to see me later. There is serious intrigue against Joffre— to be replaced by Galliéni. This is bad.

Next day the entry appears:

Foch came to see me ¼ to 6 to tell me that Millerand had sent him a copy of the precious document sent by Winston, K., Grey and Asquith, about our going on the left (see yesterday). Foch much, amused. Millerand put this down to Kitchener; but Foch is right in putting it down to Winston. Of course, Foch treats it with the greatest contempt. We went down to see Sir John; he was quite apologetic about the left flank scheme, and said it was Winston's idea!

Next day, December 12, Wilson wrote:

Meeting at Bailleul at 11.30 a.m. to discuss final arrangements for attack on Monday. [The date had been postponed from the nth to Monday, the 13th.] Sir John held forth at length, explaining that the attack was to be in echelon from the left — if the line was broken he meant to pursue with cavalry I After the meeting I tried with some success to get three matters focused, viz., artillery, cavalry, and our arrangements with the French. When I got back here I found Sir John in rather a stew. A letter from Winston came in by this mail to say he had made elaborate arrangements for sending ships (and replacing when sunk or damaged) to shell Ostend and Zeebrugge and to land forces to take these places. This is not quite in Foch's mind. A wire was at once sent to say that Nieuport was only secondary operation, and bombardment such as had been done on previous occasions was all that was necessary. Huguet went off to Foch to explain the situation, and I got him to get Foch to send D'Urbal a message to say that he was to put his action' on Monday on paper and give a copy to Smith-Dorrien, who would do ditto. I am sure a wise and necessary precaution between Allies.

Wilson was indeed profoundly dissatisfied with the arrangements that had been made for the Expeditionary Force to take part in this joint offensive, seeing that only 9½ battalions were to share in the operation and that there had been no adequate concentration of artillery to help these units in their task. Nor was he mistaken in his anticipations, for the British effort effected nothing, although repeated on three successive days. He wrote home on the 16th:

> Our attack to-day was no more use than yesterday, and we make no progress at all, which is maddening. We put no weight into it and so can't expect to get on. We want a thorough overhauling here, otherwise we won't do any good. Also we shall get into trouble with the French if we are not careful, as they are attacking over miles of front and we over some 500 yards.

It would seem, however, that Sir J. French had no belief in the possibility of getting forward. And there certainly was a good deal to be said for this view, for, although the French did gain some ground, there never was any question of their inflicting a serious defeat upon the enemy or of their improving their position to any appreciable extent, except quite locally. But this attitude on the part of the commander of the B.E.F. made relations with the French somewhat uncomfortable, and Wilson was hard put to it in his mediatory capacity to obviate serious friction.

His appreciation of, and sympathy with, Gallic mentality was most beneficial on occasions such as this, while his intimacy with General Foch was of almost incalculable service to the cause. The pair of highly accomplished soldiers, seeing each other almost daily, could always realize each other's point of view, and they were in the habit of discussing such questions as came to be in debate, frankly and without reservations. Wilson's candour delighted Foch, who keenly enjoyed his British comrade's ready humour, boisterous spirits and epigrammatic raillery. It is true that when it came to chaff the Frenchman proved no match for Sir J. French's expansive Sub-Chief of the General Staff— according to Wilson's own account indeed, Foch, in an access of excitement at the badinage to which he was being subjected one day, kicked his tormentor round the room. But important decisions would often be arrived at under cover of such banter, acute differences of opinion were smoothed over, and relations between the French and British High Commands could be, and were, kept on a reasonably satisfactory footing.

Nor should the exertions of General Huguet to ensure goodwill between G.H.Q. and the French commanders and General Staff be forgotten. Entirely in Wilson's confidence, and a most popular figure at St. Omer, his work when divergences of view manifested themselves between the forces fighting side by side, and at this time indeed inconveniently intermingled, was invaluable. The French were disposed to regard him as unduly pro-British, just as there was a tendency in the British camp to regard Wilson as unduly pro-French. But the truth was that Huguet could always understand the British point of view and he made allowances for it, just as Wilson did in the case of the French, and it was this that made their joint labours so effective and their co-operation so complete. What difficulties Wilson had to contend with at times is illustrated by an entry in his diary on December 17, which reads as follows:

> Foch, who had been down all day long watching Maud'huy's attack near Arras, came to see me at 5.30. We had a long talk I made the best case I could about advancing in echelon from the left, and he listened without saying a word. At the end he said, "*Mais mon cher Wilson nous sommes militaires pas avocats*."* That exactly expresses the straits I was pushed to. We discussed everything, and he was as nice as could be; but "*Pére Joffre n'est pas commode*,"† and it was dear that Sir John would be in a very difficult position if he did not put up some fight.

Thanks to representations tactfully conveyed by Wilson to his Chief after the above quoted conversation between himself and Foch, orders were drafted at G.H.Q. under the terms of which the attack to be undertaken by portions of the B.E.F. was to be carried out on a considerably broader front than had previously been contemplated. But there was another question, and one in which Wilson was personally interested, that was also at this time coming to a head at St. Omer. This was the decision on the part of Sir John

---

* "But my dear Wilson we are military not lawyers."

† "Father Joffre is not easy."

that the Sub-Chief of the General Staff was to replace Sir A. Murray at its head, a matter that was generally understood amongst subordinate officers at G.H.Q. to have been definitely settled. Wilson wrote in the diary on the 19th:

> Saw Sir John twice this morning and again this evening. He talked as though it was settled that I was to be C. of S. He told me that late last night K. had wired saying that Asquith would like to see him if he could come over, and after some hesitation he agreed to go. When post came in this evening he read me two letters from Kitchener. The first about unsatisfactory state of affairs in Russia, shortage of ammunition, the second about me. Kitchener said, "I will not oppose the change, although I do not like it. It seems as though Cambon was right after all." This seems all right. The rest of the letter was devoted to Winston and his "wild cat schemes," which K. said he could not stand any longer, and he has asked Asquith to put Winston in charge of the War Office and to let him resign! What a happy family the Cabinet are.
>
> Sir John goes over 7.30 to-morrow. K. meets him at Folkestone. They motor to Walmer where they meet Asquith, and then Johnnie goes to London. The change will do him good. I don't know if he has told Murray yet. We took 5 trenches last night, but we have been put out of 4 of them, chiefly by bombs, and we lost some 1,300, I am afraid. The movement was good, but the expense was great.

Next morning the Indian Corps, demoralized by the continuous wet weather, by the deplorable condition of the trenches, by the big guns, and by finding themselves in so strange a country, lost about a mile of the front line. They were relieved by the Ist Corps, which had been resting in reserve; and a good deal of the ground that had changed hands was regained — but not all of it. The general result of the offensive operations on the part of the B.E.F. during the month of December indeed merely tended to indicate that, under the conditions then prevailing as regards strength and artillery potentialities, there was little prospect of breaking, or even of denting, the German line in the water-logged Flanders sector. The French had gained some ground in their offensive operations near Arras and near Rheims, but they had achieved no real success at any point. Still, if results had been disappointing, the activity displayed on the part of the Allies had at least prevented the

Germans from sending troops from France and Flanders to the Eastern theatre, where the Russian offensive, which had made so promising a beginning, had now been brought to a standstill.

Sir J. French returned to G.H.Q. from England on the 23rd. But even before Wilson saw his Chief next day, he had already been made aware that he was not after all to succeed Sir A. Murray, as he had been led to expect. Lambton,* who had also been over to England, had brought back the news that neither Mr. Asquith nor Lord Kitchener liked the idea of his being appointed Chief of the General Staff at the front. "This is very flattering," he wrote in his diary that evening. "For myself I really care very little and find it difficult to get up any enthusiasm." He had a prolonged conversation with Sir John next day, and of what passed between them he gives the following account in his diary:

> He began by saying he would speak very openly. He said no man had ever given another more loyal and valuable help than I had given him. He said that so long as he was alive and had power, my future and my promotion were assured. He went on in this way for some time, and then came to the real point. He said the Government and Kitchener were very hostile to me. They said my appointment would be very repugnant to the Cabinet and would shake confidence in the army! That I was the principal cause of all the Ulster trouble and was, therefore, dangerous. In short, neither Kitchener nor Asquith will have me. I feel highly complimented, and told Sir John so. I care not a rush for the opinion of either of these men. Asquith said I was particularly active after Sir John had resigned over Ulster. I don't know what this alluded to, but I expect that Asquith gave the poor man to understand that I had kicked him out. Anyhow the net result is that Murray is more firmly established than ever, and Sir John hinted that the less work I did the better. I might go to Russia and see what they were doing there. How funny!
>
> When I remember Sir John's conversation with me a week ago, I can't help laughing. He knew he was on difficult ground, so he was as charming as he could be. I said little till the end, when I said that I was prepared to go at any moment, and had several times discussed the matter with Billy Lambton, and that I was rarely of use, or of

---

* Colonel (now Major-General Sir W.) Lambton, Sir John's military secretary.

> value for my pay, except occasionally when things were going all wrong, and also in our work with the French. He told me I was absolutely necessary to the rest of the staff. I don't know what this meant, and had not the curiosity to inquire.
>
> I cannot get up any sorrow at not serving him or Asquith or K. as Chief of Staff. He said this Government would soon be out, and then it would be all right. So there are politics in our Army!

Although Wilson made light of the matter in his diary, there can be no doubt that he was disappointed and hurt at Sir John's acquiescence in the veto apparently placed by the Prime Minister and Lord Kitchener on an appointment that had been definitely promised. It is difficult, moreover, to believe that, had the commander of the B.E.F. insisted, the veto would not have been withdrawn. Mr. Asquith's action in the matter is readily intelligible. He could not but be aware that the somewhat ignominious position in which his Cabinet and he himself had been placed at the time of the Curragh incident was mainly due to the skill with which Wilson had handled an unprecedented situation. A politician, thinking politically, he objected to Wilson on political grounds — and it is possible that there are other politicians who, similarly situated, might have done the same.

Lord Kitchener's attitude was not unnatural. From the date of his taking up his appointment as War Minister, Kitchener had decided to make the multiplying of our military forces the basis of his policy. He had satisfied himself that the estimates formed by the foremost British soldiers, other than himself, as to the nature of the conflict which had broken out, and as to its duration, were utterly at fault. The experiences of the first four and a half months of warfare had not only served to confirm him in his views, but had made manifest that those views had been substantially correct. He had foreseen that this was not a struggle lasting merely for months, but that it was a struggle that was to go on for years. Long before any prominent figure in the country thought of such a thing as America intervening in the conflict on the side of the Entente, he had already taken certain preliminary steps calculated to smooth the way when that desirable event should take place.* He was creating the "New Armies," and — in so far as personnel was concerned — those armies were actually in being. But the attitude of G.H.Q. towards this great creative effort of the War Minister's had from the outset been undisguisedly hostile, and no member of G.H.Q. had been more declamatory in his condemnation of the project than had Wilson — as everybody in the War Office well knew. Wilson had, as he himself noted in his diary at the time, scoffed at the "shadow armies" to Churchill at Fère-en-Tardenois; and, if the First Lord informed Lord Kitchener of the views entertained by Sir J. French's Sub-Chief of Staff on returning to England, no one had right to complain. Taking all the circumstances into consideration, it does seem that the Secretary of State for War was not without a certain military justification for hesitating to magnify the power at the front of so influential and so outspoken an opponent of his plans.

Sir John, accompanied by Wilson, started for Chantilly on December 26, to visit General Joffre at his head-quarters, and they arrived there next day after spending the night at Amiens in the same rooms as they had occupied on August 14. Wilson gives the following account of the meeting:

> We started at 8 a.m., got to Chantilly at 10 a.m. and had 1½ hours with Joffre (just Joffre, Sir John, Huguet, and I). Sir John gave Joffre Kitchener's and Asquith's message that the Germans would defeat the Russians and bring 4 million over here and take Paris. Joffre much amused and said they were "*affolés*."† Joffre told us of the enormous increase in output of French gun ammunition; from 10,000 a day to 100,000 a day, all but one tenth in high explosive. Bombs of all sorts being made. Great success of gun fire against wire

* The presence at G.H.Q. and with the B.E.F. for several weeks about this time of Colonel Squiers, the United States Military Attaché in London — scientist as well as soldier— when the presence of Military Attaché of other neutral Powers would not have been permitted for a moment, was Kitchener's handiwork; as was, furthermore, the skilful method by which this special privilege accorded to the American representative was camouflaged.

† "Distraught."

at 1,400 yards. Joffre thinks Russia quite safe for defence, but not enough ammunition for offence for 6 weeks.* If Bulgaria and Rumania join us we will send Russia ammunition through Salonika. I have never seen Joffre so well or in such good form.

Next day the entry appears in Wilson's diary:

Sir John very full of my idea of taking over from La Bassée to the sea. Tom Bridges† sent for from Furnes, and Sir John, Archie, Tom, and I talked it over with result that Tom has to go back to approach the King with a proposal to incorporate the Belgian Army of 6 divisions of 70,000 men in brigades into our army. When the others were gone, I warned Sir John not to be in such a hurry, and never to take over a long line without having good reserves.

At 8 o'clock Huguet arrived from Paris with an amazing story. It appears that Fitzgerald‡ told him the whole story about Kitchener, Asquith, and me, when running down to Chantilly in the motor yesterday. After our interview with Joffre yesterday Huguet remained on, as he was going to Paris. Joffre spoke to him about Murray, and Delcassé (Foreign Minister), who was there, joined in the conversation. Delcassé told Huguet he was wrong, because on the previous day Francis Bertie had told him that Murray was going to be given an Army Corps at home, and I was going to succeed him as Chief of Staff. Huguet thereupon said that this was not so, and related what Fitzgerald had just told him about Asquith and Kitchener. On this Delcassé said he would see Bertie at once, and that if this interview was not satisfactory he would go over and see Asquith, that it was intolerable that I should be ruled out for political reasons. Now, here is rather a dangerous development. I had hoped that the matter would rest quiet for the present anyhow, and for Delcassé to rake this up into a semi-international question is rather dangerous. Delcassé had sent for Bertie, and was crossing to England to-night, so it looks

---

* It is not quite clear what this means; but it may be assumed that the passage should read "for an offensive lasting six weeks." The French information as to the condition of Russian munitions was defective, and they were disinclined to believe, when told, how bad the situation in reality was.

† Bridges was British Military Representative at Belgian H.Q.

‡ Lieutenant-Colonel Brinsley Fitzgerald, Sir J. French's private secretary.

as though he were moving.

The upshot was that Sir F. Bertie wired to Lord Kitchener from Paris to say that the French were much disappointed with the British co-operation during the Wytschaete operations in the middle of the month. A copy of this message was sent over to Sir John, who called in Wilson, and they had a conversation which Wilson records in his diary:

> I told him that when he, Kitchener, and Asquith thought they had solved the problem by allowing things to remain as they were, they made a great mistake. I analysed the objections to myself as C. of S., and pointed out that, whereas Kitchener's objections were a matter of opinion, viz personal dislike and a belief that I was rather a mischievous fellow, Asquith's objections were political, because of Ulster and this War, and that here was a matter of principle.
>
> I said that in my judgment he *must* remove Murray. He must beat Asquith on the matter of principle, and he *must* offer me the appointment. I then told him that I had been thinking over his position, and that to make matters easier for him, when he offered me the post, I would refuse it. He could then appoint whom he pleased. I can do no more than refuse the appointment that I have worked for and dreamt of for years. Finally I told him that 5 minutes after Murray was told that he was going to be given a Corps he would thank God that the strain was over. Sir John was charming and grateful, and I think perhaps will use this loophole.

The question of the B.E.F. taking over the extreme left of the line, and in so doing absorbing the Belgian troops in a measure, had not been settled by the end of December. But one subject had been effectually grappled with during the closing days of the year. This was the formation of the B.E.F. into two Armies, the First under Sir D. Haig and the Second under Sir H. Smith-Dorrien, each to consist of three Army Corps. The 27th Division had recently arrived from home, and the 28th was expected early in January; these two were to form the Vth Corps, making up the six. Wilson wrote in his diary on the night of the 31st:

> And so the year goes out in wind and rain and sobs. Uncle and I had a good gallop in spite of the weather and heavy going. Foch came

to see me and to wish me a happy New Year. I dined with the French Mission, they were all so nice. I stood outside my house here (7 Place Victor Hugo) and listened to the old church clocks.

Chapter XII – 1915: January to March

The Project of advancing on Zeebrugge — Sir W. Robertson becomes C.G.S. at St. Omer — Wilson, Chief Liaison Officer — His name struck out of list of K.C.B.s for the "Honours Gazette"—His difficulties in preventing a breach between G.H.Q, and G.Q.G. — The Battle of Neuve Chapelle — Wilson and Joffre at Chantilly — Lord Kitchener comes over to meet Joffre and Millerand.

"All quiet along our front from Givenchy, on the right, to opposite Wytschaete on the left," — so Wilson opened his diary for the year 1915.

> The corps stand in line, Ist, IVth, IIIrd, IInd, with the Indian Corps in reserve and the 27th Division of the Vth Corps which has just arrived out and the Cavalry Corps and Indian Cavalry Corps also in reserve. So we start the year. Since the war broke out in August we have lost 100,000 men, and in my judgment once saved the whole situation and defeated the German hopes of dominating Europe (this was at Mons — Le Cateau), and once saved an awkward situation for the French at Ypres.

In a letter home on the same day he remarked:

> The water and mud increase and are getting horrible. The longer days will be very welcome when they come, especially to officers; the men do not mind so much.

On January 2 he wrote in his diary:

Sir John sent for me this morning, Murray and Tom Bridges there. All the plans of incorporating the Belgian Army into ours by brigades have fallen to the ground, because their King won't have it. We discussed how to get more troops, and in the evening Sir John sent for me and showed me a memorandum he had written to Kitchener, Winston, and Asquith, in which he says he wants guns, ammunition, and men, at least 50 battalions, and that with half-trained troops nothing higher than a brigade is possible and single battalions are much better. This will be a facer for Kitchener with his ridiculous armies, the commands of the six armies being in to-day's paper — Haig, Smith-Dorrien, Hunter, Johnny Hamilton, Rundle, Bruce Hamilton. During my interview this evening Sir John leant over to me and said to me in a whisper, "You are such a brute, you will never be nice to people you don't like. Now I am going to get Asquith out here, why don't you make love to him?" By which he means that he still wants to have me as Chief of Staff.

Paid Foch a long visit at Cassel, and I had a long talk with him. He agreed with me in thanking that the French Army of to-day is much better than that of August last. He agreed in thinking that this was due to great changes in superior commands, to the mental effect on both French and German minds in August of the events of 1870, and to the consequent gain in moral on the French side and loss on the German as the campaign developed. For the English, the voluntary system is quite sufficient to account for the marked deterioration.

Having been granted leave of absence, he proceeded by car to Rouen on the 4th, and there he went round the enormous base camps of the British force; he then drove on to Havre and crossed the Channel during the night. He remained ten days in England, and during his stay saw numbers of prominent people, such as Mr. Palmer, the representative of the whole American Press, Lord Northcliffe (who was very bitter on the subject of the embargo placed on Press correspondents at the front). Lord Milner, Mr. Bonar Law, Mr. Austen Chamberlain, and others. Mr. Gwynne of the *Morning Post* also came to see him one evening at Draycott Place, and Wilson wrote in his diary:

He told me of a War Council -which has been formed of Asquith, K., Haldane [?], Crewe, Grey, and Balfour, and these beauties are contemplating withdrawing the E.F. from France and sending us to

Austria! Were ever such demented fools!

Sir John followed his Sub-Chief of the General Staff to London on the 12th, and remained some days; Wilson did not, however, see him during that time, but he obtained a good deal of information with regard to what was in progress from Gwynne and others. He learnt from various sources that a serious difference of opinion had developed between Sir John and Kitchener with reference to the "New Armies," their grouping, their employment, and so forth. In this connexion the following significant entry, which appears in his diary on the 13th, deserves to be quoted:

> At 9.30 a.m. Gwynne rang me up. He said he was going to see Johnnie at 11 o'clock and would have a good talk and advise him strongly to see me. He told me Johnnie had already had a meeting with Winston and Lloyd George. I gave Gwynne the substance of what I was told last night, and he promised to let me know what happened at his interview with Johnnie. At 11 o'clock I saw Lord Lansdowne at his house; he is much better than when I last was over. I spoke freely about our relations with the French, and my proposal that they should send some representative men to see what Kitchener was doing, also of the strained relations between Sir John and K., and of the vital necessity of preventing a rupture, also of my suspicions of Winston's intrigues, also of our lack of H.E. shell, and so forth. He was charming as usual.
>
> I saw Gwynne at 7 p.m. He told me of his 10 a.m. interview with Johnnie. Johnnie discussed me. He wants me as C. of S., but said the difficulties were insurmountable, though he did not tell Gwynne about Asquith and Ulster.

Wilson returned to St. Omer on the 14th, and Sir John on the 15th and they met next day, when Sir John showed him a letter from Lord Kitchener saying that Sir John's memorandum [mentioned in Wilson's diary on the 2nd, *vide* p. 238] had been discussed at the War Council on the 7th and 8th, the three principal points considered being: 1. Advance on Zeebrugge; 2. Organization of New Armies; 3. Different theatre for our forces. The Council had deferred decision as to 2 and 3, but, as regards 1, had come to the conclusion that the advantages gained would not be commensurate with the loss and with the difficulties likely to arise from the consequent extension of the line. Moreover, 50 additional battalions, which Sir John regarded as indispensable for the execution of his plan, could not be made available without upsetting all arrangements for making good wastage, for home defence, and for the New Armies. It was impossible furthermore to provide the necessary ammunition; and the Council also thought that the Germans were likely to resume the offensive, so that in their opinion the existing line ought to remain as solid as possible. Sir George Arthur in his "Life of Lord Kitchener" quotes this communication in full, and he suggests that, by the date of the War Council of the 7th and 8th, Mr. Churchill, who had been a one-time keen supporter of the plan to advance on Zeebrugge, may have allowed his attention to be drawn elsewhere, and may therefore no longer have wished to employ warships on the Belgian coast.* General Joffre arrived at St. Omer on January 17 and a long discussion took place in which Sir John, Murray, Robertson, Wilson and Huguet participated. At this Sir John, to Wilson's surprise, announced that the War Council in London which he had attended on the 13th had decided that he was to carry out his proposal to take Ostend and Zeebrugge. General Joffre, according to Wilson, expressed himself as entirely opposed to the operation, being of opinion that the troops that were available for such an undertaking were altogether insufficient to carry it out successfully. It turned out that the War Council of London had completely changed their minds during the interval between the 8th and the 13th — as Wilson speedily ascertained. The conclusions arrived at on the 13th had been as follows: x. Arrangements to be made to dispatch two Territorial Divisions by the middle of February to enable Sir John to throw forward his line to the coast up to the Dutch frontier; 2. The Admiralty to consider the possibility of action in the Adriatic, or 3. To prepare a naval expedition in February to "bombard and take the Gallipoli

---

* Mr. Churchill had cabled to Admiral Carden in the Mediterranean on the 2nd asking if he believed it to be practicable to force the Dardanelles by the use of ships alone. The Admiral had replied on the 5th that they could not be rushed, but that they perhaps might be forced by extended operations. On the 6th, the First Lord had cabled asking for detailed particulars.

Peninsula" (*sic*); 4. A sub-Committee of the C.I.D. to be formed to consider to what other theatres British forces could be dispatched.

"So this absolutely futile paper of 'Conclusions' is the sum of strategical knowledge of the War Council, Heaven help us," Wilson remarks in his diary; and he goes on to give an account of a prolonged conversation which he had that afternoon with Robertson on the subject of the morning's work. The question of who was likely to become C.G.S. also cropped up, and Wilson informed Robertson that he had decided to refuse to accept the appointment should it be offered him, and that he expected it would be offered to Robertson. Robertson, however, showed himself as most unwilling to accept it either, supposing the question to arise. "He begged me to put Johnnie off offering it to him," Wilson concludes, "because he must refuse. The chance of a lifetime, and two men in one car, both refusing it. It is something of a tragedy. "

The Ostend-Zeebrugge project was finally given up by Sir John two days later, after a meeting at which he, Murray, Robertson, Wilson, and Huguet were present, and at which Murray, Robertson and Wilson all expressed themselves as opposed to the idea. Then at a meeting which took place at Chantilly on the 21st, an understanding was come to that the B.E.F. should relieve two French corps which were holding trenches in front of Ypres, thereby considerably lengthening the front to be under its charge, but that the rest of the line beyond Ypres to the sea should continue to be occupied, as it was at the time, by French and Belgian troops. From Chantilly Wilson started for a trip right along the French front, and at its conclusion he wrote home to his wife:

> My trip was a great success. I went to Amiens, Chantilly, Chagny, Villers-Cotterets, Rheims, Epernay, Bar-le-Duc, Remiremont, Gerardmer, and Belfort. Everywhere met by the generals, who took the greatest pleasure in showing me things and making me as comfortable as they could. We ran into snow in the Vosges, and had deep snow on the tops, where the troops were on skis or snow-shoes, or in sledges. I went right down to Switzerland and quite close to Altkirch, which the Germans still hold (that place where you saw all the sidings) and which the French were shelling when I was there. I had one curious experience, as after dark one night we

> walked through the French lines at an old frontier fort which the Germans had taken, and for ½ an hour stood between two lines of outposts. Snowing heavily all the time. I called at Chantilly on my way back to thank General Joffre, and he was so nice to me. No other officer in any army, not even a Russian, has been allowed to go down the French line except me.

Wilson had been handed the following message at Remiremont on the 26th: "*Du Général Robertson au Général Wilson. Commandant en chef me charge de vous faire connaître que le Général Murray va partir pour Angleterre a cause de son état de santé et que je suis nommé en son remplacement. Le maréchal vous a nommé officier principal de liaison avec l'armée Française. Votre successeur est Perceval.*"* This announcement came upon Wilson as rather a surprise after the conversation that he had had with Sir W. Robertson in the car on the 17th,† and the receipt of the message made him anxious to get back to St. Omer and to make himself acquainted with the new situation at G.H.Q. He mentions in his diary that, when he saw General Joffre at Chantilly on his way through, the French Commander-in-Chief held out both his hands and said, "You are the best known and best beloved officer to the French Army " When Joffre asked him about Robertson and the new state of things at G.H.Q. he "scrambled round the corner"

---

* "From General Robertson to General Wilson. Commander-in-Chief charges me to inform you that General Murray will leave for England because of his health and that I am appointed in his place. The Marshal has appointed you as principal liaison officer with the French army. Your successor is Perceval."

† Sir William mentions in his "From Private to Field-Marshal" being asked to become Chief of the General Staff by Sir John in place of Sir A. Murray, who was about to return to England. "The offer was a tempting one," he writes, "as it meant an increase of pay as well as of position, but I did not wish to accept it. I had become interested in my work, I knew that the Commander-in-Chief had previously asked for another officer to succeed Murray, which was sufficient proof that I was not his first choice, and, although he had appeared quite satisfied with me as Quartermaster-General, there was no certainty that either of us would be equally happy if I became his Chief of the General Staff. I, therefore, asked to be allowed to stay where I was, and, after further discussion, a final decision was, by my request, deferred for a day or two. In the end I realized that it was my duty to put personal considerations on one side, and on the 25th took up my new post."

by declaring that he really did not know what had happened. Wilson wrote home to Mrs. Wilson on the 31st:

> I had my interview with Sir John this morning. I put my three alternatives to him. He was perfectly charming. He said that Robertson would not hear of the first, i.e. that I should remain on as Sub-Chief with altered duties, that he (Sir John) would not hear of the third, i.e. that I should go home, but that he liked the second, i.e. promote me Lieutenant-General and that he would put me in Orders to-night. He said that nothing that he ever could do for me for the work I had done would be enough, and that, so long as he held power, etc. So, as I said last night, all this fuss has indeed, as I felt sure it would, ended in making me much bigger and more powerful than I was before. I told him that he had not the power to confer the temporary and local rank of Lieutenant-General on anyone, and that he must get W.O. approval, which in my case might not be forthcoming. He said he did not care. He would put me in Orders and then, if the W.O. or the Cabinet objected, we would go home together. So Messrs. Asquith and Co. have not done much good this time.
>
> My duties will be pretty much what I like to make them, and will, in point of fact, be much what they have been, but with the additional rank, which will, of course, in due course give me additional power.

The arrangement thus decided upon had certain obvious merits. Wilson was so essentially a *persona grata* at French G.Q.G. and amongst French superior commanders in general, that he possessed altogether exceptional qualifications for filling the post of principal liaison officer between Sir John's head-quarters and Chantilly. That, in view of the relations existing between the leaders and the General Staffs of the two allied hosts, such liaison work needed to be in skilled and tactful hands had been plainly demonstrated during the previous months, when Wilson had in reality been virtually duplicating the function of Sub-Chief of the General Staff with that of principal intermediary between G.H.Q. and G.Q.G. The plan was also in all probability the one which would have best commended itself to Joffre, next to that of Wilson having been appointed to be Sir John's C.G.S. But there was also something to be said on. the other side. Wilson's seniority in itself, as also the fact that (as everybody at St. Omer was well aware) he had been first choice for the position of C.G.S., could hardly fail to render his position *vis a vis* Robertson awkward for both of them. The newly appointed Chief of the General Staff with the B.E.F., who must by right of his position be the first and principal adviser of the British Commander-in-Chief, now found alongside of him in a sense a rival, unhampered by responsibility, whose relations with Sir John were especially close and cordial, and who during the past three months had actually been more in Sir John's confidence than any member of the Head-quarters Staff.

The question just at this moment came up of transferring two British divisions to Serbia. This project emanated from a Cabinet Committee of which Mr. Lloyd George was a member; and M. Briand would appear at this time to have strongly favoured the dispatch of troops to this new theatre of operations. Mr. Churchill crossed the Channel to try to persuade Sir John to agree that the 29th Division and the Canadian Division, which were now ready to be dispatched from the United Kingdom to some front, should be detailed for this duty — so Wilson at all events, according to his diary, understood when consulted by his Chief. Wilson wrote:

> I told him that if the Foreign Office said that two divisions in Serbia would raise Greece and Rumania on our side, and would keep Bulgaria quiet, it would be real good business; but personally I did not believe this, and I was in favour of sticking to the old principle of decisive force in decisive theatre. Sir John told me to get the French to combat the idea for all they were worth.

Wilson wrote in the diary on February 2:

> Allenby in to see me about a story that Capel [his interpreter]* had told him of the feeling which is arising in France against us for various causes, partly because of our present want of enterprise, partly from our hunting and shooting, partly because of our not having conscription, etc. I have often heard these things lately, and it was for

* Mr. Arthur Capel was an Englishman of wealth, living in Paris, and a great friend of M. Qemenceau's. Wilson came to know him well later on and reference will be made to him in other chapters. His health broke down and he had to resign his interpretership in the field. He died shortly after the close of the struggle.

this reason that, when I was home last, I advocated our Government asking over half a dozen representative and trusted Frenchmen to see what we are doing now, but I think they only asked M. Millerand over. This feeling of hostility must be stopped.

Next day he wrote:

I went out to see Foch at 6 p.m. He had not seen me since all these troubles and he was as nice as he could be. He said he would have resigned if I had gone, etc. I told him I thought Robertson would do very well. We discussed the situation. He does not expect the Russians to move till the end of March. He thinks that the Russians can hold Warsaw, and as they will slowly get stronger their position becomes better. He hopes the Germans will attack here, and he thinks after the mud is gone he will be able to blow down opposition with guns. He said a curious thing. "You English must not invite a long war by dilatory action; we French cannot go on for years, so send everyone you can as fast as you can." This has set me thinking, and I am not sure what it all means. Can France be getting tired, as well as getting cross with us? Sir John told me that "at home" they had agreed to my promotion, so I suppose it will come out in the *Gazette* presently.

A day or two later Wilson had a pleasant surprise in the shape of Mr. Bonar Law walking into his room unexpectedly, and they had a long talk; Bonar Law had come over on purpose to ascertain how far politics had been allowed to stand in the way of Wilson's being made Chief of the General Staff, and was staying with Sir John. Wilson had another long talk with him next day and seized the opportunity to deprecate strongly the project of diverting any troops to the Balkans, and also to convey the intimation that Joffre and Foch were both entirely opposed to anything of the sort.

The shortage of artillery ammunition, and in particular the insufficiency of high-explosive shell, was at this tim e beginning to cause anxiety, seeing that a lack of material such as this was bound to hamper any attempt on the part of the B.E.F. to assume the offensive. Wilson wrote in his diary on the 10th:

The figures are exceedingly bad. In no case have we 800 rounds a gun in this country, and probably not more than 40 of these are H.E.

> Nor is our daily output at home of any real use, for, in the case of the 18-pr., which is the most favourable, we are only getting 12 rounds a gun a day, of which 4 are H.E. Now this is a scandalous state of affairs.

But Wilson is on rather dangerous ground here; for the reason why the output of high explosive shell for the field-guns proved such a difficulty during the early stages of the war was that this form of ammunition had not been adopted in our artillery before the outbreak of hostilities, whereas it was in use in practically all foreign field artilleries. That was largely the fault of the General Staff, who ought to have insisted upon its being introduced after its value had been proved in the Balkan War of 1912.

A day or two after this, Robertson informed Wilson in the course of conversation one afternoon, that his name had been struck out at home from the list of those who were to be awarded K.C.B.'s in the forthcoming Honours *Gazette*, and that Sir John wished him to know this. Sir John, who had been home on a short visit, had been indignant when he had heard of it and had made representations to Lord Kitchener, who, however, had declared that nothing could now be done as the King had signed the list. Wilson, moreover, heard from Lambton that same evening that he was now going to be granted his temporary lieutenant-generalship as an "Honour" in the Honours *Gazette*. This quaint reward was actually conferred in that publication, which duly appeared on February 19. In view of his outstanding services in having made it possible for the Expeditionary Force to reach the theatre of war in time, in view of his work during the dark days of the retreat from Mons, and in view of his success in maintaining reasonably satisfactory relations between G.H.Q. and the French, Wilson had ample grounds for irritation at such treatment. But he nevertheless made light of the matter in his diary and in his letters to his wife. He had an idea, it is true, that he would eventually be in a position to claim permanent promotion to the rank of lieutenant-general from the date of this *Gazette*, seeing that it was an "Honours" *Gazette*. Whether such a claim would have held good, however, seems extremely doubtful. The question happily never had to be put to the test; but the fact in any case remains that he was the victim of a trick, and that he probably was not far wrong in assuming that the perpetrators of the trick were politicians.

Nearly all the officers who had constituted the General Staff at G.H.Q. as it had been formed at the outset had now disappeared — moved on for the most part to higher appointments — and Wilson missed their society. But some junior staff officers who had long been members of his mess remained at St. Omer. They used to go out with him on his rambles beyond the outskirts of the sleepy little town, and they have treasured up some of his original reflections and sayings at this time of disappointment. One of them writes:

> In the first "Honours" list of the Great War, H. W., who had done more than anyone to smooth over the difficulties prior to, and during, the concentration of the B.E.F., received nothing. Not unnaturally there was much comment on this at G.H.Q., and, rightly or wrongly, the omission was attributed to political influence. H. W. rode with me on the afternoon after the *Gazette* appeared and I think had some feeling about it, from what he said. He finished with the remark that he was now going up in his balloon. I did not understand. So he explained:
>
> "When I was young, my father, who was a very shrewd man, used to say — 'Now, whenever you are a bit down and things don't seem to be quite what they should be, just go up in your balloon. As the world recedes, you will look over the side and will note how all objects, which bulked so large, and all the funny little men who seemed so prominent when you were on the earth, gradually diminish and diminish till they matter not at all. You will then regain your sense of proportion, and a true perspective of the things that really matter.' So I am now going up in my balloon."

Another writes:

> When at G.H.Q., H. W. often took me for long walks, and he used to discuss methods of government amongst other things. He would often stop dead in his stride, while his companion shot forward on the next pace, and would give vent to some aphorism or some remark that stuck in one's memory. On one occasion he suddenly pulled up in this fashion and said, "Asquith hates me after the Ulster pogrom and says that Wilson is the sort of man who would head a

revolution." Then, after a pause, he added, "I'm not sure that he isn't right."

Another time he remarked: "Whether Asquith drowns himself in a bucket, or whether Lloyd George becomes Premier, or whether Winston kicks out K., doesn't matter a hang. The country is determined to see the thing through. And so, you buy yourself a copy of *The Times* and put up your feet and, from a front row in the stalls, you see the little marionettes dancing." "Stand back from the picture if you want to see the true perspective," was another favourite saying of his.

Wilson's judgment and his good understanding with the French were somewhat severely taxed shortly after this by the strained relations that temporarily arose between British and French head-quarters in the field. General Joffre was elaborating plans for an offensive which he proposed to put in execution during March. The plan was that the principal operation was to be an attack to be delivered by French troops in the Arras region, but that a minor operation was to be undertaken simultaneously by the British in the neighbourhood of La Bassée. In view of what was contemplated, Joffre had written to Sir John on February 18, requesting him to effect the relief of two French corps in the north by extending the British front; and in support of the overture he had made reference to the fact that reinforcements in the shape of the Canadian Division, of a Territorial Division, and of 24 independent battalions were about to join the B.E.F. The proposal to take over more of the line from the French had not been welcomed at G.H.Q., and Sir John's attitude gave rise to an extremely uncomfortable situation — as is made apparent by the following entries in Wilson's diary under date of February 20 and 21:

On the 20th. Yesterday's Gazette reached us. I head the list of Honours and Rewards as Temp. Lieutenant-General, so the fools have (I think) given me another opening. I wrote to Robb, the Military Secretary, saying I supposed this Gazette gave me permanent date? Belin arrived from Chantilly with a further letter from Joffre. It is a very stiff one, asking for the relief of the IXth and XXth Corps, as agreed to, as soon as possible, and for the relief of the IXth and half the XXth by -the 28th of this month. This is, of course, impossible.

Belin and Foch came to see me at 4.30 before going to Sir John. I had told Robertson that a *non possumus*[*] attitude about any relief would be very difficult, but he never showed me Joffre's first letter, nor Sir John's answers, till the day after they had been dispatched; so I was not able to help. Sir John continues to say that he won't relieve any of the IXth Corps. This won't do in face of the reinforcements, giving a total of 36 battalions, exclusive of the Canadians who have just finished arriving.

On the 21st. A meeting in Sir John's house of Sir John, Robertson, Huguet and self, at which Sir John showed much anger at the tone of Joffre's letter, brought by Belin last night; and Sir John who had arranged to meet Foch and Belin at Cassel at 11 a.m., refused to go.

The letter from Joffre was a stupid one, inaccurate in some important details and rather hectoring in tone. Robertson, Huguet, and I to Cassel to meet Foch and Belin, and Robertson told Belin that Sir John flatly refused to relieve anybody before April 1, and even then did not promise. This was difficult. Foch asked again for one division of the IXth Corps to be relieved, and I lean very much to this solution. Foch says that this division is essential to the success of his operations at Arras. Coming home in the motor I told Robertson I thought he ought to relieve this one division before March 7, and he says he will try. I advised Robertson to draft a clear letter for Sir John's signature to Joffre, restating the whole case.

The feeling of irritation that evidently existed both at Chantilly and at St. Omer was no doubt to some extent aggravated by the disappointing intelligence that was just at this time coming to hand from the Eastern theatre, where the Russian forces had been suffering somewhat serious reverses at the hands of the Germans in northern Poland and East Prussia. Wilson was not, however, disposed to take the news too seriously, and he believed that the German reports exaggerated the measure of their successes.

He wrote in the diary on the 22nd:

Saw Sir John again in the afternoon, he is fussy about Russia, but I can't say I am. The Russians have a habit of piling up as they go back, till they become immovable.

---

[*] "We can not."

Berlin had that day claimed that Von Hindenburg's troops had taken 100,000 prisoners, and it was at the same time given out that the German pursuit of the Russians was finished. But, on the other hand, the Austro-Hungarian forces seemed to be making no progress in southern Poland or Galicia. Wilson felt much more concerned about the difficulties that were coming to a head between G.H.Q. and the French than about what he believed to be merely a temporary set-back to the Allies beyond the Vistula, for it turned out that Sir John's reply to Joffre had intimated that no relief of the French troops could take place before April 1. So he went with Huguet to see Foch, and he wrote in his diary:

> We told him what had happened, and he was distinctly upset and annoyed. He said he thought that Pere Joffre would be angry, that he would say that to declare that no reliefs could take place till April, when in February alone, the Field-Marshal would have received a Cavalry Division, a Territorial Division, and 24 T.F. battalions, over and above the 28th Division, was to talk nonsense, and that he (Joffre) would not stand it. Foch was afraid that Joffre would take up this stand.
>
> I asked Foch as a personal favour to me to write to Joffre at once and to send it down through the night by special officer, begging Joffre not to be angry, but to write a private line (through me) to Sir John, saying how disappointed he was, and begging him to reconsider and to help if he could, as success at Arras depended upon it. Foch promised to do this at once.

The French Commander-in-Chief did not, however, fall in with Wilson's suggestion; he wrote instead to Foch to the effect that he had better come to an understanding with Sir John direct. Wilson welcomed this arrangement, but a fresh difficulty now arose. There had been an agreement that the attack by the B.E.F. in the La Bassée region, which was to synchronize with the mote ambitious offensive of the French from about Arras, was to commence on March 7. He now, however, learnt that G.H.Q. proposed to defer the La Bassée operations till the 10th, and the whole problem was furthermore complicated by the doubt that existed as to whether the 29th Division, which was ready for embarkation in England, was, or was not, to join the B.E.F. on the Western Front. Definite information, however, reached G.H.Q. from Kitchener on the 27th announcing that the 29th Division was going to be utilized in the Near East. The Secretary of State, moreover, at the same time pointed out that, inasmuch as the French were likewise sending a division to the Near East, it was evident that they considered themselves safe along their front at home.

All this afforded Sir John some excuse for adhering to his refusal to take over any more line, in spite of the fact that he had received appreciable reinforcements from England and that the French were about to embark on a serious offensive for which they required some additional divisions. Wilson was strongly of opinion that the withholding of the 29th Division by the War Office ought not to prevent the relief of at least some French troops in the Ypres region by the B.E.F. But, so far from concurring in this view. Sir John was now actually proposing that the French should reoccupy some lengths of trench which our cavalry had taken over from them some weeks before, and there appears in Wilson's diary on February 28:

> At 3 o'clock Huguet and I went out to Cassel to see Foch, to tell him, not only that Sir John would not take over any IXth Corps trenches, but that he wanted the cavalry relieved. Foch took it in the most wonderful manner, and I told him as much as I thought wise. I dictated a wire, which I suggested he should send Joffre, and he took it down himself. It was to the effect that Sir John had not informed Kitchener of the reason why it was so necessary to send the 29th Division; that, although this division would take over trenches, it was so as to relieve French troops urgently needed at Arras for the attack; that this attack might very well fail without the aid of the IXth Corps; that the IXth Corps could only be relieved if the 29th Division came out at once, and that therefore K. and the Cabinet had better reconsider and send out the 29th. Foch, when I left him, was already putting all this into shape to send at once to Joffre. I cannot do any more, and this is our last chance. Sir John has not told Kitchener about the projected attacks, beyond the vaguest outlines, so it is possible that when Kitchener realizes all this, he may change.
>
> When I got back I went to see Sir John and to tell him that I had been to Foch and given Sir John's messages. Sir John said that he had told Asquith and Haldane what he thought of Kitchener. He was charming to me personally, and said he had written officially about

> the K.C.B. To finish up with, Huguet showed me a letter from Joffre to Foch in which Joffre gives Huguet a nasty wipe for being too pro-English.

The month of February, in fact, closed with the development of what amounted to a grave difference of opinion between British G.H.Q. and French G.Q.G., a difference of opinion which might have led to an open breach but for the continual exercise of Wilson's soothing influence. "We have fallen on rather difficult times," he wrote home to his wife, "what with the French, Sir John and K.; but it will work out, I hope, although it requires rather delicate handling." The truth about the 29th Division was that its destination had not yet been decided. The attempt to force the Dardanelles by naval power alone, unaided by military effort, was, after a week's delay due to bad weather, making some progress; but the Cabinet were beginning to realize, somewhat late in the day, that, even supposing the ships to be successful in their arduous task, troops would also sooner or later be required. Mr. Churchill was doing his utmost to secure the 29th Division for the ffsgean venture. Lord Kitchener would not give a final decision as to its destination, and its disposition was consequently hanging in suspense at the very juncture when Sir J. French had persuaded himself that, without its presence under his command, he could not safely relieve French divisions which Foch counted upon for the Arras offensive. There would seem to have been little real justification for this attitude, and that clearly was the view not only of Wilson but also of other members of the staff at G.H.Q.

Sir John, two days later, showed Wilson a letter he had received from Joffre, wishing him luck in the attack he contemplated on the 10th, but saying that, owing to the IXth and XXth French Corps not having been relieved by the B.E.F., he could no longer undertake the Arras offensive. The letter wound up by saying that only the enemies of the Allies would profit by the disagreement that bad taken place. The consequence was that the IVth Corps and the Meerut Division, under the orders of Sir D. Haig, embarked on their offensive, which has received the title of the Battle of Neuve Chapelle, unsupported directly or indirectly by the French. They nevertheless made a satisfactory beginning, securing 3,000 yards of enemy trenches and a depth of 1,000 yards on the first day, without suffering any great loss. But the next day proved foggy, and no further progress was made, while additional loss was sustained; so Sir John ordered the Second Army to undertake an attack on the morrow at a point near Ypres, by way of assisting Haig. ""I don't like this," Wilson wrote in his diary, "as no attack of a serious nature can be made without most careful artillery preparation and lots of ammu nition, and as far as I know, both these are lacking in the Second Army." Little progress was again made on March 12 at Neuve Chapelle, the spasmodic effort on the part of the Second Army farther to the north, as was only to be expected, came to nothing, and Wilson wrote in his diary on March 13:

> I went out to Cassel at 1 p.m. to pick up Foch, and we went on to the Shaffenberg to see Sir John. He was up there to pitch into Smith-Dorrien for his attack of yesterday having failed; but my sympathies are with Smith-Dorrien, who had not sufficient time to prepare, nor guns, nor ammunition, nor infantry to carry it out. His little attack in front of Wytschaete, therefore, failed. Foch came to say he was collecting 8 batteries of heavy artillery and some infantry towards Vermelles to help Haig in his attack on La Bassée, and he wanted to know where to put these troops, and so on. Sir John would not tell him anything, said he wished to keep his moves and Haig's secret. As far as I can judge, our fight at Neuve Chapelle is finished. We have neither infantry nor gun ammunition to go on with it. This is a disappointing business.

There appears in the diary next day:

> Our fight at Neuve Chapelle is over. We have lost about 12,000 men in the 7th, 8th, and Meerut Divisions, and we reckon the enemy's loss at 15-16,000. We have pushed back the Boche line on a front of 3,500-4,000 yards, with maximum depth of 1,000 yards. We ought to have done more. During the attack the Meerut Division on the right inclined to its right, attracted by the fire from the Bois de Biez; this made a gap between the Meerut Division and the 8 th Division. Each division, finding its flank uncovered, was afraid to advance, and this gap remained all day, no one reporting it. As it occurred between Corps it was the business of the Army to rectify it. Now, I put this

down to faulty liaison work.*

There was some sharp fighting at St. Eloi in the Ypres section on the 14th and 15th, in the course of which the Germans wrested that village from the Second Army; but it was speedily retaken. During nearly the whole of this month of March the French were acting on the offensive in Champagne, where they gained some ground at first, but in the end were wholly unable to effect anything like a real breach in the enemy's lines. Wilson summed up the situation to Sir John on the 16th in a few words: "The French were stopped in Champagne, and they had not even started in the Arras country for want of men. We were stopped for want of ammunition. There is the whole story, and as far as we are concerned, a very scandalous story. After 7½ months of war we have exhausted all our available ammunition in an attack by three divisions." He wrote:

> Out to Foch and discussed matters. He told me Kitchener was coming over to discuss in Paris some question of the action of Italy. Foch seems to think that Kitchener may send his New Armies down there, either to the Dardanelles, or Adriatic or Trentino. My own fear is, and has been, that these S.E. ventures will withdraw men and ammunition from us here, which will be bad. Already we have dropped to half the ammunition we were promised, and only one round per gun landed yesterday.

---

* Wilson's gifts of original illustration were demonstrated a few weeks later with regard to this fight at Neuve Chapelle, when he came to see me in the War Office — "gossiping" as he used to express it. He was stalking about the big room told off to the D.M.O., describing the combat, while I sat at my writing table, when he suddenly ejaculated, "Just come over here a minute 1" I came over as directed. "Now, shove up against me," he ordered, and we lay up against each other, striving for the mastery. (Had anybody come in — the C.I.G.S., say, or a War Office messenger — and seen a pair of general officers in uniform comporting themselves in this unwonted fashion, we should have been set down as crazy). "Shove! Shove hard!" he urged as, being the heavier man, he pressed me back. "Now step back quickly!" I did — and he fell flat on his face.

"There you are," he panted, as he struggled to his feet, "that's how it was. Our sportsmen went push, push, push. Boche wouldn't give way. Sportsmen went on pushing. Boche suddenly did give way. Sportsmen weren't ready, didn't know what to do, fell flat on their faces. They'll know better another time." — C E. C.

Sidney Clive[*] up from Chantilly also says Kitchener is going to Paris to-morrow and meets Joffre. A letter to-night says that the ships in the Dardanelles are being delayed by hidden guns. Obviously. Now they will have to land troops and then. Cecil writes that Bonar Law has been in to see her and was upset to hear I was opposed to the venture. I will write her something to show him.

This letter he wrote the following day, and it ran as follows:

I said I would write you something you could read to B. L. As regards the Dardanelles the problem presents itself to me under two forms. There is the question of high policy, and there is the question of strategy. In all preliminary examinations of the subject these two should be kept absolutely separate. It is only when we come to the question of making a decision that they must be put together and their respective claims weighed and balanced.

Now, as regards high policy, obviously I am not in a position to judge, not being posted in the latest situations. It may be that forcing the Dardanelles, a by no means difficult operation if gun and rifle fire are not too great, may lead to a political *coup*. For example, one need not know much about the Balkans to realize that it may mean a revolution, the assassination of Enver and Djemal and other kindred spirits; it may mean that Turkey will conclude peace; it may mean that Italy, out of love, jealousy, or suspicion (or all three) may be galvanized into action on our side; it may mean a safe Egypt, a well-secured Persian Gulf and Mesopotamia; it may mean that Rumania will actively join us; it may mean a Greek army marching through Belgrade on its way to Buda Pesth, and that Bulgaria will actually remain neutral. It may mean all these things. I have not been studying the Balkans for years without realizing that a shell falling on either side of the Dardanelles may mean all these things and other things, too. It may mean raising the thorny question of the Ægean Islands, and of Constantinople, Smyrna, and Asia Minor, at a moment when all diplomacy and all energy ought to be devoted to killing Germans and finishing the war. Yes, the high policy of forcing the Dardanelles is not for me to discuss. But when we come to the strategy of the operation I am on ground that I know sufficiently well to venture an opinion.

I preface the few remarks that I am going to make by this

[*] Colonel S. Clive was Sir John's representative at French G.Q.G.

> assertion. We (French and English) have now reached a stage when to break the German line is not only an operation of war, but a certain operation of war, given sufficient troops and sufficient ammunition. At this particular moment we engage in operations in the Dardanelles. Now, to force the Dardanelles and to keep the passage open, it is essential to hold both banks. True, if the Gallipoli Peninsula is cleared of the enemy, the whole of that spit of land can be held by occupying the Bulair lines. Even this means a certain number of troops. But the Asia Minor bank is quite another thing. If we land there we must be prepared to fight and beat whatever troops the Turks can bring against us. What this means, I don't know, but it may mean one or more corps. When Constantinople is reached, if the Turks don't make peace, we shall have to occupy the town, hold the lines of Chatalja, hold both banks of the Bosporus. This will mean several more corps. Now, the way to end this war is to kill Germans and not Turks. The place where we can kill most Germans is here, and therefore every man and every round of ammunition we have got in the world ought to come here. All history shows that operations in a secondary and ineffectual theatre have no bearing on major operations — except to weaken the force there engaged. History, no doubt, will repeat her lesson once more for our benefit.*

G.H.Q. was a few days later afforded serious grounds for concern by the arrival of a letter from the C.I.G.S., dictated by Lord Kitchener, which conveyed an unmistakable hint to the effect that certain divisions of the New Army, which were nearly ready for dispatch to some theatre of war, would not be allotted to the Western Front because too much ammunition was being expended by the B.E.F. "High strategy," Wilson remarked caustically in his diary after having read the letter, and he gives a graphic account of a visit which he paid to Joffre, at Chantilly, by arrangement on March 23, in company with Huguet. His record in the diary of what passed reads as follows:

---

* One point Wilson overlooked in this comprehensive appreciation — the strategical importance of opening a way into the Black Sea, so as to ensure the munitions supply of Russia and thereby to influence operations in the Eastern theatre, which was not at that time in any quarter — and least of all at G.H.Q. and G.Q.G. — regarded as a secondary one.

Joffre was waiting dinner for us. I noticed that Belin was not in the hall, but Pellé was. (Joffre afterwards told me that Pellé has succeeded Belin). As we sat down (I sat on Joffre's right) Joffre said in rather a loud voice, "*Eh bien, votre chef est assomnant.*"* This met with general approval and was not a good beginning. I kept off the topic of Sir John as much as possible during dinner, and all went fairly well. After dinner Joffre took me back in his car to his office. Huguet joined us a few minutes later, and we began; Pellé came in a little later and remained.

First Joffre described his meeting with Ministers at the Elysee on Sunday; how he described the general situation and that we should soon be in a position to break the line; how Ministers were rather doubtful, and favoured Dardanelles or Adriatic, which found favour in England; how he (Joffre) said, "If you take away one single man that I can use on my front *I will resign*;" how Poincaré said, "On the contrary you will obey orders;" how he (Joffre) said, "M. le President, if you order me to go to the trenches and get shot, I will go, but if you order me to uncover the heart of France I shall disobey;" and how, as a result of this and more, he got absolute *carte blanche* till May, when the situation would again be reviewed.

Next came a strong attack upon Sir John, "who calls me C. in C. and disobeys my orders," that he (Joffre) was going to write to Sir John "*carrement*,"† and so on. By degrees I got him to look at the picture in a different way. I insisted upon dispelling the poisonous idea in Sir John's head and at home that the French had 800,000 more men in line then the Germans — many misunderstandings date from that. Joffre promised to make out a dear statement and to give it to me. Next I enlarged without exaggeration on the relations between Sir John and Kitchener, Winston, and Haldane. Then went on to say that Sir John's one idea was to collect ammunition and men for another attack, but that this must be combined with a French offensive. Next, mentioned the difficulties Sir John had in finding out what our Government and Kitchener intended to do, and whether this was to remain the principal theatre of war. Next, what changes, if any, there were in Joffre's plans, and the necessity of telling Sir John. Next, the importance of not repeating to politicians like Millerand things that Sir John thinks ate secret, which Millerand passes on to Kitchener,

---

* "Well, your boss is amazing."

† "Definitely."

who shoots them back at Sir John. And so on, by this and by that, I got Joffre round to quite a different frame of mind. I told him to give us orders, but without appearing to do so, not to refer to our numbers or dispositions but to refer to Sir John's loyalty, and to leave the rest to his good heart— and me.

Then he went on to talk of his own plans, how he calculated that by the end of April he would be in a condition to *attack* and to *break* the line, because he would have enough men, ammunition, trench mortars which were now being made by the thousand, and so on. He had stopped the Champagne attack, having got all he could out of it, and was well satisfied although he had lost 40,000 men in a month.

And so, after 1½ hours, I came away well pleased with my work. Huguet in delight. A very important meeting at a critical moment has, I think, gone off *well*. Joffre was really charming to me.

Next day Wilson again saw Joffre, who showed him a letter addressed to Sir John asking for the relief of the IXth and XXth Corps and for co-operation in a decisive attack at the end of April. On getting back to St. Omer he read Joffre's letter, asking for the relief of the two French corps, to Sir John, and preparations to carry this out were taken m hand. Information had been received that Lord Kitchener was coming over to Chantilly to see the French Commander-in-Chief, and it was arranged that Sir John and Wilson should be present at the meeting, which eventually took place on the 29th. But Wilson had returned to Chantilly on the previous day at Joffre's special request, and he had taken with him notes of a number of matters that Sir John wished Joffre to bring up with Kitchener, e.g. the ammunition question, the danger of becoming seriously involved in secondary theatres of war, and the fact that the B.E.F. was not wasting ammunition on the Western Front— as appeared to be assumed in Whitehall. At their meeting that evening Joffre suddenly announced his intention of raising the question of the command in France and Belgium. He meant, he said, to propose that the command should henceforward rest in his hands, and that he should be placed in a position to give orders to Sir J. French. Wilson realized that the raising of such a question under the circumstances then existing would be in the highest degree inopportune, that the British Government would be unlikely to assent to such an arrangement, and that the matter being even

Marshal J.J.C. Joffre

mentioned was to be deprecated. He therefore pointed out that, if Joffre were to be granted the power to give orders to the B.E.F., he must also possess the power to discard any commanders in that force with whose handling of the troops under their orders he felt dissatisfied. "He agreed," Wilson wrote in his diary, " so the matter will not be brought up at to-morrow's meeting. Good."

Wilson, it should be mentioned, continued to hold the view that this question of a Generalissimo being by his position empowered to deprive subordinate commanders of their appointments, effectively disposed of the idea of such a post being created, and he held it almost up till March, 1918. The plea partakes perhaps rather of the nature of an excuse than of a justification for deprecating unity of command. In actual practice this particular point would not seem to have given rise to any difficulty, either during the brief space of time when Sir D. Haig was placed under the orders of General Nivelle, nor yet during the closing months of the war when General Foch had been appointed Commander-in-Chief of the Allied Armies on the Western Front. Joffre, however, evidently concurred in Wilson's opinion when he heard it. Of the very important meeting that took place on the 29th, Wilson gives tike following account in his diary:

> There were present, M. Millerand, General Joffre, General Pellé, General Graziani (Chief of the General Staff in Paris), General Huguet, Lord Kitchener, Sir John and I. The meeting lasted 3 hours and much was discussed. Kitchener began about Holland, and what should be done if Germany went to war. Kitchener favoured sending a lot of troops and making it the decisive theatre. Joffre, of course, would not hear of it.
>
> Joffre then gave a general review of the situation, ending by declaring this to be the decisive theatre and that, by May 1, he and Sir John would attack and break the line. Wanted — all the ammunition which could be given, and all the troops. Kitchener told at length of his labour troubles. I did not know they were so bad. Kitchener said we had already increased our output 3 times over our peace output, and he had established plant which, if fully worked, would give us 9 times present output — i.e. he is now making 45,000 18-pr. shells a week; he could make 370,000. The workmen would not work. His appeal at Liverpool did good for 2 days only! Kitchener said, and repeated, and Millerand made a note, that the only way out of the

difficulty was by conscription, and that if we had conscription none of these troubles would have occurred. Kitchener was very open about, and the Frenchmen much shocked at, our condition. We are getting 6-7 rounds a day; the French are getting 17-20; but with our small number of guns we should be getting 30.

The date (approximate) for next big attack was fixed for May 1. Kitchener promised Sir John two more Territorial Divisions within three weeks. Sir John promised to relieve the IXth and XXth Corps by April 20. Discussion about Russia, where Joffre said they had sufficient though not abundant ammunition. He and Grand Duke had now a secret cypher, and they thus avoided F.O.s where there was always leakage. Dardanelles discussed. Millerand asked if there was any plan. Kitchener said, not much of one; only plan was to occupy height on Gallipoli overlooking the Narrows. Sir John hoped no more troops would be sent. Kitchener said *none*, there were already 67,000 available down there. Kitchener said Italy and Rumania looked like joining soon, but Bulgaria and Greece, no. Kitchener back again to Holland as decisive theatre, with Joffre and Sir John (and all of us) deadly opposed. Curious this ignorance of true strategy. Kitchener wants the loan of Dunkirk now we have so many men. Joffre objected. Small talk, and we broke up. Kitchener and I stayed for lunch, and K. then went off by train to Boulogne. He was quite nice to me all the way through. Huguet and I got back here at 8 o'c.; I copied out my notes and gave to Sir John at 10.30, as he goes off to London early to-morrow. A good day's work.

This meeting brought the month of March to an end in satisfactory fashion from the Allies' point of view, in view of the discord that had marked some of its course, and Wilson was entitled to look back with complacency upon his share in composing the differences that had occurred. To-day, after the event, Joffre's confidence that he would be able to break the German line may seem strange. But the Allies — and also the enemy — had still many lessons to learn with regard to the changes and the chances of warfare under the latest conditions. For the French misapprehension as to Russian potentialities there was at this time the excuse that, although our eastern Ally's operations against the Germans had made practically no progress, the campaign in Galicia had, on the 22nd, been crowned with the capture of the great fortress of Przemysl — in appearance the most gratifying success gained for the cause since the Battle of the Marne. It is also evident from Wilson's account of the Chantilly meeting that more friendly relations had been established between Lord Kitchener and himself than had been prevailing between them during the preceding eight months, and this was in itself a matter for congratulation.

Chapter XIII – 1915: April to June

Plans of attack — Wilson pays a visit to England — The reverse north-east of Ypres — Opening of the Arras — La Bassée offensive — Fresh difficulties with the French — Further offensive in the Arras — La Bassée region, with little result — Wilson telegraphed for by Lord Kitchener.

Sir J. French had asked Wilson to join his mess at St. Omer, and on one of the first evenings he met Lord Northcliffe, who was staying with Sir John; of their talk at dinner he wrote home to his wife:

> Northcliffe made me laugh last night, he was so fearfully pessimistic. Nothing was right, either here, or in Egypt, or India, or Russia, or at the Dardanelles, or in the U.S., or at home with the labour troubles. He was quite upset at my laughing so much.

Wilson was indeed in an optimistic mood just at this time, although dissatisfied about the Dardanelles venture; and he still wrote home anticipating an early victorious ending to the struggle. On April 5 an important meeting with Foch was held at Cassel, at which Sir John and Foch explained their respective plans of attack when the contemplated joint offensive should start in a few weeks' time on either side of La Bassée, the object of the discussion being to ensure that the two armies should deliver their strokes simultaneously. Wilson wrote in his diary on the 7th:

Foch came to see me this morning about a criticism I had made of his secret note of yesterday, describing the operations he was going to undertake at the end of April. I was most anxious that, between the attacks (French and English), there should be a portion of the XXIst Corps sitting quietly in its trenches doing nothing, so that there should be no chance of either of our attacks waiting on the other. Foch agreed, and amended his note accordingly. I translated it this evening and gave it to Sir John, with whom I had a talk after dinner. I told him I was going home on Wednesday. Then we discussed the Dardanelles. He showed me a letter he had just received from Johnnie Hamilton, dated from Lemnos. Johnnie had returned from a cruise in the Bay of Saros, he had gone so near the coast that he had seen the rows and rows of trenches. He had gone to the *mouth* of the Dardanelles, where he was at once shelled. This all sounds like going through! Sir John agrees now that to employ troops for this enterprise is madness. I think I must see if I can't do something to stop it. As I always say, I am not clear that, even if successful, it would be a good thing to do. Winston ought to be, and must be, *dégomméd*[*] over this.

He wrote on the 10th:

This morning Robertson came to my room and we had a long discussion about the coming attacks. We have 10 divisions and 600 guns, of which 100 are heavy. Foch has 14 divisions and 950 guns, of which 230 are heavy. I can't help thinking we ought to succeed. On the w T hole line from Ypres to the southern point of the Tenth Army, including all troops in repose, Macdonogh calculates only 180,000 Germans. We have at least 300,000 men with which to attack a small portion of this line, and ample men over to hold the remainder.

Robertson gave me Sir John's reply to Foch's letter of the 6th, I took this out before dinner and we had a long talk. I told him I thought that, if we broke the line in our next attempt, it was quite possible that, as the Germans had no serious reserve, the fighting might become one of localities and no longer of line, a number of isolated actions, and that in this case cavalry might push through and seize Douai, or even Valenciennes, and that this would mean a general retirement of this part of the line. He told me that Castelnau was also going to attack, with a corps at least.

---

[*] "Sacked."

Wilson proceeded home on April 16. The question of a possible Coalition Government was already attracting public attention at this juncture, and he met several of the Opposition leaders — Lord Milner, Lord Lansdowne, Mr. A. Chamberlain, Lord Edmund Talbot, and others — besides paying several visits to the War Office. It was while Wilson was in England on this occasion that Mr. Asquith delivered the strange speech at Newcastle, in the course of which he declared that the B.E.F. was not, and never had been, hampered by lack of ammunition, a speech which aroused much indignation at the front and wherever the facts were known. Wilson was in a position to give Chamberlain chapter and verse as to the real state of the case. "Now that the Dardanelles are not doing well, Winston and Fisher are preparing plans for landing a force in the Baltic, and another of 8 divisions at Rotterdam" — so he heard in the War Office — "and Fisher is spending enormous sums on flat-bottomed boats for the former venture. It is incredible." But, while becoming aware of much that displeased him and caused him anxiety, he also saw something of the "New Armies," and, in view of the criticisms with regard to these creations which he had indulged in during the previous autumn, an entry in his diary on April 17 is of no little interest:

> Cecil and I motored to Aldershot and saw the whole 12th Division of Kitchener's Army file by, at the end of a 12-mile route march. Undoubtedly a fine body of men in a good hard condition, and Fred Wing (G.O.C.) and Tit Willow (1st Grade G.S.) both say they are in excellent heart, and ready to take the field in 3 or 4 weeks. Most units commanded by regulars, 4 or 5 regular officers to each battalion, all O.C.s batteries regular officers, men all much better class than our regulars heretofore. Horses excellent, and beautiful mules. All musketry finished. All guns fired 25 rounds a gun, and good practice according to Wing. Howitzers still incomplete, and only 2 machine-guns per battalion; telephones incomplete. But another month ought to suffice, and I was very agreeably surprised.

He also saw something of the 17th Division at Wareham; but this division, which belonged to the 2nd New Army and not to the 1st, was naturally not so far advanced in training and armament as was that of General Wing.

On his return to St. Omer he was much concerned to learn the details of the serious reverse which the French and, although to a much less extent, the Canadians had met with on the 22nd and 23rd to the north-east of Ypres — the first German gas attack. But he could not withhold his admiration of the enemy's General Staff for accomplishing so much under the conditions that existed at the time. "The Germans did this by those noxious gases and without reinforcements, for they have none," he wrote home that night to Mrs. Wilson, "and so it was a very fine performance." He was, however, seriously disturbed at so much ground, in what happened to be a portion of the Ypres salient that seemed to be of almost vital importance, having passed into the enemy's possession. He was even disposed to think that its loss might render the hold of the Allies upon the salient as a whole extremely precarious. He, moreover, feared that this serious discomfiture might upset the plans that had already been decided upon for an offensive farther to the south. He was worried by finding that Sir John was angry with the French for having given way, with the loss of 36 guns, and for their having completely exposed the flank of the Canadians, who had nevertheless gallantly stood their ground. "Although the gas no doubt has something to do with the panic," Sir John wrote to Lord Kitchener, "this would never have happened if the French had not weakened their line a great deal too much" — a complaint for which there seems to have been some justification.

Wilson saw Foch next day and they both agreed that the old line must be re-established at once; Foch had indeed already brought up two divisions for the purpose, and another one was coming. The effort to restore the position was initiated next day, on which Joffre and Foch arrived at St. Omer to visit Sir John. Wilson wrote of this in his diary:

> A most disappointing conversation. Present Joffee, Foch, Huguet, Sir John and I. They scarcely touched on Ypres or this afternoon's attack. Joffre said he was being heavily attacked at Eparges [in Champagne], Italy and Rumania were coming in, attack at La Bassée and Arras must be postponed to May 6-8. I asked what was to be done if this afternoon's attack was unsuccessful. Foch said we must drive Boches back to the old line or else we cannot hold Ypres. No one else

took much interest. Extraordinary. Later in day and during the evening reports of attack show that the fighting is rather indecisive. We must go on till we drive Boches back, as the *boucle*[*] is untenable as it is.

Resolute attempts were made during the next three or four days by the Allies to recover the ground that had been lost, and some little progress in that direction was made. Sir John had declared from the outset that, unless the portions of the line farther to the left that had been lost were recovered, he would find himself obliged to draw in his front to the east and to the north-east of Ypres — that he would, in fact, have to contract the existing salient. Foch and Wilson were at one in holding that if such a withdrawal were actually to be carried out, Ypres would probably be lost and that, this being so, the ground that the Germans had captured must be retaken. In view of the virtual failure that attended the efforts of the troops on a succession of days to restore the *status quo*. Sir John, however, decided to order the proposed retirement, and this was effected on the night of May 3 without incident. Foch had warned the British Commander-in-Chief at a meeting held on the 1st, that his project of shortening the line within the salient was to invite attack, and had begged him not to lose Ypres. "It is a real bad business," Wilson wrote in his diary. But no evil results, as it turned out, ensued during a period extending over more than two years, apart from the approaches to the lines within the salient becoming more exposed to hostile artillery fire than had previously been the case, and apart from the fact that a somewhat stronger force had to be retained on the spot for defensive purposes than would otherwise have been necessary.

Arrangements for the coming offensive by the B.E.F. north of La Bassée, and by the French to the south of that point, were in the meantime being perfected, but not without the occurrence of somewhat serious friction between G.H.Q. and Foch, friction which exercised all Wilson's tact to overcome. He proceeded to Chantilly on the 4th to see Joffre, and the French Commander-in-Chief on that day, according to the diary,

---

[*] "Loop."

...was very hopeful of Foch's coming attack on Friday. Said he was bringing up even more troops and really thought he would break the line past mending, and that it might be, and ought to be, the beginning of the end. He talked of getting to Namur and the war being over in 3 months. I am hopeful, but not so much.

Wilson also heard that day from Joffre about the Italians joining the Allies.

The offensive had been fixed to commence, in so far as infantry were concerned, on May 9. Foch proposed to start with a prolonged bombardment on the 8th; whereas Haig, who was in immediate local charge of the British effort, only meant to start his gun-fire just before the infantry advanced on the 9th. "At last this great attack of 100,000 British bayonets and 600 guns, and of 210,000 French bayonets and 1,100 guns is off," Wilson wrote on the previous evening, and his account of the opening of the operations in his diary is of particular interest:

Huguet and I at St. Pol at 7 a.m. and then on to Savy, where I saw General D'Urbal and General Messe (Gunner). They advised me where to go, so we went on in the motor and got to near St. Eloi, passing through rows of guns, including 4 guns on rail trucks, and some immense old mortars, and batteries on batteries of heavy guns. We got into a long trench which took us over St. Eloi hill to the most forward observing station on the eastern slope. There, in front, was the whole panorama. All the French and Boche trenches, the wire, communicating trenches etc., with the tremendous roar of the artillery and shells bursting ceaselessly over the Boche lines, and away back over their batteries.

The Frenchmen began to fire at 6 a.m. and fired till 10 a.m. I got to this observation post at 9 a.m. The gunning was incessant; from 9.30 to 9.40 an increase, from 9.40 to 9.50 less, from 9.50 to 10 o'c. appalling. Twelve hundred guns served by Frenchmen and lashing to their utmost. No living person has ever before heard or seen such a thing. The shells passing over my head made one steady hiss.

At 10 o'clock, to the second, the guns stopped and the whole long line of French infantry, as far as I could see to the north and south, rose up out of their trenches and went forward. The next minute the guns opened again with a barrage. A most wonderful sight. I watched the infantry take all the trenches within sight without too much loss, and then, at 11 a.m. I came away. We were shelled all the time up on the hill, but not much. I then went to Hautes Avernes and saw Balfouriez, who commands the XXth Corps. He was quite pleased with his reports, then to Foch at Brias, also pleased, then to Sir John at Hazebrouck.

Joffre came at 6 o'c. He was also well pleased, but none of the French were in the least boastful. Sir John quite nice to Joffre, and this was difficult as Haig's attack had been a complete failure. Neither the Ist Corps, Indian Corps nor IVth Corps could do anything, we lost some 10,000 men and never gained a yard. Now whose plans were right? Foch or Haig? I heard later that the French fired 176,000 rounds of "75" shell and in the last ten minutes of bombardment they were firing 46 shells a second. We fired 50,000 rounds.

Kitchener wires wanting us to send some ammunition to the Dardanelles. Whew!

The attack carried out by Haig's three corps is in this country known as the Battle of Festubert. The losses were extremely heavy, and it was after returning to his head-quarters on the first day of the fighting that Sir J. French found a telegram awaiting him from Lord Kitchener, directing him to dispatch 20,000 rounds to the Dardanelles. He has in his book, "1914," recorded the steps that he straightway took, how he sent two A.D.C.s to England to see Mr. Bonar Law, Mr. Balfour and Mr. Lloyd George, to bring to their notice the inadequate amount of ammunition that was reaching him, and the fact that he was being called upon to deliver up some of what he had got. He claims that this was a main cause of the substitution of the Coalition for the Liberal Government, which took place a few days later. As it happened, the 20,000 rounds were replaced within twenty-four hours. But there can be no doubt that insufficiency of ammunition had contributed largely to Haig's lack of success on the first day, and that it most gravely hampered the British offensive on subsequent days.

Foch's operations farther to the south, although their course at no time favoured the idea that he would achieve a break through, gained ground from the outset, and they continued to gain ground slowly on succeeding days, if at heavy cost. The British failure to make progress was so pronounced that the question arose whether it would not be better for the B.E.F. to confine itself for the time being to helping the French, either by taking over some of their line or else by transferring some divisions southwards to act as reserves to Foch's troops in their offensive. But no satisfactory understanding was arrived at. Wilson makes it quite clear in his diary that he found his task as principal liaison officer very far from being a sinecure. According to the diary, for instance, Haig suspended his operations on the 10th and nth, but proposed to resume the effort on the 12th; the attack was, however, again put off till the 14th, and was ultimately only launched on the 16th. Nor did the fact that one French division (the one that had been on the right of the B.E.F.) was relieved by British troops, suffice to allay the French irritation. Wilson gives an account in his diary of a meeting that took place on May 12 at Brias, Foch's headquarters, between Sir John, Joffre and Foch, which serves to show how difficult it sometimes was to prevent a serious quarrel:

> Sir John said that he would begin Indian attack Friday (14th) night, and Ist Corps would attack Saturday morning. Joffre said this was very late. Sir John then said that, as he could not begin earlier, there was no alternative but to bring his troops down to join the French. General Joffre laid out his plan. Sir John agreed to relieve the 58th. Division, but would not hear of relieving up at Ypres, said he had no troops, that it was dangerous to change troops there even if this strengthened the force there; then the next minute he produced four divisions for an attack on Loos, which the French don't want. Joffre pointed out that we should be doing very little if we only relieved the 58th Division, and hinted at Government action, which luckily Sir John did not quite catch and I got the chance of interpreting wrong; but as both were getting hot, I got Sir John to go away, saying he would send an answer later. I had a few words with Joffre and Foch after Sir John left, and then went back to Hazebrouck.
>
> Sir John, Haig and Robertson had a talk; then I was sent for and Sir John told me he had decided to begin the attack on Friday night and main attack on Saturday morning. I asked if this was certain. He said it was. Huguet and I then went off to Brias and gave this message to Foch. He took it amazingly well, and all the more so when one remembers that both yesterday and to-day the French have had very heavy fighting and made very little progress. In fact what we have done is this: We attacked on Sunday with a ridiculous artillery preparation of 40 minutes. We took a few trenches, which we lost that

night, so we gained not one inch of ground. We lost about 10,000-12,000 men. Since then we have done nothing. We said we would attack again on Tuesday, then on Wednesday (to-day), now we say we will attack Saturday. And all this time the French are fighting *hard*, and we have at least four fat divisions doing nothing.

Wilson learnt on the 16th that a letter had come from Lord Kitchener intimating that H.M. Government were now afraid of invasion and that no more troops would therefore be sent out. He also heard that the force landed on the Gallipoli Peninsula had been brought completely to a standstill close to the shore and had suffered heavy losses. On the day following he moreover learnt that the reasons put forward for withholding the remaining five divisions of the 1st New Army — the first of them, the 9th Division, had just arrived — were: 1. That the offensive had failed to break the line; 2. That there was danger of invasion; 3. That there was so serious a lack of ammunition. Wilson was highly indignant. "He promised us all six divisions at 5 days intervals," the diary on that day (the 17th) records, referring to the Secretary of State, "and our plans were laid accordingly, and he knew it." He wrote in his diary on the 20th, after hearing that a Coalition Government was being formed:

I went to Hazebrouck and saw Robertson. I then went over and saw Sir John and walked half an hour in the garden with him. He burst out once or twice, but not badly, and I was able to make him laugh the next minute. He seems to think Winston may remain and Kitchener go, but I don't. I got letters to-day from Callwell and Gwynne. They both say the same thing — that Kitchener is going to be made G in C and Bonar Law to be Secretary of State. Now this would be worse than the present arrangement. We want Kitchener to remain S. of S., but to confine his energies to his own work, we want to restart the General Staff. Making Kitchener C. in C. will crush out the last spark of life in the G.S. Both Charlie and Gwynne say that Sir John had better walk warily, or he will be out.* Saw Arthur Lee, who goes over to-morrow, and gave him all my ideas. He will see Austen to-morrow. Discussed after dinner with Billy Lambton and Guy

---

* This was owing to Sir John's Press campaign.

> Brooke [Lord Brooke] how we can warn Sir John, but could not think of anything that would not do more harm than good.

Next day Wilson went to see Joffre at Doullens, as Sir John had received a telegram from General Hanbury Williams (our principal military representative in Russia) asking what the strategical policy was. Joffre said that the answer was "active and aggressive operations," but he at the same time made it clear that the decision must be on the Western Front, not in Russia, nor in Serbia, nor in Italy. In spite of his intimation of a few days before. Lord Kitchener was now sending over a third division of the 1st New Army, the 12th. Excluding this, Wilson on the 27th calculated that the B.E.F. now had 8½ battalions per mile of front, which, taking the German strength into account, seemed to him excessive. General Joffre that day told Wilson that he wanted the B.E.F. to attack at Loos as soon as a stretch of line to the south of La Bassée that was at present occupied by the French 58th Division had, as already arranged, been taken over.

> Joffre said this was a great opportunity, Germans very thin, Italy joined, etc., and we must put every man and round into it. I do so agree. I begged him not to ask us to take over a division up at Ypres. He agreed to leave that subject alone.

The question of relieving the 5 8th Division, however, gave rise to fresh difficulties, because Foch happened to mention that he might, later on, want to withdraw another division from Ypres. Wilson, however, managed to compose differences, the 58th Division was relieved, and the question of attacking towards Loos was fully considered at a meeting of Foch with Sir John on the 30th, at which Wilson was present. Foch hoped to deliver a big attack on June 3, and he asked Sir John to attack all along the line from La Bassée to Loos on the same day, but Sir John objected to acting before the 6th or 7th, and also to undertaking operations on so wide a front.

Mr. Asquith, accompanied by Lambton, arrived at St. Omer on the 30th for a visit and remained for some days, and on the last day of the month Wilson wrote in his diary:

I rode with Billy Lambton in the evening. He says I am to get the K.C.B. this time. He has come back with the impression that the Government will not bring in conscription. He saw Milner, who was fairly hopeful. I don't agree with Billy. Of course, the great stumbling-block is Ireland and Johnnie Redmond's prohibition, but this really ought not to frighten the fools. Sir John is in very bad odour at home, especially because of his Press campaign against Kitchener. Kitchener forbade a counter-campaign against Sir John. Foch wrote to-night to say he would postpone his attack from June 3 to June 7.

Next day the entry appears:

In answer to General Foch's letter of last night, Sir John writes that he won't attack opposite Loos, which is where Foch wants him to attack, but will attack on the 8th, 9th and 10th astride the La Bassée canal. Considering that he told Foch the day before yesterday that he would attack on the 6th and 7th, we have here another cause of quarrel. It is very disgusting, with a real decision hanging in the balance all the time. Huguet and I went out to Foch at 5 o'c., and I tried to soften his disgust by saying he might get the relief of a division up at Ypres early next week. Asquith goes to see Foch and Joffre to-morrow, and I warned Foch what sort of man he is and to ask for more troops and more relief.

On June 2 Wilson wrote:

Saw Billy early and told him to tell Asquith to thank Foch in the presence of his C. in C. for the work he had done for us. Billy told Asquith, but Asquith forgot to say this at the meeting. At n a.m. Sir John sent for me to ask if I would meet Asquith at dinner. I said I would if it would please Sir John. Freddie Guest was then sent to see Asquith if he would meet me. He said — yes — also. So I dined.*

---

* An officer who was present at this feast gives the following account of an incident that occurred during its progress which, when the story came to be known, gave considerable satisfaction at G.H.Q., and in billets and trenches:

"Mr. Asquith was on Sir J. French's right at dinner, and Henry Wilson was sitting some two or three places away from Sir John, on his left. Mr. Asquith, with a singular want of tact seeing who was his host, remarked to Sir John, 'It is a curious thing, Field-Marshal, that this war has produced no great generals.' The

> Johnnie Baird in at 11 p.m. on his way home finally. He and Percy and I talked till 1 o'c. and I impressed on him once more that, until a General Staff is formed and a Chief of Staff appointed, you *cannot* get a military opinion. There was a meeting at Sir John's house to-day of Sir John, Robertson, Asquith, Joffre, Foch, Millerand and Huguet. Nothing decided, of course, but Sir John and Joffre both impressed on Asquith the necessity of sending all available troops, and Sir John offered to take over a French division up at Ypres.

Wilson would have liked to have proceeded to London, so as to have an opportunity of discussing the situation with the Unionist leaders who had joined the Cabinet, with almost all of whom he was personally acquainted. But he realized, as is noted in bis diary, that this would be inadvisable unless he was invited to do so. He was, however, also anxious that certain members of the Unionist party who held seats in the House, such as Arthur Lee and Sir J. Baird, should be at home at this juncture, and he had, moreover, urged that a seat should be found for Lord Percy. He was beginning to feel solicitude concerning the Russian ammunition question, in view of what he was constantly hearing from the War Office on the subject — the more so owing to the tidings that were coming to hand from the Eastern Front. For Przemysl had been retaken by Austro-Hungarian forces on the 3rd, and the whole of the Tsar's legions which had penetrated into Galicia in the winter were being pushed back rapidly eastwards. Joffre had hitherto been disposed to pooh-pooh what at French G.Q.G. were regarded as alarmist reports from this quarter. But Wilson found that Foch was becoming perturbed, and afraid that the Russians were going to be pushed yet farther back unless the Germans should decide to transfer some of their troops operating on the Eastern Front to another theatre. That troops which had carried out an offensive against the forces of the Dual Monarchy a few months earlier so successfully should now show themselves palpably unable to hold their own against the same antagonists was particularly disquieting. This, moreover, was occurring at the very moment when Italy was

---

rest of us at table naturally cocked our ears at this. But Henry Wilson chimed in with, 'No, Prime Minister, nor has it produced a statesman.'"

about to embark on offensive operations from Venetia. Fresh delay had in the meantime taken place in restarting the La Bassée-Arras offensive, and on the 10th Wilson wrote in his diary:

> Huguet and I to see Foch at 5 o'c. Foch has a preliminary attack of the XXIst Corps on the 12th, and then his big attack on the 15 th, so we |will have ours the same day. On my way back I called to see Sir John at his new house at Blondecque. He told me he had just got news that four more divisions were to go to the Dardanelles at once (10th, 11th, 13th and a Territorial Division). It is simply incredible. This makes. I think, 9 there and 22 here, and not a single Boche facing the 9. How they will laugh in Berlin. I wonder who the fools were who decided this, and on what evidence. This will prolong the campaign for some months, and may even lead to serious consequences.

The postponed offensive commenced on June 16, and the French again gained some little ground; but the operations undertaken by the IVth Corps of the B.E.F. practically effected nothing, after a temporary success at the very outset. "We don't seem able to 'mount' an attack." Wilson complained in his diary after having witnessed the advance of the French farther to the south, and he was rendered uneasy by learning from liaison officers that our Allies were much dissatisfied alike with the proceedings of H.M. Government and with the performances of the B.E.F. "We don't fight, we don't take over, we don't send out our New Armies," he wrote, echoing the sentiments which appear to have been entertained by the French. Our Allies, moreover, could not at this time understand the difficulty experienced in the United Kingdom in connexion with the production of munitions. For they did not realize (any more, indeed, than did G.H.Q.) that, what so terribly hampered those responsible on our side of the Channel was the fact that the plant for making ammunition had in great part to be created, whereas in France and Germany the plant had existed from the start. Those countries had always contemplated placing huge armies in the field, and they had been prepared for supplying such huge armies with war material when war broke out. The British Government, on the other hand, had never even considered placing more than six divisions in the field; but it was already maintaining nineteen (besides two Indian) on the Western Front, as well as two in the Gallipoli Peninsula. Anxious to reassure those at Chantilly with regard to these matters, Wilson repaired thither on the 22nd, and he recorded his experiences there on this occasion as follows in his diary:

> Long talk with General Joffre (Pellé being present). Explained situation at home. New Cabinet, anxious to do what is right, grossly ignorant, no military advice except Kitchener's, which is distrusted. Difference in my -position with arrival of Bonar Law and his men. I am anxious about future, about strain on France, about Dardanelles, about Russia. Necessity for defined policy for autumn and winter, and no longer hand-to-mouth — therefore suggest that Joffre draws up a paper for his Government and Sir John for his. Each to show the other his paper and then send them in — regular state papers.
>
> Joffre agreed. He meets his Ministers to-morrow, Foch and Castelnau also present, to discuss future, and Joffre is going to raise the question of general direction and command again. This is a very delicate question, and we shall see. This talk was good.
>
> Lunched with Joffre. Then at 1 o'c. started back and called on de Castelnau at Chazy near Amiens. He takes over the group of Armies of the Centre to-morrow at Chateau-Thierry, and I am glad. Three groups: North — Foch; Centre — Castelnau, East — Dubail.
>
> Castelnau very open (though he said he would not speak to any Englishman alive like that except me). He thinks the English are amazingly slow in helping in men and ammunition, and cautious to a degree in action. He wants a wider outlook and "motor service between the brains of the Allies." He is very much opposed to attacks like this Arras one which cost 100,000 men and did no good except shatter four corps — IXth, XXth, XXIst, XXXIInd. He is for big guns, lots of ammunition, deep entrenchments, wait for the English to appear, stop all attacks till some chance of real decision, and so on. I agree with much, but a sitting policy here might throw Russia into Boche arms. Castelnau told me he was going to speak in this sense at the meeting of Ministers to-morrow, and I am sure he will carry great weight. He confirmed absolutely my fears of French suspicion of us, and of the possibility of their getting tired, and he spoke at length on losses and no advance, and the consequent depression in France.
>
> All this makes me more anxious than ever to go home for a few days. Got back to St. Omer at 7 o'c., found letter from Edmund Talbot saying he was anxious about state of affairs and would I come

over. I said I wanted to, but must be sent.

Wilson paid a fresh visit to Chantilly two days later, driving thither in advance of Sir John and Robertson; and he had a talk with Pellé during the forenoon which afforded him further evidence of the extent to which the French were disposed to criticize us. He, moreover, heard, while there, the bad news that Lemberg had been retaken by the Austro-Hungarian forces, and that furthermore there was likelihood of Warsaw also falling. At the conference in the afternoon Sir John stated that his Government were in favour of a defensive policy being maintained for the present on the Western Front. Joffre thereupon declared that, were such a course to be adopted, the consequence would be that the Russians would first be beaten in the east, and that the Franco-British armies would then be beaten in the west — a view in which Wilson entirely concurred. He had seen in a newspaper at Amiens the *Gazette* awarding him the K.C.B., which naturally pleased him, as also did a telegram from Lord Kitchener on the 29th, asking that he should be sent over to acquaint the Government with the French view of the situation. So he proceeded to London next day and spent all that first afternoon with the Secretary of State. Of what passed he records in his diary:

> He talked incessantly, and told me how Winston started the Dardanelles show, and how he (K.) agreed, thinking that Fisher and A. Wilson* also agreed. How these two never uttered a word until things went wrong, and then said they had always been opposed to it. How Kitchener then turned on them, and afterwards recorded the whole thing in writing.
>
> On my urging him to clear out, he said it would mean trouble in India, loss of Egypt, in addition to loss of whole force while trying to do it. He would resign. It must be gone on with. Even more troops might have to be sent. On my stating very plainly what this would mean to the French and what they would say and do, he showed me three papers which he was going to produce at a meeting which he was attending with the P.M. at Calais on the 5th July, where Poincaré, Joffre and others were to be present. First paper showed the dates on

* Sir A. K. Wilson was assisting Lord Fisher (First Sea Lord) at the Admiralty.

which the New Armies would be ready, second gave forecasts of ammunition, third gave numbers available to meet wastage, etc.

On my saying that the French must be given a programme, he said he could reinforce us by 25 divisions by December 31 — viz. 3 New Armies, making 18, plus 1 Canadian Division, plus 6 from the Dardanelles! And then he said that after clearing the Dardanelles, i.e. after taking the Gallipoli Peninsula, he was going to withdraw all his troops and bring them to France. This was a staggerer for me. He said he could, and would. I said he couldn't, but if he could it would entirely alter complexion. He repeated over and over again that he would. I went back, and said that if he told the French that by Xmas we would have some 50 divisions in France, and could, therefore, take up about 100 miles of front, both the French army and France would be quite content, but that, short of a programme, they would not.

He repeated that he would tell the French on Monday at Calais about 18 of the divisions, but probably not about the Dardanelles, as this might get out. I agreed. He then spoke of a pure defence all along the Western line, which he advocated at great length and over and over again. I said that, if he could get France and Russia to agree, it would be all right, otherwise it was obviously impossible.

These were the principal points of our three hours' talk. He was most civil and allowed me to contradict him as much as I liked. I had an hour with Bonar Law after dinner. Much the same ground again.

Wilson, who paid several visits to the War Office during the next few days, was naturally pleased at having established such friendly relations with Kitchener and at finding him so ready to listen. Although he makes no reference to the matter in his diary or in letters home, there can be no doubt that his views had undergone a transformation as regards the merits of the "New Army" scheme, to which he had a few months before been so strongly opposed. He was now prepared to give the Secretary of State the credit that was due for having, at the very outset of hostilities, initiated a huge expansion of the nation's military forces, and for having realized at that early stage of the struggle that this was bound to be a protracted one. However mistaken Kitchener's views and actions in connexion with the strategical conduct of the war at a later date may have been, his judgment in regard to those fundamental questions had by the event been proved to have been sound.

Wilson could not but perceive the advantages that the British forces in France would derive from his establishing cordial relations with the War Minister, and from his keeping the responsible controller of the national military forces as a whole fully informed on the subject of French opinions and susceptibilities. He was already in close touch with most of the Unionists who had recently joined the Cabinet, and he had now arrived at a satisfactory understanding with the one Cabinet Minister who belonged to neither of the two great political parties.

Chapter XIV – 1915: July to September

Wilson attends a Cabinet Meeting — Joffre insists on an offensive on the Western Front to help Russia — The Coalition Cabinet and the Dardanelles — Wilson's advice to Kitchener — Difficulties in connexion with the contemplated offensive — Wilson accompanies Kitchener on a tour of the French lines — General Sarrail — The Battle of Loos.

Wilson was knighted by the King at Buckingham Palace on July 1, and he afterwards had a long talk with His Majesty. From there he went to see Lord Kitchener at the War Office, who sent him on to Downing Street to see Mr. Asquith. The Prime Minister began by telling him that a strong agitation had been set up in France against Millerand and Joffre. Wilson wrote in his diary:

> He asked me my opinion, and I gave him my view of the French mind. This nettled him a good deal, as I did not spare him French remarks about our unpreparedness before the war, their doubts as to our participation, their amazement that after eleven months we had not sufficient ammunition for a "push" of four divisions, their doubts as to what we were going to do in the autumn and winter, their hatred of the Dardanelles, and their insistence on a programme for the coming months. He listened very attentively and in the end was very civil.

Later in the day Sir Henry paid visits to Mr. A. Chamberlain, Lord Milner and Lord Lansdowne. He had a long conversation with Mr. Lloyd George on the 2nd, and there is recorded of this in the diary:

> He also thinks we are going to be beaten. I went over all the same ground with him: Dardanelles, Serbia, defensive idea must have approval of Russia and France, dissatisfaction and suspicion of France about us. He agreed. He is entirely opposed to Dardanelles, but says that Kitchener is so mixed up with Winston over it that he, Kitchener, will never agree to quit. At 4 o'clock we had a meeting at Bonar's house of Bonar, Walter Long, Carson and self. We talked for two hours, and I got all three to agree to oppose sending further troops to Gallipoli, and to send all troops to France on programme.

Later in the evening Wilson saw Lord Milner again, who, he found, was opposed to going on with the Dardanelles undertaking; and he met Mr. Chamberlain at dinner, who said the same thing.

Sir Henry attended a Cabinet meeting on the following day (July 3), and he records in his diary:

> Full Cabinet discussed future plan of campaign. I represented French view of us as "not being cross, but dissatisfied and a little suspicious," and pointed to Dardanelles and shortage of ammunition as chief reasons. Much discussion, and a good deal of nonsense; but in the end Kitchener said he thought that the 2nd New Army should be sent out at once. This was good. It was agreed that a programme should be submitted at the meeting which is to take place on Wednesday at Calais.

For taking part in a sitting of this kind, in a conference with dialectically disposed associates gathered round a table, Wilson could lay claim to qualifications that are not commonly found amongst naval men or soldiers — even when these are masters of their respective crafts. Gifted by nature with a talent for explicit statement, and possessing the happy faculty of, as a general rule, gaining the upper hand in any controversy that he became engaged in, an encounter with politicians practised in debate offered no terrors to him whatever. A mind quick and resourceful, coupled with a thorough knowledge of the art of war in its various branches, enabled him, when professional subjects were at issue, to assort his arguments in a form and in language almost bound to carry conviction to such an audience as was assembled on July 3, in the big room in 10 Downing Street where Cabinet meetings are wont to be held. Sir Henry felt well content with what he had accomplished on this occasion and he so expressed himself in his diary. He wrote on the 5th:

> Went to War Office and had a talk with Kitchener, who was most friendly, about this meeting at Calais to-morrow. He wants me to prepare Joffre for his proposals, then he wants to see Joffre alone and to tell him of all his fears, show him his whole hand, and come to an agreement as to what he shall say in front of the politicians whom he (Kitchener) hates and distrusts as much as, I told him, Joffre did. I then said that I meant in future to come over oftener and expose the situation as I see it. He said at once that I could not come too often. What a change! Kitchener is frightened. He has nobody he can talk to or trust, and he finds that I am not afraid of him. I left by 2 o'clock train. Clive
>
> Wigram came to see me off, and I explained whole French mind to him, so that he may pass it on to the King.
>
> The broad result of my visit and the impression that I gained are these: The Cabinet is frightened. Kitchener is frightened. The Cabinet is ignorant. Kitchener is ignorant. No one knows what to do. Result and feeling m my mind are that, with the advent of the Coalition, the Old Firm is completely bankrupt and out-classed, and we now have a lot of men who are anxious to do what is right, but are ignorant and feel that they are already committed to many things that are wrong. I can get over this.

Sir Henry's record of the Calais discussion on the 6th reads as follows:

> Huguet and I went to Calais at 6.50 a.m. and met General Joffre as he arrived by train. I explained situation and then went off to the Gare Maritime, got Kitchener and brought him to the Gare Centrale to Joffre, and these two had an hour alone. On our way, Kitchener and I passed Sir John, which led to much trouble.
>
> At 10 a.m. there was a meeting, which I was not allowed to attend, in the Gare Maritime of Viviani, Delcassé, Millerand, A. Thomas, Joffre, with Asquith, Arthur Balfour, Crewe, Kitchener and Sir John. Heard afterwards that Kitchener exposed his hand and set

out a programme. *Good.* Meanwhile I had two hours with Fite [Colonel O. Fitzgerald, Lord Kitchener's Personal Assistant] about Kitchener, his work, his position, his feelings, the General Staff, etc., Fitz all the time nibbling round to get me as C.I.G.S. But I kept him off and told him I would come over oftener. This has been a good day's work.

He wrote to Lady Wilson on July 8:

The Calais meeting went off quite well, and a meeting between K. and Joffre, which I arranged and which took place in Joffre's train in the early hours, was a great success. K. was all smiles, both then and again last night when I went to have a talk with him while he was dressing for dinner.

A military conference took place at Chantilly on the day after the Calais meeting. At this General Joffre read a long appreciation; he ended by asserting that it was necessary to act on the offensive because of Russia, because of the importance of stimulating morale, and because the Germans were not in great strength along their line. He impressed upon the Serb and Italian representatives who were present that this applied to the Southern as well as to the Western Front. Sir John agreed, and moreover promised that, as the divisions of the 2nd New Army were beginning to come out, he would take over more line from the French. Finally it was agreed that the offensive on the Western Front should take place in August?

The situation on the Eastern Front was becoming ominous, and the total inability of the Russian forces, short of munitions as they were and dwindling in numbers for want of rifles, to check the steady advance of the German and Austro-Hungarian hosts in Poland and Galicia, was causing grave concern to the two Western Governments and to the British and French military authorities. Even the French G.Q.G. was at last beginning to grasp the seriousness of the situation in that quarter.

It was agreed a few days later that troops under Sir J. French's orders were to take over charge of a stretch of front immediately north of the River Somme, and that these were to be separated from the rest of the B.E.F. by the Tenth French Army. This army was holding the line on either side of Arras, and the intention was that, when the offensive was resumed in August, it should continue the operations that it had already been engaged on. Sir John decided that the corps detailed to occupy the detached section of front north of the Somme were to constitute a Third Army, to be commanded by General Monro.

In common with the majority of the general officers forming part of the B.E.F., Wilson had been provided by the Quartermaster-General's department with a car and a soldier chauffeur, and he had been fortunate in having a fine Rolls-Royce placed at his disposal from this source. This car he almost invariably drove himself, and he took pleasure in doing so — differing in this respect from most officers in high places, who preferred to be driven by the expert charged with the duty. Sir Henry's bent for the wheel and his skill as a motorist indeed attracted a good deal of attention — particularly so amongst the French superior officers whom he so often visited or met on the road. Only when he happened to be accompanied by someone with whom he wanted to hold serious discussion by the way did he call upon his chauffeur to take control. He continued to make a practice of driving himself during the whole of the time that he was serving in France, as also later, after the Armistice, when he spent considerable periods in attendance on the Peace Conference in Paris. He displayed that same apparent immunity from fatigue as a motorist which those associated with him in other forms of activity, mental and bodily, used to note with admiration and wonder. He wrote in his diary on July 17:

> I went out to Foch, with Huguet, at Frévent at 5 o'clock. He was quieter than usual, and we discussed some questions of ground and of boundaries between our new Third Army and his Tenth and Second Armies. Then he said he had given up hopes of breaking the line, but he still hoped to get Vimy, which would be a "*rude secousse*."* I told him of my latest Dardanelles news, and that I thought a success would be a disaster. I told Huguet on the way home of what I had said to Kitchener as to our two great dangers being (1) not sending out all our

* "Rough shake."

men to France, thus annoying France to danger point; and (2) that when we got up to 50, 60, 70 divisions there would be jealousy on the part of the French. Both these must be watched and avoided.

Suggestions were being put to him from various quarters on the subject of his possibly becoming C.I.G.S. at home, where considerable difference of opinion was beginning to manifest itself within the ranks of the Coalition Cabinet, particularly in respect to the Dardanelles operations. Even the Ministers who were most opposed to the venture, however, recognized that, now that five additional divisions* were arriving, or had arrived, in the Ægean Islands, Sir I. Hamilton must be allowed to carry out his plans. But it had already been proposed that yet further reinforcements ought to be sent, and this naturally excited apprehension. Wilson's views with regard to the inexpediency of proceeding with the undertaking were well known, he was at all times prepared to give a definite opinion upon any strategical problem with which he was familiar, and the need of reorganizing the General Staff at the War Office and of restoring it to its proper position was becoming apparent even to the Ministers who had been members of the Liberal Cabinet, and who were therefore more or less responsible for the unfortunate Ægean enterprise.

His presence was, however, required in France just at this time, because during the closing days of July difficulties arose between G.H.Q. and the French in respect to the point at which the British forces were to deliver their stroke during the forthcoming joint offensive. The understanding arrived at at Chantilly had been that the B.E.F. was to act somewhere to the south of La Bassée. But Haig and Robertson had come to the conclusion that the attack could be more effectively delivered to the north of that town, and Sir John had not as yet decided between the two courses. The date for operations to commence had, it is true, been deferred until the end of August, but even so a decision on the subject was required.

He recorded on the 23rd:

* A second Territorial Division had been added to the four divisions that had been arranged for during the previous month.

Went out to see Foch at Frévent. His formula before talking to the Boches about peace is excellent, because so simple and so appealing. "Get behind the Rhine and then I will discuss terms — not otherwise." He told me of overtures just made by an underling in the Boches' Ministry at Berne, to ditto in French Ministry. They were these: Very liberal concessions to France in Alsace; Boches to take Holland and Flanders; France to take Walloon; then, later, to combine to rob England and divide the spoil. Not too stupid. The same man said that Bavaria was rather inclined for peace. She had been heavily punished and now thought she would get nothing out of the war.

I discussed with Foch our coming increase. I suggested that, in order to avoid hurting the susceptibilities of the French, and in order not to stretch farther south than the Somme or the Oise and not to cover Paris, and in order not to give Sir John too big a command, we should form two groups — one where we are, and one away in Argonne or Vosges. Foch much pleased.

On July 25 the entry occurs:

I wrote Gwynne a long letter and laid special stress on the change in the situation owing to the great retreat of the Russians. Just as I finished, in walked Johnnie Baird to tell me that he had seen his old father, just back from Egypt, and that in Egypt they did not care whether we left Gallipoli or stayed on. We then discussed my letter, and Johnnie thought it so important that he is going over to-night by 10.30 boat, to make sure that Bonar Law, Austen, Carson, etc., see it to-morrow, as the House rises on Wednesday for six weeks.

Next day he went to see Joffre, and he seized the opportunity to read his letter to Gwynne to the French Commander-in-Chief, who declared that Italy was doing well, and who stated further that Rumania was now preparing to join the Allies. Wilson noted in his diary:

I confess that I could not understand why Rumania should join. He said that if the contents of my letter got to his Government they would be so frightened that they would want to make peace. Again I could not agree, for the whole letter was to make for conscription. He said that his Ministers (chiefly Ribot) had told him that, from a financial point of view, France could not last after December; but this seems rubbish to me. He, of course, endorsed all that I had said about necessity of England pulling her whole weight, but he did not think that the war would last another twelve months, although he did not meet my arguments. He was, as always, charming to me.

This appears in the diary next day (27th):

> We all left at 9.30 and got to Frévent 10.45, where we had an interview with Foch. Sir John put out his reasons for not attacking on left of French. Foch answered, and in my judgment completely upset Sir John. Concentration not dispersion, continuous and prolonged effort in one direction and for one purpose (say the heights overlooking the plain of Douai). All parts of the line equally strong. After leaving Frévent I took Sir John out to Arras to see the battlefield. It was a fine day, so he saw it well. Very quiet all along the front. A few shells here and there. Sir John told me Foch had convinced him, but that both Haig and Robertson would oppose him heavily; still, he would attack down near the French.

A wire arrived from Lord Kitchener on the 28th to say that Wilson was wanted in London, and in obedience to this summons, he crossed next day, leaving Sir John still in considerable doubt as to whether the attack by the B.E.F. was to take place up in the north or was to be delivered at the point where the French wished. He saw Lord Kitchener on the 30th, and at their meeting he expressed the opinion that, now that Russia was for the time being defeated, the French would be much dissatisfied unless the United Kingdom adopted compulsory service without further delay. To keep friends with the French, he insisted, there must, in the first place, be conscription; but it was also imperative that abundance of ammunition should be produced and should be dispatched to the front, and it was furthermore absolutely necessary that the Gallipoli operations should be abandoned. He pressed these three points home, although he could see that Kitchener did not like it.

After his discussion with the Secretary of State he had conversations with regard to the Dardanelles with other members of the staff in the War Office, and he heard from these exactly how the campaign in that quarter was proceeding. A certain amount of guarded optimism prevailed on the subject at the moment — this, in view of the offensive which Sir I. Hamilton proposed to initiate in a very few days' time, so soon as the five new divisions should be ready to participate. Sir Henry, however, speedily satisfied himself that no clean-cut strategical plan existed, governing this undertaking in the Near East, and that the sole objective appeared to be the occupation — should that prove possible — of the Gallipoli Peninsula. The idea appeared to prevail that if such occupation were to be effected this would automatically carry with it the command of the Dardanelles. Whether that anticipation was justified or not remains undecided, seeing that Sir Ian's operations in August for all practical purposes proved a complete failure and that the Peninsula remained in Turkish hands, but for an insignificant patch of ground at its toe and another patch on its outer coast-line. Wilson, however, always maintained that possession of the Thracian Chersonese did not by any means necessarily ensure control of the Hellespont, and he used to illustrate his view of the matter with a characteristic originality.

"It's just exactly like fishing rights on a river," he would declare. "I'm one side — Gallipoli side. Johnny Turk's t'other side — Asiatic side. I have fishing rights my bank and exercise them. Johnny Turk has fishing rights his bank. Now, where are we? Why, don't you see, Johnny Turk may be able to spoil my sport, and I may be able to spoil Johnny Turk's sport. But — you may say what you like — *I can't prevent the blighter fishing*."

He enjoyed conversations with many prominent people during his week's stay in London, in the course of which he impressed upon all and sundry the vital need of adopting conscription, of developing the munitions supply, and of abandoning the venture at the Dardanelles. But although he was pleased to find a disposition to agree on the point of compulsory service in many quarters, and to find a determination to grapple with the munitions problem in almost all quarters, he met with considerable opposition as regards his third contention. He saw Lord Kitchener at York House on the day before his return to the front, and later in the day he had a conversation with the Prime Minister.

This is recorded in the diary:

> Kitchener very civil, and tried to be cunning by riding me off talking of things I wanted to talk about; but I would not have it. I told

him of Joffre not allowing us in the line south of the Somme. He quite understood and agreed. I pointed out the advantage of two Army Groups — less power for Sir John, less jealousy by the French, rivalry of the two groups throwing them into the arms of the French Kitchener agreed. Fitz told me that Kitchener was only waiting for a fall in recruiting, and completion of Registration Act, to ask for compulsion.

Then I went on to Asquith. Was with him till 8 o'clock. Very civil and listened to my story about French thinking we were not pulling our full weight, because we had not conscription nor ammunition, and because they hated the Dardanelles. Asquith said conscription would not pass through House of Commons, our ammunition was getting better, and, as regards Dardanelles, no more troops would be sent there under any circumstances. He also said that conscription would not give us one extra soldier in the next 12 months owing to lack of rifles, equipment, etc. I don't agree, nor do I agree that it would not pass the House of Commons. As regards Dardanelles, Asquith said he was going to withdraw at earliest moment. *Good*. He was anxious about the political outlook of France, and the intrigues against Millerand and Joffre, and he asked my opinion. He spoke of a return of Caillaux. I replied that up to date there was no sign of bad work. He asked me to come again soon, and was most cordial and appreciative. On the whole my visit this time has done good.

All this time the Russians were daily losing ground in Poland; the Germans entered Warsaw on August 5, and on the same day the fortress of Ivangorod was taken by the Austro-Hungarian forces, so that the Vistula had ceased to be an obstacle to the enemy's progress. A few days later news began to arrive which clearly indicated that the offensive in the Gallipoli Peninsula, from which so much had been hoped, had miscarried. All this was very unsatisfactory. Wilson, moreover, now gathered from a letter written by Sir John to Joffre that there was little intention on the part of the British Commander-in-Chief of delivering a determined attack as his share of the work in the coming offensive — an offensive on which Joffre was employing twelve divisions about Arras and twenty-seven divisions elsewhere. Sir Henry therefore communicated with Pellé; and in consequence of this intervention of Wilson's, Joffre wrote a letter to Sir John intimating in unmistakable terms that the French expected the B.E.F. to play its part. Wilson wrote in his diary on August 14

> I got a copy of Joffre's letter to Sir John of yesterday. He takes for granted, and says so, that Sir John will attack with all his forces, and wishes him to settle details with Foch. Sir John wrote from Hazebrouck to Robertson to tell him to draft a very short note to effect that he would assist according to ammunition. Of course this is no answer at all. I telephoned to Foch, to come in to-morrow; he replied that he could not, but would like to see me. Huguet and I went to Frévent at 5.30. Foch, when I told him the whole story, was quite open about the deplorable effect if we don't fight. I am equally clear, and I will speak to Robertson and Sir John to-morrow. I had a long talk with Foch about Millerand, Russia, Serbia, etc., and he is not satisfied with things. Sir John had better walk warily.

Next day there is the entry:

> Robertson and I had a long talk this morning. I told him it was quite immaterial from my point of view who did what, but one thing was clear — if the French were left under the impression that a serious attack was going to be made, and then it was not made, it would lead to serious trouble. I told him I would see Sir John and tell him so. This I did at Blondecques at 3 o'c. I told Sir John exactly what the French mind was, and that if he thought that he could not attack Loos-Hulluch it would be much better to say so, and attack at Aubers, or anywhere else he liked. But a serious attack was essential. He said he would attack south of the Canal "on a front of 5 divisions." I rubbed in the danger of failing the French.

The French Commander-in-Chief had sent Lord Kitchener a cordial invitation to cross the Channel and to see something of the French army and of the French line, so, in response to this overture, the Secretary of State arrived at Compiègne on the 16th. There he was met by Millerand, as well as by Joffre, Foch and other prominent French generals, and also by Wilson, who afterwards accompanied him during his tour. They paid a visit to some of de Castelnau's troops near Chalons that same day, and then they made their way on to Bar-le-Duc, seeing the whole of the vifh French Corps on parade while en route. The Secretary of State was paid all possible honours during his stay with the French and was provided with a special train for his personal use. He had a number of conversations with M. Millerand, whose position as War Minister had come to be none too secure, and he also had a prolonged discussion with Joffre. Wilson seized the opportunity, which being so much with Kitchener offered him, to propose afresh that, when further British reinforcements should arrive, an entirely new group of armies should be created, that the B.E.F. should thus be divided into two groups of armies, and that one of the two groups should take up some part of the Allied line away to the east and entirely separated from the other group. He wrote in his diary on August 16:

> I had a long talk with him about the French political position; I found him very sensible. He listened to all I had to say of dangers ahead, of the Caillaux and Valois group, of *dégommé* of Millerand being only a preliminary to attack upon Joffre, of the Valois and Caillaux group wanting in reality to make peace, of the absolute necessity of our doing nothing to upset the French soldiers, such as Sir John not putting his back into the forthcoming attack, etc. He told me he quite agreed and would speak to Sir John. A good day's work on Kitchener's part.

This appears in the diary on the 19th:

> Poor Kitchener was much down on his luck when going away at 7 o'c. Russia's loss of Kovno, and the coming loss of Brest, Novo Giorgevsk and Vilna has upset him. Then, 6 of our 18-prs have burst, apparently with the American ammunition. Finally the Dardanelles. Kitchener asked Haig, Gough and the others about conscription, and they all plumped for it.

On the following day Sir John offered Wilson command of a corps, telling him that Lord Kitchener and he both thought that the offer ought to be made, although they both hoped that it would not be accepted. Sir Henry wrote in his diary that evening:

> Sir John was very nice; he said that he wanted to show his gratitude for all I had done. "I never would have got through the retreat without you, Henry, what with Murray fainting, and everything

> going wrong. You alone were always laughing and cheery, and I shall never forget it." We discussed my acceptance, and in the end I refused because (*a*) both he and Kitchener were anxious for me to remain on as now, and (*b*) because I thought it was hard luck on some divisional commander. I think I did what was right and fair.

A meeting was held at Chantilly on the 22nd, and at this Sir John promised to take part in the co min g offensive with all available troops, the date for its commencement being provisionally fixed as September 8. Wilson was now hearing from various sources at home, inside and outside of the War Office, that the prospects of conscription being introduced were becoming promising, and he was greatly heartened by this intelligence. Ammunition was, moreover, at last coming in in fair quantities, thanks to the greatly increased plant for turning it out that was becoming available. But he learnt, on the other hand, that the 4th New Army, which Lord Kitchener had promised to send to France in the coming November, was likely to be broken up to supply drafts.* It may be mentioned that in August three divisions of the 1st New Army and five of the 2nd New Army were already included in the B.E.F.; a Guards Division was also formed during the month; two divisions of the 3rd New Army, moreover, arrived at the very end of the month. This brought the total number under Sir J. French's command up to twenty-one divisions emanating from the United Kingdom, besides two Indian divisions and one Canadian division.

The position of the existing French Government was becoming somewhat precarious at this time, and M. Millerand, in particular, was being subjected to much criticism, M. Caillaux's sinister influence making itself appreciably felt. Wilson feared that an effort might be made to displace General Joffre, who, in spite of the virtual failure of the various offensives that had been tried since the beginning of the year, retained the confidence of the

* The original 4th New Army had already been broken up. The promised 4th New Army was the original 5th New Army, composed of the divisions numbered from 36 to 41. Three of its divisions arrived in France during the autumn, the remaining three arrived in 1916.

French troops as well as of their commanders. General Sarrail, a soldier with a political following of whom the French Government were somewhat afraid, had just been appointed to the command of the French troops at the Dardanelles, which post appeared to ensure that he would depart out of the country. But Sarrail remained on in Paris, and the effect of his presence only too speedily made itself felt.

Wilson mentions in his diary on September 2 being shown a letter from Lord Kitchener to Sir John, intimating that the French Government had decided to send four divisions to the Ægean, and stating that our ally's troops engaged on the Dardanelles undertaking would henceforward operate on the Asiatic side of the Straits. Kitchener now proposed that two divisions from the B.E.F. should also be transferred to that theatre of war. "This is all appalling," was Wilson's comment. But, on his getting promptly into communication with Chantilly, he was reassured by intelligence that there was no question of sending additional French troops out to the Near East at the present time. Sir John was ill at the moment; but a wire was drafted by Robertson and Wilson to Lord Kitchener acquainting him that no further French troops were going to the Dardanelles and that the question of sending off two divisions of the B.E.F. did not therefore arise. Sir Henry proceeded to Chantilly next morning, and he was there apprised of the real facts. The account appearing in his diary of what he learnt runs as follows:

> The story is this. Sarrail, who has not yet left Paris, persuaded the Government to go in for an enlarged set of operations. The Government seem to have agreed, and to have approached our Government, who, of course, were fools enough to concur. Hence Kitchener's letter. Pellé showed me a letter from Cambon to Delcassé, in which it was suggested that Joffre should tell Sir John that he was to send two divisions down to Dardanelles.
>
> By the way, Joffre went down to Italy last night to see Cadorna and discuss operations, and incidentally to tell him on no account to send men to Dardanelles. Pellé went on to tell us that the whole movement was brought about by Sarrail, who, although appointed to command in Dardanelles, has never left Paris. It was he who, wishing to have a larger command than two divisions, suggested three

> alternative plans to be carried out by six divisions. One was a landing at Bulair, and both the others were in Asia Minor. So the whole thing is political.
>
> Joffre went up the day before yesterday and saw the President and Ministers. He was inflexible about not sending any troops out till after the big attack (and as this has been put back to the 25th it probably solves the problem, owing to October winds down there), and when the result of that attack is known, he said he might consider the thing again. Meanwhile he examined Sarrail's proposals and found them so sketchy, with no definite objective and therefore no knowledge of the force to be employed, that he said he thought they were quite useless, and that the best thing Sarrail could do would be to go out at once and to study the problem on the spot! This gets rid of Sarrail rather neatly. So the whole thing falls down, and the wire which Robertson and I sent Kitchener yesterday did admirably.

On September 7 this entry appears:

> At 5 o'c. got a long wire from Kitchener ordering me to go and see Joffre or Millerand, and find out exactly about these four divisions and the Dardanelles, and that "no opinion of any kind must be expressed or suggested by you as to the wisdom or otherwise of whatever military policy may be adopted." After all this I am to go and report to Kitchener. Rather amuses me.

Wilson went with Huguet on the 9th to see Joffre, who had temporarily scotched the plan of sending the French divisions to the Ægean, but had not crushed it. The project was merely postponed until after the offensive that was to take place on the Western Front. Wilson and Huguet afterwards went on to Paris and had an interview with M. Millerand, from whom they learnt that a meeting had been arranged to take place at Calais two days later between Millerand, Kitchener, Joffre, Sarrail and Sir John. Wilson remarks in the diary:

> This is hot stuff. Joffre told me that Sarrail had not yet left Paris, and that only a staff officer had been sent to work out the details of the plan, and yet, here is Sarrail, sitting next to Joffre, to urge a plan about which he knows nothing. And all because he is a Radical-Socialist. Hot stuff. Joffre told me that the Grand Duke Nicholas was

dégommé and sent to the Caucasus, and that the Tsar has taken command. He also told me that Cadorna would not send "one single man" to the Dardanelles, and that his ammunition was already running short, so that an Italian offensive could not start till a week or ten days later than ours!

Sir John had gone over to England just before this. Wilson, therefore, also crossed the Channel so as to discuss matters with his Chief and with Lord Kitchener before the meeting at Calais, and he had long talks with both of them in England. Kitchener told him that Sir John was being freely quoted by Mr. Asquith as being opposed to compulsion, and also that the Government (Wilson thought that Kitchener meant himself) felt so strongly about the Dardanelles that they would send out all the troops themselves in the event of the French abandoning their intention of contributing further divisions. Wilson adds in his diary:

The gist of the talk was this: That the French Government had asked for transports for September 24 to take 4 divisions to the Dardanelles. That we had hired them and "upset the trade of the world." That in a letter dated September 2 (which he showed me) we (British Government) had cordially approved of this new move and said we would send our quota of two divisions to relieve the two French divisions at Helles, and that no doubt this would affect the coming operations in France. No one up to this point seems to have bothered about Joffre. Then came his intervention, and, of course, cessation till after our big attack. I explained to Kitchener that in my judgment the whole thing was political and Sarrail.

Kitchener's attitude is that we *can't* get out of the Dardanelles without an appalling disaster there and all over the East, without some success. He favours the French sending four divisions, and he will send four also from our line! But not till after the coming big attack. I asked him if he proposed to go to Constantinople, and he said, "By God, no. By God, no! I have been let into the thing, and never again. Out I come the first moment I can." I must say I do not agree, and I said so. I don't think there would be disasters, and I feel that the deeper we get into the place the more impossible it will be to get out. And I said all this, but Kitchener would not agree. He realizes that it is bleeding him white, and he dreads the whole thing, but he favours further operations, ending in success, i.e. clearing the Gallipoli, and then withdrawal. I don't believe this is possible.

Wilson's account of the meeting at Calais on September 11 runs as follows:

> We had our meeting this morning. Lord Kitchener (chair), Millerand, Sir John and I on his right, Joffre, Sarrail and Hankey on his left. The result of much talk (2½ hours) was this. That Joffre and Sir John agreed to send 4 French and 2 British divisions to Dardanelles if and when the great attack failed. No date could be fixed, but somewhere about October 8th-10th was imagined.
>
> Joffre was wholly and strongly against the whole thing. He said there was no proper plan, it was a pig in a poke, it would exhaust France and thus endanger her, and it would achieve no results. Sir John was inclined towards Foch [Joffre?] but said little. Kitchener's one idea is to get out of the mess he is in, and he said so specifically, and that there was now no intention of going to Constantinople. Sarrail's one intention is to get a big command — and succeed Joffre! Millerand is afraid of Sarrail and so played the latter's game. That was the salad.
>
> At the end, Millerand drafted instructions putting Johnnie Hamilton under Sarrail. This opened Kitchener's eyes, and he was very curt and settled that question at once. Now, the whole thing falls down by itself, because it will be impossible for Sarrail to land with six divisions before the end of November or beginning of December, and the weather will decide the question then.
>
> After lunch, Kitchener made me take him for a drive in my Rolls-Royce, and we talked for 2 hours. His one idea is to get out of the hole he is in, and he will withdraw the moment he can do so without disaster, i.e. directly he can draw a line across the Peninsula and thus secure his re-embarkation. He does not even care whether the ships get up to Constantinople. He thinks the Gallipoli Peninsula will give him the waterway. I don't, and said so. But, as his only object is to withdraw, I told him that I thought Sarrail should land at Suvla and not on the Asia Minor side; then we might draw a line across and get out. It is a vile and dangerous mess. Kitchener was more than nice to me.
>
> Now, what I saw at this meeting was this. Three ideas: 1. Joffre, fine soldier, great patriot with a single eye to the safety of France, fighting the others for her safety and honour, deeply, terribly impressed with the danger to her life if a false step is taken; 2. Lord Kitchener, concerned chiefly in getting himself out of a vile hole he allowed himself to be put into by Winston; 3. Millerand and Sarrail,

purely politician. They don't care for Kitchener's difficulties, they know that six divisions cannot do anything great, they took no notice of Kitchener's exclamation that all that he wanted troops for was to extricate himself; no, purely politicians. Sarrail represents the Radical-Socialists, and Millerand represents Sarrail. A curious salad. I never admired General Joffre so much. A fine, a very fine old man.

An important conference was held at Chantilly on September 14, at which the three Army Group Commanders, Dubail, de Castelnau and Foch, attended, together with Sir John, Robertson and Wilson. Joffre described his plans fully for the great offensive that was shortly to be launched, and the date of commencement of this was finally fixed as the 25th. Wilson afterwards had a conversation with Joffre about the Dardanelles, and was disappointed to find that the French Commander-in-Chief, while entirely opposed to sending out any more troops to that theatre of war, thought that the forces in the Peninsula ought to dig themselves in and to remain where they were. A few days later Sir Henry, while in Paris, met General Gouraud, who had recently returned from the Dardanelles (where he had been in command of the French troops) in consequence of a very severe wound sustained at Helles. Gouraud held the same view as Joffre as to the troops remaining on the Peninsula; but he expressed the opinion that, so long as the garrison was only to be required to maintain a defensive attitude, it was needlessly large. Wilson wrote in his diary:

He was very severe in his comments on those responsible for the whole enterprise, which he considers disastrous, on whoever ordered the landing at Cape Helles, and lastly very critical of General Sarrail who, although given a command out there, is not going to see things for himself.

Sir John was somewhat indisposed just at this time, and his illness caused a certain amount of inconvenience, in view of the preparations that had to be set on foot for assuming the offensive on the 25th. He had, however, recovered by the 20th, on which day Lord Kitchener arrived at St. Omer, when Wilson was at once sent for. He wrote in his diary:

We discussed Kitchener's meeting with Joffre, which later on I fixed at 5 p.m., at Monro's H.Q. Saw Kitchener again at 6.30 and had a good talk with him about Dardanelles, and I think made some impression on him as regards Gouraud's plans of holding on, but reducing garrison considerably. He said he did not think our Cabinet, and especially Asquith, would agree. Good Lord 1 He is anxious about the result of the coming battle, and said a failure would be very bad both at home and in Russia, where things were not going well. Kitchener showed me a long wire from Johnnie Hamilton. It was his considered opinion of what to do with six French divisions if they went down to the Dardanelles. Kitchener is going to show this to Joffre to-morrow, Huguet and I having translated it. What Joffre will think, I know well.

Kitchener says that if our great battle here is not a success, and if the French refuse to send four divisions to Dardanelles (and I hope they will), it would create a bad impression on our Cabinet! Our Cabinet!

Early on the morning of the 25th that prolonged and costly offensive, which is generally spoken of in this country as the Battle of Loos, was at last set in motion. An attack on a great scale under de Castelnau was launched simultaneously in Champagne. The British troops started in highly promising style, for they gained ground almost all along the whole of their front of attack and they secured possession of a number of important tactical points. The French on their right, on the other hand, made very little progress this first day. The fighting continued on the 26th; but, while the French pushed their line forward at several points, the British divisions to their left were hard put to it to maintain their grip upon the ground which they had made good on the previous day. For the Germans had brought up substantial reinforcements, and they were carrying out resolute counter-attacks to recover what had been lost. Fighting continued on the 27th and 28th, and then, on the night of the 28th-29th, the French made a notable gain of ground — as Sir Henry, who had been disappointed at the results hitherto achieved in the northern sector, records in his diary with an exultation which as it t urn ed out was not altogether justified by the event.

Last night the French took Hills 119 and 140. This is splendid. Foch has been aiming for those heights since March, and the Dame de

> Lorette fighting, and that of May 9 and June 16 and the present battle, have all been for this object. It has cost the French at least 250,000 men since the beginning. Later in the day we heard that Castelnau had broken the line in Champagne with three divisions, but we have no details so cannot judge the value. But all this is very good.

The triumph proved, however, to be not nearly so pronounced as Wilson had at first supposed. "Hill 140" was the famous Vimy Ridge; but this height had not by any means been captured. The French had only gained a footing - on its near slopes which, as Sir Henry himself was to find some months later, was far from easy to maintain Nor, although tactical success could be claimed by de Castelnau, had the German line in Champagne been effectually broken, or even driven in to any great extent. The great autumn offensive, about the results of which the French and also Wilson had been very sanguine, had, in fact, by the end of September accomplished far less than had been anticipated. The operations were, however, still in progress, and there seemed to be at least a possibility that something really important might even yet be achieved.

Chapter XV – 1915: October to December

Allied troops sent to Salonika — Disappointing results of the offensive on the Western Front — Wilson summoned to London — Talks with Kitchener and Bonar Law — His anxiety as to the Greek attitude — Joffre's visit to London and its results — The Salonika imbroglio — Question of quitting the Dardanelles — Resignation of Sir J. French — Wilson quits G.H.Q.

The British and French Governments found difficulties to be gathering thick at the beginning of October, and they were especially concerned with regard to the position of Serbia. That little kingdom, which had hitherto opposed a successful resistance to the efforts of the Dual Monarchy to crush it, was evidently about to be invaded by formidable Austro-German hosts, and there, moreover, appeared to be every prospect of Bulgaria seizing the opportunity to wipe out old scores with her rival of 1913. A decision was therefore arrived at to dispatch one British and one French division from the Gallipoli Peninsula to Salonika, and advance parties from the two divisions began to land at that port on the 5th. This, as had been foreseen in London and Paris, created a somewhat irregular situation, seeing that Salonika was situated in Greek, and therefore in neutral, territory. Although disposed at the outset to deprecate the Allies thus becoming committed to a new oversea undertaking, Wilson comforted himself with the reflection that the troops to take part in it were coming from the Dardanelles. He wrote to Lady Wilson on the 7th:

The whole of the Salonika business is political, and as usual the fools at home, Asquith, Grey, K., have been taken in. If they have a very modest modicum of brains they will jump at the chance of transferring our troops from Gallipoli to Salonika. Much as I hate the idea of Salonika, I prefer it infinitely to Gallipoli.

On the following day Kitchener had an interview with Joffre at Chantilly, the results of which Wilson learnt from Clive.

It appears that, much against Joffre' s wishes, another expedition is to be undertaken, now to Salonika, the French sending one division from Helles and three from Joffre, and we sending one from Suvla (10th) and three from here, i.e. eight divisions, of which six from here. This will mean a total of twenty divisions in the Near East. We have already lost 130,000 in Gallipoli, the equivalent of 10 divisions, so the amateur strategists have cost us 30 divisions — and not one Boche. A good detachment!

Two letters that he received from the War Office on October 12 he also found very confusing. He wrote in the diary:

They accuse the French and Joffre of having let us in over Salonika, and both of them declare categorically that we are not going to send a man there, that, so long as the offensive here lasts, no troops will be withdrawn, but if any troops are taken away they will be sent to the Dardanelles. In no circumstances to Salonika. Now the whole thing is in a muddle, and these old men — Kitchener, Joffre, Delcassé, Grey, etc. — have made a proper pie. I quite believe that Sarrail and Delcassé pushed the Salonika idea, but why did we fall in with it, and promise troops, and then, apparently, back out? My fear that we would go to the Dardanelles with more troops, and that the French would send an expedition to Salonika, looks like coming true.

Wilson, in consequence of this, decided to pay Joffre a visit on the 13th, and he spent some time with the French Commander-in-Chief, talking the whole situation over. Of what transpired he wrote the following account on getting back to Amiens that night:

The French under Delcassé, and we, agreed to send 150,000 to Salonika if the Greeks mobilized and came in. The Greeks mobilized, but have not come in. Thereupon Venizelos fell off his perch. Joffre is in favour of sending the 150,000; we are backing out. Viviani made a speech last night, saying the French and English were in perfect accord and had settled everything. It may be so, but information from Callwell and Percy is quite different. Joffre is in favour of sending 150,000 to Salonika, because he thinks this force could hold the railway to Uskub, would thus keep open communications with the Serbs, and would thereby keep the Serbs on their legs. He estimates Boche and Austrian forces at 150,000, Bulgars, 350,000, and Serbs, 250,000; and he thinks that our 150,000 would save the situation. If the Serbs are knocked out, he sees the Boche and the Bulgar at Salonika. He can only send two divisions and one cavalry division, but he has no objection to three of our divisions going from here, as they will be replaced so soon by Kitchener's 4th Army, though he thinks we could, and ought to, get all the troops we want from Gallipoli, which he detests.

I told him I had grave reasons for thinking that we were not going to send a man to Salonika, and that if we sent anybody anywhere it would be to Gallipoli. He said our strategists were fools. I told him I cordially agreed with him.

This appears in the diary next day (October 14):

We went to Frévent 9.30 a.m., to see Foch and tell him all our gossip, which he loves. Back at 1 o'clock, to find an amazing post. It appears now that our people at home have decided not to send a man to Salonika (the 10th Division is on its way there) in spite of Viviani's declaration of the night before last. Not only that, but we are sending a large force from here to Egypt! To be used how, where and when the Cabinet may decide later! Of course, this simply beggars imagination, especially when I understand that probable destination is to be Gallipoli.

At 6 o'c. I went down to see Sir John, and he then showed me the General Staff minute on the whole position, ending with two weak paragraphs giving the whole position away.* He showed me a letter,

* The Cabinet had been bringing pressure to bear upon Lord Kitchener to restore the Genetal Staff at the War Office to the position that it was supposed to hold, and that it had held prior to the outbreak of war. Sir A. Murray had, therefore, at the end of September, become C.I.G.S., and he, with his assistants, was being called upon for considered views on questions such as that which was agitating the

just received, ordering him to pull out two corps (six divisions) and the Indian Corps, and prepare to send them to Marseilles, then to Egypt, ultimate destination to be decided later, their places in the line to be taken over by the French. Lord! How I laughed!

I then told Sir John of my long talk with Joffre last night, and said that I would send Joffre a wire to say that we had been ordered to pull out eight divisions to go to Egypt, and when would he relieve? This I did, and we shall see the answer to-morrow. Now what did Viviani mean when he said the night before last that we had agreed on the number of troops we would send to Salonika, etc.? The result of all this business is that Delcassé has resigned and that the whole Government is rocking. Viviani succeeds Delcassé.

I wrote a long letter describing Joffre's position, and how I agreed with him as regards the necessity of saving Serbia, and that this must be done by the Gallipoli troops — their withdrawal, incidentally, saving a disaster, saving Serbia, saving Salonika from the Boche, saving the Greeks from joining the Boche, saving the Near East in fact. Pointing out that it is time we stopped paying any attention to Grey, Kitchener, Asquith, etc., as they have *always* been wrong.

Joffre's reply to Wilson's wire came to hand on the following day, and it was to the effect that he regretted having no troops to spare to relieve eight divisions of the B.E.F. which it was proposed to dispatch to. Egypt, and that, so far from reducing the strength of the B.E.F., he thought that it would be well if this continued its offensive. "Now," remarks Wilson in his diary, "the whole inane scheme of sending eight divisions to Egypt falls to the ground," and Sir John hastened to sign a rejoinder to the War Office intimating that, as the French could not relieve the divisions, the divisions could not be spared. It must be understood that during this first half of October the offensives had been proceeding in Champagne and about Arras, but the operations were dying down. The object striven for — breaking the enemy's line — had failed at all points and heavy losses had been sustained.

That the home Government was beginning to consider the expediency of withdrawing from the Gallipoli Peninsula seriously

---

British and French Governments.

was made evident at this time by the recall of Sir I. Hamilton, and by the dispatch of General Monro (whose place at the head of the Third Army in France was taken by General Allenby) to take over charge of the Dardanelles operations. Bulgaria embarked on hostilities against the Serbs on October 11, and the Hellenic Government on the following day acquainted that of Serbia that the Greco-Serbian treaty of 1913 was considered at Athens to be purely of a Balkan character, that this pact did not cover the contingency of Serbia being attacked by Germany and the Dual Monarchy, and that Greece was not in consequence proposing to take up arms. This made the position of the Allied troops ashore at Salonika all the more unsatisfactory. Hostile forces were now pouring into Serbia from the north in overwhelming strength, and the flank attack from the side of Bulgaria placed the Serb army in an almost impossible position, so that the situation of the sorely tried kingdom was becoming extremely critical, while the French and British troops at Salonika could afford it no effective aid.

A meeting was held at Chantilly on the 19th in consequence of Sir John, who had been over to London, having been charged by the British Government to arrange with the French for the relief of two divisions of the B.E.F., which would then be dispatched to Salonika. This was agreed to by the French Commander-in-Chief.

Certain of the Unionist members of the Cabinet had hoped that Wilson would have been appointed C.I.G.S. at the time when Sir A. Murray was called upon to take up the appointment early in October, and the question must assuredly have been seriously considered. Mr. Asquith and the Liberal side of the Cabinet probably objected; but it is a reasonable assumption that Lord Kitchener also may not have favoured the idea of Sir Henry assuming the position of First Military Member of the Army Council. Kitchener had for some months past been finding Wilson extremely useful, and had undoubtedly been giving ear to his counsels; but a very sharp divergence of view existed between the two soldiers as regards what was at the moment the most pressing subject for consideration — the question of the Dardanelles campaign. Sir Henry had, in their numerous discussions, always insisted upon the need of abandoning that ill-starred enterprise. Kitchener, on the other hand, was opposed to withdrawal from the

Gallipoli Peninsula, partly because he dreaded the effect which such an admission of failure might exercise in Egypt, India and the East in general, and partly because he felt persuaded that an evacuation could not be carried out without incurring something at least approaching to a military disaster. That the Secretary of State, however, set store by Wilson's opinions is made manifest by the fact that the latter was called upon by a message from Kitchener to cross the Channel again on the 20th, and that they had prolonged conversations that evening and again on the following day. The following entry, in respect to these, appears in Wilson's diary on October 21:

> Kitchener is frightened of Egypt, of India, of Mesopotamia, of going on with the Dardanelles, of coming away, of going to Salonika, of not going. He has no plan of any sort. I insisted on making Greece declare one way or the other by threatening to bombard Athens and all coast towns. He was frightened of that. I saw Monro, who starts for the Levant to-morrow to take Johnnie Hamilton's place. Monro is very unhappy about his job. Carson came to see me after lunch and told me the whole story of his resignation. Absolute chaos and indecision reign in the Cabinet, all due to Asquith who has now gone to bed to gain some more time.
>
> Bonar breakfasted with me. I put the Greek case to him,, as I saw it. It was impossible for us to go to Serbia unless our base and line of communications were secure. We could not know this without forcing the Greeks to show their hand; therefore Tino, who had asked us (through Venizelos) to come to his assistance and then broken his word, who had also broken his word with the Serbs, must now be forced to decide for or against. He seemed rather horrified; but as a matter of fact he came in again at 7.30 p.m. and showed me a paper he had written, which was printed, and which he read at the Cabinet this afternoon, exposing my ideas. He told me that he had then said that a Cabinet of 22 was quite incapable of dealing with such a matter, and that he proposed that a small Cabinet of 5 should take over the show, the small Cabinet being the Prime Minister, War Office, Admiralty, Foreign Office and Munitions. To this. Cabinet agreed, and Crewe (who was in the chair) was deputed to inform Asquith. I wonder what Asquith will do? Bonar Law also showed me another capital paper he had written in favour of the evacuation of the Dardanelles. I was pleased with Bonar Law, and told him so, and then advised him at to-morrow's Cabinet to do another thing, namely to get

the British and French Governments to agree never to plunge into these ridiculous ventures like Antwerp, Dardanelles, Asia Minor, or Salonika, until the problem had been thoroughly discussed at a meeting of six men — the two Foreign Ministers, the two War Ministers and the two C. in C.s* Bonar Law thought this an excellent idea and said he would bring it forward. I rubbed into him again the fact that at the moment we had absolutely no plan of any sort for all this trouble in the South East.

After his return to the front. Sir Henry saw General Joffre at Chantilly on the 24th, to whom he put three points: 1. Would he "take the King of Greece by the throat," so as to make Salonika secure before there was an advance to Uskub? 2. Did he approve of the plan of six men examining all problems before embarking on oversea ventures? 3. Was he prepared to relieve any British divisions if Lord Kitchener wanted to withdraw them for the Near East? Joffre promised support as regards the first two points and declared that he was not prepared to relieve any British divisions under the circumstances suggested. "He was tired and worried and disgusted with our want of a definite plan," Wilson wrote of their interview in his diary. Sir J. French had been summoned to London, and he came back on the 28th — so Wilson wrote in his diary that night:

His story is this. He was in front of a so-called War Council yesterday, which, however, developed into a full Cabinet. It is evident he was much heckled, and, as far as I can see, gave in to the proposal to send 6 divisions to Egypt. What for he does not know! It appears also that Kitchener's 4th Army is promised here, so I suppose we shall get it next month and in December. Well then, this precious War Council decided that the two General Staffs, ours and the French, should meet and discuss what should be done in the Orient. Sir John declared that he did not know what they were to discuss; but Percy, who came to see me off at Victoria, told me it was the complete abandonment of Serbia and Salonika, possibly of Gallipoli, and then

* This was the germ of the idea which during the coming two years Wilson developed into his plan for a Supreme War Council, as was set up at Rapallo in November, 1917.

vague plans for future operations in the East. Now, what becomes of Monro who went out only last Thursday to give advice on these very points? By Jove, our Cabinet is the limit. Sir John told me that Kitchener told him how Asquith got ill at the Cabinet last Tuesday. The previous afternoon Asquith had promised Kitchener to announce to the Cabinet that we must have conscription. Sir John appears to have been severely pushed about by the Cabinet, and the Lord knows what he agreed to.

Sir John got a telephone message to say that Millerand had resigned, Galliéni replacing him, Briand to be Foreign Minister, and a crisis in the French Cabinet.

The meeting of the General Staffs, so called, took place at Chantilly on October 28, Sir A. Murray having crossed for the purpose, and Sir John, with Robertson and Wilson, being present. Wilson wrote in his diary:

> It is clear that this meeting can do no good, as poor Murray has come out simply to show port and rail difficulties. No plan; nothing. I had 10 minutes with Joffre before the meeting to warn him that it was only a talk on difficulties. Murray and Joffre differed about port possibilities of Salonika, the railway facilities inland, the hostility of Macedonia, the immobility of our troops, the trip to Egypt and rest, and the necessity for prompt action.

Joffre at this meeting maintained that Venizelos was working for us, that Cadorna had promised Italian help, and that there were great hopes of bringing in Rumania; and he finally proposed that all the troops from Gallipoli should be moved to Salonika and that steps should be taken to compel the Greeks to declare themselves. Sir John agreed, and Joffre intimated his intention of going over to London next day and of expressing his views to H.M. Government. Wilson entered in his diary next day:

> I saw Sir John in the morning and again at 7 o'c., and I put a problem to him then. If we don't take strong action against Tino, both by the Fleet and by heaping up troops at Salonika, he will certainly join the Boche, and he will do it in this way: He will say to us and the French, "Look here. This benevolent neutrality is going to get me into an infernal hole. I protested against your landing at all, but you would

> do it. Now I must ask you to stop and to take your troops out of Greece either into Serbia or back to your ships. I will give you 10 days to complete this business, after which anyone left behind in Greece will have to lay down his arms and be interned." What should we do? There are now two French divisions landed and gone up the line, and we have one division. Obviously we can't fight the Greek army.
>
> Now compare that with taking Tino by the throat and, with Venizelos's assistance, getting the Greeks on our side, followed by Russia snaffling Rumania. Now where are the Bulgars and all Boche intrigues? It is surely worth a try.
>
> At 10.30 p.m. came a wire as follows: "Cabinet has decided on urgent representation of Joffre to co-operate energetically with the French in opening and maintaining railway communication between Salonika and Uskub."

Wilson was pleased to learn this, although he remained anxious with regard to the attitude of Greece, and he wrote home to Lady Wilson:

> Old Père Joffre seems to have done wonders. Whether he got the Cabinet to agree to the *whole* programme he and I sketched out I don't know. If they carry out only half of it, it will lead to disaster. In my opinion it is *all* or nothing. We shall see.

Anyhow he galvanized the Cabinet into some life and action, the requisite orders were issued, and the military forces of the British Empire in consequence became definitely committed to the Macedonian venture, although neither H.M. Government nor yet British military authorities in general regarded it otherwise than with serious misgiving. Fortunately for the Allies, the Hellenic Government accepted the situation of French and British troops making Greek territory into a base of operations, and it maintained an attitude of more or less benevolent neutrality up to the time when, two years later, it converted this neutrality into active partnership with the Entente. Wilson, however, for the first few weeks feared that King Constantine's somewhat equivocal attitude would bring disaster upon the fighting forces which had been so unceremoniously planted down in his territory, and he continued to advocate the adoption of robust coercive measures as against that monarch. He insisted upon the imperative necessity of "taking Tino by the throat" in influential quarters on his crossing the Channel on November 1. But although he found a certain amount of concurrence in principle with the drastic policy that he was advocating, little inclination was displayed by his hearers for translating opinions into action. This appears in his diary on the 3rd:

> Gwynne came for me at Travellers, 4 p.m., and we went to Lloyd George. On the way he told me the amazing news that Kitchener and Johnnie French were both going to be *dégomméd*. He (Gwynne) had been commissioned to ask Kitchener which he would like: 1. C. in C. at home. 2. C. in C. France. 3. Viceroy India. Kitchener said he would fight. He seems to be going to France. Gwynne tells me Johnnie French is done. I suggested Kitchener going to Egypt and Johnnie remaining where he is. Gwynne rather liked the idea.
>
> Then we had an interview with Lloyd George. I told Lloyd George my alternatives, and impressed on him that if we did not take Tino by the throat he would play the neutral card and we were done. He understood, but did not think our Government would do it. I left Gwynne with Lloyd George and went to Bonar Law. I put my alternatives to Bonar Law. He told me Lloyd George was going to succeed Kitchener, but he did not tell me where Kitchener was going.

The truth was that Sir C. Monro's report, recommending the evacuation of the Gallipoli Peninsula, had arrived, but that the Government, instead of accepting the recommendation and cabling instructions to Monro to carry it out, had hit upon the expedient of deputing Lord Kitchener to proceed to the Ægean and to examine into, and report on, the situation. Whether in arriving at this comical decision the Government were actuated by their habitual inability to make up their minds, or by a disapproval of the policy advocated on the part of Monro, or by eagerness to snatch at an opportunity for getting rid of Lord Kitchener, is not apparent. All. three factors probably assisted to bring about the result, which was that, although winter was fast approaching, bringing with it the likelihood of rough weather in the Aegean, no orders for withdrawing from the Peninsula were sent to Monro for a period of five weeks. Wilson heard of this on November 5, and he thereupon wrote in his diary:

> I went to see Bonar Law at Colonial Office. It appears that at yesterday's Cabinet it was settled that Kitchener should be sent out to report. Hence his departure at 8 p.m. last night. On reflection, Bonar Law came to the conclusion that this last attempt to "wait and see" was too much. So he has written, and sent, a letter to Prime Minister to say that he could not agree to this further postponement, and he therefore wished a Cabinet assembled and a decision to retire from Gallipoli at once come to, failing which he could no longer remain. He showed me a copy of the letter. This will help to bring matters to a crisis.

On the 7th he wrote:

> Lunch with Bonar Law. Then a long talk with him about whether he should resign to-morrow. Austen came and was much opposed to it. He argues that Bonar Law will "cart" his colleagues and make them look ridiculous if he goes before Kitchener reports. It seems to me that Bonar Law's simple course is to say that he made a mistake when he agreed to let Kitchener go out, but that on reflection now he is clear that he must back Monro's opinion, and if the Cabinet don't agree with him, then he must go.
>
> We dined with the Austens, Edward Grey the only other. After dinner I went bald-headed for the vital necessity of bringing in Greece before marching into Serbia, and the madness of the adventure from a base which is not secure. To my astonishment later on when I pressed on Grey my Committee of Six, he objected to the two Foreign Ministers dictating to the soldiers and said that the soldiers should dictate to the Foreign Offices. I pushed Grey about the Committee of Six, and it was as a result of this attack that he said he wanted soldiers a the top, and he said he had already submitted proposals to Cambon. Both he and Austen were loud in saying that this Salonika business was Joffre's fault, but they were wrong in dates and in facts.

Next day he wrote:

> Bonar Law rang me up and asked me to go to his house. He showed me a long dispatch from Bertie in which Kitchener's visit and interviews with Briand, Joffre, Galliéni and Lacaze [the Minister of Marine] was described, clearly showing that Kitchener had made up

his mind already to remain in Gallipoli (and Lacaze even said it was possible to force the Dardanelles by ships alone), and had already got Briand's and Joffre's concurrence. So it is now quite clear what Kitchener is going to report.

Bonar Law then read me a draft letter that he was writing to Asquith. He said he must adhere to his letter of Friday, that he fully realized that he was open to fair criticism for having agreed to send Kitchener on Thursday, then for changing again on Friday. But this was a small matter, and in substance he was so opposed to the Dardanelles that he could not agree to remain there. All this made it impossible for him to stop in the Cabinet. Bonar Law asked me if I approved. I did, and said so. I also advised him to draw Austen's attention to Bertie's dispatch, as showing in clearest manner that Kitchener was going to report in favour of Dardanelles, and that therefore Austen had better get out before the report came in.

At 6 p.m. Bonar Law telephoned to me to say that he was not sending his letter, as both Carson and Edmund Talbot said he would smash the Unionist Party if he did.

On November 9 the entry appears:

At 9.30 Edmund Talbot, Bonar Law and Walter Long came in. We talked for 2 hours. I made the position, as I see it, as clear as I could, viz. that we had not sufficient troops, and never will have, to engage in operations at Salonika and on Gallipoli. We cannot go away from Salonika owing to our arrangement with the French, but we can leave Gallipoli whenever we like, and Monro advises it. Now if we go on with the two operations we shall have two disasters; but if we empty Gallipoli into Salonika we save a Gallipoli disaster, we save a Salonika disaster, we bring in the Greeks and possibly even the Rumanians. The one difficulty to this course is Kitchener who, without waiting till he gets to Mudros to report, has already in Paris committed our Government to remain in Gallipoli, and, as far as he was able, has got French approval.*

All this time the Serbian forces were being pressed back

---

* In his "Life of Lord Kitchener," Sir G. Arthur writes, "Kitchener was obliged to stay two days in Paris; at a long interview at Chantilly he discussed anxiously with Joffre the recalcitrance of Greece, and learnt that the abandonment of Gallipoli would be to the French High Command a subject of 'poignant regret.'"

steadily by the vastly superior forces of the Central Powers and Bulgaria. Nish had fallen on the 5th, which opened up the line of railway from Belgrade through Bulgaria to Constantinople to the enemy, so that the Germans in due course would be able to push munitions through to the Turks for employment against the Allied force in the Gallipoli Peninsula. Sarrail was pushing French troops up the Vardar valley from Salonika. But, quite apart from the risk of the Greek Government raising difficulties, or its actually assuming a hostile attitude as Wilson feared, there were as yet insufficient Franco-British forces on the spot to afford the hard-pressed Serbs effectual aid. As to whether Greece was bound in honour and by treaty obligation to support Serbia in the situation which had actually arisen, neither the British nor yet the French Government were impartial judges. The Entente Powers were scarcely in a position to claim that they were the victorious side in the great contest, and King Constantine and his advisers had good grounds for doubting whether the interest of their country would be served by openly taking sides against the Central Powers. A reluctance to compel a small state to become a belligerent was in the circumstances at least excusable, however inconvenient from the purely soldier's point of view. Wilson's strongly expressed opinions on the question consequently found only modified favour in and around Downing Street. He wrote in his diary:

> I saw Arthur Nicolson this morning, but got little out of him, except that he is not in favour of clearing out of Gallipoli. Then I went to Archie Murray. He assures me that the four divisions will go to Salonika as fast as they can be sent, although he is much opposed to the whole thing. On the other hand, he is in favour of remaining on Gallipoli. I told him we would have two disasters unless we emptied Gallipoli into Salonika. He does not know whether Kitchener is War Minister or not. Marvellous state of affairs.
>
> At 6 p.m. I went to see Asquith at the House of Commons. We discussed the Salonika and Gallipoli situations. I told him I thought we were in for two disasters and that the only way of saving them was to empty Gallipoli into Salonika and bring in the Greeks. He did not seem to approve, but was full of criticism of the French, and how they dragged us into the Salonika business. I defended their action, but asked how Lord Kitchener had got Joffre to agree to our remaining in

Gallipoli, and I suggested that Kitchener had said we should lose both Egypt and India. Asquith said that Briand and Galliéni had said the French would lose Morocco, Algiers, etc. All these worthy old gentlemen — Kitchener, Briand, Galliéni — are equal fools in this respect. Asquith wants me to find out what is going on with Joffre, Galliéni, etc., and to write to him or to come and see him. He told me that Johnnie French had written suggesting that Robertson should come over and explain our position in France. Asquith said the whole Balkan business was like an opera bouffe; I hope it will play him off the stage. I told him that I had told Charlie Monro that he was bound to be *dégommé* in any case; because, if he reported in favour of evacuation, he would be up against Kitchener, and if in favour of staying on he would be in for a disaster.

Two days later Wilson learnt that after examining into conditions in the Ægean., Lord Kitchener had recommended evacuating the Gallipoli Peninsula, but that he now wanted to send an expeditionary force to Alexandretta. Sir Henry also learnt that the General Staff were entirely opposed to the latter project, and that the question of removing Sir J. French and replacing him by Sir D. Haig was under consideration of the Cabinet. He was much gratified by his being appointed Colonel of the Royal Irish Rifles, dating from November 11; and from that time forward he took a very keen interest in everything connected with his regiment. He returned to St. Omer on the 14th and on arrival there he had a long talk with Lord Esher (who was on a visit), especially with regard to Sir John's position. Wilson maintained that the only possible reasons that could be alleged for removing the Field-Marshal were that he had lost hie confidence of his troops, or else that the French could no longer work with him, and neither reason had any existence. Sir John was, as it happened, indisposed at the moment, and Sir Henry wrote in his diary on November 15:

At 10.30 I went up to Sir John at Blondecque. He was in bed, but better. Esher was in the room. Esher led off by saying that he had been suggesting to Sir John that he should draw up a paper showing that it was the detachments to Gallipoli and Salonika which had ruined our offensive power in the West, and that if this continued he could not remain responsible for the operations in this theatre. Sir John and Esher asked my opinion. I said that in the present condition of the Cabinet they would jump at this and ask him to resign, but that, if we could get Joffre to endorse Sir John's views, we had got the Cabinet fixed. This was much approved. We finally settled that Brindsley Fitzgerald should go over this afternoon and do the private letter business by word of mouth, while Sir John settled down to write the big dispatch, and I said I would take it down to Joffre to-morrow night. Sir John took the whole thing most awfully well.

Wilson proceeded to Chantilly next day with Sir John's letter, but he found that Joffre had been summoned to Paris to take part in a big conference between members of the British Government and the newly-constituted French one. So he followed to the capital. There he heard that the meeting had taken place and, when he saw Joffre in the evening, he found his old friend worried and indignant, as Galliéni's attitude at the meeting, backed by Briand, had been unpleasant. Wilson had previously seen Lloyd George and Robertson, and both of them had told him about the line that Galliéni had seemed inclined to take up, more or less thrusting Joffre on one side. He wrote in his diary:

I did all I could to impress Lloyd George with the danger of doing anything to upset Joffre, and we are going the right way to do it. I am profoundly dissatisfied with the whole of to-day's work. I spoke to Lloyd George about Sir John and Haig. Also spoke to Lloyd George about Haldane and Kitchener, and he was quite clear he would not have either of them in the Cabinet.

This appears in the diary on the 17th:

Got to Chantilly at 9.45. Spent an hour with Joffre. He told me that, as a consequence of my conversation yesterday, he had told Lloyd George last night that, in view of the fact that neither the English nor the French had troops available to relieve those now on Gallipoli, also in view of great sickness, also in view of possible arrival of more Boche guns, gas, etc., he was in favour of evacuation, and that steps should at once be taken to make the necessary arrangements.

I told Joffre that he was our only fixed point and that we must have no more meetings like yesterday's, which did an infinity of harm, exposing to each Government the ignorance and vacillation of the other, and in addition, owing to Galliéni's action, undermining Joffre's authority and position.

Sir John now anticipated that Robertson would take Murray's place at the War Office as C.I.G.S., and Wilson mentions a conversation which he had with his Chief, in which reference to this possibility was made by Sir John who, moreover, said, "If Robertson can only do that, then I want you to become C.G.S. here, and we shall beat the Boche. Would that suit you, Henry?"

During a conversation which he had with Joffre on November 26 Wilson urged the French Commander-in-Chief to advise clearing out of Salonika, and he also represented the vital importance of his "Committee of Six" being set up. Joffre agreed with regard to the second point, but he held that, so long as there remained any Serbian troops to be saved, the Allies must remain in Macedonia.

Wilson wrote in the diary on the 27th:

> Went out at 8 a.m. to see Foch at Dury and told him all my gossip. He is still in favour of Salonika and he does not seem able to visualize the position, which is curious. He impressed on me in the most earnest manner the necessity for England to stiffen France in her resolve to fight the war right out. It is dear that he is getting a little anxious and wants all the support we can give him. He repeated this several times. There are cursed peace proposals floating about again.

On his return to St. Omer from Dury, Sir Henry found that Sir John was crossing the Channel to England and that Lord Esher had arrived, and in the afternoon he learnt from Esher what had actually occurred. Sir John was to be asked by the Prime Minister to resign the command of the B.E.F. and to take up the appointment of Commander-in-Chief of the forces at home, and Esher had been deputed by Mr. Asquith to convey this information to Sir John. It had not apparently yet been definitely settled who was to take up command of the B.E.F., but the choice seemed to rest between Sir D. Haig and Sir W. Robertson. Wilson commented in his diary on the strangeness of the procedure that was being adopted in the matter, for Lord Kitchener, who was Secretary of State for War, was only returning from the Ægean to Paris on the following day, and the presumption, therefore, was that he had not been consulted. Sir John returned to St. Omer on December 3, and he had not then finally decided whether to resign or not. But he eventually did so on the 6th, having asked Wilson to become his Chief of the General Staff at home. Wilson wrote at St. Omer on December 1:

> Dined with Winston and Esher. Winston's open contempt and exposure of the Cabinet was quite refreshing. When passing through Paris, Kitchener said we must get out of both Salonika and Gallipoli, but he apparently wants to go to Alexandretta. Winston wants to get out of Salonika, but to reinforce Gallipoli and also clear the Asia Minor bank! I told Winston what I thought of all these idiotic schemes, and of him, and of Asquith. This "Cabinet of all the Indecisions," as I call it, will lose the war. They will certainly do their best.

A day or two later Wilson heard that General Joffre had been gazetted. Commander-in-Chief of all the French forces except those in the colonies; also that Briand and Viviani were going over to London to ask for 100,000 more men for Salonika, and, moreover, to intimate that if the request was not complied with, the Entente would be dangerously strained. But he, at the same time, received a message from M. Clemenceau to the effect that the Entente would not be imperilled as the two Ministers were going to allege, and that "The Tiger" was entirely opposed to further troops proceeding to the Near East. Wilson, thereupon wrote letters to Bonar Law and Carson reporting this, and he sent them over by Robertson who had been summoned to London by Lord Kitchener. The visit of Briand and Viviani was, however, deferred and it eventually did not take place. Instead of it, there assembled what Wilson calls a "mass meeting" at Calais on the 4th — Asquith, Balfour, Kitchener, Briand, Joffre, Galliéni, Murray, etc. — and, going up to Paris next day, he heard from Murray that as a result of the discussion that had taken place there was a prospect of withdrawal from Salonika. This visit of his to Paris was carried out on purpose to meet M. Clemenceau, and he wrote in the diary:

> I spent a most interesting hour with him. A real character and

personality — one of the few I have ever met. He was not over-anxious about the Entente, thought he could hold that up, thought that Briand was done when Salonika state of affairs came out, thought they might try Barthou, thought the real crux was the coming fight between him and Poincaré. He thought but little of Poincaré and thought he would have to resign, thought he himself could perhaps just manage a year of strain although he knew he was old and already "seriously ill," thought Joffre estimable as a "figure-head" and as "Buddha," but no use otherwise, and quoted many serious mistakes, chapter and verse. He thought in fact that both in England and France we must make a dean sweep if we wanted to win the war. He was very complimentary to Carson and Milner and said he had often heard of me from Milner and Leo Maxse.

Wilson wrote nest day (December 6):

Met Sir John between Chantilly and Creil and drove to Chantilly with him. He opened by saying that yesterday, on the advice of Walter Long, he sent in his unconditional resignation. I told Sir John I would send in my resignation to-day, but he asked me to wait and see what happened to his, and I agreed.

Then we had our big C. in C. meeting, Joffre in the chair. We settled down to business at once, and Joffre made out that the French would be ready in men, guns, ammunition, gas, etc., for the largest offensive of which they were capable by the middle of March. But we then got off on to Salonika, and there we remained arguing for and against on a subject which was supposed to have been decided last Saturday in favour of complete evacuation. Murray was against remaining, though he said we could defend Salonika. I think we cannot. But Joffre and the Russian and Serbian representatives were all the other way. My own opinion is that we can't remain without the active assistance of Greece. However the whole thing was pure waste of time, as no decision was reached — nor could a decision be reached as we had no Foreign Affairs people with us.

On the 8th there appears in the diary:

Principal thing to-day was that Joffre read our conclusions, which said roughly:

1. Main theatres are east and west, not south.
2. Decisions can only be reached in the main theatres.

3. Simultaneous action necessary, date to be fixed later.

4. All (except England) agree to remain in Salonika, and all agree to fortify it now.

5. All agree to clear out of Gallipoli.

6. Egypt to be defended by minimum of troops.

Some other discussion, and we broke up. Sir John, who had received a letter from Asquith just before the meeting, then asked me to clear the room and then tell Joffre that Asquith had created the post of C. in C. at home and offered it to him, and he had accepted. He did not yet know who his successor was. He then went off to Paris, and Huguet and I came back to St. Omer. Now all this means that I go too, and probably also Huguet. Sir John will be back here to-morrow and I will hand in my resignation, and, after I have said good-bye to Joffre, Castelnau and Foch I will go home.*

Lord Kitchener (who had resumed his duties at the War Office), Sir E. Grey and Robertson, however, now journeyed over to Paris, and, after prolonged discussions with M. Briand and Generals Joffre and Galliéni, they settled that the British troops should remain at Salonika after all, and that General Sarrail was to act as local Commander-in-Chief. The military situation out there was somewhat critical at the moment, for the French troops under Sarrail had got into difficulties, and the British 10th Division had suffered a reverse at the hands of the Bulgarians. But the arrival of French and British reinforcements restored the situation, and Wilson's fears with regard to the Allies remaining in this theatre of war unless the Greeks should declare in favour of the Entente were not justified by the sequel. He learnt from Paris that the French were well pleased at the conclusion that had been arrived at, that they, moreover, hoped to extract yet more troops out of us for Salonika, and he commented in his diary:

> If Kitchener and Grey did not make it quite clear that under no circumstances would any more troops be sent they ought to be shot, because if this whole position is not made perfectly clear now it will lead to further trouble later on.

---

* On this day, the 8th, orders were at last sent to General Monro to proceed with the evacuation of the Gallipoli Peninsula.

He had been given to understand that he was likely to be offered command of an Army Corps and had also learnt that Sir D. Haig was succeeding Sir J. French at the head of the B.E.F.

Having been summoned to London by the Prime Minister, he crossed on December 15, and he saw the announcement of Haig's appointment and of a peerage for Sir John in the paper next morning. After visiting Bonar Law and Sir John during the course of the day he had an interview with Mr. Asquith at Downing Street in the evening. He reports in the diary:

> Asquith was quite charming! He said that he realized that my position was changed with change of C. in C. and he proposed I should have a Corps. He was evidently anxious to please me, and on my saying "Yes," he said, "It is understood, then, you get a Corps." I went over much the same ground with him as I had with Bonar Law, and I thought he was bored! We discussed Robertson, and he was looking forward with amusement to the clash of Kitchener and Robertson. Thought it "very disagreeable to *dégommé* Murray, who had done excellent work in bringing the General Staff to life again," but "all personal considerations must be sunk in order that the war might be prosecuted, etc."

The entry closes with a particularly acid comment concerning the Prime Minister, and this appears in the diary next day:

> Kitchener telephoned for me at 10 a.m. He was very nice, said he had told the Prime Minister I was to have a Corps, but that it "would only be temporary pending something better." I said I was overwhelmed with everyone's kindness! He then told me that Castelnau was going out to Salonika, which was sure to mean a large force. This was the opposite to the decision reached at Chantilly. Could I help to get the French to talk sense? I said I was now in command of a Corps and could not go racing to Paris, etc. But he wished me to do so and to come back and report. I said that I would tell Haig, and then would go to Chantilly and Paris and talk to Clemenceau.

He returned to St. Omer next day and then learnt from Sir John that General Monro was to be brought home to take command of the First Army in Haig's place. Sir A. Murray replacing Monro in the Near East; Rawlinson was taking over the First Army as a temporary measure. Huguet and he accompanied Sir John and his personal staff to Paris on the 19th, visiting Foch on the way for Sir John to bid the commander of the French Left Army Group good-bye. Next day they lunched with Joffre at Chantilly, which gave Wilson the opportunity of discussing the Salonika question with the French Commander-in-Chief, who was confident of being able to hold the place with the five British and thr ee French divisions that were there or were about to arrive. On returning from Chantilly to Paris in the afternoon, he went to see Clemenceau and of this visit he wrote in his diary:

> The old man very well and very cordial. He is quite satisfied with the heart of France, and with the troops, and with the women of France, but not with the generals, from Joffre downwards, and if he gets power he v ill have a much younger set. He is, of course, profoundly dissatisfied with Salonika, and cannot understand why Poincaré stays there. He puts it down chiefly to Sarrail and his political influence. He was amused at Castelnau going out, none of the Ministers having been told. He was shocked at 20 heavy batteries going when we have not guns enough here. He said that the slightest reverse on our line would upset the Government for ever. He wants my Committee of Six, and suggests that it should be formed to go into the Salonika business and to determine a date on which we shall retire. He is quite happy about the Peace Party, and the only thing he seemed afraid of was gas, for which the French soldiers were not prepared.

On the day following, December 21, Wilson and Huguet accompanied Sir John and his personal staff on their way by train from Paris to Boulogne, where they- saw him off. "Guards of honour, etc., and rather sad after 18 months of war" — so Sir Henry wrote of the ceremonial that took place at the station, and of the enthusiastic send-off given to their departing Chief by swarms of officers and men who had gathered for the purpose on the jetty and at the pier-head. He then proceeded to St. Omer and there saw the new British Commander-in-Chief, from whom he learnt that he was to have the IVth Corps. Sir L. Kiggell, who was replacing Robertson, arrived at St. Omer in the evening, a number of other changes were taking place, and Wilson, who was now at last after a year and a half bidding adieu to G.H.Q., admits in his diary to wondering how this body would fare in their new guise. Of the value of his own services as one of its foremost members, first as Sub-Chief of the General Staff and afterwards as Principal Liaison Officer with the French, it seems difficult to speak too highly, and no one realized this more clearly and appreciatively than did the Chief whose departure he had witnessed that day at Boulogne. It will therefore not be out of place to close this chapter with the eloquent tribute which is paid to Henry Wilson by Lord French in his "1914":

> In those many weary, anxious days we passed together during my term of command in France, I cherish a most grateful remembrance of his sincere, loyal, and whole-hearted support. Of iron nerve and frame, nothing seemed to tire him. Having passed through the Staff College early in life with high honours, he was marked out for the most important staff work; and, after filling many minor positions with distinction, he became Commandant of the Staff College, where his great talents were employed in reforming and much improving that institution. His *magnum opus* in peace time was done when he was Director of Military Operations at the War Office during the four years preceding the war. His countrymen have never realized, and probably may never know, the vital importance and invaluable results of the work he did there, not only in regard to the share that he took in the preparation of the Expeditionary Force, but also in establishing those happy relations with the French Army which have proved of such help to Allied operations throughout the war.
>
> Fearing no man, it was the very essence of his nature to speak his mind openly on all occasions, and when the great Irish crisis in the spring of 1914 was at its height, he sided openly with his native Ulster. He accompanied me to France as Sub-Chief of the General Staff and, when Murray's health broke down in January, 1915, I selected Wilson as his successor; but owing to his candid expression of opinion in the Irish imbroglio, he had many enemies, and his appointment was vetoed. It was this bad luck alone which prevented his valuable services then being used for his country's benefit in the best direction, and in a position for which he was better qualified than anyone else.

Chapter XVI – 1916: In Command of the IVth Army Corps

The Corps — Wilson's lectures — His temporary command of the First Army — The Corps loses some ground on the Vimy Ridge — Commencement of the Battle of the Somme — Wilson directed to prepare for an attack on the Vimy Ridge — IVth Corps Head-quarters shifted farther south — Wilson and the Government Crisis — Learns that he is to go on mission to Russia.

The IVth Army Corps, when Wilson took over the command from Rawlinson on December 22, 1915, was in the line to the south of Béthune and it consisted at the time of four divisions, the 1st, 15 th, 16th and 47th, making up a force of about 70,000 of all ranks. Brigadier-General (now Lieutenant-General Sir A.) Montgomery was B.G.G.S. and Brigadier-General W. L. White was in charge of the staff on the administrative side. Corps head-quarters were at a village called Labussière, to the south-west of Béthune. The troops that were in the front line were holding the ground near the Hohenzollem Redoubt and Loos, with stretches on either side; this had been the scene of the fighting of the First Army in the previous September, 'when a certain amount of ground had been gained by it between La Bassée and Lens. The enemy at the moment was comparatively quiet; but mining and counter-mining were in progress, which demanded the utmost vigilance in the trenches.

Wilson drove in to St. Omer on the last day of the year to be present at a farewell dinner given by his old mess to Huguet, who was about to take over a command. He wrote in his diary:

Huguet made a charming little speech, and when I was going away kissed me on both cheeks. I part from 1915 with no regret. To me, personally, it has been an unkind year, commencing with the offer by Sir John of C.G.S. and Asquith's refusal to allow, finishing with Robertson getting C.I.G.S., which at one time it looked as though I was certain to get, either when Murray got it or, later, before Robertson got it. On the other hand, the command of a Corps of four divisions is a fine command and I shall enjoy it immensely. The year as regards the war has been equally disappointing. Two great offensives on our part — May and September — both failed to break the line. In addition we have had the disgraceful affair of Gallipoli, and the almost as disgraceful business of Salonika. It was apparently settled at the Cabinet on Wednesday last that we must have compulsion for single men. This is a bright spot; but so long as we keep Asquith as Prime Minister we run a serious chance of losing the war. Wars cannot be won by indecision.

On January 1 he wrote:

My mind is travelling this way, that the thing of first importance is to make safe our line, and the thing of next importance is the education and training of officers. I mean to fasten on to these two things.

And what of this year? I don't think the war will be over during this year. It seems to me that we in the West should not try our next big attack before the Russians are really ready with men, guns, rifles, ammunition, equipment, railways, etc.; and from all I hear I don't think this can be before July or August. Then, when Russia relieves us of about 20-25 divisions, then we can commence. We stand to-day roughly — 96 French and 34 British divisions, and opposite to us 104 Boche; and only 48 Boche opposite Russia, with about 10 down Serbia way. Well, when Russia begins and we follow, then we must drive the Boche to the Rhine and to the Oder before he will agree to our terms. But if we don't start till August we shall never get to the Rhine by the end of the year, consequently it looks to me as though we have two summers' work in front of us before we finish.

A very noteworthy entry appears in the diary two days later, as indicating Sir Henry's views on a subject of considerable importance:

> Rawly on the telephone told me he was in at G.H.Q. yesterday. He told me that Haig had been down at Chantilly last week at a meeting of Group Commanders, and that Haig had been treated entirely as a Group Commander. To me this is very unwise, and if he begins to take orders from Joffre there will be serious trouble later. It appears that Poincaré, Briand and Galliéni were there and put the Group Commanders through their facings, asking questions about strength, lines, reserve, etc. I confess that I don't like it.

Wilson was assuming that the report was correct, which may not have been the case, as Rawlinson apparently had not been actually present at Chantilly and was merely repeating what he had heard. But, be that as it may. Sir Henry was entirely opposed to the B.E.F. being considered as definitely under the orders of the French Commander-in-Chief, and he clearly realized what difficulties such an arrangement was likely to give rise to. In view of controversies as to "unity of command" his attitude in the matter at this time is highly significant. He proceeded to England on leave on the morrow, and he remained for ten days in London, where he had interviews with a number of prominent people, and where he also arranged with Viscount Duncannon (now Earl of Bessborough) of the Bucks Yeomanry* and with Lieutenant G. L. T. Locker-Lampson of the Wilts Yeomanry to come as his A.D.C.s.

Getting back to Labussière on January 30 he wrote in his diary:

> From my visit home it is perfectly clear to me that, so long as we keep Asquith as Prime Minister we shall never go to war. And this is a most dangerous thing. He will do nothing himself and will not allow anyone else to do anything.

A day or two later, Brigadier-General (now Major-General) H. De Pree took over the position of B.G.G.S. from Montgomery, who had been given a rise. Sir C. Monro also just at this time came back from the Near East to command the First Army in place of Rawlinson, who was to be placed in charge of a Fourth Army that

---

* Sir Henry in his diary almost invariably refers to Duncannon, who was to be constantly with him for the next three years, as "the Lord."

was about to be formed north of the Somme. The 16th (Irish) Division was, moreover, at this time transferred from Wilson's corps to another, leaving him with only three divisions.

He was taking special interest in the schools for training officers and was placing these on a thoroughly sound footing, convinced that these winter months of comparative quiet ought to be made the fullest possible use of for promoting efficiency in the, at present inexperienced, commissioned ranks. The 1st Division, which was under command of Sir A. Holland, was at this time out of the line, resting, after several months in the trenches. So Major Lewin, who was serving in it, well aware of Wilson's gifts as a lecturer and anxious that numbers of the officers of the division should see their new corps commander and acquire some idea of his arresting personality, proposed to Wilson that he should give the division a lecture on the frontiers of Europe such as he had given to the company present at Englemere at the end of 1913.

Lewin writes:

> Henry was very diffident. Said, "Oh, the boys don't want to be lectured at. Let them have a good dinner and talk to any pretty girls they may be able to find." However, I persuaded him at last. He fixed a date and secured the theatre at Lillers, and officers flocked by lorry from all the surrounding villages and billets. Sir A. Holland was in the chair, and, after a few introductory remarks from him, Henry climbed up on to the stage from the orchestra pit, with a pointer about 12 feet long in his hand.
>
> Standing well forward on the stage, leaning on the pointer, with a vast sketch map of Europe arranged on the curtain behind him, he began his lecture, speaking very slowly and distinctly as though carefully weighing each word. He said:
>
> "A distinguished officer of your division has told me that I ought to inflict this lecture upon you, because the general view of all young officers is that Corps Commanders are fat, old, pot-bellied blighters, who live far back in safety in 'chattoos,' eat and drink a great deal, and know nothing of the realities of war. This being the case, I felt that if any of you were kind enough to avail yourselves of my invitation to come here this evening, you would at least realize that I am *not pot-bellied*. And I venture to hope that when I have finished the few observations that I propose to make, you may perhaps believe me when I say that I have given some thought and time to the study

> of this war, and am not altogether without experience of our allies, our antagonists, and the theatre of operations in which it is being waged."
>
> These prefatory remarks produced a wild burst of laughter and applause, during which Henry stood, tall, gaunt, and whimsical, propped up by the pointer and regarding his audience with affected surprise. He then proceeded to grip the three or four hundred assembled officers and to keep them spellbound for an hour, while he traced the causes which had led up to the war, and the course of the operations that had followed. To show them that his knowledge was not merely gained from books and reports, he mentioned that he had made no less than 17 trips up and down the Franco-German and Belgian frontiers on a bicycle during the years preceding the War and added, "On a *push*-bike: a *push*-bike. I did not say a *buzz*-bike."
>
> The lecture created tremendous interest, and the discussion over it lasted for several days. A very clever young chemical engineer, who had just become my adjutant and who, up to the War, had devoted his time to science and had never so much as heard of Henry's existence, remarked to me, "I could not have believed that any man in one short lecture could have so imbued his audience with a sense of his profound mastery of his subject, and could at the same time have made an even greater impression on them by the magnetism of his personality."

So great indeed was the impression that this address of his at Lillers made upon his audience, that his renown as a lecturer speedily spread through his corps and beyond it, and during the next few months he was frequently besought to oblige other divisions and audiences with a similar discourse. He generally consented. When, moreover, he had agreed, and the place and hour had been fixed, generals and staff officers who had cars at their disposal would arrive from distant localities to hear what he had to say and to swell the local audience. A story told of the unconventional, but, on that account none the less effective, fashion in which he began one of these addresses, deserves to be repeated.

The incident took place some months after that just recorded. It had been arranged that this particular lecture was to take place in the afternoon; the streets of the little township furnishing the venue had for some time before the hour fixed been congested with lorries and cars and bicycles converging upon the appointed hall, and this was speedily packed with swarms of officers, many of them coming from afar off. Wilson's appearance upon the platform evoked a burst of applause, and then there followed a tense, expectant silence. It was a still, hot summer's afternoon. The throbbing of the motors outside had ceased. The whole neighbourhood was steeped in drowsy repose, and the only sound to be heard within the hall was the gentle drone of winged insects flitting lazily about its precincts. Wilson stood there facing his audience, wearing a puzzled expression such as he liked to assume, and apparently in a state of doubt as to how to begin and what to say. Then suddenly, as though it were by some prearranged signal, a cock crowed. "That's a d— fine cock! " ejaculated the lecturer, and before the burst of laughter which this elicited had died away, he was already plunged into his subject and — in a phraseology and garnished with metaphors all his own— was telling his audience about the strengths and the objects of the belligerent forces in the various theatres of operations extending from Basrah to Boulogne.

One most valuable service General Huguet had performed on Wilson's behalf at the time when their pleasant association at G.H.Q. had come to an end. The French military representative on. the staff of Sir John French had captured the departing British Commander-in-Chief's highly efficient chef, and had forwarded him to Labussière; and the presence of this artist at the head-quarters of the IVth Corps enabled Wilson to exercise his bent for hospitality in a manner most grateful to those entertained. Few days there were on which, as recorded in Sir Henry's diary, there were no guests at luncheon or at dinner, or at both; and he was always delighted to put up any of his friends, military or civilian, for a night or two and (if they showed curiosity in that direction) to dispatch them under charge of one of his A.D.C.S to see what there was to be seen up near the front line. A member of his Staff writes the following appreciation of him at this time:

> Sir Henry was a delightful man to live with, witty and ever full of good stories. Unlike so many amusing people, he was not wont to be jocular at one moment and down in the dumps at another. I never

came across anyone else with so even a temperament, nor one who could remain so unperturbed in times of stress. It was ever a pleasure to hear his buoyant, "Good morning, soldiers 1" when he came in first thing, or his demand, "What's the gossip?" when one turned up again after having been to confer with some other head-quarters or to pay a visit to some unit.

The following was a very favourite yarn of his, as illustrating "the optimist and the pessimist": Shortly after "Proficiency Pay" had been introduced during the reign of Mr. Haldane in Whitehall, two old soldiers, fervent supporters of the "wet canteen" both of them, were one day taken down to the range to undergo musketry and with a view to their qualifying for this desired largess. The situation, towards the close of their test, was such that it behoved each of them to hit the target with every round he had left— else all would be lost.

The first of the pair lay down, puffing and blowing, perspiration pouring down his countenance, and a prey to almost paralyzing anxiety. But he nevertheless planted shot after shot upon the target with a regularity worthy of a King's Prizeman. Then, rising to his feet, dusting himself down and proudly squaring his shoulders, he ejaculated triumphantly "Mr. 'Aldane's beat!"

The second old soldier thereupon took the victor's place. His first two or three shots were signalled hits, and the prize almost looked within his grasp, when the final and decisive bullet struck the ground, knocking up the dust about half-way down the range, and ricochetted off noisily into the unknown. His anticipations of an extra beaker of beer each evening dashed, as it were, from his very lips, the discomfited marksman got slowly up and was heard to murmur in tones of acutest distress: "There goes my money! 'Oppin — 'oppin — 'oppin — to 'ell."

News from the Lorraine zone of the long Allied front was at this time indicating that a gathering of great German forces was in progress in that region, forces that evidently were assembling for an effort on a formidable scale directed against the fortress of Verdun, and on February 23 tidings arrived that this offensive had been launched. On that same day Wilson was ordered to take over the length of front at present held by the French division on his right, south-east of Loos, and he was given the 2nd Division from the Ist Corps for this express purpose; two days later he learnt that his corps was, as he expressed it in the diary, to start "sideslipping" to the south, i.e. giving up some of the line on the left and taking over more on the right, losing the 15th and 1st Divisions, and taking over the 23rd in addition to the 2nd in their place. Sir D. Haig had agreed to take over the stretch of line about Arras from the French, which had intervened between the Third and the First Armies, so that the British front would henceforward extend from the Yser to close to the Somme, Rawlinson's Fourth Army being on tide right, then the Third Army, then the First Army, with Plumer's Second Army on the left, up in Flanders.

These changes were all carried out gradually during the early days of March, and on the 12th, the IVth Corps headquarters was shifted from Labussière to Ranchicourt, farther to the south. There the corps commander, with De Pree and the two A.D.C.S, occupied a delightful chateau, planted down in a fine park traversed by a trout stream. Just at this same time the corps was put on a strictly limited allowance of gun ammunition, much to Wilson's chagrin. "The Boches fired more 6-inch shell to-day than we are allowed in two months — and this after twenty months of war," he wrote in his diary on the 14th. On the 20th there appears in the diary:

> To-night the 2nd Division telephone that the Boche put 300 (5.9) shell on the right battalion of our left brigade in 8½ minutes, and another 300 shells on a dummy battery we put up in front of Bouvigny. In other words, they again put 600 big shells upon us in one evening, this being our allowance in big shells for two months! It is perfectly maddening to have to undergo these things, while old Asquith and his crowd sit in London and do nothing.*
>
> There is only one solution to our impossible position, and that is to get rid of Asquith. He will lose this war if he possibly can, by simply doing nothing. No ammunition, no trench mortars (big ones), no rifle grenades, no anti-aircraft guns, no sausage balloons, no recruits, no huts, no light railways, no war. And the whole of this, and no blockade, no foreign policy, no Irish policy, no tariff policy, no

---

* Wilson was so much alarmed at this that he wrote to Sir A. Lee at the Ministry of Munitions, who was able to send him reassuring information. In his acknowledgment to Lee, he wrote: "I see. The limitations imposed come, therefore, from G.H.Q., and not from you, and come from a fit of saving up and not from a fit of fear of empty lockers. This, of course, is a very much brighter outlook and I am much happier. Why the devil G H.Q. couldn't tell us this I don't know. You would think we were all children!"

peace policy after the war, no financial policy, no savings nor retrenchments, no Zeppelins, no *going to war*, no *intention to go to war*, these and a thousand other things are due entirely to Asquith and his brood of Wait and See.

On April 7 Wilson had a long talk with General Joffre, who expressed himself as well satisfied with the situation at Verdun, and as hoping that an offensive, which was shortly to be undertaken by 300,000 men at Salonika, would pin the Bulgarian forces down and would bring in the Rumanians as allies. Joffre declared that he could not understand out difficulty about men and munitions. Wilson wrote:

> I told him that the answer to all his questions was Asquith. He told me he had written a strong letter on all these points to Rriand two days ago, which Briand was to show Asquith as Asquith passed through Paris on his way back from Italy, and he added that more divisions should be sent from England, and from Egypt where large forces were lying idle. There was one rather disquieting thing about Joffre to-day. He kept on hinting and indicating that he thought an early decision was necessary. He gave no date, but I am left with the impression that he meant June or July rather than August or September. Knox* puts the earliest moment for Russia at August, or preferably September.

Sir Henry was able to proceed to England for a few days' leave towards the end of April — as it happened, just at the time when the Irish rebellion so suddenly broke out. He, as usual, saw a number of prominent men during his stay. He was telephoned for one day by Mr. Bonar Law to go down to the Colonial Office, and this appears in the diary:

> I went down, and he told me the Irish thing was serious, Conky Maxwell† had been given command and went over to-night. He (Bonar Law) and some others wanted me to go, but agreed my Ulster

---

* Colonel W. A. Knox, Military Attaché in Russia.

† Lieutenant-General Sir J, G. Maxwell.

record made it impossible. He asked me if I would take command of the Canadian Corps. I said I was afraid there was too much politics in it, but he pressed. He will get Aitken to come and dine to-night and I will hear what he has to say. I dined with Bonar, but Aitken was not able to come, so I heard no more of the Canadian Corps.

Bonar Law really believes that the Coalition is the best possible Government at this time. I told him that if we did not get rid of Asquith we should lose the war, but he remained obdurate. The Irish affair gets worse. Conky should arrest Birrell and get him shot if convicted. An amazing day. Bonar Law told me that Townshend (at Kut) was bound to surrender.* Then the miserable Bill for semi-compulsion was withdrawn this afternoon. Then the fighting in Dublin was severe.

Wilson found a good deal of activity in progress when he returned to Ranchicourt on April 29, for the enemy were using their guns freely; and he also learnt that he was shortly to be weakened by the loss of the 23rd Division, which was to be moved south to take part in the contemplated offensive north of the Somme. A week later he was delighted to receive a visit from M. Clemenceau, who arrived at 7 a.m. by appointment. A sumptuous breakfast had been prepared for the eminent Frenchman, although Sir Henry and his staff rather expected that at that early hour their guest would, after the manner of his countrymen, merely toy with a cup of coffee and a rusk. But, in spite of his three score and fifteen years and of his up-bringing, "The Tiger 55 made his way through the elaborate menu, from porridge, by way of kippers, to bacon and eggs, and he tamped this snack with a generous portion of strawberries and cream — to the unbounded admiration of his hosts. Wilson did not mention this feat in his diary, but he wrote:

I had a long talk with him. Most disquieting. Russia is more backward even than I thought. Grave difficulties in the interior. Strikes in Putilov works, which can turn out 450 guns a month, and last month turned out only 35. Clemenceau does not think that Russia will be ready for an offensive before next spring. He thinks an early offensive on the West on our part sheer madness. He told Haig so. He

---

* Kut surrendered next day.

thought Haig was impressed. He asked Haig if he was under Joffre. The reply was No — though nearly, as Clemenceau gathered. He urged Haig to stop all great offensives until Russia was ready — right on to this time next year if necessary. He also told me about French financial troubles, which are great.

He said that we (English) must find the men and the money. The French have lost just on 1,000,000 dead, and over 2,000,000 wounded and prisoners, and they could not go on at this rate either in men losses or in money losses. A great offensive now, or later, which was not a real success would lead to "*une demie paix*"* — which was fatal. He told me that Turkey was talking to France about peace, that she would make peace the day Russia said she would agree not to take Constantinople, that France and England were hampered by the promise that Winston got Grey to give Russia that we would give her Constantinople when the Dardanelles was fixed, but that the French were now trying to get the Russians to agree about not wanting Constantinople. The Turks promise to massacre every Boche in their country the day they make peace. This would be a very fine stroke, and would be a real blow to Germany. But on the whole I had never seen Clemenceau so anxious about the future. He fully realizes about Asquith and the terrible danger we run from keeping him as Prime Minister. He begged me to work hard at home to make them realize the dangerous position into which we are drifting, and the crying danger and madness of another unsuccessful attack.

Next day (May 6) the entry appears:

Robertson came to see me, and lunched. He is over for a couple of days. He thinks Lake and Gorringe ought to be quite safe, as they are as strong as the Turks.† He thinks that Russia will not forgo her claim to Constantinople, and we cannot come to terms with Turkey. He wants to clear out of Salonika, but the French not only won't, but want to take the offensive (this tallies with what Joffre told me). He can only produce another 40 or 50 divisions from home and Egypt. He seemed rather in favour of an early offensive.

Here I joined in. I told him that there was no reasonable chance of success with the balance of forces as they are, and that a failure

---

* "Half a peace."

† Referring to Mesopotamia.

might, and probably would, mean an inconclusive peace — absolutely fatal — and that it was his business to get that balance changed before allowing an attack. He said Joffre was pressing for it, being himself pressed, but I said I did not care a rush who pressed. We must stand firm. It was mad to gamble in that way. When we had added 10 divisions to our forces and the Germans had withdrawn 25 to 30 to send to Russia then try an attack. I put all my weight into my arguments against an offensive until Russia helped, and I think that I did good.

He says Ireland is squashed. Old Robertson seemed in good form and pleased with himself. He is putting much faith in Lloyd George and Carson, and I think he is right.

General Monro went on leave on May 9, whereupon Wilson took over command of the First Army as a temporary measure, with head-quarters at Aire; but he continued living at Ranchicourt, retaining command of his corps and motoring to Aire when necessary. Foch came to see him a few days later and expressed the view that the Allies must mobilize and organize their resources more fully, that infinitely more guns and ammunition must be turned out by France and Great Britain for themselves and for Russia, and that then, perhaps a year hence, it might be possible to secure victory. He entirely agreed with Wilson that the balance of forces must be altered and that the number of guns must be increased if success was to be assured. The views of both had, in fact, undergone a considerable modification since the previous year, when they had been intent upon offensives on a great scale although the relative strengths of the belligerents of the Western Front were, if anything, less favourable to the Entente then than they were now. "On occasions like this," writes General De Pree, "General Foch and Sir Henry used to be closeted together for hours, discussing, gossiping and chaffing. They used to exchange caps, and in this get-up they would stride up and down the drawing-room, laughing heartily and exchanging experiences."

It had been arranged some time before that the IVth Corps was to take over some line about the western slopes of the Vimy Ridge at its northern end — an awkward bit overlooked by craters and generally under heavy fire — from the corps under General Byng alongside, which belonged to the Third Army. This transaction was effected without incident on the nights of May 19 and 20, on which latter day Wilson had taken the Archbishop of Canterbury on to the Notre Dame de Lorette heights to watch the gun-fire. The trenches taken over proved, owing to the peculiar nature of the soil, to be very shallow and unsatisfactory, and the corps commander realized that until they could somehow be improved, this must constitute a danger spot in his line.

He was on his way out to this ground so recently come under his control on the following afternoon when, as he and Duncannon were walking up a long communication trench towards the front line, the enemy suddenly started a very heavy bombardment and barrage. "The Boche was shelling everywhere, at the batteries round us, on our front line, on Souchez, Carency, Ablain, Lorette, Servin, Bouvigny, Hersin, etc. — very heavy," he wrote in the diary. On their way forward they encountered a young soldier, a cheery Yorkshireman, who came striding towards them, whistling blithely and in high good humour. "They're doin' of 'em in, they're doin' of 'em in" was all that could be got out of this happy warrior; so, after waiting some little time, and as the hostile gun-fire was growing even hotter, they turned back to head-quarters, so as to get into general telephonic communication with the command. The blow had fallen upon the 47th Division, which formed Sir Henry's right, alongside of the Third Army. He could only get contradictory and unsatisfactory reports as to what had actually been happening in the front line, so he ordered up a brigade of the 2nd Division by omnibus from its rest-billets, to be ready for action. Only late at night did it transpire that about 1,200 yards of the trenches which had just been taken over had been lost, and that the whole line at this point had been thrust back from 300 to 600 yards, and Wilson admitted in his diary:

> It is a nasty little knock, our casualties about 1,200 to 1,500. By a savage bombardment I have been knocked out of rotten trenches which we only took over on Sunday morning.

The lie of the ground within the German lines in this section of the front had lent itself admirably to a surprise bombardment such as the enemy had so suddenly opened. The Vimy Ridge towered abruptly from the Lens plain and the enemy after a fashion held its crest, so that on Wilson's side of it there was, except at one point, no direct observation beyond the height. The scattered townships and villages and slag heaps and woods of the Lens colliery district provided innumerable concealed gun positions for the use of the German artillery. The steep eastern face of the ridge enabled the enemy to plant down trench-mortars under cover, close up to the British front line. The Germans had secretly assembled large numbers of these short-range weapons, as well as of guns and howitzers of all kinds, for delivering their effective stroke. Wilson's gunners had promptly put down a protective barrage; but their available ammunition was already used up before the hostile bombardment had ceased, and the enemy infantry then, presumably, advanced. Owing to the dust and smoke that obscured the view, some doubt has ever since existed as to the hour at which the assault was actually delivered, for no one from the doomed companies in the front line returned to tell the tale.

Sir Henry at once prepared plans for retaking the lost trenches on the following night, and Allenby came to see him and to offer the help of the Third Army if desired. But, after the necessary orders for the operation had been issued, General Monro (who had just returned from leave) persuaded the corps commander to defer the undertaking for another twenty-four hours, by which time he would have four additional heavy batteries at his command. Wilson would have preferred to carry out his own plan; but he gave way. Officers from G.H.Q. came next day to say that Sir Douglas suggested yet further delay and was proposing to send up yet more guns to help; but Monro, Allenby and Wilson himself all favoured making the effort that same night. It was so decided, and Monro instructed Sir Henry to carry on.

But when the counter-attack came to be delivered as contemplated, after dusk, a serious hitch occurred. One of the two brigades that were to carry out the operation did not start, while the other, after being at first successful and recovering some of the lost trenches, was driven out of them again. So Monro at 12.30 a.m. sent orders to stop any further attempt, as it seemed to him to be too late by that hour to effect anything. Wilson thought this a mistake. He gives a full account of what occurred in his diary, and of certain misunderstandings that contributed to bring about the failure; but the record could not be readily followed without a large scale map showing the details of ground and the trenches. There was at first some idea of making a yet further effort, to be carried out with fresh troops, and G.H.Q. gave serious consideration to the matter. But it was eventually adjudged best to leave the enemy in possession of the ground captured in preference to undertaking a serious operation to regain it — the more so as arrangements for the great offensive that was to take place about the Somme were already in progress, and as any spare troops available were already being moved in that direction. "Rather than weaken my offensive," Sir D. Haig wrote in regard to the incident in his Dispatch dated December 23, "by involving additional troops in the task of recovering the lost ground, I decided to consolidate a position in rear of our original line." But it was something of a misfortune for Sir Henry that the one really important occurrence that signalized his term of command of the IVth Corps should have been this minor set-back.

The plans for the great offensive which was to take place on either side of the Somme were in the meantime being gradually completed, and on June 1 Wilson learnt that the Naval Division from home was coming to him, but that he was shortly to lose both the 2nd and the 23rd Divisions. Of this he wrote in his diary:

> It seems as though early next month G.H.Q. expect me to hold my line with the 47th Division and Naval Division, and no reserve and no big guns. This is impossible if Boches keep troops and guns in front of me. For the 47th Division are about 4,500 fighting strength, and the Naval Division has only 6 battalions, quite untrained, no musketry, no Maxims, no Lewis guns, no bombers, nothing. We shall see.

Two days later news of the Battle of Jutland arrived, whereupon he remarked sardonically in his diary:

> Our navy is just beginning its course of instruction. Very expensive, but very necessary. This will wake up the English people and do a lot of good, and put a long Whitsun Holiday in its true perspective.

This appears in the diary a few days later:

I see signs of the Boche plunging about and losing his head. These futile, but terribly costly efforts at Verdun, the ineffectual and rather costly attack on me at Vimy, this attack now going on at Ypres, and this fleet action. None of them lead to anything except increase of weakness and loss of morale. Moreover, I really believe that food is getting rather scarce in Germany and that this is having a depressing effect and is pushing the Government to this, or that, or any action. Yes, I see signs of loss of head.

Of a conversation which he had with Clemenceau on June 11 he wrote:

He told me that he (Clemenceau) was going to get rid of Joffre, who was too old and too slow, who had taken no precautions to safeguard Verdun, witness Pétain's first orders on going there and other documents, all of which Clemenceau had in his possession. He told me Joffre and Briand had gone to London and were there now to try and get more English troops sent to Salonika — a ridiculous proposal. He agreed with me absolutely in thinking that we ought to clear out of Salonika, but is not quite sure we can, now that Bulgaria is moving down. When Joffre is moved out he thinks the choice lies with Castlenau, Foch and Pétain. He personally favours Foch, and so do I, telling him I knew all three and that Foch was the most brilliant by far, Castelnau the best staff officer, and Pétain a fine dogged fighter but without Foch s drive and wide outlook.

He was as insistent as ever that we should not attack prematurely and that it was mad to do so. There was no hope of breaking through unless we had unlimited ammunition, which we have not got, and were prepared to face a loss of 250,000, which we aren't.

On another day he wrote:

Milner sees no chance of getting rid of Asquith and thinks, like me, that his continuance as Prime Minister is a great danger. He looks on Lloyd George as the only chance, but a broken reed as he cannot make up his mind to resign. Ireland, of course, is very serious, and Jemmy [Wilson's brother] has been working all day to get Walter Long to resign. It seems that Lloyd George is trying to get Ulster in by saying that the cutting out of Ulster is permanent, and trying to get

Redmond in by saying that it is only provisional! That won't last long.

The disaster to the *Hampshire* had occurred a few days before this and Sir Henry had hoped that Lord Milner might succeed Lord Kitchener as Secretary of State for War; Mr. Lloyd George was, however, appointed to that office a few days later. Wilson spent a night with Rawlinson on June 22, heard de tails as to the contemplated offensive by the Fourth Army and Foch, and wrote in the diary:

> On the whole it seems to me that we run a serious chance of doing something considerable here. If we get Bapaume and Péronne we really might crack the line and cause the retirement of the Boches as far north as Arras and as far south as the Compiègne salient. This would be substantial. I understand that the Boches have now only about 15 floating divisions, and that 7 or 8 of these have been in at Verdun and are very tired.

He wrote in his diary next day, after getting back to Ranchicourt:

> Haig came and paid me a visit at 3.30, also Kigg. He told me about there being only 32 battalions opposite Rawly, that Foch was, of course, not ready and that Joffre wanted a further delay, but he was opposed to it. He said he had been in London at the meeting of Briand and Joffre 10 days ago, when our people would not hear of a campaign at Salonika, but he now hears we are weakening. Haig had no other gossip.

The great Somme offensive was launched on July 1, but the results of the opening day were disappointing. It is true that Foch's troops, as also Rawlinson's two right corps and his centre corps gained, and retained, ground to a considerable depth. But the two left corps of the Fourth Army, and also a corps of the Third Army, on their left again, failed to hold what they had captured. This ill-success along half of the front allotted to the B.E.F. was no doubt partly due to lack of adequate heavy artillery — the French had relatively a far larger number of heavy pieces to help them, away on the right — but it appears to have been still more due to the insufficient training and the inexperience of the troops concerned. Of the seven divisions on the left which failed to make good, four had not previously taken part in any offensive operations on a large scale; they had only arrived in France during the previous winter and spring; and one consequence of their inexperience had been that no effective arrangements had been made for clearing up and securing ground after it had been won. The Germans facing Rawlinson's left and centre were, moreover, folly prepared and were expecting the onset, whereas those facing Foch had not anticipated attack and offered but a feeble resistance. Wilson heard an account of the operations from Foch, whom he visited at Dury on the 5th, and he wrote in his diary:

> Foch was full of gossip, and well pleased with his attack, and well he may be. He has the XXth Corps north of the Somme and the Colonial Corps south of it, i.e. 5 divisions. With this he has captured first and second systems, he has advanced 4,000-5,000 yards, he has taken 9,000 prisoners and 60 guns, and all this at a loss of under 8,000 men. It is the finest attack performance of the war, and Foch and Weygand can well be proud of themselves. Result is a very high moral tone in his men.
>
> Compare with our work. We have done well on the right, but badly from La Boiselle to the north. We have captured 5,000 Boches and 15-20 guns, we are still in our trenches on more than half our line, and our estimated loss is 1,900 officers and 61,000 men. Now, most, if not all, of this comes from our inability to "mount" an attack. Foch told me that two days ago there was a meeting at Beauquesne, at which he and Weygand were present, also Haig and Joffre. At this Haig showed that he was upset by his losses, that he was responsible to his Government, etc., and that therefore he was not much inclined to attack again at Thiepval — Serre, but proposed to exploit the success farther south. This infuriated Joffre, who simply went for Haig and, as Foch said, was quite *brutal*. Haig said he was not speaking as one gentleman to another, and old Joffre said he would have no further dealings with Haig over this matter and that Haig must work it out with Foch.
>
> On the whole, then, Foch is very pleased with his own advance and displeased with ours, but does not think that Haig yet understands in what ours failed, viz., not nearly sufficient concentration of fire

before infantry attack.

Foch's account of the interview between Joffre and Haig at Beauquesne, quoted above, is of interest; but it by no means tells the whole story. The five corps under Rawlinson had attacked at a re-entrant in the front — the two corps on the right advancing in a northerly direction, that in the centre advancing at the angle, and the two on the left (with the one corps of the Third Army) advancing in an easterly direction. The result of the first day's fighting, and that of the next dav, had been to push forward the whole of the right in a northerly direction, capturing the enemy first and second systems. The re-entrant had been, if anything, accentuated, and the actual angle had been pushed some 3,000 yards farther to the north. Haig wisely decided to devote his reserves and his available artillery to pushing the newly-won line on the right still farther forward northwards, and, by so doing, to take the Germans in flank along the front where they had, in the end, repulsed all attacks on the opening day. Joffre, on the contrary, wanted Haig to repeat the effort along that front — this, although that effort had signally failed when to some extent enjoying the advantage of surprise, and although the enemy had in the meantime already received substantial reinforcements. Haig very properly refused; and he adhered to his refusal. The result was that, when the fighting on the Somme many weeks later came to a conclusion, five miles of enemy lines, which had defied the onset of four divisions in the frontal attack delivered by them on July i, had been captured by the B.E.F. almost automatically, in virtue of successive outflanking operations.

In furtherance of his plan Haig now placed the two left corps of the Fourth Army (which were at first to stand fast), under General Gough, as a Reserve Army; and he left Rawlinson the other three, reinforced by divisions which had been kept in reserve at the start, to continue their offensive in a northerly direction. They pressed forward gradually during the next few days, and on the 14th they delivered a highly successful attack along part of their front, which secured to them possession of points of tactical importance that greatly facilitated yet further advance from commanding ground. "A really remarkable day's work," Wilson wrote of this in his diary: "and getting cavalry out is very remarkable, as it shows a certain amount of collapse in the Boche defences." The enemy was, however, now facing Rawlinson in formidable strength, and the offensive could thenceforward only be continued at the cost of heavy sacrifices, of occasional checks and of much hard fighting.

The question of losses had indeed already become a serious one. The total of casualties suffered by the British divisions launched into these operations on the Somme was mounting up most ominously, and Wilson, who managed to keep himself well informed of what was occurring in that quarter, was impressed by the relative difference between the battle wastage which was taking place amongst our troops and that which was taking place amongst the troops under Foch. Sir J. Shea, who had been a student at the Staff College when Sir Henry was commandant, tells of a conversation with him shortly after the opening of the offensive on July 1. Shea's division, the 30th, advancing on the extreme right of Rawlinson's forces, next to the French, on July 1, had gained all its objectives without suffering very heavy casualties, and its commander naturally felt well satisfied with what he had accomplished. He was consequently a little disappointed when Wilson's only comment amounted to an unmistakable hint that the losses of the 30th Division had been excessive. The division was, moreover, thrust afresh into the protracted Somme struggle more than once at a later date, and, whenever Shea saw Sir Henry after one of these efforts — as he generally did — the same procedure was repeated. Sir Henry referred pointedly to the question of casualties, and Shea at last began to perceive that this attitude on Wilson's part was intentional and was designed to convey to him that there must be something radically wrong in the tactical handling on the British side. The story is a typical one. Wilson — a corps commander not immediately concerned in the proceedings — would not directly criticize to a junior general the handling of their troops by other corps commanders and by the army commander set over them; but he nevertheless, contrived to make the junior general examine into the matter for himself.

Sir Henry was getting the 37th Division in place of the 2nd; and on the 22nd he heard that his 47th Division was to go south to the Somme and that he was to receive the 9th, from the Somme, in its place. The 37th and 9th Divisions both proved to be much below their proper establishment owing to losses, and the Naval Division had always been weak. "It will be a difficult business," Wilson remarked in his diary, "to hold the Vimy Ridge with very few infantry and somewhat indifferent artillery." He did not, of course, actually hold the ridge, but merely claimed a footing on the lower slopes, where his trenches were overlooked; and he made it clear to Monro (as he says in his diary) that he could not stand "even a moderate form of attack." He was constantly busying himself all this time with training questions and with promoting the efficiency of officers' schools, and he felt well satisfied with the result.

Sir Henry learnt on August 5 that his immediate Chief was about to proceed to India as Commander-in-Chief, and that General Haking, commanding one of the corps in the Army and who was junior to Wilson, was to take over the command. This news was confirmed next day, and Wilson wrote in his diary:

> It is quite true that Richard Haking gets this Army as a "temp" measure, but it is obvious that it is not "temp," as I would naturally officiate, and Monro asked that I should; but Haig would not have that.

Although he makes only brief reference to the matter in his diary, Wilson was deeply hurt at this supersession. He was mistaken in thinking that it was not a temporary measure; but the fact of its only being a temporary measure in reality made the slight all the more significant.

The King saw some of the troops of the IVth Corps on the nth, and a few days later Wilson learnt that G.H.Q. might call upon him any day, at short notice, to attack the Vimy Ridge so as to pin the enemy troops and guns holding it down to their ground, and that he was to prepare a plan for carrying such an operation out if required. After due consideration, and after full discussion with his divisional generals, he intimated that he would be prepared to attack, at four days' notice, on any date after August 28, but that he would prefer September 7 because of the moon. He had been given some heavy artillery for the purpose, and he at once set to work to have an exact copy of the Vimy trenches marked out on suitable ground in rear, so that an attack could be practised beforehand by those who were to take part in it. Haking informed him on the 17th that Haig wanted the attack to take place before September 1. He wrote in his diary:

> I said I could not do it with even a moderate chance of success, Of course, I could lose 5,000-6,000 men any day Haig liked, but I could not take and keep the Vimy trenches before September 1.

This was duly represented to G.H.Q. by the Army commander. Wilson learnt a few days later that General Horne was to get the command of the First Army as soon as he could be spared from the Somme. Then, on the 30th, he was informed that the attack upon the Vimy Ridge would not be asked for by G.H.Q. before September 10, and he was at the same time promised 18 additional heavy guns and howitzers to help in the task. But on September 7 he heard that he would not, after all, be required to carry out his operation against the Vimy Ridge till the end of the month; the attack, when it came to be delivered, was, however, to be on a larger scale than previously contemplated, and he was to be given one or more additional divisions to carry it out. Two days later a meeting of the corps commanders of the First Army took place, and of what occurred at this he wrote in his diary:

> Haking explained that there had been another change of plans.. When, and if, the Somme attack has been so successful that the German line up to Arras has been rolled up, then we are to attack the Vimy Ridge on a front of about 3,000 yards, with 3 divisions, of which two are to be in my corps and one will be lent by the XVIIth Corps. This is a good, sensible plan, and under the conditions postulated it ought to succeed. If, on the other hand, the Somme does not succeed, then Haig seems to contemplate an attack on the whole Vimy Ridge (9,000 yards) with some 4-6 divisions. I said I thought it would take at least 14 divisions, and a great mass of artillery.
>
> I held out for having my two divisions, and the one of the XVIIth Corps, in the line for 10 days before the attack; and this was agreed to.

Progress was made with the necessary arrangements for this important operation, but Wilson was somewhat put out by receiving an order next day to send two of his heavy batteries down to Gough on the Somme. "This is not hopeful," he observed in the diary, "as I want 106 heavy guns for my attack, as well as the guns of my three divisions." He also, not unnaturally, thought that the one division of the XVIIth Corps, which was to attack on the right of his own two divisions, ought to have been definitely transferred to his command. He nevertheless proceeded actively with his preparations, although he also contrived to pay a visit to Foch at Villers-Bretonneux on August 12, on which occasion he moreover saw Joffre, who happened to come in for a few minutes. This appears in the diary:

> Foch told me all his secrets. In the first place he is dissatisfied with his relations with Haig. Haig is always civil and nice, but tells him nothing, and the relationship between them is not such that Foch can converse freely with Haig and tell him all his plans and hopes and experiences. Then there is no one on Haig's staff senior enough to go between them, as I used in old days to work between Sir John and Foch, seeing Foch often twice a day— for example, during all the 1st Battle of Ypres, and possessing Foch's entire confidence and also Sir John's. Foch is worried about the present state of affairs.
>
> Foch wanted to know how we could get back to the old happy relations and wanted me back, but realized this was impossible. Then Foch told me of his long interview with Lloyd George, who came to see him yesterday. Lloyd George asked innumerable questions about why we took so few prisoners, why we took so little ground, why we had such heavy losses, all these in comparison with the French. Foch played up well as regards Haig and would not give him away. He simply said he did not know, but that our divisions were green soldiers and his were veterans. Lloyd George said he gave Haig all the guns and ammunition and men he could use, and nothing happened. Foch said that Lloyd George was *trés monté*[*] against Haig, and he did not think Haig's seat was very secure. Lloyd George is staying at Hôtel du Rhin, Amiens, and not at our G.H.Q. Arthur Lee is with Lloyd George. During the conversation my name turned up,

---

[*] "Very mounted."

and Foch let fly about me, about my work before the war and during the war, and said all sorts of ridiculous and charming things, Arthur acting as interpreter.

Foch said that if Somme attack was unsuccessful the French would ask us to take over more line for the winter, but he thought I was right a year ago when I said we ought to break in two — not prolong south of the Somme, but go to Lorraine.

Foch was launching a heavy attack while I was there, from Combles to the Somme, on a front of kilometres. This attack started while we were at lunch at 12.30 p.m. and at 12.40 the first reports began to come in. An amazing performance. To-night we hear that they got along the Péronne-Bapaume road from just south of Rancourt, then all Bouchavesnes, and then down to the Somme short of St. Quentin. They took 1,500 prisoners. A fine fight. Foch told me that since July 1 he had captured 42,000 prisoners and has only lost 58,000 men. This shows the very highest class of soldiering both for infantry and artillery, and for command and staff. He told me all about his methods of attack and of how he worked his guns, infantry and aeroplanes, and I got a lot of wrinkles for my Vimy attack, which I shall apply.

On getting back to Ranchicourt that evening Wilson found a wire from Lee to say that he was bringing Lloyd George over on the following day. The party consisted of Sir Rufus Isaacs (Lord Reading) as well as Lloyd George and Lee, and they spent an hour at the chateau. Wilson mentions in his diary that Lee told Duncannon during the drive over, "how nearly I was *dégommé* after May 21, and how I was saved by Charlie Monro putting in a tremendous report in my favour." The diary goes on to say that Lloyd George asked Wilson exactly the same questions as he had asked Foch on the previous day, and got the same answers, i.e. that our troops and artillery were new to the game, and could be nothing else seeing that the B.E.F. had been swollen from six divisions to sixty.

Two days after this visit of the Secretary of State for War, Wilson learnt that the division of the XVIIth Corps which was to have co-operated in his attack on the Vimy Ridge was ordered off to the Somme, and that his own Naval Division was likewise to move south — changes which rather upset his plans and necessitated an entirely fresh distribution of his troops for the purpose. Two days later, again, he heard that he was losing the 9th Division as well as the Naval Division, and that he was getting the 24th, which was 5,000 under strength. "A nice lot to hold the Vimy with," he remarks in his diary. Then on the 21st he had a visit from Robertson. The C.I.G.S. was encouraging as regards guns and ammunition, saying that plenty of both would soon be coming over, but he was most dissatisfied at the way in which exemptions from service were being allowed at home, and also dissatisfied with the situation at Salonika, and with Sarrail, whose offensive in that quarter was at this time in progress. This appears in the diary:

> I told him that, after the Somme, the French would want us to take up more line, and that Joffre might object to our prolonging to our right because of Paris, and might suggest that we should take over a bit of the Vosges. Personally, I told him, I favoured this, not, of course, from the military point of view, but from the point of view of the future, so that we should not be too strong in one place and make the French jealous.

Wilson does not mention how the C.I.G.S. took this suggestion, but it is at least conceivable that Robertson would have been more impressed with the obvious military objections to such an arrangement than influenced by an altruistic tenderness for French susceptibilities.

Wilson wrote on August 28:

> The brothers Gwynne (Bishop of Khartum and *Morning Post*) came for the night. Henry Gwynne tells me that Robertson is having a tough fight against the politicians about this fantastic idea of sending an expedition to Mecca to help the Yemen Arabs against the Turks! It is simply marvellous!
>
> Haking rang me up on the telephone at 10 o'clock to say that Home comes to-morrow to take over First Army, and he (Haking) goes back to the XIth Corps. I hear also to-night that Greece has joined us. What will the Boche King and Queen do now? And was I not right to advise Grey on October 21, 1915, to take Tino by the throat and find out what the fool was going to do?

Wilson proceeded home on leave on September 30. Lady Wilson had undergone a very severe operation, and he had been extremely anxious on her account; but he found her to be making satisfactory progress. On getting back to Ranchicourt on October 10 he heard that his head-quarters were to move south in a few days and that he was to join the Reserve Army under Gough — thus putting an end to any idea of his being charged with an attack on the Vimy Ridge. This was a disappointment after the labour he had expended on framing plans for that operation; but the redistributions of troops under his command had already rendered his being called upon to make the attempt unlikely. That evening he wrote in his diary:

> The general impression on my mind after my trip home is one of dissatisfaction. The Cabinet as a whole has not gone to war, and many of them are now definitely not going to war, and some are thinking and talking of peace. I mean that the Cabinet are not in earnest about getting recruits, and some are frankly obstructive. They will not, if they can possibly avoid it, apply conscription to Ireland. They will not carry out the Paris Conference. They *will* talk of our losses being unbearable, of the enormous expense, of armistice, of not beating the Boche to the ground, as we shall want him against the Russians — and so forth.
>
> If, then, we don't get sufficient men, in sufficient time, for next year's fighting — if we are not in a position to take punishment of *at least a million between April and October* of next year and still have our divisions full up to the brim — it seems to me that we really shall have reached a condition of stalemate, in which case the war is lost.

The IVth Corps head-quarters quitted Ranchicourt on the 15th and became victims of some vexatious counter-ordering before their destination and the duties and composition of the corps were finally settled. In the meantime Wilson was able to stay for a couple of days with the Baron de Neuflise (Lord Duncannon's father-in-law) at Chantilly, and while he was there General de Castelnau one evening came to dinner. Wilson noted in his diary:

> Castelnau was perfectly charming to me, and in front of everyone at dinner said that, only for me, England would never, could never, have gone to war, and therefore it was the literal truth that I had saved France. A proud moment.

Corps head-quarters were finally fixed at Domart; but Wilson, with De Pree and his personal staff, located themselves at the Chateau de Vauchelles, some little distance away; the corps for the moment consisted only of head-quarters, having no divisions, and this gave its commander a good deal more leisure than he had been recently enjoying. The Somme operations were still continuing, and the Reserve Army (which about this time came to be called the Fifth Army) was about to take its share of the' task, acting on the left of Rawlinson's army against some of the German line which had withstood the attack of July 1. But the weather was, as usual at this time of the year, becoming very unfavourable for fighting owing to bad visibility and to the sodden condition of the ground, and Wilson wrote in his diary on October 21:

> Here on the Somme we are gradually coming to a standstill, and I don't think there is any chance of getting Bapaume. What then should we do? My own opinion is that we should gradually settle down to winter conditions, i.e. in a month's time, then hold the line as lightly as we can, do a lot of gunning and mortaring, and *rest* and *train* our divisions, so that we may start a spring offensive with full divisions, well trained and in good heart. The moment the winter comes we should all turn on to the schools.
>
> The alternative to this course is to go on fighting all the winter and to start the spring offensive with tired and ill-trained and ill-disciplined divisions. This would be bad. We shall see what is decided.

Next day he wrote:

> Hugo de Pree, who had called in at G.H.Q. this afternoon, said that he was told that Lloyd George was playing the devil in the War Office, and that he was hunting Robertson and Cowans and so on. Duncannon and Locker-Lampson quoted Lloyd George's invariable procedure on taking over a new office, which apparently consists in kicking out all the people he finds there and replacing them by others, and they (the Lord and Locker) thought Robertson had better be careful. Hugo said that he heard at G.H.Q. that Lloyd George was going to replace soldiers to a certain extent by civilians. For example, this Eric Geddes, a railway manager, has apparently been made a sort of G.O.C. L. of C., and has blossomed out as a major-general. Rather

a startling innovation — but I don't know enough about it to form an opinion.

On the 24th the entry was:

Just as I go to bed I hear that the French have retaken Douamont Fort at Verdun, have advanced from 1,000 to 2,000 yards along the whole front, and have captured 3,500 prisoners. What a fine performance. This Verdun success shows what I have been preaching for two months, that an attack anywhere except on the Somme would be instantly successful.

On the 26th, after seeing Gough, he wrote:

Haig had just been to see him. Haig says the Russians are sending several corps to help the Rumanians, which is damnable as being a detachment not pulling its own weight. Haig said that the Russians were now intent on flattening out the Bulgars, and proposed to do it now. This is worse and worse, for if the Russians engage in serious operations against the Bulgars they will forget the Boches, and if they succeed against the Bulgars the temptation to go to Constantinople will be irresistible. The only thing worth talking about is killing Bodies..

To add to this miserable business, we are sending another division from here to Salonika, and no doubt the French are doing the same. The Boches have 7 divisions in Transylvania and one-third of a division in the Dobruja, 127 divisions against the west, 61 against Russia, and two-thirds of a division in Macedonia. That one-third of a division in the Dobruja is a perfect example of what a good detachment can do.. The 7 divisions in Transylvania and two-thirds of a division in Macedonia are pulling ten times their weight.

If we go on walking from one cess-pit into another we shall get drowned. I dread a Russian campaign against Bulgaria now, If we beat the Boches, all else follows. If we beat the Turks and Bulgars and Greeks we shall be beaten by the Boches. And serve us right.*

* It is interesting to compare the views here expressed with the attitude taken up by Sir Henry a year later, as recorded in Chapters XIX to XXI. [Publisher's note: these appear in Volume II.]

Corps head-quarters were shifted to Beauval on November 10, and two days later Wilson had a long conversation with Foch, who declared that the war must be finished next year, otherwise there would be an inconclusive peace as France would be worn out. He entirely agreed with Wilson that as many divisions as possible ought to be withdrawn out of the line during the winter, so as to be rested and to undergo training in view of the campaign of 1917. Wilson went home on leave next day, and he was at once sent for by Lloyd George, who asked him if he still held the view that we could defeat the Germans. He wrote in his diary:

> I said that I had not a doubt of it, if he would give us the men so that we could "mount" two Sommes at once. He horrified me by saying, "We shall never beat the Boches." I said, but what nonsense, because our side could produce far more men than the Boches. He did not agree. He said that with Bulgaria and Turkey and Poland the Boches would outnumber us — but this in my judgment is absurd.
>
> He says the Russians can't get guns from anywhere but from us, and Haig won't agree, and he wanted to know what 1 thought. I told him that Haig ought to be told exactly how many men he was going to be given, and when, and then he could calculate what fronts he would attack on, and, from that, how many guns he would require. When these were given to him, then all others should go to Russia. Lloyd George was clearly dissatisfied with Haig and also with' Robertson, but did not, of course, discuss either of them directly.
>
> I told him we should want at least 1,700,000 in drafts in the next twelve months, and he said we could not get anything approaching to that number. I asked him why he did not clap conscription on to Ireland, and he said it would have a bad moral effect abroad to see the Irish members carried squealing out of the House, and that there would be serious trouble in Ireland. I said that on the contrary there would be serious trouble in Ireland, but that nobody abroad cared if Johnnie Redmond acted the part of a baby, whereas on the other hand it would be serious, and might easily be fatal, to lose 200,000-300,000 good Irish soldiers. And so we discussed for half an hour, and then he had to go.

He heard at the War Office that there was a strong party in the Cabinet who were in favour of sending ten or fifteen divisions to Salonika, but that to carry this out would require a million tons of shipping, in addition to the half million tons already absorbed by that theatre of war, and that this was prohibitive.* Then, one day (November 16) he went by arrangement to *The Times* office to see Lord Northcliffe, and he would not seem to have been adequately impressed, for this appears in the diary:

> I could not get him to talk sense. He would not consider my offensive of two Sommes. At one moment he said the Boches were on their last legs, in the next he said they had an inexhaustible supply of men. He thought they were starving because eels had gone up from 4 marks to 21 marks! He agreed that Bukarest might be taken, that Sweden would attack Russia, that the long-range submarine was a real danger, and said that Ireland would give any number of recruits if there was a settlement, i.e. Home Rule! Devlin would get hundreds of thousands of men then — and so on and so on. Haig and Robertson were perfect, and had now full power as he (Northcliffe) could "force the Government to do anything!"

Sir Henry found Bonar Law in a very pessimistic mood and to be of opinion that the Coalition Government was on its last legs and that there was no hope of success on the Western Front. Wilson noted:

> Apparently we are sending a brigade to Yemen, or somewhere, and Robertson objects very much. Also we are going to arm all merchantmen and give precedence to this, and Robertson and Haig object to this also. But here they are wrong, and I explained to Bonar Law my opinion of the Navy as being, in time of war, L. of C. troops, and I pointed out that to conduct war at the front you must have a secure base and secure L. of C., and these two services take precedence. Bonar Law was pleased with this and understood it. He told me that Asquith had told him that he [Asquith] had had a letter from one of his sons in which a lecture I had given was described as the "most brilliant he had ever heard."

---

* Owing to his being away in London, Wilson would not seem at the time, judged by his diary, to have heard anything about the important military conference which took place at Chantilly on November 15, at which Joffre and Haig agreed upon their plans for 1917, plans which were modified after Nivelle replaced Joffre.

In the meantime, the news coming to hand from Rumania was bad; but some progress, on the other hand, was still being made on the Somme. Wilson had an interview with the King at Buckingham Palace one day, and there he urged the need of more men, as also the vital importance of introducing conscription in Ireland. He discussed matters with Lord Milner, and of his conversation with him he wrote in his diary:

> He is just back from ten days in France. He is lost in admiration of our Air Service and also of the working of the whole military machine, but he sees no victory ahead of us. He does not believe we can beat the Boche army. Altogether he is thoroughly depressed and depressing. I had a long talk with him about the state of affairs at home, and here also he was depressing and saw no daylight, although he thought that, if Lloyd George broke with the Government and went boldly to the country he would sweep the Government out. Milner would be quite willing to join Lloyd George and Carson. Meantime Asquith sits and does nothing.
>
> After dinner Conky Maxwell came in. He was interesting about Ireland. He had been hampered from the beginning, and was never given a fair chance. He says he thinks there would be serious trouble in north and south if conscription were put on — in this I don't agree.

Two days later Gwynne rang him up to say that certain members of the Cabinet were considering the question of an armistice. Wilson wrote in his diary:

> I urged Gwynne to push along and turn this Government out, and he promises to address Carson's committee next week and give them the figures I gave him, and thus force the pace and force Bonar Law and Co. to leave the Cabinet. Locker came in next, having arranged a meeting between Lloyd George and me. Lloyd George told Locker that he could not make me out, and was never sure whether I was in earnest or not, and Locker begged me to speak my mind to-morrow. This I will do, except that I will not criticize Haig or Robertson.

He also made a point of seeing Gwynne (who had been with Lloyd George) next morning (November 26) before starting to go down to Walton Heath for luncheon, and this appears in the diary:

After lunch a long talk with Lloyd George. I told him that I had not met a single man in high position since I had been home this time who thought we were going to beat the Bodies, and that he alone could save us from the defeat which must follow on such a train of thought. I told him that the present Government stank in the nostrils of the whole army, and that if he was to break away and raise the standard of victory he would have a unanimous army behind him.

He agreed — I think — and thought the margin of safety between victory and indecisive peace was daily becoming narrower. It is. He then went on to tell me that there was a meeting to be held in Petrograd in a fortnight or so, at which next year's plan of campaign was to be decided. The French were sending Castelnau and others, and the choice of our representative lay between me and Lord French. Grey was also going. He had spoken about me to Haig yesterday and Haig was nice about me and agreed to my going. Kiggell is also to go. Lloyd George favours me rather than French, and is going to speak to Robertson about it to-morrow. It looks, therefore, as though I should be off to Russia soon. I said I was willing to go if he thought I was the best man, and he said most emphatically I was. We are to have *carte blanche*.

He wrote next day:

At 12 o'clock I saw Robertson. He was very nice, and quite open in his views about Asquith and the present Government. The Cabinet had asked for his views as to when the war would be over, and what chance there was of winning it. On this Robertson wrote a most admirable paper, in which he made the soldier position clear and said that no one but "cowards, cranks and philosophers" could doubt the final result, provided we did what we ought to do, and could do, and did it in time. A really strong and lucid paper. It seems to me that his position is so strong that nothing but good can come out of it. I was pleased with Robertson's outlook and told him so, and if he stands firm he will get his way.

I dined with Fred Oliver, also there Milner, Carson, Geoffrey Robinson and Waldorf Astor. The most interesting dinner. Carson asked what he should advise Lloyd George and Bonar Law to do, as a crisis was coming. Our unanimous advice was that he should get Lloyd George to smash the Government and get Bonar Law to come out, so that Lloyd George should get the Unionist machinery for a general election, should one come about. I think he agreed, and after

> a long discussion we broke up in that mind, i.e. that Lloyd George should smash, that Bonar Law should come out, and that a real fighting Government should be formed round Lloyd George, Carson and Milner. My last words to Milner were that he should bear a share and take a part. Carson drove me away and sent me on to Arthur Lee, who had telephoned that he wanted to see me. Arthur told me that Lloyd George had decided that I was to go to Russia as the head of the Mission to decide on next year's campaign. I am glad.

Wilson saw Lloyd George on the 28th, who confirmed the information as to his going to Russia, was very complimentary, and said that it was ridiculous his still commanding a corps and reporting to Haig that he had raided trenches "and taken two prisoners." He found out at the Foreign Office that Mr. George Clerk was coming as representing that department, as well as Grey, and he afterwards went to the War Office to obtain information as to the terms of reference and so on. On the 29th he rejoined his corps head-quarters, together with Duncannon; but he only did so for the purpose of bidding good-bye to the staff, and of formally handing the corps over to his successor, which he did on December 1.

During his year in command of the IVth Corps he had fully carried out his intention, expressed in his diary on the previous January 1, of devoting himself especially to making the line, wherever entrusted to him, safe, and to doing what was possible to improve the training and education of his officers. Fate had ordained that he was not to take part in any important offensive, and, although he had hoped at one time that he would be called upon to attack part of the Vimy Ridge and had made elaborate preparations for doing so — preparations which he felt confident would ensure success — circumstances over which he had no control had intervened and had deprived him of the opportunity of putting his plan into execution. The loss of a stretch of front in occupation of his corps below the Ridge on May 21, coupled as it was with ill-success in the effort to recover the ground that the enemy had captured, had been an unfortunate episode; but similar incidents had occurred in the experience of other general officers situated like himself. The reverse had been due to sheer bad luck, and yet it may have been one cause of his still holding a position in the B.E.F. no higher than that of corps commander in the month of November, 1916.

Chapter XVII – The Mission to Russia

General situation in Russia at this time — Fall of Mr. Asquith's Coalition Government — Wilson accompanies Lloyd George to Italy for a Conference about Salonika — The Mission starts for Russia — Conferences in Petrograd — Wilson makes a prolonged tour of the Russian Front — Return of the Mission — Wilson accepts the appointment of Liaison Officer between Haig and Nivelle.

If, at the time when the Allied western Governments arranged to combine in sending joint civil and military Missions to Petrograd for a conference on the spot, the conditions in Russia were in some respects most unsatisfactory from the Entente point of view, they were in other respects tolerably reassuring. The political situation undoubtedly gave grounds for grave anxiety — stronger grounds indeed than the western Governments appear to have realized or to have made adequate provision to deal with. But the purely military situation was by no means unpromising; for the vital problem of munitions was being, at least to some extent, solved, and the position of affairs in this connexion, if still unsatisfactory, was rapidly improving. It was with the military situation that Wilson was immediately Concerned; and when he had made himself acquainted with this, in so far as the various departments of the War Office in touch with the facts were able to assist him, he found that there was much in it that was encouraging.

The Russian offensive of the previous summer had, taken as a whole, achieved a gratifying measure of success. The position in regard to munitions had, moreover, considerably improved since that time, and it was now improving from day to day. The output of the Russian factories was developing fast, and even heavy howitzers were now being produced in fair, although still in entirely insufficient, numbers; rifles, field-guns, machine-guns and ammunition |were, furthermore, being turned out on a totally different scale from that which had prevailed in the years 19x4 and 1915 and even in the early months of 1916. Nor were the Tsar's military forces any longer dependent for armament upon the resources of their own country alone. The French had already provided a handsome supply of field-guns. The United Kingdom was dispatching a substantial consignment of field howitzers, as well as a few pieces of heavier calibre. Most important of all, vast contracts which Lord Kitchener had placed in the United States on behalf of the Russian Government (but for which the British Government was lending the money) were beginning to materialize; and freight ships were arriving almost daily at Vladivostock, and had been arriving at Archangel in numbers in anticipation of the co min g of the ice, crammed with munitions of all sorts — direct result of forethought and willingness to assume responsibility on the part of the great British War Minister, who had passed away before his labours in this direction had really begun to bear fruit.

It must be understood that a very close relation had come to exist between the military position in Russia and the military position in Rumania, and that (apart from Pacific waters) the Russian Empire was now entirely deprived of maritime communication with the outer world, except by way of the Arctic Ocean and the havens presented by the White Sea and the Kola Inlet. The Rumanian military forces had been faring ill during recent weeks, and, at the time when Wilson came to take special interest in Eastern theatres of war, the entire western portions of King Ferdinand's dominions were already being overrun by the enemy. Bukarest fell on December 6, and before the end of that month not only practically the whole of Wallachia, but also considerable portions of Moldavia, had passed into the hands of the invader. Then, the fact that the White Sea is always closed for four or five months in the year, and that the avenue of entrance via the Kola Inlet had only recently been rendered of effect by the opening of the hastily constructed Murmansk Railway, was of vital consequence. Goods of all kinds, as well as war material, moreover, kept accumulating at Archangel during the months of open water far more rapidly than they could be conveyed into the interior of the country by the inadequate railway communications existing. The Murmansk Railway — partly owing to the improvised character of the permanent way, partly owing to the inadequacy of signalling arrangements, sidings, passing stations, etc., on the single line, and partly owing to lack of rolling stock — was only capable of moving a relatively insignificant amount of freight during the twenty-four hours.

During a prolonged period of delay before the Mission actually started, Wilson studied this somewhat complicated subject exhaustively. He also made it his business to discuss very thoroughly the various aspects of the different questions that were involved with technical and other experts at the War Office.

The purpose for which the military members of the joint Allied Mission were supposed to be going was to arrange for the co-ordination of offensives in the coming year, and also to come to an understanding with the Russian military representatives as to what munitions the Western Powers were to supply. But Sir Henry learnt that Russian military administration left much to be desired in the matter of securing that the armament coming from America, as also such armament as the Allies might be prepared to furnish, should reach the troops in the field with reasonable dispatch. He was informed that, owing largely to the unsatisfactory condition of railway communications, but owing even more to defective organization and administration, munitions were accumulating in vast quantities at ports and important railway junctions, and that war material was not being "assembled" on arrival in the country, but was being dispatched in parts into the interior. The consequence was that the armies in the field were being deprived of the use of armament, of mechanical transport, and of other urgently needed requirements for the effective conduct of operations, owing to administrative ineptitude and to sheer lack of system, although the material was actually in the country and would be available for use but for the prevailing mismanagement.

Even before starting, therefore, Sir Henry had made up his

mind that this problem of organization was one to which he must devote special attention, and he had secured the services of an artillery officer who had been under him in France, Colonel (now Major-General Sir F. C.) Poole, whom he hoped to leave in Russia with powers to give effect to such recommendations on the subject as he might in due course find it desirable to make.

Wilson's arrival home from the front practically coincided, as it happened, with the fall of Mr. Asquith's Government and the setting up of that under Mr. Lloyd George, and he watched the progress of the political situation with the keenest interest from a position to some extent behind the scenes. The day after he reached Eaton Place was a Sunday, and Miss Bonar Law told him after church that the crisis had arrived. On getting home, he found Gwynne at his house, who told him the news; and this appears in the diary:

> Lloyd George Las given Asquith a final decision that a small committee of himself, Bonar Law and Carson will take over the conduct of the war, and have no portfolios, but absolute power, and that, if he [Asquith] did not agree to this, he [Lloyd George] and also Bonar Law would resign. Personally I don't like this proposal, because it will leave the Cabinet to intrigue and bring down this trio, who will fall to a certainty if things go wrong, as they are sure to do for some time. Moreover it has no representative of Foreign Affairs nor of Finance. No, I don't like this. However, it will be better than Asquith.
>
> Kiggell came at 2 o'clock and we talked till 5 o'clock. He is quite hostile to this Mission and wants everything (practically) to go to France. He had no answer to my query as to what would happen if Russia refused to play. I don't know in detail what Haig's demand in guns, aeroplanes, etc., is, but I shall not be surprised to find it excessive in view of the situation in which we now are.
>
> Then the Lord telephoned to say that the troops we had landed in Athens to enforce our demand on Greece for the surrender of guns, had been attacked and driven back on to the ships, and that a fight was now going on in the streets between Venizelists and Royalists! What a commentary to our foreign policy.

Next day the entry occurs:

> *Asquith is out.* Hurrah. Bonar was sent for at 8.50 p.m. to form a Cabinet. Bonar Law appears to have behaved like a man, and I am delighted, but, of course, the real credit is due to Lloyd George.

On December 5 Wilson wrote

> In the afternoon it was seen that Bonar Law could not form a Government, and so refused the offer of Premiership. Lloyd was then sent for, and to-night after dinner I went over to see Lady Carson and she says Edward thinks it will be all right. Then I telephoned to Leo Masse, who said Asquith was done. Then I telephoned to Miss Bonar Law and told her all this good news. I am confident myself that, if we manage things properly, we have Asquith dead.

By the 10th the constitution of the new Government was known.. Wilson was well satisfied with the arrangement of a small inner War Cabinet, acting as the authoritative nucleus of an outer Cabinet, and he felt confident that this novel arrangement would work well. Just about the same time news began to arrive from France of certain important changes that were taking place as regards command, that Nivelle was succeeding Joffre as Commander-in-Chief on the Western Front, that Foch was being pushed into the background, and that General Lyautey had been appointed War Minister. Sir Henry wrote in the diary on December 11:

> I saw A. J. Balfour on Horse Guards Parade. I asked him if he was coming out to Russia with me, and he said, no. I asked if he had taken over the Foreign Office, and he said he had only agreed to do so on condition that he should have ten days' holiday, and he was off to-morrow to Brighton. Marvellous. One would think there was no war.

He wrote next day:

> It seems that Bethmann-Hollweg made a speech this afternoon to say that he is now prepared to discuss terms of peace, and has so informed the Allies. This frightens me. I am afraid he is going to get President Wilson to move, and then by degrees try and drift us into an armistice. This is what I have long been afraid of. After dinner I

telephoned to Milner (he was out) and to Carson (he will see me to-morrow at the Admiralty), to Gwynne, who promised to put an article in the Morning Post warning of the danger of an armistice, and to Leo Maxse to the same effect. I am afraid of an armistice. Duncannon telephoned to say that George Clerk had telephoned to him that we are not going to start till the day after Christmas. What a sinful waste of time.

Sir Henry spent the remainder of the month in London, having frequent discussions at the War Office and with Lord Milner and others in regard to matters connected with the Mission, and keeping himself acquainted with the general situation in the various theatres of war. He heard the whole story of the recent political crisis from Mr. Bonar Law one day:

How Asquith had no idea of the reality and weight of the attack, how the right thing for Lloyd George to do was to go to the country now, but how this would be made impossible by the Opposition voting with him until it was organized in the country, and then attacking him! Real patriotism!

Wilson was somewhat disconcerted by finding that Bonar Law, and also Lord Carnock (formerly Sir A. Nicolson) were less disposed to scout the idea of peace than he was. He, moreover, found that the C.I.G.S. was, like himself, growing somewhat disturbed at all the talk of peace that was making itself heard. Robertson was indeed disposed to think that, if the Germans were to offer to withdraw from France and Belgium and also from Alsace and Lorraine, our position might become difficult, and Wilson wrote in his diary:

When I left Robertson, I had a long talk with the Monument [Major — now Colonel— C. C. Lucas, the C.I.G.S.'s private secretary], who thought that Robertson might have to stand an attack about Rumania. According to the Monument, old Robertson has been right all along about Rumania, and I can quite believe it; he had told the Monument he was sure to be downed the moment he made a mistake. But all this is very unsettling. Robertson told me that Russia was still shouting for us to send more troops to Salonika; but 23 divisions are the utmost which our shipping can compete with, so it is impossible, as well as childish, to send troops there.

"That ass President Wilson has barged in and asked all belligerents for their terms," he wrote on December 22, when news of this uncalled-for intervention from across the Atlantic came to hand; but he felt confident that the effort at mediation would come to nothing, and in this he proved to be right. He learnt with the utmost satisfaction on the 30th that Lord Miln er was to be head of the British section of the Mission, and he, moreover, heard at the same time that Lloyd George, Milner and Robertson were about to proceed to Italy for a conference, and that after this the Mission would at last start. Later in the day he received a message instructing him to be ready to accompany the party to Italy, and on the 31st he entered in his diary:

> The last day of a year of indecisive fighting. Verdun, Somme, Greece and Rumania all indecisive, both sides claiming victory; on the whole, victory inclining to us, and the final decision brought nearer. A very disappointing year. The answer to Germany's peace proposal is published to-day. It is admirable and conclusive, and I hope that President Wilson will stop his nonsense or take [his courage in both hands and join us.

The Italian trip was being undertaken because no decision had been arrived at at a meeting, held in London a few days before, with regard to the Macedonian theatre. Lloyd George had thereupon proposed a meeting at Taranto, at which Sarrail and General Milne (who was now in command of our troops at Salonika) were to be present. The matter at issue was that, whereas the Italians agreed with us that no more troops ought to be sent to this theatre, M. Briand was pressing for the dispatch thither of reinforcements amounting to two more British divisions and four more Italian divisions, besides two French divisions. The dispatch of reinforcements on this scale was, in reality, quite out of the question from the shipping point of view; but an impression prevailed in military circles that Lloyd George was, as ever, hankering after the East. So Wilson wrote in his diary:

> I confess that all these changes in France upset me rather, and I

am not sure that the best way would not be to knock Briand off his perch, he is so deeply committed to the Salonika business.

Of a conversation which he had had with Lord Derby, who was now Secretary of State for War, he wrote:

> I impressed on him the importance of allowing the French to give the *coup de grâce*, but on the other hand of not allowing Haig to take over so much extra line that he would render himself impotent; for the French are sure to call on us to attack, no matter how much line we take over, and we must be in a position to do so or else the French will say nasty things. [Dealing with people who always want to have it both ways is bound to prove awkward.]

The party for Italy started on January 2, its principal members being Lloyd George, Milner, Robertson, Wilson, Clerk and Rennell Rodd, Wilson taking Duncannon with him; they were joined in Paris by Briand, Albert Thomas and Lyautey, with their assistants. Discussing matters in the train with Milner and Robertson, Wilson found that both were entirely opposed to any more troops being sent to Salonika, and he wrote in his diary on arriving in Rome:

> We arc now the most important of the Allies, in money, in fleets, in shipping, in coal and (almost) in armies, and yet we allow our Allies to do things of which we entirely disapprove, and, although it is quite true that we cannot dictate, still we can get our own way to a great extent by bargaining.

He continued:

> A lot of people at the station — Sonnino, Tittoni (an Italian Caillaux), Cadorna (who looks old to my eyes), Delme-Radcliffe, Charlie Lamb, and so on.* Radcliffe tells me the Italians have only 8 million field-gun rounds and 3 million heavy. There is a fierce pro-Boche and anti-English campaign going on at this minute, which

---

* Brigadier-General Delme-Radcliffe was British Military Representative with the Italian armies at the front; Colonel Lamb was our Military Attaché in Rome.

makes our people uneasy. Long talk with Fairholme,* just in from Athens. He is of opinion that we are wrong in backing Venizelos, and ought to change and back Tino. He says our Foreign Office has been absolutely hopeless — never once a decision on any point. He gave his experiences in Athens during the riot last month, when the French and we lost 60 killed and wounded and made prisoners. Very interesting. There seems no possible doubt that we have behaved like fools. It is quite clear to me that the French and we are entirely wrong in backing Venizelos. One great stumbling-block is Sarrail, who, according to Fairey, is determined to go to war with Greece. But I can't see why Sarrail should not be curbed and ordered to work within certain limits. Undoubtedly we have played fast and loose and *false* with Tino. He may have done the same with us; but Fairey is clear that he does not want to go to war with us.

Milner and I had a talk till midnight. He said that at the meeting of Ministers to-day nothing had been settled, that Sonnino made a good speech in favour of Tino and the Italian policy of backing him, and that Lloyd George made a speech about the solidarity of the Allies! The real fact being that the Italians are backing Tino, the French want to attack him, and we are backing both Tino and Venizelos.

Next morning (January 6):

Lloyd George weighed in with a Memorandum on Strategy as regards Rumania, Salonika and the Italian front. An amazing document, written without Robertson's knowledge or approval. Robertson very cross.

Then the first Plenary Conference took place, after which the assemblage broke up into two parties, one politicians, the other soldiers. The following entry in Wilson's diary obviously refers to the proceedings of the latter body:

Sarrail spoke well, but was not logical. He expects an attack by the Bulgars and Boches within 4 to 6 weeks; he must have reinforcements, but he could not get even the two promised French divisions for 10 weeks! He wanted to attack Greece at once and

---

* Colonel Fairholme was now our Military Attaché at Athens.

without warning of any sort. He intended to stand on his present line even up to the point of disaster. He is an attractive personality, but not a very practical soldier.

We broke off for lunch and met again at 4 p.m. This meeting was the devil. Lyautey led off with three-quarters of an hour of platitudes and contradictions, finishing off by asking for 3 divisions (British and Italian) to save Monastir — although exclaiming, with hand on heart, that the West was the only place of importance. Pelikini (Russia) backed Lyautey. Cadorna and Robertson both refused to send any more troops; and, incidentally, there is no shipping. The result was a distinct cleavage, and I don't myself see how we can be brought together. As Cadorna very rightly said to Lyautey, "If you think Monastir is so important you had better send three divisions there yourselves."

Meanwhile, the Frock Coats in the next room, having settled in the morning that they would not go to war with Greece, decided this after noon to give Greece a 48-hours' ultimatum, and then let Sarrail loose! Wonderful! The result of the day's work is exceedingly unsatisfactory The Frock Coats are being led by the French into war with Greece, and we soldiers are in clear disagreement, the English and Italians versus the Russians and French. By the way, we never touched on Lloyd George's paper all day.

Next day there is the entry:

Another conference at 10 a.m. I went with Milner to the Embassy before it, and found that Lloyd George had got Sarrail there, and he got Sarrail to make a bargain that he would not attack the Greeks. They shook hands over this. We soldiers were not allowed in at the conference this morning. Robertson showed me a letter he had sent to Lloyd George saying that he would not be a party to sending any more divisions to Salonika. Robertson and I went for a drive after lunch, then another conference. The net result is this:

1. A 48-hours' notice to Greece to agree to our last note.
2. No attack by Sarrail during this 48 hours. Nor afterwards without the consent of the Powers, unless Greece rejects the note.
3. No reinforcements for Salonika.
4. The Italians to study the question of opening a road from Santi Quaranta to Monastir.
5. Milne to be put rather more under Sarrail's orders.

The outcome of this particular conference was that a compromise was arrived at as between the views of Robertson and Cadorna on the one hand and the views of the French and Russian Governments on the other hand — whether the latter views enjoyed the genuine support of the French military authorities as represented by General Lyautey seems open to question. So far from entertaining any desire to send additional British divisions to Macedonia, Robertson was most anxious to reduce the number already there in the interests of the Western Front; but in this he could not count upon support from Lloyd George. Briand had consistently favoured the giving of a first-class importance to the Salonika undertaking from its commencement, and he now wanted to send additional troops thither so as to enable Sarrail to embark on a comprehensive offensive in the spring. The decision of the conference practically amounted to leaving matters as they were and virtually to imposing a defensive attitude upon Sarrail, while declining to sanction an actual reduction in the forces serving under mat commander.

The Prime Minister and Robertson, together with the French representatives, started for home in the evening; but Milner and Wilson remained in Rome, and on the following day Sir Henry had a prolonged discussion on the subject of the Santi Quatanta road to Monastir with Cadoma, whom he then found quite ready to undertake responsibility for inspection and labour so long as the parties were not attacked. They also went into the question of British troops, guns and so forth possibly being sent to help the Italians in their operations against Laibach and Trieste.

Wilson noted in the diary:

> He is still anxious — almost very anxious — about an attack coming in the Trentino, like last year; and I too would be anxious if this attack were to be made by some Boche divisions, for the Italians are simply terrified of the Boches. I have been much struck during my visit here in Rome with the amount of Boche and of Boche sympathy here, and with the terror of Boche soldiers.

He got back to London, with Milner and Duncannon, on January 11, only to find that the start for Russia was further delayed in consequence of the fall of Trepoff, who had for some months been the principal Minister of the Tsar. He met General Nivelle, who had come over from France to discuss matters, at dinner a day or two later, and he wrote in his diary on the 17th:

> Met the Monument before breakfast, who told me that, at a War Committee meeting yesterday, at which Nivelle was present, all had not gone well, and that Nivelle and Haig had had some words, but nothing serious.

He heard from Robertson next day that it had been agreed at this meeting that the offensives on the Western Front should start somewhat earlier than had been agreed with General Joffre at Chantilly in November, and he also heard that news from Russia forecast a revolution and even possibly the dethronement of the Tsar.

A party of fifty British, French and Italian representatives, forming the personnel of the joint Allied Mission, assembled at Euston on the evening of the 20th (January), and they sailed from Oban next day at noon* in the *Kildonan Castle*, escorted by two destroyers. H.M.S. *Duke of Edinburgh* replaced the destroyers after passing the Shetlands. M. Doumergue and General de Castelnau were the heads of the French portion or the Mission, Signor Scialoja and General Ruggeri of the Italian portion, and Milner and Wilson of the British portion; the British portion included, amongst others, George Clerk of the Foreign Office, Lord Revelstoke on the financial side, Mr. Layton of the Munitions Ministry, General

* Great secrecy was maintained with regard to their starting point and date of departure, when the party embarked in the armed yacht. H.M.S. Eriska. "I was ordered to Oban one January day," Captain C. Brooks writes, "and arrived there in the afternoon. No one knew what was to happen until 10 a.m. next day, when a special train arrived bringing Lord Milner and his Mission for Russia. I took them on board and steamed outside the harbour, where I found one of the Castle Line. I went alongside and put my passengers on board. The whole proceeding only took about an hour. Sir H. Wilson joined me on the navigation bridge, and I and my officers were much impressed by his very strong personality and charming manner, and we all regretted that his stay on board had been so short." It is said that mines were found to have been laid a few hours later, near where the Kildonan Castle had been at anchor.

Headlam (as artillery expert). Colonel Sidney Clive, Lord Brooke and Lord Duncannon.

Wilson was very anxious that no serious conference should take place in Russia until after the military members of the Mission had been to the front, going as separate parties; and he found that de Castelnau was of the same mind and was opposed to "*un voyage Cook*."* Milner, he found, had no hopes of a decision on the Western Front, but this was by no means his own view. "I have enormous hopes if we can get a real move on the Russians," he wrote in his diary, and he proceeded:

> Later in the day I got General de Castelnau and General Ruggeri into my cabin, and we discussed what we would do on arrival at Petrograd. We all agreed, in principle, to split up. Castelnau wants to go south to see the Rumanian position and Berthelot; Ruggeri does not care much where he goes, and I must go wherever the big attack is going to be. We then discussed what we had to do, and I explained that I had a certain number of guns in my pocket, and mortars, aeroplanes, etc., but had no intention of giving them until I was convinced that the Russians could and would use them.
>
> Then we discussed the Chantilly Conference, the Rome Conference and Nivelle's visit to London. As regards the Chantilly Conference, I pointed out that the whole Russo-Rumanian attack on Bulgaria, as well as the Salonika attack towards Sofia, were things of the past, and that therefore the Chantilly Conference had for the most part fallen to the ground. As regards the Rome Conference, I said that, in the main, the only military decision had been not to send more troops to Salonika. Ruggeri said that there was a proposal to send English guns to help the Italians on the Isonzo; but I explained that this was only a tentative proposal of Lloyd George's to lend 300 guns until our offensive began in May, but that Cadorna had quite agreed that we could not send either guns or men for an offensive. Then we got on to Nivelle's visit to London, and when Castelnau told Ruggeri that the French and British attacks were to be made "as soon as possible" Ruggeri was much upset and wanted to wire this to Cadorna. This we begged him not to do. I told him I was certain that Cadorna had already been informed.

---

* "A Cook journey." This is a reference to the explorer Captain James Cook (1728-1779).

On January 24, when they were due north of the North Cape but a long way out, the *Duke of Edinburgh* went about and steamed for home, and that day a wireless message came to hand, of which Wilson wrote indignantly in his diary:

> President Wilson has made an amazing speech about peace without victory — all countries to have access to the sea, and much other dangerous nonsense. Doumergue and Castelnau, and all Frenchmen, are furious with "my Cousin."*

The heads of the Mission afterwards met, and all went off well at their conference. It was finally agreed that the members of the Mission should, at first, lay themselves out to gain and not to give information, that the Mission's proposals should come at the end and not at the beginning of the visit, that the soldiers should go down the front or not as they pleased, and that the heads of the Mission should meet and should pool their knowledge and information before the final conference with the Russians took place. Next day they entered the Kola Inlet, and the *Kildonan Castle* anchored near the terminus of the new railway at Romanoff. Complimentary visits were paid, that same evening the party started by train for Petrograd, and Wilson wrote in his diary:

> This port of Romanoff has boundless possibilities, but the Russians won't open it up for a hundred years. It is at the end of a long and very sheltered bay, with great depth everywhere. It is always open, and it ought to be the greatest port of Russia next to Odessa.

The journey by the somewhat ramshackle railway, laid down in haste during the war, took over three days, a deputation from the Emperor meeting the train during the first night. Its principal member, General Nostitch, had been Russian Military Attaché in Paris during the Agadir crisis in 1911, he knew all about Wilson's activities at that time, and they had a long and interesting conversation. Wilson notes in his diary:

---

* Wilson from this time forward frequently refers to the President as "my Cousin." No relationship, needless to say, existed.

> General Nostitch said that, if it had not been for me the Germans would have been in Petrograd. In November, when I was staying at Chantilly, General de Castelnau told everyone at Les Tilles that 1 had saved France. I ought to be satisfied with these two expressions of opinion. And I am.

Of a discussion which he had with Milner on the day before reaching Petrograd, and which is of interest in view of the attitude which he assumed during the following winter, he wrote in the diary:

> I told him I should have to tell Gourko, or somebody, what our plans are for the coming great battle; and he quite agreed. It will he impossible to negotiate unless I do so, though I shall find out what their plans are before I disclose ours. Then we discussed what would happen in the event of the great attack being a failure. Milner is opposed to our trying again, and I agree with him. I think that, by helping the Italians and Russians, we might knock out the Austrians; and also in the autumn we might knock out the Turks, who are already showing signs of distress. These two blows would be fatal. Milner is at last getting quite hopeful!

The train arrived at Petrograd on the morning of January 29, and the party were met by a distinguished Russian gathering and by several British officers. Sir Henry arranged with the military members of the Mission under him, and with our military representatives permanently accredited to Russia, that nothing was for the present to he discussed with the Russians except the existing state of affairs, so as to find out exactly how this stood. He heard at the Embassy of the ominously strong feeling that had sprung up against the Emperor and the Empress, and he learnt with astonishment that even the possibility of their assassination was quite openly spoken of in leading Russian circles. Next night a gala dinner took place at the Foreign Office, and of this entertainment he wrote in his diary:

> I wore the Grand Officer of the Legion of Honour and the Star and Necklace of the Bath, and my medals; also Russian shoulder-straps, and grey Astrakan cap, and altogether I was a fine figure of a man! I created quite a sensation at the Foreign Office dinner and the

reception afterwards. I was much taller than the Grand Duke Serge, and altogether a "notable" — as I was told. Superb! The Admiral-in-Chief told me that a Boche submarine had turned up in Kola Bay the day after we arrived there I Just one day too late.

Next day there is the entry:

At 9.30 we all started for Tsarskoe-Selo. It was a beautiful Swiss morning. The Emperor was most affable, and talked to every single one of us. I was astonished to find much more character in his face than I had imagined, and quite a twinkle in his eye. We were received in a charming suite of rooms, with court officers in quaint uniforms, and some servants in marvellous Catherine clothes and feathers in bonnets. What a murderous pity that the Emperor is so weak and so under the Empress's thumb, for, according to all the accounts I get, he and the Empress are heading straight for ruin.

We got back at 1.30, and at 2 o'clock I went to Gourko for my private talk, only to find that he had invited both Castelnau and Ruggeri, and he then gave us if hours of a lecture on the reorganization of the Russian Army. Gourko showed and explained at break-neck pace a large number of graphics, from which he made what seemed to me to be quite erroneous deductions. He talked volubly of road transport, of lack of horses, of manufactories, etc., etc., and wound up with a criticism of the Rumanians, claiming, however, that Russian action in helping Rumania had saved Sarrail at Salonika. We were then bowed out. I must get a hold of the man and shake him into some practical frame of mind.

Layton told me afterwards that the Munitions Sub-Committee had got on better to-day and had nearly got to grips. The Russians had asked for 4,000 of the 75 s, and only 100 of our 6-inch, instead of 600! But 200 of the 9.2-inch, instead of 30 or 40! They are difficult gentlemen.

The first Plenary Conference was held at the Russian Foreign Office on February 1, when de Castelnau, by agreement with Wilson, asked that a Military Committee or the generals should be set up. This proposal was agreed to and, on the adjournment of the Plenary Conference, the committee met — Gourko, de Castelnau, Ruggeri and Wilson — and, as Wilson remarked in his diary, "did good work." It was settled that 1917 must be made decisive; that attacks must be brought off simultaneously; that "side shows" must

Tsarskoe-Selo, February 3, 1917

be avoided; that the troops at Salonika were simply to be regarded as a retaining force; that no big attack was to be undertaken in Rumania; that the Rumanian army was not to be absorbed by Russia; that, if the Germans should attack any one of the Allies, the others were to join in. Dates when offensives were to be launched were also specifically mentioned and were agreed to. In the meantime Sir Henry was also arranging about how Poole was to perform his duties; and he was agreeably surprised to find the Russians quite prepared to fall in with his far-reaching proposals on this subject, as also was de Castelnau. Milner had audiences of the Emperor and Empress on the 2nd; Wilson heard of their very unsatisfactory result next day, and he refers to the matter in his diary as follows:

> Milner tells me that yesterday the Emperor and Empress, although very pleasant, made it quite clear that they would not tolerate any discussion of Russian internal politics. On the other hand, the Emperor was quite sympathetic about my proposals about Poole. He asked Milner whose proposals they were, and when told —

Wilson's — he said, "That is the very tall man. I hear he is of the first order."

We all dined at Tsarskoe-Selo with the Emperor. Very well done in flowers, silver plate, etc., but all the wonderful things are in Moscow. After dinner the Emperor saw a few of us, one at a time.

I was taken down a long passage to the Empress's own boudoir — a room full of pictures and bric-a-brac and flowers, and a large gallery. She was very pleasant and nice to me. I reminded her of our tennis parties in the old days, 36 years ago, at Darmstadt, where I said I used to play tennis with her and her sisters. She was so delighted with the reminiscences, and remembered some of the names I had forgotten. After this it was easy. She said her lot was harder than most people's because she had relations and friends in England, Russia and Germany. She told me of her experiences, and her eyes filled with tears. She has a beautiful face, but very, very sad. She is tail and graceful, divides her hair simply at one side, and it is done up at the back. The hair is powdered with grey. When I said I was going to leave her, as she must be tired of seeing strangers and making conversation, she nearly laughed and kept me on for a little while. What a tragedy there is in that life.

Sir Henry prolonged his stay at Petrograd for another four days before proceeding to the front, and during these a number of meetings with individuals and meetings of committees took place. Both Genera! Gourko and the War Minister agreed to the proposed arrangement with regard to Poole; so that Wilson was placed in a position to cable home and to ask that the requisite staff should be got together and sent out. Sir Henry informed Gourko of the British intention to continue offensive operations on a modest scale on the Egyptian frontier and in Mesopotamia so long as the weather permitted, but that it was in contemplation to carry out attacks on a much more ambitious scale in those two theatres in the following autumn and winter, with the object of settling the Turks once for all. But he added that this must depend upon the Russians doing their share of harassing the Osmanli in Armenia. In reply to this, Gourko promised that as great activity as was practicable would be displayed by the Russian forces in those quarters. Then, at a formal meeting of the Military Committee, de Castelnau inquired of Gourko whether he proposed to embark on active operations in Rumania, but he received the reply that this hinged upon how far the Rumanians helped with their army; and what was said indicated that little faith was reposed in its affording effective assistance.

A meeting of the Plenary Conference was held on February 6, and at this the decisions of the Political and the Military Committees were read and were agreed to. Wilson wrote in his diary:

> Castelnau then raised the question of the Japanese helping us more, and, after *messieurs les civiles* had tried to give *un enterrement de première classe*,* he got his way that the subject should be taken up seriously. Sazonoff told us how, 18 months ago, he had tried, and that the Japs gave a flat refusal.

Next day the entry appears:

> Guy Brooke, Duncannon and I lunched with Grand Duchess Vladimir, mother of Boris, and others. Lovely palace overlooking the Neva. Guy and Duncannon were plotting with Boris to have me made Hon. Colonel of a regiment of Cossacks. Great fun if they would. Boris commands all the Cossacks.

Sir Henry, accompanied by Colonel Knox, our chief Military Attaché and some of the military staff of the Mission, arrived at Pskov, General Russki's head-quarters, on the 8th. Russki, who commanded the northern group consisting of thirteen corps, showed them the maps of the trenches all along his front and explained his dispositions and intentions; as he did not know French or English the conversation had to be carried on through Knox. He explained that he had been appreciably weakened owing to troops of his having been sent off down to the Rumanian front, and he admitted that he was not very hopeful of undertaking a big offensive. But he held that East Prussia ought to be the goal of Russian offensives, and Wilson notes in his diary that he was favourably impressed by what he saw of this Russian leader. The party went on to Riga next day, arriving during the night, and in the morning they met General Radko Dmitrieff (the Bulgarian who had

---

* "Civilians/civil servants" and "a first-class funeral," respectively.

played so important a part in the campaign in Thrace in 1912-13), who was in command of the Twelfth Army. They were taken out by motor to the front and they drove to a locality where the Russians had recently taken a strong pivot in the German line by assault without preliminary gun fire. Wilson wrote in his diary:

> The Russian original positions were very strong, and in several lines with a good deal of wire. Miles and miles of corduroy roads, several light railways, and a fine bridge, 2,000 yards long, over a river. Altogether I was much more pleased with the front system and organization than I had thought to be. The men were well fed and well clothed, the little horses in perfect condition, long lines of sleigh transport moved along the side of the road in excellent order, the hospital arrangements were good, there were organizations of a voluntary character right up in front for supplying the men with rations. All this was good.
>
> We lunched with a dear old general, Vasiliev, who commands the VIth Siberian Corps. He was over 60 and was the father of this very fine corps, having commanded it right through the war. This was the corps that had done the recent fighting. After lunch he came with me, and we inspected the 11th Siberian Regiment and the 6th Letts Regiment. I had to shout to each battalion "*Sdorovo molatzi*" (Welcome my braves), to which they replied, "Long life and health to Your Excellency." Then the general made a little speech and called for cheers, which they took up like children. Then they filed by in fours or sixes, and I called out "*Spazebo molatzi*" (Well done my braves).
>
> Then back to Riga. Knox and I took a walk. A fine town with good shops, but very Boche. Then he and I had an hour's talk with General Radko Dmitrieff before dinner. Radko is a shrewd, hard, bullet-headed Bulgar, now a naturalized Russian. He has great hopes of breaking through the Boche lines with three divisions by surprise, and then pushing through with three or four corps, and getting cavalry out to break railways and communications. He says the Boches are very thin opposite to him, and cannot collect any serious force for at least ten days. We also discussed heavy guns, aeroplanes, trench mortars, etc. He is a stout-hearted little fellow, and I feel happy that the Boches will now never take Riga.

Next morning the party proceeded by tail to Minsk, a two-days
5 journey, and were there met by General Ewart, who was in

command of the Western Section and had fifty divisions under him, and with whom Wilson had a long talk. Ewart expressed h im self as confident, although he was anxious for more artillery, aeroplanes and trench mortars; he moreover appeared to have a good staff. "I was well pleased with the outlook of these men/ 5 Wilson observes in the diary, "they understood all about Salonika and President Wilson. 55 Ewart gave the party a fine lunch, at which he and Wilson made speeches, and in the afternoon he came to see them off at the station on their journey to Moscow. "The visit was a complete success," was Wilson's verdict.*

They arrived at Moscow on February 14 and were met on arrival by the Governor. They found de Castelnau there. He was, however, going to start back to Petrograd in the afternoon, so Wilson had a long talk with him, and of this conversation he wrote in his diary:

> He was very down on his luck. He saw no way by which these Russians could take the offensive this year, and he did not believe that they could do anything before May at the earliest, and not very seriously even then. He was not impressed by their men, nor officers, nor staff, nor by such of their lines as he had seen; but he said that he had not been up in the front line. He thought the railways were in a hopeless mess, and, in short, he did not think they were in a position to hold the Boche divisions in front of them; so he doubted the success of our offensive. He repeated that we must have the Japs to help. He said the Russians were not more advanced in their ideas and methods than we were 18 to 20 months ago, and had no more chance

---

* At one locality an incident occurred during the progress of this tour of Wilson's along the Russian front, of which he makes no mention in his diary, but which, nevertheless, greatly impressed him, for he often referred to it afterwards. He got into conversation with a party of Russian soldiers in the trenches, the parley, of course, being conducted through an interpreter. He made inquiries of the men concerning various matters, and they returned the compliment by questioning him; and the one point that they asked about with a quite particular insistence was whether the British soldiers who were fighting on the French and other fronts were called upon to tear down barbed-wire entanglements with their hands. Their anxiety for information on such a subject brought vividly home to him the rare difficulties under which the Russian troops were — or, at all events, hitherto had been — carrying on the war.

> against the Boches than we had at that period. I tried to hearten him up, and succeeded, I told him what I had seen, and how much better I thought it than what I had expected, and I reminded him that even 18 months ago we could have whipped the Boches had we then the numerical superiority which the Russians now have over them. Undoubtedly we must get help from the Japanese, especially of the fleet and shipping— I don't see how we are going to get many men because of shipping. But we ought and must be at the Boches, even without them, and the Russians ought certainly to hold what they have now got in front of them.
>
> I had an interesting talk with General Vogack, who once was Military Attaché in London, and also elsewhere. His chief concern was the internal trouble of the Emperor and Empress, next was the Russian mind which had not yet gone to war, next the total lack and power of organization. He said that he himself frankly could not see the end of the war under another two or three years. Meanwhile he dreaded the submarine. Not at all an encouraging picture. After we got back to the hotel I had a talk with one of our Naval officers, who has been four years in submarines and is on leave from Reval, where we have 8 of them. He considers our return journey will be excessively dangerous.

Wilson mentions in his diary going next day to a meeting of the Moscow Municipal Munitions Committee, a private and local, although also municipal, association for making shell and war material, which had been established in view of the Government failure. He was told that there were 220 similar committees scattered over the face of Russia. The chairman, after describing the work and indicating the difficulties under which the committee laboured, launched out against the Government. But Sir Henry pointed out that he and his party were soldiers, who had nothing to do with Russia's internal troubles and who had only come to offer help and to assist in devising an effective organization with regard to supplying war material for the army in the field. He learnt from another source, however, that this committee had done splendid work, and he found the opinion to prevail in Moscow, as it prevailed elsewhere, that the Emperor and Empress were a danger to the country and would very likely be assassinated. "They have lost their people, their nobles, and now their Army, and I see no hope for them; there will be terrible trouble one day here," he wrote in. his diary. He and his party received an ovation when occupying, the Imperial box at the Opera that night — such celebrations in honour of Allied representatives were always most admirably stage-managed in Russia in the days antecedent to the Revolution of March, 1917.

This appears in the diary next day (February 16):

> It seems as certain as anything can be that the Emperor and Empress are riding for a fall. Everyone— officers, merchants, ladies — talk openly of the absolute necessity of doing away with them. If the poor Emperor would only choose the best man, make him Prime Minister, then go to the Duma and say he would trust himself to the people, he would have the whole of Russia at his feet. It is a tragedy.
>
> We left Moscow at 2.30 p.m. I must speak to Milner about the necessity of his putting the case of the state of the country and the army before the Emperor. I feel that we shall not have done our best until we do that.

Back in Petrograd he wrote:

> I find Milner in depression, tired and worried and listless. I got to work on him at once. Castelnau had depressed him beyond words. I told him that Castelnau had no reason to be depressed, he had seen nothing and so had got the wrong point of view. He had been put on a siding for half a day. These things had depressed him. I, on the contrary, was far from being depressed. I related some of my experiences and I did Milner good. I also insisted that Buchanan should send a good stiff wire about precautions necessary on the sea, and I will send one to Robertson.
>
> Before dinner one of the Emperor's A.D.C.s came to warn me that we were running grave risks in returning as we were doing, and that we ought to take far more elaborate precautions for secrecy.

Next day, the 18th, the entry occurs:

> Milner went down to Tsarskoe-Selo with the other *civiles* and saw the Emperor. He gave the Emperor a paper he had written, showing how we had found it necessary to enlist all voluntary enterprise, etc., and suggesting the same for Russia. The paper was quite good, but was not nearly strong enough, and Milner told me on

> his return that he had not been able to rub it in as I wanted him to do. He found the Tsar tired and looking ill.
>
> At 4 o'clock, Milner, Doumergue, Castelnau and I had a meeting till 6 o'clock to discuss our experiences. The *civiles* are anxious about the internal state. I am not, as, even if the Tsar and the Tsarina are assassinated, it will not make for a separate peace. Castelnau was very critical of the army. He says their value is only 9 against French 20, and the utmost we can expect is that the Russians can hold what is now in front of them. I don't quite agree, as I pointed out — an army which completely recovered from the disasters of 18 months ago may, and will, do good things. Neither the French nor our army could have made such a recovery. Then, the Boches are very thin opposite to the Russians, and I can quite imagine a crack in the Boche lines and then masses, of Cossacks. The Russians have 52 Cavalry Divisions. My own opinion is that, with luck, the Russians may do great things, just as I think that we may do great things if we have luck.

Upon the whole agreeably surprised with what he had seen of the troops, Sir Henry was also well satisfied with the readiness of the Russian military authorities to fall in with his plan of organizing a commission under Poole to deal with the war material that, as it was, we were sending out, as well as the further war material which he proposed that we should send. A meeting of the Military and Munitions members of the Mission with the Russians at the War Office on the 20th did not, however, proceed altogether satisfactorily. This meeting was especially assembled to discuss a report that had been furnished by Layton, and Wilson wrote of it in the diary:

> Gourko was in the chair and in his opening statement he was quite unfair to the Allies. For he said that at Chantilly it had been agreed that all Allies should have equality of treatment as regards materials, but that this principle had not been applied here, probably because the delegates had been instructed not to supply it. The truth, of course, is that the amount of stuff we could send is strictly limited by the shipping and by the railways over here.
>
> I was going to object to Gourko's presentment, when the War Minister, Belaieff, did it for me, which was much better. Gourko said later on that, if the Russian offensives were not so successful as they might be, it was because of our not sending them all they asked for.

However, Layton's report was agreed to.

At the final plenary meeting, which took place later in the day, all the work that had been done during the visit was passed and confirmed except Layton's report, of which all the constructive paragraphs were cut out and were put in as "considerations" at the end. "This was brought about," Wilson notes in his diary, "by that vain, talkative devil Gourko, who got quite warm about Layton's proposals, as he had done at the 2 o'clock meeting." Next evening Gourko came to present to Wilson the Insignia of the Order of the White Eagle, and before midnight the Mission left Petrograd by special train for Romanoff taking three days over the journey. This appears in the diary:

> At Sotoka, the south-western port of the White Sea, we walked down to the harbour and saw some 40 ships frozen up in the ice, and Layton and I went on board one. A wonderful sight, the White Sea all frozen, and quite flat and covered with snow. The sun setting in the west gave a wonderful pink colouring over the sea to the east.

And another day:

> Revelstoke tells me that we [English] cannot go on financing Russia after this year. We have lent her 500 millions, and arc now going to lend another 550 millions. Doumergue offered 5 million francs.

At Romanoff:

> Here we find that things are very different from what we heard at Petrograd. We can land 1,500 tons a day, and the railway can only take away 200 tons a day. The wharfs are congested, the shipping is held up, the labour arrangements are puerile, and altogether the Russian railway authorities are carting everybody as usual.

They sailed in the Kildonan Castle on the evening of February 25, which happened to be the anniversary of the day on which General de Castelnau had arrived at Verdun in 1916 and had saved the situation there. Wilson therefore proposed the General's health at dinner, and he gives the terms of his speech in the diary, which ran as follows:

> *Madame* (Lady Maud Hoare) *et Messieurs. Aujourd'hui est l'anniversaire d'un des plus glorieux jours de la guerre. Le 25 me février 1916 le général de Castelnau est arrivé a Verdun. La situation était grave, le fort de Douamont perdu, les troupes françaises tres éprouvées. Cette situation a éte retabli par le général de Castelnau, dont la presence a donne un élan immediat et merveilleux a la contre-attaque qu'il a commandée. Je leve le verre au général de Castelnau, a son état-major, au XXme Corps d'Armée, et a tous les défenseurs héroiques de Verdun.**

They were escorted at first by the cruiser Vindictive, but she was unable to keep up against a heavy sea, and they were without escort for 36 hours till picked up by the cruiser Shannon. Later on they were escorted by an additional cruiser and three destroyers. Wilson was able to discuss many matters with de Castelnau, Lord Milner and others of the Mission during the voyage, and also to make a start on his official report for the War Office. On the last day before getting into Scapa Flow he had a long conversation with Milner, who was disposed to think that Russia might be prepared to agree to the Turks remaining in an internationalized Constantinople, and to an autonomous Poland under the Russian double-eagle, provided that she was assured of access to the sea. Wilson wrote in the diary:

> There is no doubt that if we could detach Turkey from the Germans it would be a great blow to them. This would surely be followed by the secession of Bulgaria, who is already nibbling, and the German dream of the East would be shattered. Therefore I think that Milner is tight. But, on the other hand, Milner considers the

---

* "Madam (Lady Maud Hoare) and Gentlemen. Today is the anniversary of one of the most glorious days of the war. On the 25th of February 1916 General de Castelnau arrived in Verdun. The situation was serious, the fort of Douamont was lost, the French troops were very hard hit. This situation was restored by General de Castelnau, whose presence gave an immediate and marvelous impulse to the counter-attack he commanded. I raise my glass to General de Castelnau, to his staff, to the XXth Army Corps, and to all the heroic defenders of Verdun."

defeat of the Boches in the field as impossible, and therefore he is prepared to consider terms of peace, which I think quite impossible. It seems to me that if our offensive this year is unsuccessful in getting real decisions, we ought, as Milner suggests, to try and detach the Turks, then the Bulgars, and then the Austrians. If we succeeded in this, then we could, for certain, beat the Boches in the field and impose our own terms.

Milner and I also discussed the question of the Dominions. He had a sort of vague hope that, in future, we might be able to keep out of European complications, saying that the Dominions have vast potentialities and that if we link up closely we would be strong enough to defy all comers. Here, too, I don't agree. We shall never be strong enough to stand alone, until the population is vastly increased.- With only 7 or 8 millions in Canada, and 5 or 6 in Australia, we are helpless. When Canada has 50 millions and Australia has 30 millions, and when we really have command of the sea so that our common action can be certain, then we may consider Milner's proposals. But not now. And all this will take 100 years if we confine ourselves to English breeding. Meanwhile what is to be done? It seems to me that we must have alliances in Europe. But if we have alliances in Europe how are we to keep out of complications?

The *Kildonan Castle* arrived safely at Scapa Flow on March 2. Good news greeted the travellers, for they learnt that our Fifth Army had made an appreciable advance on the Ancre, and also that General Maude had advanced and had retaken Kut in Mesopotamia.

Sir Henry, during the immediately following days, paid visits to the Foreign Office and the War Office; on the 6th he saw the King and afterwards attended a meeting of the War Cabinet, at which he made a military statement about Russia. He saw Lord Derby, and afterwards Robertson, that afternoon at the War Office, and during their conversation the C.I.G.S. asked him if he would like to go to Salonika, or if he was prepared to go back to Russia, or if he would accept the position of acting as Principal Liaison Officer between Haig and Nivelle. He replied that he did not wish for any one of these three positions, but that he would like to have command of a corps. He had on the previous evening heard details as to the strange position which Haig now occupied with regard to Nivelle — as is shown by an entry in his diary written at Eaton

Place that night, which runs as follows:

> When I got back here at 7 o'clock the Monument [Lucas] turned up to warn me of an amazing story. He says that there was a meeting last Saturday week, February 24th, at Calais of Briand, Lyautey, Nivelle, Lloyd George, Haig and Robertson. Previous to this meeting Lloyd George and Briand had laid a plot, and at the meeting Lloyd George suddenly sprung it upon Haig and Robertson. He said that Haig was to be put under Nivelle, and that I was to be a British Chief of the Staff under Nivelle. Haig and Robertson refused to agree. Nivelle was not enthusiastic (at least Monument said so). On that Lloyd George said that Haig and Robertson must agree or get out! They agreed!
>
> So apparently Haig will now pass under Nivelle's orders. A dangerous game. Of course, the whole of this is new to me.

He wrote in his diary of a conversation with Milner:

> I explained the whole position as I saw it. The dangers of the new arrangements, the inability on my part of acting as Liaison with Haig. He agreed. He thinks that Lloyd George wants to get Haig out, and I told him that I would not help Lloyd George in that sort of work and that, if the War Cabinet did not think Haig good enough, then let them remove him, but not do so at Nivelle's orders, which would raise an impossible situation in the whole army. I told him of Robertson's proposal that I should go to Russia or Salonika. He will keep me informed of how things go on.

In the meantime Sir Henry was busily engaged in connexion with the carrying out of the arrangements necessary to complete Poole's staff in Russia. Then, on March 12, he met Haig (who had come over with Kiggell for a meeting at which Briand, Lyautey and Nivelle were to be present) by appointment; he was told the whole story of the Calais meetings, and he wrote in the diary:

> It amounted to this, after I had read all the papers. Two decisions were reached at Calais. At first Haig was put under Nivelle for the coming fighting, and Nivelle was to be given an English Chief of the Staff with a General Staff and Q.M.G. under him, and through this Chief of the Staff Nivelle would issue his orders to Haig. This Chief

of the Staff was to be *me*. This decision was subsequently modified, and a fresh agreement come to, in 5 paragraphs, which in truth was the old position of Haig, "conforming," but being an Ally and not a subordinate.

A couple of days later, Nivelle wrote Haig two letters containing *orders*, and in rather curt language, showing that Nivelle was acting on the first decision and not on the second. To this Haig took exception and he wrote two notes to the War Office. In the first he said that there were only two courses possible, one was the *status quo ante*, and the other the complete subjection of the British Army to the French and the elimination of the British C. in C. The second letter was much longer, and in this he objected to the disappearance of the British C. in C., and he defined in some 8 or 9 paragraphs the safeguards against French future interference, which he thought essential.

There was the position as I found it. As regards myself, Haig made an apology about filling up my corps— owing to pay difficulties— but assured me that I should have the first one that fell vacant. But as we talked on I found that he was in an uncertain frame of mind about his own position, and he listened more and more to what I had to say.

I first made my own position quite clear — viz., that I knew nothing of all these manœuvres. I thought them stupid, and I would not be mixed up in any way. I said that what was wanted was a perfectly clear definition of his position *vis-à-vis* Nivelle, and that once this was done there would be no place for me, and that, rather than accept an equivocal position, I would prefer going on half-pay, and I would go on half-pay. Haig said that he would not hear of such a thing and begged me to accept the post of Chief Liaison Officer.

I refused point-blank under the present conditions, and I told him that I would go and see Lord Milner and explain the situation as I saw it, and insist on the meeting this afternoon coming to an absolutely clear definition of Haig's position. So at 1.15 1 was at Downing Street, where there was a War Cabinet sitting, and I sent in a note to Milner saying I wanted to see him as soon as possible. He sent for me at 2.15 at his house,

I told Milner of my talk with Haig. I told him that the relative positions of Haig and Nivelle must be clearly defined, and that, when this was done, it would be found that no one would want me. I told him that I did not wish to go to French Head-quarters, and that I thought Sidney Clive could do the work much better. Milner told me that Lloyd George was now much more friendly to Haig, and was

> going to side with him in the controversy with the French; but that he [Milner] was going to do all he could to get me to go to French G.Q.G., because he did not think that any other man in the world could hold the two armies together. I repeated my conviction that, if the positions of Haig and Nivelle were clearly defined there would be no place for me, but he would have none of it.
>
> So after my talk I went back to Haig again, and this time Kiggell was in the room. I told Haig of Lloyd George's changed attitude, and I repeated once more that, when the position was made crystal clear there would be no need and no use for me, and that Sidney would do perfectly well. But I added that if, after all these pieliminaries had been made clear, both he and Nivelle still wanted me, then I was prepared to go, although I did not want to. He thanked me for what I had done.

Wilson was called up by Haig on the telephone next morning, and asked as a favour to go to French G.Q.G., to which Wilson replied that he would like to know more before accepting. For, as is made clear in his diary, he had made up his mind that, if he agreed, it must be on the condition that he could resign the appointment at any time that he liked. That afternoon he was in the first place approached by a representative of a small group in the House of Commons who wanted him to become C.I.G.S. He notes in his diary:

> I said that in my opinion the only people who could, or who ought to, make this change were the War Council, as they alone were the responsible people, and that I could not, and would not, join in any agitation to depose Robertson, more especially as in my opinion he had done really useful work.

Sir Henry then went off to see the C.I.G.S. at the War Office, and of this interview he wrote in the diary:

> I at once made the position clear. I would *not* go unless certain conditions were fulfilled, viz: 1. Clear definition of Haig's status. 2. Clear definition of my duties. 3. A personal request on the part of Haig, Nivelle and the War Committee asking me to go. 4. My own power to resign at any moment. I added that, as he knew well, neither he nor Haig would, voluntarily, have me near them, that even when

> I was in Russia evil tongues had spread reports that I had engineered all these troubles so as to get Haig or him out and to slip into their places, and that, if this was said when I was in Russia, what would not be said if I went to Beauvais. I said that I was against taking up this appointment and would do so only if the conditions already enumerated were fulfilled. Robertson said that he would write to Haig.
>
> I went back to No. 36, and Nivelle arrived, with Berthier, before 5 o'clock. After we had had tea, Nivelle and I went into my study and had three-quarters of an hour alone. He enlarged upon the present futility of the connexion between him and Haig, and added that Lloyd George would like to get rid of Haig but, for the minute, the Northcliffe Press was too strong. Finally, after much talk of this description, he appealed to me " in the name of God" to accept the post offered as I "was the only man in England who could save a most dangerous situation." To this I replied that I was going to see Haig at 6 o'clock, and that I had certain conditions to put forward. If these were accepted I would agree to go to Beauvais.
>
> I then went to Haig's. Kiggell was present throughout the interview, at which I was very glad. I put the same case before him that I had already done to Robertson, and I said that unless I could have, and retain, his complete confidence I would not accept. I told him that within a month of my going to Beauvais any number of people would tell him that I was intriguing to put him out — that in point of fact I probably could put him out if I wished — and so I advised him not to have me but to keep Clive. Nothing that I said — and I was most open — shook him, and he agreed without hesitation to my condition that I should be allowed absolute discretion about resigning at any moment if I saw fit.
>
> And so to-night my conditions are all fulfilled, and I really believe I could impose any others I like as regards pay, rank, staff, etc. For I am clear that they are all frightened and that they all *really* believe that I am the only man who can save the situation. The more I look at it, the less I like it, and yet I must not refuse to try. So it is settled. Nivelle asked me and my A.D.C. to live in his mess, but I refused.

Nivelle returned to France next day and, before leaving, sent Wilson a message asking him to follow as soon as he could. Wilson saw Derby at the War Office, who also begged him to take the appointment, and he afterwards saw Robertson.

This appears in the diary:

> He showed me still further draft agreement between Haig and Nivelle, and I told him that, if my advice was followed, the whole of these cursed agreements would be torn up and thrown into the fire, my right hand would go out to Nivelle, and the trick would be done. I think that Robertson agrees.

Next day he saw the King. He afterwards had a conversation with Lord French, and he notes in the diary:

> I told him that I thought our only plan was to support Haig, and I meant to do all I could. I am going to be in an increasingly difficult position, and I am so thankful that I put the whole case so plainly before all of them, and that I have reserved my power of freedom about resigning.

News of the Russian revolution had come to hand three days before this, but up to the present all appeared, at least on the surface, to be going satisfactorily enough from the point of view of the Entente. Most people in this country and even the War Cabinet — failing entirely to appreciate the nature of social conditions in Russia — were disposed to think that the overthrow of the existing form of government in this huge territory, inhabited as it is almost entirely by an uneducated, ignorant peasantry, would actually be beneficial to the Allied cause. Sir Henry found that Milner, like himself, was inclined to take an optimistic view of what had occurred in the country they had so recently quitted, and Milner, moreover, expressed cordial approval of the attitude which Wilson had taken up in the matter of his new appointment. "He said that in his judgment I was 'by far the ablest soldier in our army,' but that I had two faults — I was too pro-French and I was too clever and summed up people too quickly," so Wilson wrote in his diary. He had by this time completed all the arrangements necessary in connexion with the organization and the staff of Poole's Mission, for the War Office had accepted his recommendations in their entirety, and had also approved his suggestions in reference to establishing a more systematic distribution of duties as between the various other British military representatives in Russia.

Chapter XVIII – 1917: Liaison Officer with General Nivelle and General Pétain

The situation on the Western Front — Nivelle's plan — Nivelle and his Army Group Commanders — The French Government intervene — The offensive for all practical purposes fails — The question of replacing Nivelle — Strange position — Pétain replaces Nivelle — Wilson and Pétain — His alarm at lack of co-ordination— Wilson in London— He resigns his appointment — Discouragement of the French Army and the French People.

Wilson re-assumed military responsibilities on the Western Front at an interesting juncture. The B.E.F. had taken over some miles of front south of the Somme from the French during the winter, Gough with his Fifth Army had gained ground on the Ancre early in February, and the Germans had in the latter part of that month suddenly begun a deliberate retirement from the line which they had previously occupied, stretching between the vicinity of Arras and the vicinity of Soissons. This retirement of theirs was being steadily followed up by the British Fourth and Fifth Armies, as also by French troops on the immediate right of these, and villages were being recovered daily. The date of the great offensives that the British and French Governments had agreed upon was, moreover, drawing near, so that everything pointed to stirring events taking place in the early future.

Expressed in very general terms, Nivelle's scheme of operations was as follows: The British were to deliver an attack, in a more or less easterly direction on a wide front, on either side of Arras. The French Northern Army Group under General Franchet d'Esperey was to occupy the attention of the enemy between the right of the B.E.F. and the vicinity of Rheims. Two French Army Groups, under Generals Michelet and Pétain respectively, were, a few days later, to carry out the main offensive on Franchet d'Esperey's right, attacking in a northerly direction. The broad strategical idea was that the B.E.F. engaged about Arras were, together with Franchet d'Esperey's troops, to draw off enemy reserves and to hold the attention of as many German divisions as possible as a result of their preliminary offensive operations, while Micheler and Pétain, farther to the right, burst through the enemy front by a sudden attack which was to be delivered in great force and with the utmost vehemence. Under the project of operations for the year 1917 which had been agreed upon at Chantilly in November, the more important r6le during the offensive to be undertaken on the Western Front, then examined into by Joffre and Haig, had been allotted to the B.E.F. But Nivelle's plan awarded the principal role to the French. The deliberate German retirement between Arras and Soissons was, however, a strategical development for which no provision had been made in the plan, although some such move on the part of the enemy had not been wholly unexpected at British G.H.Q.

General Nivelle had carried out an extraordinarily brilliant operation on a restricted front before Verdun in the previous October, and he had followed this achievement up by a still more successful offensive operation near the same point on December 15. As a consequence of these encouraging experiences he was confident of not only breaking the German line to the east of Rheims, but also of making decisive use of the gap when this had been created. Mr. Lloyd George and his War Cabinet had, no less than M. Briand and his Government, been enormously impressed by the boldness of the successful soldier's plan, by the skill with which he had elaborated it in the council chamber, and by the confidence which he had displayed in his designs and in himself. But neither Sir D. Haig, nor yet certain of Nivelle's French subordinates who were to participate in the undertaking, felt satisfied that the coming operations were going to be crowned with the triumph anticipated by their designer. And even before Wilson arrived upon the scene considerable anxiety was already beginning to manifest itself in public circles in France, in view of the heavy losses that the French Army might be expected to incur during the progress of the effort, should this not prove (as Nivelle had promised himself) immediately successful

Wilson crossed the Channel to take up his new appointment on March 17, he stayed the night with Haig at Montreuil, and he mentions in his diary having had a prolonged conversation with the British Commander-in-Chief on this occasion. He goes on to say:

> The withdrawal of the Boches continues and is spreading north and south. It is spreading up towards Arras and down towards the Oise. We take scarcely any prisoners, but we walk slowly and solemnly after the Boches. Haig thinks it portends going back to the Hindenburg Line of Arras — St. Quentin — Laon and then massing for an attack at Ypres. I don't quite agree, and it is too early yet to see what it means. Cadorna thinks it means an attack on Italy! Alexeieff doubtless thinks it means an attack on Russia!

He went on to Beauvais on the following day, he dined that night with Nivelle, and this appears in the diary:

> I brought him a wire we received from Robertson last night, which said that Jellicoe could not prevent a landing of "considerable forces" to the west of Dunkirk, What does command of the sea mean?
>
> I started my new work by assuring him whole-heartedly that Haig would play right out to the end. This pleased him, though he could not help showing me a codicil that Haig had added to the recent agreement, in which he said that he must be treated as an ally and not as a subordinate. This rankles in Nivelle's mind, for he assured me that he never dreamt of any other course. Briand resigned the night before last, and no one yet appointed. So Russia is in revolution and has no Tsar, and France has no Government. Nivelle and his staff absolutely indifferent, even amused, at the fall of Lyautey and Briand,

If Nivelle and his staff were at the first blush indifferent to the fall of Lyautey and Briand, they were only too soon to find grounds for altering their point of view. M. Briand was succeeded as the head of the Cabinet by M. Ribot, while Lyautey gave place to M. Painlevé; and Painlevé was no believer in Nivelle's ambitious plan of campaign. Nor in this estimate of his did the new War Minister stand alone. A growing lack of confidence in the recently appointed Commander-in-Chief had been finding expression for some weeks past amongst French politicians and in certain organs of the French Press, as also amongst some French soldiers of prominence and of high repute. Nivelle had been loyally supported in his proposals by the Briand Government, and he had, as we have seen, found no little favour in the sight of the British War Cabinet; but, with the advent o£ Ribot and Painlevé and a new Ministry, the doubts and misgivings that existed in the minds of many of his countrymen began to find voice in the councils of the Executive. Indeed, even M. Poincaré, the President, appears to have entertained qualms as to whether the great Aisne offensive, which was the central feature in Nivelle's strategical design, would really prove so triumphant as was anticipated at the French *Grand Quartier Général*. The extent to which the French Commander-in-Chief was to be hampered and discouraged by the dubious and critical attitude which those set in authority over him were about to adopt will become apparent in later paragraphs of this chapter.

Haig drove over to pay a visit to Nivelle next day, and a meeting then took place at which, besides Wilson, Generals Franchet d'Esperey and Micheler, as well as other French commanders, were present. The German retirement was at this time still in full swing, and Nivelle asked Haig what he proposed to do. In the circumstances the Field-Marshal intimated that his idea was to continue following the enemy up, as he was already doing; he demurred to undertaking an attack at once, as it was his hope to strike home in some sector where the enemy would not simply walk away. Franchet d'Esperey then described the manner in which he was following the retiring Germans up on the right of the British, just as these were doing. Then Micheler indicated his arrangements for conducting the great offensive on Franchet d'Esperey's right. The question of possible eventualities in Italy was also considered, and Nivelle announced that Cadorna had estimated that he might want 20 French divisions; this Nivelle pronounced to be absurd, and he declared that in any case not more than from 4 to 6 could be spared for such a diversion. Wilson wrote in his diary:

> How then do we stand to-night? Bapaume and many villages

north of it, as also Péronne, Ham and Noyon, arc in our hands, and Vimy looks like coming to us. Of the three Boche objectives that I saw, viz; Calais, Paris, Venice, I am inclined to rule out Paris. If Vimy and La Bassée fell to us, I will rule out Calais. And, as for Venice, we have still 5 or 6 weeks in which to make plans. There remain Boche objectives of Odessa, Kiev, Moscow and Petrograd. In the present state of revolution in Russia would a heavy blow towards any of these four places make the Russians make peace? I can't say to-night.

Cadorna is already withdrawing guns from the Gorizia front to put them along the Trentino front, so poor Nivelle was rather harassed about Russia and Italy. Also, he was yesterday in Noyon, and further forward. There were 12,000 people in Noyon, the peace population being 6,000. These people had been put there by the Boches, who as a last act carried off 50 girls between 15 and 25 years of age. Nivelle was not satisfied with the way the corps under Franchet and Micheler were getting on, so he was going to move up to Compiègne and establish his head-quarters there; which is very wise, I think, for, as I said, it is only natural that after 2½ years of sedentary warfare the minds and habits of men should get slow and inelastic.

Sir Henry drove to Montreuil on March zz to spend the night. The Field-Marshal, he found, was like himself much puzzled by the German retirement, which was still proceeding, although more deliberately than at first. The resistance of the enemy rear-guards was also gradually stiffening. Of a discussion between Nivelle and Haig that took place on the following day Wilson wrote in his diary as follows:

Nivelle came to see Haig at 8.30 a.m., and had if hours interview with him, I being present. All went most amicably. We discussed the situation, and we all agreed that appearances now pointed to the Boches standing on the Hindenburg Line, and therefore that Michelet's attack from about Soissons — Rheims, and Haig's attack Arras — Vimy will hold good. The difficulties of roads, rails, river crossings, etc., etc., all well discussed.. Then Haig explained his alternative of attack Messines — Ypres, which will take two months to prepare. Then we discussed the Belgians. Then the Italian situation, where Cadorna seems to have given up his promised offensive on the Carso because of his fear of a Boche attack from the Trentino. A nuisance. The whole tone of Haig and Nivelle was as good as it could be.

On occasions such as this Sir Henry generally visited any commanders and staffs of the B.E.F. that were within reach, so as to keep himself acquainted with the view that appeared to be generally entertained on the British side as to the progress of events. He loved what he called "gossip" — that is to say, hearing the news and discussing the course of the campaign with military friends and acquaintances. He moreover believed in officers in very high positions, like himself, keeping in close touch with subordinate generals, and he always acted on this principle as far as he found practicable. Sir W. Orpen writes of him about this time in his "Stories of Old Ireland and Myself":

> I never saw him from those early days until the spring of 1917. I had been lunching at Advanced G.H.Q. near Arras, and Sir Henry strolled up to us under the trees where we were having coffee. After a time he said, "Ah yes. I remember you. You used to draw for the *Jarvey* in Dublin." "No, sir," said I, "I was too young to do that; that was my brother." He answered, "Bless you, you look old enough for anything." I replied, "Not old enough yet to have a word contest with Rake-faced Wilson, sir." And I bolted before his boot got me. Later I had the pleasure of seeing a lot of the Field-Marshal. A most brilliant man, with an unsurpassed sense of humour and knowledge of his own countrymen.

After returning to Beauvais, on the 24th, Wilson was rung up by G.H.Q. with news to the effect that the Admiralty were evidently becoming seriously concerned as to the possibility of a landing on the part of the enemy taking place in rear of our lines in Flanders. Sir Henry replied, suggesting that Sir Douglas should take the line of pointing out that the defence of the coast was a matter for the French, and of intimating that if the French were satisfied, he also was satisfied. The telephone message from G.H.Q. was followed up by a telegram from the War Office direct to Wilson, and referring to the same question. This appears in the diary:

> It said that the Boches had now collected "over 30 Destroyers"

> in Belgian ports, with which we could not compete, and therefore a landing might take place west of Nieuport. Dunkirk might be taken, the Channel lost, and all communication with England cut! An amazing proposition. What did Nivelle think?
>
> I will ask to-morrow, but I hope that he thinks, as I do, that the Admiralty and the War Office are a set of d—— fools. To my mind it would be easier to get a lodgment in England (say Dover) and *keep* it, than it would be to get a lodgment upon our coast here and *keep* it.

Nivelle, when asked by Wilson about this coast question, expressed himself as feeling no anxiety, and he explained the dispositions that existed for meeting such an eventuality as a hostile attempt to effect a landing. This Wilson passed on to the War Office and to G.H.Q. That afternoon an important meeting was held by Nivelle with the French generals who were charged with carrying out the coming offensive, and Nivelle very courteously invited Sir Henry to be present at the discussion. After Franchet d'Esperey had made his statement, Pétain was called upon, and he argued that three German divisions were equal to four French or British divisions. He asked why, that being established, we were attacking or going to attack in the manner proposed, seeing that there was no chance of success. Wilson thereupon expressed the opinion that, inasmuch as a German division had only nine bat tali ons, while a British or French division had thirteen, so far from three German divisions being equal to four Allied ones, two Allied divisions were equal to three German ones. "Nivelle was very forbearing and good about this, for Pétain's argument was belated and untrue," Wilson remarked in his diary, and he went on to write:

> Nivelle impressed me at this meeting as being tactful and firm, and capable of giving a decision to generals who were *guerriers*[*] and masterful men.

On the following day the entry occurs:

---

[*] "Fighters."

Nivelle spoke to me about Pétain's attitude yesterday, saying that he was always like that, always against the offensive, and adding that "luckily there were no foreigners in the room" — for which I thanked him, for it really was a charming remark!

Wilson wrote in the diary on March 28:

This morning when I got to the office I found two difficulties. The first was a letter from Nivelle to Haig, which began "I order the English Army of the 1st, nird and vth Corps to attack on April 8th, the G.A.N.* to attack on the 10th, etc., etc." Now it had already been agreed that Haig would attack on April 8, so that it would have been more courteous to say, "In accordance with our agreement, you are going to attack on April 8, and I have now ordered G.A.N. to attack on the 10th, etc., etc." The letter as now drafted may annoy Haig, and we could have got the same result by another formula without any friction.†

The other difficulty was an order giving a certain road to Franchet d'Esperey which apparently ought to have been allotted to Rawlinson; but it turned out that Haig had already agreed to this.

A message came through from Robertson this day to the effect that General Alexeieff reported that the revolution in Russia was creating all manner of difficulties in the army and was causing delays, and that he proposed that the offensive on the Western Front should therefore be deferred. The C.I.G.S. wanted to know Nivelle's and Haig's views with regard to this suggestion. Wilson found that Nivelle had received a similar message direct from Russia and had already sent a reply to Alexeieff to the effect that the arrangements on the Western Front were now too far advanced for the offensive to be retarded, that it was therefore desirable that the Russians should adhere to their engagement to attack at the

---

* Franchet d'Esperey's "Northern Army Group."

† It was not the first time that something of the kind had occurred. Nivelle's directives, sent to Haig, had taken the form of orders on other occasions, and he had even tried to send orders direct to Haig's subordinates. Wilson's presence at Beauvais had, however, soon put this right.

same time, and that an offensive on the part of the Russian troops was the best way to maintain their discipline and at the same time to restore order in their country. Sir Henry notes in his diary:

> I was very much pleased with his decision and clearness of view, as he said, "What condition will Russia be in in June or July? Probably at peace."

Wilson moved from Beauvais to Compiègne, where Nivelle was now installed, on April 4. Heavy snow fell that day, which was particularly unfortunate seeing that the 8th, the date fixed upon for commencing the offensive, was drawing so near. A meeting therefore took place between Nivelle and Haig on the morrow (at which Wilson was present), when a decision was arrived at to postpone the start of the operations for twenty-four hours. Sir Henry had met Painlevé by arrangement on the previous day, and he was therefore able to give the Field-Marshal an account of what had passed on that occasion. Of his conversation with the French War Minister he had written in his diary:

> I had not met him before. I was not much struck with his appearance, but he seemed sensible. What I did not like was the attitude towards Nivelle. Not that he said anything against him, but he insisted on the right to discuss matters with Nivelle's subordinates, and named Pétain, Michcler and Franchet. If he discusses Nivelle, or Nivelle's plans, with these men it will certainly end in trouble. lie is supposed to be an admirer of Plain's and an enemy of Nivelle's. I asked him if he was going to make Pétain his Chief of Staff, and he said that that had been his intention but that his colleagues had put him off, saying, in effect, that Pétain would run him instead of his running Pétain.
>
> He told me that Foch was going down to Italy at once, and that the French Government had written to the British Government to say that they proposed to send three divisions (starting the first on the 20th) and suggested that we should do the same, all under the orders of Foch. I told him that in my judgment we must save Italy if attacked by the Bodies, but with a minimum of troops.

A very important meeting took place in M. Poincaré's train on the 6th at which, besides the President himself, Ribot, Painlevé,

Admiral Lacaze, A. Thomas, Nivelle, de Castelnau, Pétain, Micheler and Franchet d'Esperey were present. Wilson wrote that night:

> I hear that the Government, aided by Pétain, wanted to force Nivelle to abandon his great offensive, and have a small one instead. Nivelle stood firm and won. What time of day for such a proposal, and Haig not consulted.

Sir Henry, moreover, heard all about this remarkable conference from Nivelle two days later — he was to dine with Painlevé that evening, he had therefore wanted to know what had happened at the meeting in the President's train, and he wrote in the diary:

> He told me at once practically what I had heard the day before yesterday, that the Ministers (and there were several) and Pétain urged that the great offensive should be abandoned and only small attacks made. Nivelle listened for some time and then weighed in by remarking that there were so many C. in C.s that he was confused, but as C. in C. he would not tolerate the present state of affairs, and would do as he pleased or resign. This brought them to their senses, and then he added — for the benefit of Pétain and Micheler — that if some French generals would give him the loyal support that Haig was giving it would be a good thing. So the meeting terminated, but I am quite clear that, if our coming offensive does not succeed or is only moderately successful, the politicians will unload Nivelle. What a scurvy crowd, I then discussed Foch having been sent to Italy on Thursday. Nivelle said that the War Committee got a sudden scare that Cadorna was not going to hold on, and packed off Foch, without staff, etc, Nivelle was writing to-day to the War Committee to tell them to bring Foch back and to let him discuss the situation with me, with Haig and with Robertson, and then go down decently. The whole thing is a mess.

Wilson dined with Painlevé that night, and General Smuts came in together with the Hon. F. Guest after dinner. The diary records:

> Smuts, Painlevé and I had a talk. Smuts wants the English and

> French to come to a clear understanding as to what they want when peace begins to be discussed, more especially -with regard to Constantinople. But I pointed out that Constantinople cannot be discussed in Russia's absence. We chatted about other things, and then Smuts, Freddie and I back here to the Ritz, and Smuts and I discussed till nearly 1 a.m. I impressed on him the vital necessity of our beating the Boches to such a point that we can dictate terms — not discuss them. There is a world of difference in that. We discussed strategy, etc., etc., and I was able to tell him things about the Meuse, Rhine, Holland, Bulgaria, Turkey, etc., that he did not know. It seems to me that if Smuts and Milner get together they may do good work.

Next day, April 9, was a day of triumph for the B.E.F. The Western Front offensive was commenced that day by portions of the First and Third Armies under Home and Allenby and the result was in the highest degree satisfactory. The greater part of the Vimy Ridge was captured, the remainder being secured next day, and the enemy lines were also penetrated to a considerable depth on either side of Arras. At a date prior to Wilson's taking up the post of Chief Liaison Officer between Haig and Nivelle, the latter had opposed the British Commander-in-Chief's intention to extend his offensive so far north as to embrace the Vimy Ridge, although that had been agreed upon between Haig and Joffre at the Chantilly Conference in the previous November. Some members of Nivelle's staff had, moreover, seen the intended plan of attack on the ridge, and they had expressed doubts as to the likelihood of the plan succeeding — in this they may have been influenced by recollection of Foch's failure at the time of the Battle of Loos in 1915. Haig fortunately adhered to his intention to attack the ridge, Horne adhered to his plan, and the Canadians, under Byng, achieved a notable success.

Wilson wrote in his diary:

> The news to-night of our attack is that we have got to our objectives, and have taken 10,000 prisoners and 50 guns. Vimy Ridge is at last in our hands. This is a good beginning towards the 500,000 prisoners that I want this summer.

But vexatious delays were about to occur in the launching of the great attacks to the east of Rheims by the French — as appears from an entry in Wilson's diary under date April 12, which reads as follows:

> When I got to office I found Clive rather fussy. Nivelle had sent off a long telegram at 9 p.m. last night to Haig, and we only got a copy this morning. In this telegram he said that Franchet would attack tomorrow, Micheler on the 15th, and Pétain on the 16th; he then advised Haig to strengthen Gough and to attack towards Qudant, and gave a sort of small tactical lecture. Exactly at the same time last night (9 p.m.) Franchet settled not to attack in the morning and put off his attack till the 14th, which was wired to Haig. So everyone is in a muddle.
>
> I went straight to Nivelle and told him this was all rather childish, and that in future all communications to Haig must pass through me, and that in addition, when these communications were drafted, Sidney Clive should help in the composition. Nivelle agreed at once. Niveile told me he could not get any news from Italy as to whether they had started their attacks, because Foch has to wire to Painlevé.

In the end there was yet another day's delay before Micheler launched what was meant to be the main offensive of the great French effort. His attack thus did not take place till the 16th, a whole week after the B.E.F. had started their operations. Wilson went to see the fighting at its western end; but the result of the first day's undertaking in this quarter was very disappointing, and he came away having formed the impression that success in this particular sector was almost impossible. Farther to the east the French had done better. What had been accomplished even there did not, however, in the least approach to what Nivelle had expected, nor to what, in fact, formed the basis of his whole plan — a break-through on a wide front followed up by immediate exploitation on the part of troops held in readiness for this purpose. One cause of the French discomfiture had been that the enemy was well aware of what was impending. Wilson wrote in his diary on April 17:

> It is clear now that the whole attack of the Sixth Army is a complete failure. The Fifth Army, and now the Fourth (Pétain) are getting on better, and Nivelle is going to stop the further attacks of the

> Sixth Army and to exploit the attacks of the other two. But, so far, the great attack has been a failure. Of course, all this will greatly shake confidence in Nivelle, and my opinion is that unless the Fourth and Fifth Armies pull off a real success Nivelle will fall and that we shall have Pétain here. Painlevé will certainly aim towards that.
>
> At 4 o'clock I went to see Foch who had just come back from Italy. We had a long talk.
>
> Foch was clear that Nivelle was done, owing chiefly to the failure of the Sixth Army. Foch said that he knew that the positions which this Army was told to attack were impossible — and after what I saw yesterday I agree. He thinks on all this work that Nivelle will be *dégommé* and Pétain put in his place, who will play a waiting game until the U.S.A, come on the scene, say a year hence.* I asked about a central organization of the Allies to really take hold, and he was all in favour of it and would love to be the French representative. But he was insistent on its sitting at Chantilly, or some place outside Paris. Personally, I see many difficulties in such an organization being above Robertson and Haig. Theoretically it is sound, but practically I have grave doubts.

The French Fourth and Fifth Armies continued to make a certain amount of progress, as did the British Third and Fifth Armies; even the French Sixth Army indeed also gained some little ground. But the French operations had now reduced themselves to pushing forward gradually, just as had been the case on the Somme; and the same thing held good with the B.E.F. Nivelle, on the 19th, informed Sir Henry that, up to the 17th, the losses of the French were not heavy, relatively speaking, and that they had taken 17,000 prisoners, 82 guns, and quantities of machine guns; he moreover reckoned that the Germans had already used up 21 of the 43 divisions that they had had in reserve. He also showed Wilson a long wire from Cadorna, which announced that there was no sign of a German concentration against the Italians, and which added that he did not propose to attack till the offensive on the Western Front had used up all the German reserves. Nivelle had sent a very stiff answer, calling upon the Italians to play the game, and reminding Cadorna of his repeated promises to attack at the same

---

* The United States had declared war on Germany on April 6.

time as the French and British did. Lloyd George had moreover arrived in Paris, and he was proceeding thence to Modane with Ribot for the purpose of pressing the need of action upon the Italians. Wilson went to Montreuil that evening to stay with Haig, who thanked him heartily for his services, which the Field-Marshal pronounced to be proving most valuable, and Wilson wrote in the diary:

> I told him that my feeling was that Lloyd George and Painlevé were determined to take a more active command of the major operations of the war, and that Painlevé was determined to get rid of Nivelle, and to replace him by Pétain, whose mental attitude was to sit and do nothing and wait for the Americans. I praised Nivelle, and said it would be a dangerous thing if the French Army were to think that Lloyd George had joined with French politicians to *dégommé* Nivelle. He showed me a short note that he had written to Lloyd George on the necessity of going on with the present attacks. The note was good; but I could have made a much stronger and more convincing case about the danger of Italy and Russia running out, and the danger of prolonging the war and thus giving the Boche submarines more chance.

Next day he wrote:

> Sidney just back from Paris and brought the gossip about Lloyd George's visit to Modane, and about the meeting in Paris about our offensive. Lloyd George and Ribot were down at Modane yesterday trying to "binge" up the Italians.
>
> Then a meeting to-day in Paris, and discussion with Painlevé and Nivelle as to whether the present offensive should be stopped. However, Haig's letter, and Robertson's help, and Nivelle's determination have prevented this disastrous state of things from happening. But the Frock Coats are to have another meeting in 10 days, when, I fear, unless we get a theatrical success, the matter will be much more acute. I had a long talk with Nivelle before dinner. He was depressed. We discussed the Paris work, and he realizes that he is in a difficult place. I told him that he and Haig must meet next week and put up a joint paper against the Frocks when next they meet. He had no news of his front. The Boches are fighting well. He told me that Sarrail is to have an attack next week, and then the idea is to withdraw to Salonika and greatly decrease the garrison, because the

Navy can't keep the present force going because of submarines.

On April 22 the entry appears:

Esher came from Paris to lunch. I developed my thesis — that is that there are three schools of thought:

1. Somme — i.e. wearing down the Boches.
2. Verdun — i.e. whirlwind attack.
3. Pétain — i.e. do nothing.

We have tried 2 (Verdun), which has been a complete failure. There remain Somme and Pétain. To my mind the Pétain plan is one to be avoided, and a Somme, with intelligence, is our only chance.

Esher says that Lloyd George has allowed things to go on both here and at Salonika for a fortnight, and then he and Ribot are to meet again. This does not please me. We must go on fighting, and not stop and wait for the Americans. So Esher is to see Painlevé to-morrow, and then arrange for me to give him a dinner on Wednesday in Paris. If the civilians stop this fight and squat, then any chance we have of retaking Ostend and Zeebrugge is over, because, if we can't get on while the French are all out to help us, how can we get on alone if the French cease fighting?

Next day Wilson wrote:

I saw Nivelle early, and gave him a copy of a letter I had received from Poole — very interesting — in which Poole says that we cannot expect any offensive this year, nor will the Russians be able to hold the Boches on their front; and if the Boches take Petrograd the Russians will make peace.

Then Nivelle told me of his plans for further attacks by the Fourth and Fifth Armies on the 28th. I found him much more fussy and angry with civilians than I have ever seen him before. He told me that all sorts of Cabinet Ministers, Members of the Chamber and others were getting passes for the Front and going down there and seeing Pétain, etc., then going back with fantastic tales. All this is undermining discipline and playing the mischief, and is also making Nivelle's position very difficult. I was sorry for him, although he has himself to thank owing to imagining such vain things as that he would be on the Serre in 3 days, etc., etc.

The news that Wilson had received from Russia shows that

even at this early date, and while the Provisional Government composed of moderate men of unquestionable standing in the country, which had been set up on the deposition of the Emperor, was still in being, the confusion caused by the Revolution was exercising a most sinister influence in the army, and was affecting its discipline very adversely. It could indeed have hardly been otherwise. The effect of the German unrestricted submarine campaign was, moreover, just at this time being felt at its very worst, and the maritime situation was consequently causing the British Government deep anxiety. Cadorna's delay in embarking on the promised Italian offensive was another depressing factor in the general position of affairs from the British and French point of view, although it is only fair to anticipate events by mentioning that the thrust from Venetia was launched a very few weeks later, and that it achieved most gratifying results. To aggravate the embarrassments of the Allies at this juncture there was also the disagreeable fact to be faced that Nivelle's scheme of operations, from which so much had been expected in some quarters, had for all practical purposes miscarried, and that what (to borrow Wilson's expressive phraseology) had been intended as a "Verdun" had degenerated into a "Somme." Nor did the participation of the United States in the struggle afford much promise of benefiting the cause of the Allies for many months to come, except at sea. Entries in Wilson's diary at this time afford abundant evidence that he was ill at ease, and he tells of a particularly interesting conversation with Haig on April 24 when the Field-Marshal had come to Amiens to meet Nivelle. Of what passed on this occasion Sir Henry wrote in his diary:

> He arrived before Nivelle, as I had asked him to, and so I had a talk with him. I told him that I thought the emits were determined to get the upper hand, and then to go in for the Pétain school of squatting and doing nothing, so as to avoid loss. I told him that Painlevé was dining with me to-morrow night in Paris and that, if I found that Painlevé was that way inclined, I would like to go over to England and see Milner to show him the danger. Haig was much in favour of my doing this. I advised him to see Nivelle alone and have a real quiet talk with him, and he agreed. So, when Nivelle arrived, Haig and Nivelle went off to a room by themselves and left us.

> After this talk Nivelle went away, and I had another talk with Haig. He told me that Nivelle was loud in his praises of me— which is nothing— and that they had provisionally agreed to attack St. Quentin on May 15. This is good, but it makes it all the more necessary to put off the next meeting of the Frock Coats till after that date. Haig is much in favour of my going over to London to see if I can help to that end. So I will go.

The 25th was a busy day for Wilson. He saw Nivelle in the morning and told him about the Painlevé dinner, and also about the plan of going over to London. Nivelle thereupon pronounced Wilson to be "a real comrade" and declared that his services "could never be sufficiently rewarded.'' The French Commander-in-Chief moreover took occasion to mention that a telegram from King George to Poincaré, congratulating the President on Nivelle's successes, had never been communicated to him (Nivelle) officially. Wilson afterwards went up to Paris with Duncannon, and he saw a number of people there — Lord Esher amongst others.

Esher had had a long conversation with Poincaré and Ribot that afternoon; they wanted Haig to come to Paris for a conference, and the question arose whether Haig ought to fall in' with their proposal. Sir Henry pointed out that if he did, and if Nivelle were removed from his position after the conference, everybody would say that it was Haig's doing, and that the Field-Marshal therefore ought not to come to Paris until it was dear what the object of the conference was. This was telephoned to G.H.Q. Painlevé came to dine later in the evening, the party being completed by Esher and Duncannon, and Wilson wrote in his diary:*

> We four talked till 11.30. The upshot of the whole thing is that I believe that Nivelle is done. I put my thesis to Painlevé: Three schools — Somme, Verdun, Pétain. I said that Somme was usure; Verdun was a whirlwind and a crash through; Pétain was squat, do little and have small losses. I said that Verdun had been tried and had

---

* Wilson's record of the day's doings was generally very long at this time, and also later; he used often to be up early in the morning, completing the narrative of the previous day.

failed, and there remained Somme and Pétain. I urged that the proper course was Somme, with variations, and that "squat" was fatal. Painlevé urged the advantages of Pétain, and seemed to think he could hold, and use up, as many Boche divisions by making faces as he could by fighting like the devil.

We talked and talked, and the more I got him to talk the more hostile he got to Nivelle. He said that the man who drew up the present plan of operations could never carry out any reasonable plan and must be changed, and that Pétain was a most reasonable man, who all along had said that Nivelle's plan (based on a success at Verdun on a 4 kilometre front) would not succeed, and that Pétain was right. He (Painlevé) being a mathematician, entirely ignored the question of moral. And, although I came back to it over and over again, he waved it aside and made incredulous faces and noises. He then told us that Haig had agreed to come up for a conference at 3 p.m. to-morrow at the Foreign Office.

On April 26 Wilson wrote:

Haig arrived at 2.15. He went off to see Painlevé, then Ribot, and I saw him again at 4.30. He said there was a great deal of tittle-tattle, that he had seen Painlevé, who was excited and had quoted me as saying that the Boches were fighting like devils, whereas Haig told them they were not. As I said, Painlevé did not mention that I had followed this up by saying that Rawly had only "rabbits" in front of him, and that we had used up 34 out of 43 divisions which the Boches had in reserve.

Then Haig had gone to Ribot and had told him that all was going well, and Ribot agreed that nothing should be changed, and that this was not a good moment to change the C. in C. So Haig is delighted with himself. My own opinion is that Painlevé, who was not present at the Ribot interview, spoke the Cabinet mind much more truly than Ribot, and that the Cabinet do not keep Ribot informed of the state of affairs. We shall see.

This appears next day:

Esher telephoned about 11.30, to say that Haig had had another interview with Painlevé, who had confirmed Ribot by saying that there was no intention of changing the present plan. Nothing was said about Nivelle, Incidentally, Haig cleared up his doubts about what I

> had said to Painlevé. For Painlevé came out with the fact that I had said that the Boches took our men prisoners like rabbits — instead of vice-versa. This Painlevé is a mathematical don, and not a man of affairs. So Haig told Esher to telephone to tell me that he quite understood, and that I had done good work at the dinner. But I remain always of the same opinion that Painlevé will *dégommé* Nivelle and put in Pétain, and that operations will at once be changed. Neither Ribot nor Painlevé understand what they are doing, and both are out to save their skins.

On the following day (28th) Wilson crossed the Channel, and he saw Milner that night. He had received a wire from Esher in the evening which ran:

> Painlevé and Ribot go to your billet [Compiègne] to-day to ask questions. But it was settled last night that the shift should take place. Only question being method of doing it.

This meant that Nivelle was to be replaced by Pétain, if it could be managed, Wilson read the wire to Milner, and he explained that, if Pétain were to become Commander-in-Chief, the resolute offensive now being carried on by the French would inevitably be brought to a stop, that greatly modified offensives would be substituted, and that this would vitally affect the plans of the Allies as a whole. Sir Henry went on to say that Haig was strongly in favour of continuing the offensive as now in progress, and that this was the proper course to pursue in view of Italy, of Russia and of the submarine danger. He further expressed the opinion that Paris and Calais were now safe, because the Germans were not in a position to undertake an offensive on a great scale on account of their deteriorated morale. He, however, found that Milner took a gloomy view of the position of affairs in general, and of the Russian situation in particular. Of a meeting which he had with the Prime Minister at Walton Heath on April 29, Sir Henry wrote in the diary:

> I told him that Nivelle was doomed, and showed him Esher's wire. He was very quick to tumble to all it meant. He realized that a change of French C. in C. meant a change of plan, and when I

> suggested that on that basis he could wire to Ribot and say, "Hold hard till we have had a talk," he quite agreed and said he would talk the matter over early to-morrow with Robertson and me. He frightened me a little by saying that it might be best to wait till 1918 before putting in our blow; but I hope that I edged him off by mentioning Russia and the submarine. Hankey gave me dreadful figures of damage done by submarines.

Robertson and Wilson repaired to Downing Street the next morning (30th), and Wilson went through the whole story of Nivelle, Pétain, Painlevé, and the attitude of the French people. Lloyd George declared that he must be convinced of its expediency before he would be prepared to insist on the continuance of the offensive. So Wilson and Robertson both drew up papers for the Prime Minister's information, advocating that course.

The newspapers had that morning announced that Pétain had been made Chief of Staff to Painlevé, which, as Wilson interpreted the step, made Pétain in reality Commander-in-Chief, and he wrote in his diary:

> Lloyd George understands the situation, but I was careful to point out that if he exercised the undoubted power which he now had in France and took the superior direction of the war, he was doing what in my opinion was tight, but that he was also taking a *very* great responsibility.

Sir Henry was present at a meeting of the War Cabinet on the following day, which lasted several hours, and he wrote of his experiences in Downing Street on this occasion:

> The whole atmosphere to-day was pessimistic to a degree, and Robert Cecil and others were talking of peace. The best men were Lloyd George, Robertson, and Milner.

News had come that the Russian soldiers along the Eastern Front were fraternizing with the German troops, and also that Russia was now swarming with German pacifists. Lloyd George had, however, agreed to press upon the French the need of continuing the offensive, and he moreover announced his intention of going to Paris himself with a view to carrying his object into effect; so the Prime Minister left London, with Robertson, Wilson, Jellicoe and others, on May 3. On arrival at his hotel in Paris that evening Wilson was pleased to find an invitation from a M. Jean Hennessey to dine, and to learn that Painlevé was to be the sole other guest. He wrote in his diary:

> I had a long talk with these two men. It is clear that Pétain (under the name of Chief of Staff to Minister of War) is going to be C. in C., with even this extra provision — that the War Minister himself is going (almost) to direct operations. This came out in a curious and sudden burst from Painlevé. I had said that, if Pétain was going to check Nivelle's scheme, he would have to go down to the ground and see for himself, and Painlevé said "Yes. And I go too." Pétain is C. in C. But whether he will stand constant interference from Painlevé, I don't know; if not, and if Painlevé finds that Pétain takes too much hold, then I expect to see Pétain go to Compiègne and another man put in Pétain's place. If, on the other hand, Painlevé continues to absorb power, then I expect to see Compiègne come to Paris. In both cases Nivelle becomes of no real account, and I should doubt his stopping on. It seems all the more essential that Haig should deal with Pétain — as I told Robertson when coming in the car this afternoon.

Conferences took place in Paris on the two following days, but Sir Henry did not attend them. An arrangement was come to at these with regard to the command on the Western Front — an arrangement which he did not think by any means satisfactory. The plan was that Haig was to continue to deal with Nivelle; but Nivelle was now for all practical purposes under Pétain, so that the commander of the B.E.F. was being placed in an inferior position, and Wilson foresaw that difficulties might arise in consequence. He was pleased, on the other hand, to learn that the four generals, Haig, Robertson, Pétain and Nivelle, had agreed upon the principle that heavy offensives on long fronts for limited objectives should govern operations henceforward, and further to learn that Lloyd George had induced the French Government to accept the generals' recommendation on the subject. Much discussion, it appeared, had taken place at these conferences in reference to the thorny subject of Salonika; but Lloyd George, Robertson and Jellicoe, between them, had in the end gained their object, which was that British troops should begin withdrawing from that theatre on June 1.* Sir Henry paid a visit to Pétain on the evening of the second day of the conferences and he pleased the French C.G.S. by promising to send him extracts from the paper (mentioned on p. 408) which he had prepared for Lloyd George in London on April 30. He wrote in his diary next day (May 6) at Compiègne:

> Foch came at 4.30 and spent 1½ hours with me, and I told him the broad results of Paris. He is off to the Jura for a trip, and to spend his time. It is sinful that he is not C. in C. He is far the finest soldier in France, and in remarkably good form and health.
>
> I asked Foch whether, if Russia made peace, would the French fight it out, and he said certainly, provided the Government gave a clear lead. But, as there is no Government in France, the lead must come from Lloyd George.
>
> Haig sent me his plan of operations, which I am to give to Nivelle, who is away for the day. The plan consists of this: The French are to relieve us from St. Quentin to the Omignon River at once, and Haig, while still attacking a little at Arras, will mount an attack of 16 divisions against the Messines-Wytschaete ridge for the first week in June. Then, while this attack is still going on, the French to further relieve us up at Havrincourt, and we relieve the French XXXVIth Corps up at Nieuport. Haig then, probably in July, to commence his attacks to re-occupy Ostend and Zeebrugge.

Sir Henry saw Nivelle next day for the first time since the Paris discussions and found him in fairly good spirits, although very critical of the attitude of Painlevé and Pétain on that occasion. He had just sent his Chief of Staff up to Paris to see the President and to find out what Pétain's powers now really were. Wilson gave Nivelle a copy of Haig's proposed plan of operations, and he notes

---

* Although the Prime Minister and the C.I.G.S. were in agreement as to the expediency of withdrawing a large part of the British troops from Macedonia, they were by no means in agreement as to what was to be done with the troops withdrawn. The C.I.G.S. was anxious to move them to France, realizing that the issue of the great struggle must be decided on the Western Front, The Prime Minister desired to transfer them to Egypt, or, failing that, to almost any theatre other than the Western Front.

in his diary:

> I asked him if he meant to show it to Pétain, and he said, certainly not; that he would draw out his plans to suit Haig and then, when he and Haig had agreed to their common plan, he would inform Pétain. I wonder how Pétain will take this.

Briand, it appeared, had made his way down to Compiègne to see Nivelle, and Sir Henry came to the conclusion that Nivelle, backed by Briand, was going to assert himself as Commander-in-Chief against the combination of Pétain and Painlevé. The French had captured Craonne on the 5th — a somewhat notable success, which afforded convincing evidence that their offensive was still progressing even if it was now taking the form of a "Somme" rather than of a "Verdun." Wilson wrote in his diary on May 9:

> I saw Nivelle this morning and had a long talk. He was bitter against the politicians, but especially Painlevé. He did not mention Pétain, nor did I. He said that the politicians were circulating the most awful tales of his losses, putting them at 80,000 dead and 200,000 wounded, whereas they were 17,000 dead and 57,000 wounded, and said that he had given the true figures to a lot of journalists yesterday.* He said that Barrère, the French Ambassador in Rome, had written to the Government to say that all this upset in the higher commands here, and all the wild stories of French losses, were doing a great deal of harm in Italy and ought to be stopped at once. Our King had wired Poincaré his congratulations about Craonne, and this time copies of the King's wire had been sent to Nivelle.
>
> Then we discussed Haig's proposals made in the letter 1 gave Nivelle on the 7th. Nivelle was getting out a paper in answer, and seemed to think that he could meet Haig in every way except about our relieving the XXXVIth Corps at Nieuport, which Paris was against although Nivelle was in favour. I asked him if he had sent Haig's paper up to Paris, but he said no. I wrote Haig this news.

A misunderstanding had occurred with reference to the

---

* The French total losses from April to July amounted to 279,000, but the whole of these were not, of course, encountered in the great Nivelle offensive.

question of Nieuport just at this time. G.H.Q. was under the impression that the French had, on the occasion of the Paris discussions of May 4 and 5, agreed to the B.E.F. taking over the line at present held by the French XXXVIth Corps there. Nivelle, however, assured Wilson that this was not the case and that the French Government were opposed to the proposal.* Wilson wrote in his diary:

> So here is another of those cursed misunderstandings, due probably to my not being present. Haig and Robertson think that they understand the French — they don't and they never will. Then they don't take me into their confidence at these conferences.

But that evening, at 7.45, an urgent telephone message arrived from Nivelle's aide-de-camp, begging Wilson to go up at once to Paris to see Nivelle at his flat, as he was going to be removed from his command on the day following. Of what passed, Wilson wrote in the diary; —

> After a bit of dinner Duncannon and I started in the Vauxhall and got to Paris 10.30. Found the Ritz full, so went to the Continental. Then on to see Nivelle at his flat, 35 Rue de la Tour, Passy. He was out when we arrived, but came in in five minutes. Nivelle told me that Painlevé had summoned him at 5.30 p.m. and had practically ordered him to resign his C. in C.-ship. This Nivelle flatly refused to do, so a War Committee has been summoned for 9 o'clock to-morrow to put Nivelle out.
>
> I could not quite make out from Nivelle whether he thought that the vote to-morrow would go against him; but I think so. Nor was he quite sure who was going to succeed him, but he thought Pétain, I telephoned from Nivelle's flat to try and catch Pétain, but he had gone to bed so I will see him to-morrow. Nivelle wondered what I could do to help, but I was very guarded and said there were points I wished to talk over with Pétain, and that neither our War Office, nor Haig, nor our Ambassador could possibly move in the matter. Nivelle is quite dear in his mind that Pétain will not agree to take over our line up to

* The French, ever since the First Battle of Ypres, had shown a marked disinclination to assent to the front between Ypres and the sea being occupied by British and Belgians alone.

Havrincourt, nor allow us to take over Nieuport, and in addition he was quite clear that French offensives would die down to very small affairs.

Esher, from the Crillon, rang me up at Nivelle's and I told him to wait for me at the Continental, where I got back to at midnight, and he, Duncannon and I had a long talk in my bedroom. I told him I thought of tackling Pétain to-morrow about the change of C. in G, which is no concern of ours unless it changed the plan, and of asking him if I might say that no change would be carried out. Esher was against my saying anything about change of C. in C., and asked if I could not come at it in some other way. After a long discussion it was agreed that I should go to Pétain and tell him that I had come up to Paris to see Nivelle and find out what all this business about Claville was* as G.H.Q. had telephoned urgently about it to-night, and also to ask him for a decision about Nieuport, and that, as I could not get a clear answer about either matter, I had come on to him (Pétain). Both matters required an answer without delay, seeing that I had given Nivelle Haig's paper on the 7th and that, the broad arrangements having been agreed to *en principe* in Paris last Friday (4th), the C. in C. had been ordered to work out the details, and that to-morrow is the 11th.

Next day Wilson wrote:

Duncannon telephoned to Plain's office at 9 a.m. to ask for an interview. The reply was that Pétain had very important meetings all the morning, but could see me at 2 p.m.

Lunch with Esher at the Ritz. Esher says that this morning's War Committee only decided to define Pétain' s duties and did not discuss Nivelle's position. He said a thing that is very true, i.e. that at no period of this war have we been more out of touch with the Allies, and at no period have attacks and strategical plans been less co-ordinated.

Then at 2.30 I went to see Pétain. He was quite civil, but not expansive. He said that changes in the High Command were going to take place to-morrow, and that from to-morrow he (Pétain) was the man responsible for plans, and that he would send Haig an answer to his letter of the 5th on Monday next. Pétain is against relief of our

---

* A change of Staff in connexion with railways, which was causing G.H.Q, inconvenience.

divisions by French divisions even up to the Omignon River. This, I pointed out, was only a matter of one division and had already been settled for Monday next, to which, after argument, he reluctantly agreed. He is opposed to Haig's plans of attack. He is opposed to our taking over from the XXXVIth Corps at Nieuport. He is opposed to big attacks, and favours small fronts and great depths, and some successes which, he says, the Army and France require. He is very pessimistic about his effectives of 6, 7, or 8,000 to the divisions, and says that if he can't get men from America or Poland he must reduce the number of his divisions. He is going to consider whether we should not take over line from the French, instead of the French from us, as he thinks that we do not hold nearly enough front. He told me that the Belgians would not allow us to go to Nieuport, and that Poincaré had thrown up his arms in dismay at the proposal, and that Poincaré and the King of the Belgians were agreed on this point.

I summed up by telling Pétain some home truths. I said that the two Prime Ministers, the two C. in C.s, Robertson and he, had come to certain clear decisions *en principe* on May 3 and 4, and that the two C. in C.s were to work out the details without further interference. Now, on the 11th, he admitted that there was absolutely no one in France who could answer Haig's letter of the 5th. But he told me that to-morrow (12th) he would have the power; and at the same moment he told me that he disagreed to every single thing agreed to on the 3rd and 4th, and did not propose to carry these decisions out. I pointed out that we could not carry on like this, nor could we beat the Boches by such procedure, and therefore it was essential that Haig and he should meet as soon as possible. He then agreed to Monday, saying he would telephone to Haig on Sunday, fixing the hour, and he asked me to be present. And then I left.

After seeing Esher, I motored down here to Compiègne and telephoned the substance of all this to Kiggell, and wired it to Robertson. Then, at 10.30, 1 got a telephone from Esher to say that Nivelle was to remain C. in C. At 10.3 5 Weygand telephoned to say that, at a meeting in the morning, it was practically settled that Pétain should come down here and that Foch should succeed him in Paris. Lastly, at 10.45, Nivelle rang me up from his house asking me to come and see him; he told me that he was going to remain C. in C., and he laughed like a boy when I told him that Pétain had said he was taking supreme command to-morrow. Of course, all this is most unsatisfactory and can't last.

Next day (12th), to test whether Pétain was in command or not

Wilson telephoned to him to ask at what hour he would like to meet Haig on the Monday. The reply came that Pétain was not going to Amiens at all; so Wilson saw. Nivelle later in the day and told him of this message to Pétain, and of the answer. Then, when Sir Henry asked Nivelle about sending some reply to Haig's letter of the 5th, the latter answered that the reply was drafted and that it was going to be sent that afternoon to Pétain to see — a procedure which by no means pleased Wilson. He wrote to Robertson on the subject; and he also sent a copy of his letter to Sir Douglas to see, entering in his diary:

> As I said in my letter, it all comes to this. Haig sends proposals to Nivelle. On this, Nivelle puts up his complementary proposals, which he submits for approval to Pétain and Painlevé. In effect, therefore, Haig submits his proposals for approval to Pétain. This is exactly the situation which I foresaw when I went to London, and against which I warned both Lloyd George and Robertson time after time; it is a state of affairs which I would not tolerate for a moment. I said in my letter to Robertson that I hoped to see daylight in a few days. Till then we must go carefully, as Nivelle may assert himself, or go away, or anything may happen.
>
> At 8 p.m. to-night I got the following dictated telephone message from Pétain: *L'entrevue projetée aura lieu mardi le 15me mai entre le maréchal Haig et le général Nivelle. Le général Pétain n'assistera pas, la question à traiter n'étant pas de son ressort. Le général Wilson voudra bien en consequence s'entendre directement avec le général Nivelle.** Duncannon ran down to Nivelle's to know if he had arranged this; and later, 9.30, I telephoned to Kigg, and he said that Haig knew nothing about it. So it looks as if Pétain was trying on some sort of "senior officer" game.
>
> Esher telephoned to-night that Painlevé had been seen with Caillaux, and Paris was all agog, and Painlevé was at 1,000 to 1, and Pétain was mixed up, and Nivelle had become a god! So like Paris.

On communicating with Pétain' s office next day, the 13th, it

---

* "The planned meeting between Marshal Haig and General Nivelle will take place on Tuesday 15th May. General Pétain will not attend, the question to be treated not being within his competence. General Wilson will therefore agree directly with General Nivelle."

was ascertained that the "*aura lieu*"* in Pétain's message was not supposed to convey an order. When shown the message by Wilson, Nivelle was highly indignant until reassured by learning that the point had already been referred to Paris, and that the apparently objectionable words in reality meant nothing. Sir Henry had a long talk with Foch in the afternoon. It transpired at this interview that Foch had been sent for by Painlevé at 10 o'clock on the night of the 10th (the night when Wilson had dashed up to Paris and had seen Nivelle at the flat), and had been with the War Minister for two hours. During these Foch had been offered the post of Chief of Staff, vice Pétain, who was to become Commander-in-Chief on the 12th. Foch had agreed, but had at the same time said that he must have it in writing, and on the nth it had been definitely settled that Pétain was to go to Compiègne next day, Foch taking his place in Paris. But all this had been reversed that very same evening, and Foch had heard nothing more since. Foch also declared that at the conferences on the 3rd and 4th absolutely nothing had been settled, nothing had been defined, and no objectives had been decided upon. Each side, according to him, had hidden its hand from the other, and his view was that the business must therefore be begun all over again so that a common plan should be concerted. "The whole thing is a pie," Wilson wrote in his diary, and he went on:

> I saw Sidney after lunch, on his return from Haig's, and it is quite clear that Haig is annoyed with me and does not want my opinion on the state of affairs; for I gave Sidney a copy of the letter that I wrote to Robertson yesterday, but Haig said that he did not want to hear what I said. So to-night I have written to Haig to say that, for some reason which I cannot guess, I seem to have lost his confidence since April 24, and, if I had, I would go back to England, I also wrote to Kigg and said that, if Haig wanted me at his meeting with Nivelle on Tuesday he could say so, otherwise I would not go.

The immediate effect of this letter was that Sir Henry got next morning a telephone message from the Field-Marshal's advanced head-quarters, asking him to come and stay the night and then to

---

* "Will take place."

accompany the Field-Marshal to the conference at Amiens next day. So he drove over with Duncannon in the afternoon, receiving while on the road a reply to his letter of the previous evening. The reply is epitomized in Wilson's diary as "Haig tells me not to be stupid and to come and stay the night." While they were at dinner that evening a message arrived to the effect that the discussions in Paris had not settled Nivelle's position, but that, as nearly all Nivelle's and Haig's proposals with regard to reliefs and so forth had been vetoed, the French Commander-in-Chief could now see no advantage in his proceeding to Amiens to meet the Field-Marshal as had been intended. On his getting back to G.H.Q. news reached him from Compiègne to the effect that a definite decision had at last been arrived at with regard to the French Higher Command. Under this Pétain was to become Commander-in-Chief vice Nivelle, Foch was to become Chief of the Staff, and Nivelle was to be removed to the command of a Group of Armies. After returning to Compiègne on May 16 Sir Henry wrote in his diary:

> I saw Nivelle, who, I think, in his heart is very glad to be off. He told me of his meeting yesterday with Poincaré and Ribot, when Poincaré frankly told him he was against the change, but it must be done or the Ribot Ministry would fall! So, to save Painlevé and the Cabinet, it was necessary for Nivelle to be removed. Nivelle gave me a charming photograph of himself, with a still more charming inscription.

While Wilson's personal relations with Nivelle had from the outset been particularly friendly, he had at no time felt any great confidence in the ambitious plan of campaign which had been prepared and had been actually put in execution by the now-superseded French Commander-in-Chief. He none the less felt a keen sympathy for the fallen soldier in view of the attitude that had, even before the great offensive had been launched, been adopted by the Ribot-Painlevé Government, as also by French Army Group Commanders who were cast for prominent parts in the operations. The plan which had been gladly accepted by the Briand Government and had been so enthusiastically welcomed by the British Prime Minister, had in fact, as Sir Henry fully recognized, never been given a fair chance of succeeding except by

Sir Douglas and the B.E.F.; and their share in the proceedings had in any case only been a secondary one.

After having parted with Nivelle on the evening of May 16, Wilson received a telephone message from G.H.Q. to the effect that the new French Commander-in-Chief, Pétain, had asked Haig to meet him at Amiens some day soon, and that, before consenting to do so, the Field-Marshal wished to learn from Sir Henry whether Pétain was in a position to treat on equal terms. This Wilson promised to find out, and he saw Pétain (who had just taken over from Nivelle) on the following day. Asked the question, Pétain at once explained that he was invested with full powers, and he went on to indicate what he proposed to say when he should meet the Field-Marshal.

He began by announcing that he wished to discuss the question of the length of line held by the B.E.F., which, taking the British and the French effectives into account, he considered to be much too short. "Surely you don't propose to wrangle about this instead of going on with the offensive," Wilson, according to his diary, remonstrated. Pétain said that he did not; but he explained that he would like to thrash the question out and have it equitably settled, and that he was prepared to meet Haig as to relieving the B.E.F. up to the Omignon stream and handing over Nieuport, but that he could not consent to relieving the B.E.F. up to Havrincourt as G.H.Q. had requested. "He is very gloomy about Russia, and, to my horror, said that if Russia ran out then we might have to make peace. To which I indignantly said 'Never' " — so Sir Henry concludes his account of this interview with the new French Commander-in-Chief. He was, however, able to telephone to Montreuil that Pétain had full powers to treat, and he went that afternoon to see Foch, who, he found, was opposed to the Allies quitting Salonika, holding that if enemy submarines were established at the Piraeus and about the Greek islands maritime communications with Egypt would be cut. Foch was also anxious to know whether our Admiralty insisted upon Ostend and Zeebrugge being taken.

This was a point that Wilson appreciated, for he was beginning to doubt whether, in view of the likelihood that the Germans would bring strong forces across from the Eastern Front consequent on

Général de Division R. Nivelle

the rapid deterioration in Russian belligerent potentialities that was setting in, Haig's plan for recovering the Belgian littoral would prove feasible.

Wilson met the Field-Marshal next day at Amiens, before Pétain's arrival there; and the formal meeting afterwards took place. It passed off very well, the two Commanders-in-Chief coming to an agreement, after Haig had read out a wire from Robertson to the effect that the British Government would only agree to the B.E.F. continuing the offensive on the distinct understanding that the French used all available troops to help. Sir Henry, however, considered Pétain's proposals as to French subsidiary offensives to be vague; and on this being represented to the French Commander-in-Chief Pétain promised to put what he contemplated undertaking into writing. Wilson, it should here be mentioned, was now disposed to take a very long view in respect to the political and strategical aspects of the struggle as a whole. This is indicated by an entry which appears in his diary on May 19, after he had driven over from Compiègne to Soissons with his brother-in-law. Colonel Price-Davies, to visit Huguet, whom they had found "in the depths of despair."

> I soon roused him by showing him that, if the Boche succeeded in knocking out the Russians, I did not see how he could keep the Austrians in the ring, since they had gone to war against Serbia and Russia; nor the Turks, because they had gone to war to save Constantinople, which was no longer threatened if Russia fell down; nor Bulgarians, since they had gone to war to pinch Macedonia from the Serbs and to save Sofia from the Russians. So, as Italy likewise might fall out, we should be in the following condition: England and France, plus America, versus Germany, plus submarines. If the submarine won, we were beaten. If we mastered the submarine, Germany was beaten.

Next day he wrote in the diary:

> I had a very interesting interview with Pétain. I wanted to impress upon him the danger of allowing Haig to carry out his big offensive towards Ostend, an operation which will cost him very heavy losses over many months' fighting, if the French are not going to do

> likewise. I told him that he must either do the same as Haig, or else must state now, in the clearest and most emphatic manner, that he is not going to do so, and specify what it is that he is going to do. This was all new to him. But he agreed and thanked me for speaking so openly.
>
> He said that he could not attack like Haig, because he was already holding far too long a line and we were holding far too short a line; that he entirely disagreed with any idea of distant objectives; that he was opposed to the Somme procedure; that he would make three or four small attacks for strictly limited objectives, and when the objectives were reached fighting would cease. In short, he made it clear that all I had written in my Memorandum to the War Cabinet on April 30 was absolutely correct. This pleased me. He told me that, in his opinion, Haig's attack towards Ostend was certain to fail, and that his effort to disengage Ostend and Zeebrugge was a hopeless one. So I replied that this made it all the more imperative for him to make his position and his plans absolutely clear. He entirely agreed, and said that he would not sign the letter he was writing to Haig until he had shown it to me, and I had approved.
>
> Before dinner he sent me up a *directive* which he was sending out to his Army Group Commanders, and which embodies all that I have said and what I wrote in my Memorandum of April 30, as to Pétain's mind m regard to small attacks on small fronts for limited objectives. I feel rather proud of my forecast.

Wilson now learnt that there was some idea of Lord Esher becoming Ambassador in Paris, and of himself in that case going to the French capital as military adviser. There did not, however, seem to be grounds for supposing that the idea emanated from the War Cabinet in London. Lord Derby was in Paris, and a big dinner took place at which Sir Henry was present; but he could not discover what exactly was likely to occur at the Embassy, although a change of some kind appeared to be in prospect. He, however, learnt the truth next day from Lord Esher. The proposal was that the Embassy should be split in two. There were to be two Ambassadors or Ministers; Esher was to be one, watching the military work, with Wilson as chief expert adviser; Colonel Le Roy Lewis, the Military Attaché, was to be the other, charged with looking after civil matters. Derby, primed with this project, had gone back to England and was to press it upon Lloyd George. So

Wilson wrote in his diary:

> Yes. On the whole, I think I like this scheme, and we discussed it for an hour walking round the Tuileries Gardens. I told him again — what I was saying last night to Derby — that if Russia falls down, then we must start a dry-rot in the Bodies' alliances, by detaching Bulgaria by offering her Salonika, thus making a virtue of necessity since we are going anyhow; or by detaching Turkey by offering her Baghdad, or money, or both; or by detaching Austria by offering her Rumania, or the Albanian coast, or something, and thus reduce the coming war to one of England and France plus America, versus Germany plus submarines.

Two days later, May 23, there is the entry; —

> I read this morning Pdtam's answer to Haig's paper given to Pétain on the 18th at Amiens. This answer apparently went to Haig yesterday by De Vallières, although Pétain had promised to show it to me before he sent it. I object strongly to this answer, both to its tone and to its substance. In tone it smacks a little of a superior writing to an inferior, and in substance it absolutely ignores Haig's suggestions as to dates for French offensives, and he only has two attacks (Craonne and Verdun) instead of the three (Craonne, Rheims and Verdun) which he promised at the Amiens Conference. Finally, he fixes the last (Verdun) attack for July 15th, without consulting Haig who had asked for August 1. Then he comes to a dead stop, never mentioning any further operations during the autumn, nor even that he cannot carry any out.
>
> Of course, this is quite hopeless. There is no sign of combined operations at all. No mention of the Boches being able to bring over divisions from Russia, no subordination of the French plan to ours, nothing but Haig's plan and Pétain's plan, which happen to come off in the same year.

The Italians had commenced their great offensive of the year on the previous day and an important victory had been won, 9,000 prisoners and several guns being captured. But, if Wilson was pleased to hear the good news from that quarter, he was becoming more and more apprehensive of what the lack of co-ordination between the Allies in general, and particularly the lack of co-ordination between the French and British, might lead to, now that Russia was becoming less and less of a factor on which any reliance could be placed. He wrote in his diary on the 25th:

> I read this morning the *Procés Verbal* of the Paris meeting on the 3rd and 4th, and I have never read a more amazing document. Not one single member of the Conference had come there with a clear mind as to what was good, what was practical, what was possible, with the result that not one single thing was settled either as to the Western Front, or Salonika, or Greece. An amazing state of affairs after nearly three years of war, that our Chiefs, civil and military, should assemble and discuss all these subjects as though they had cropped up since breakfast and been finished. We certainly don't deserve to win, nor won't if we go on like this. It's terrifying. Then I read again Pétain's answer to Haig, and the more I study it the more unsatisfactory and incomplete I find it.

On his visiting G.H.Q. on the 26th the Field-Marshal agreed with him that Pétain's letter had been by no means satisfactory, and of their conversation he wrote in his diary:

> I pointed out strongly that in my opinion the French would help very little in August, September and October, just when we were fighting our hardest, and that we must get out of them what their minimum and maximum effort would be, as otherwise it might have a deplorable effect on the two countries and on the two armies. At the present moment Haig does not see farther than his attack on the Messines Ridge,
>
> I also asked him what he thought of Pétain sending his letters via the French Mission, at Montreuil, instead of through me. He thought that Pétain was right. This does not make my place any easier, as one of the reasons for which I was sent out here was to see that rude or curt or unintelligible letters were not written. He read me a letter he had just received from Robertson. It said that Haig must not expect many men as drafts, because of agriculture, shipping and strikes, which were very bad, and said that the state of the country was very bad, and that there was already talk of Workmen and Soldiers Committees as in Russia.

Two days later Wilson had an interview with Pétain and pointed out to the French Commander-in-Chief that his answer to

Haig had stopped short in the middle of July. Pétain explained that the diminution of his effectives would prevent his carrying out attacks after that date, or soon after it, and that he in consequence could not promise anything more. “Very well, then say so,” was Wilson’s rejoinder. Then, with Duncannon, he went up to Paris. Our Guards Bands had been brought over by Sir F. Lloyd, and Wilson had heard them play at a concert two or three days earlier. This day they were performing in the Tuileries Gardens, and he wrote in his diary:

> Enormous crowds, and we were just in time. We took part in a sort of circular march round the gardens, walking with Frankie Lloyd between the band of the Republican Guard and our bands, Frankie with some woman I did not know and I with Lady Pembroke; the Lord, having got mixed up with a baby, lost the walk. So French.

They were in the President’s box at the Opera Comique that night, and were greeted on arrival with “God save the King”; the Guards Bands then played on the stage and sang “Tipperary.” Next day (May 29) Wilson and Duncannon lunched with Esher; Churchill, who was in Paris, was also of the party. According to the diary:

> Winston in great form, and evidently in high favour with Lloyd George. He is very keen (and rightly so) that the Navy should fight instead of doing nothing, and he has great plans for bringing on fights by laying mine-fields close up against enemy ports. Then, his great plan for the moment is to delay any attempt at a decision on this front till the Americans come over — say 12 to 18 months. He developed this at length, using both good and silly arguments, all mixed up.
>
> I was not prepared to agree to a postponement until I knew more about our own man-power, and about what our shipping will allow us to transport from America next year. But I said that I would, in any case, disagree to a postponement, unless our diplomacy succeeded in detaching both Bulgaria and Turkey, and if possible Austria. This detachment of Turkey was difficult for Winston, and he never quite swallowed it. And yet, as I told him, he will have to "in spite of the fact that the Right Hon. Winston Churchill and the Right Hon. Sir Edward Grey had promised Constantinople to Russia.” To this Winston, rather nettled, answered “Yes, and we took care to get the

> signatures of the Right Hon. Mr. Asquith and the Right Hon. Bonar Law," Which is an interesting fact.
>
> Winston was very keen to get half the Salonika garrison on flat-bottomed boats, to be used for sudden descents here and there. There is the germ of a good idea in this, but I besought him not to come out of Salonika without bargaining about it. So we had a great lunch and a long talk, and it always amuses me to talk to Winston.

Sir Henry had a further discussion with Churchill on the 30th, and wrote of this in the diary that he had

> earnestly begged him not to bother his head about mechanical details as to the best form of tank, and rubbish of that sort, but to fix his eyes on a long view, and on the vital issues, and he would find that, owing to Russian action, or inaction, the old war was over. We were starting a new war, and it was essential that we should realize this and should cut out (diplomatically) Turkey and Bulgaria, which we could do, and which at one blow would destroy all the German Eastern dream.

Churchill incidentally mentioned during their talk that Lloyd George was bent on the capture of Jerusalem "because the Welsh people would like it."

General Foch had been over to London with Ribot and Painlevé for a conference, and on his return he gave Wilson an unfavourable account of the attitude of the British representatives at this gathering. The upshot of the discussions had been that only a small portion of the force under General Milne in Macedonia was to be withdrawn, and that some of Milne's troops were to participate in the operations now contemplated by Sarrail for coercing King Constantine. After hearing all about this conference, Wilson elaborated his ideas as to the imperative necessity of detaching Turkey and Bulgaria from the Central Powers by diplomatic means; these appear to have impressed Foch, and Sir Henry wrote in the diary:

> Then Foch began to talk about myself. He said that Pétain was opposed to my remaining at G.Q.G. as he looked on me as a Nivellite, though in truth, as Foch said, all that had happened was that I had accurately diagnosed Pétain's mind and character. Foch rather astonished me by telling me that he had spoken of this to Robertson,

who had said that no doubt Haig would fit me out with a Corps; to which Foch had replied, "Is that your idea of making use of Wilson?"

Sir Henry had already felt doubtful as to remaining on in his present position, and he now decided that he must leave Compiègne, But it occurred to him that Duncannon had better go to London and explain matters to Milner before any definite action was taken as regards resigning. So Duncannon left for England next day (June 1) taking with him letters from Wilson for Milner and for Robertson.

Of a further meeting with Foch, which took place on the 2nd, Wilson wrote in his diary:

> He wanted to know who it was who wanted Haig to go on "a duck's march through the inundations to Ostend and Zeebrugge." He thinks the whole thing futile, fantastic, and dangerous, and I confess I agree, and always have. Haig always seems to think that when he has got to Roullers and Thorout he has solved the question. So Foch is entirely opposed to this enterprise, Jellicoe notwithstanding.
>
> Then I discussed my own position here, and Foch was quite dear that I ought to go and ask for a command. He said that Pétain did not particularly want me, and that with Nivelle's departure all had changed, It is abundantly clear that 1 cannot stop here. But when I told Foch that Haig wanted me to go to Paris, I found that he was against that also.
>
> So he does not want me — and he really is my friend.

On June 4, the entry occurs; —

> I saw this morning the notes made at the conference the day before yesterday, when Debeney went up to see Haig. They are disquieting. The French attack for June 10 is cancelled, because the *moral* of the French troops is such that it cannot be earned out. Debeney said that the fighting at Moronvillicrs and the Chemin des Dames had used up a very large number of divisions, that in consequence of this all leave had had to be stopped, and that the men wanted leave and must have it. He hoped that the attack for July (Verdun) would still be carried out, but said that the Marshal must understand that no infantry attack would take place anywhere for at least a month. Gun and aeroplane attacks, yes; but infantry attacks,

no. This endorses and underlines all that 1 have been saying for the last month or more, and I think, and hope, that it will finally dispose of Haig's idea of taking Ostend and Zeebrugge. For if the French continue to feel the strain like this, we must expect them to ask us to take over some more line.

After lunch I came up to Paris and went to see Marshal Joffre by appointment. He was so glad to see me — both hands — and was looking very well indeed. He told me a great deal about his American trip; of the tremendous reception he got — so much greater than Viviani that it was "embarrassing." He is quite sure that the Americans mean business, and that they will help us, first with money, then in shipping, then in food, and last — 12 to 18 months — in men. The American C. in C. and his head-quarters staff come over next week, and the first divisions in a month, followed by the other six or seven Regular divisions as soon as they can. He (Joffre) is going to mother them and arrange for their training at the schools.

Then we spoke of the condition of the French Army, and Joffre is under no illusions about the loss of *moral*, which he puts down to the changes in command and to the active interference of the politicians. He thinks that it is a very grave state of affairs, which requires most anxious watching and attention. I asked him what he thought of my plan of buying out Turkey and Bulgaria, and he was delighted with the idea, provided Serbia was safeguarded.

Duncannon had reported from across the Channel that Milner was anxious for Wilson to pay a visit to London, so Sir Henry made the necessary arrangements and he proceeded on the 5th to Haig's temporary head-quarters at Blondecques, where he spent the night on the way through. He found the Field-Marshal very confident that he was about to gain an important success on the occasion of his offensive immediately south of Ypres, which was timed to start on the 7th. The British Commander-in-Chief, moreover, showed himself less disconcerted than Sir Henry had expected at the inability of the French to second his efforts in Flanders by attacks elsewhere. That Pétain had good grounds for the attitude that he had taken up with regard to such efforts was becoming manifest. The information reaching Wilson from various quarters as to the condition of the French Army had latterly been most disquieting, even if he was disposed to discount some of the stories that were told as to mutiny and insubordination being rife.

He did not like the gaiety noticeable in Paris; he was anxious about the coal question, which was giving trouble; and he was becoming apprehensive as to the spirit of the French nation at large. He remained in London from June 6 to the 11th, and, while there, he did his best to impress upon members of the War Cabinet and upon Robertson the vital importance of gaining a striking success somewhere — either in the field or else as a result of robust diplomacy — owing to the state of despondency that existed amongst the French. Robertson told him that Lloyd George wanted Jerusalem to be taken, and that the Prime Minister also proposed that assistance should be sent to the Italians to take Trieste, but that neither of these projects found favour at the War Office. Wilson wrote in the diary:

> I told him with all the strength I could that it will be impossible to keep the French in this war for another 12 or 18 months, waiting for America, without a victory of some sort, and that if we can't get a military success, then we must get a diplomatic success. We must. I certainly impressed him with the absolute necessity for this to be done. He is going over to France to see Foch, and I told him he would find the ground prepared, and that Foch and he must work together on the two Governments, and at once.

Wilson repeated the same thing to Lloyd George — while he was at Downing Street news came in of the success of General Plumer's attack on the Messines-Wytschaete ridge, although only the first report — and the Prime Minister was so much impressed that he directed Sir Henry to see Milner and Carson, to tell them the same thing, and to attend the War Cabinet on the following day. Besides seeing Milner and Carson, Wilson also managed to have interviews with Lord Curzon and Lord Robert Cecil, in each case driving his contention home; and of the meeting of the War Cabinet on the 8th, he wrote in his diary:

> I went through it all again, and I have no doubt now that I have focused the whole case for them in a way that has never yet been done, and they are impressed with the necessity of action. Milner and Smuts whispered to me that they must see me before I went back.

While in London Sir Henry heard reports to the effect that Painlevé was accusing him of having tried to take charge of the French Government, and of having insisted on Pétain being removed from the position of Commander-in-Chief. So he wrote in the diary:

> When I go and say good-bye to him in a few days' time, I shall remind him of the night that he dined with me, when I told him. specifically that it mattered not in the least to us who was C. in C. provided always that plans were not changed, and when I told him that I was afraid the plans would be changed if Pétain came in. He swore that they would not; but, of course, they have been entirely altered.

On getting back to Compiègne with Duncarmon, Wilson found an early opportunity to call on Pétain and to announce his intention of leaving; but he asked that, before taking his departure finally, he might be allowed to go and see General de Castelnau who was commanding the Eastern Group of Armies, and to continue the trip on to the Vosges. To this request, Pétain readily assented. He therefore started with Duncannon on June 15 and, on the way to Chalons, they paid a visit to Huguet, and they also spent some time with General Gouraud. Next day they proceeded to Mirecourt, where de Castelnau had his head-quarters; Wilson had a long talk with his old friend after dinner, and this is entered in the diary:

> He is anxious about the future. He says that there is no doubt that the moral of the men is not good, that the two Russian brigades, who will now neither fight nor work, are doing great harm, that Painlevé is useless and dangerous and chiefly to blame for the present state of affairs. Nivelle offered to resign on April 6,[*] and Painlevé would not have it although all the generals were against Nivelle's plan. Next to Nivelle, he thought Lloyd George was most to blame, for having backed up Painlevé and Nivelle against his own people, and for not adhering to the Chantilly Conferences of November-December, 1916.
>
> He said that the constant changes in command were playing havoc, and he absolutely agreed with me that victories, military or

---

[*] *Vide* page 398.

diplomatic, must be obtained. He did not believe in anything better than Messines-Wytschaete being possible on this front, and that was not enough. He thought that deposing the Greek King was futile,* and told me that when he was down at Salonika last year he had reported that we ought to grab all we could, and then bargain with Bulgaria — which is exactly my thought. When I was saying good-bye to him, having told him that I was going to resign, which shocked him very much, he kissed me. I was very much touched.

They had a very interesting trip through the Vosges and on as far as to the Swiss frontier, receiving every civility from the various commanders along the front, and making themselves acquainted with the feeling of officers and of the people of the country, the results of their investigations being noted in a number of striking passages which appear in Wilson's diary — as, for instance:

All day, the Lord and I talked with no end of people of all sorts of rank, and always the same story. The fighting army (i.e. the younger men) are tired and depressed; the women are ditto; be careful.

Just the same story. Be careful, don't ask too much, and gain some successes. Always the same story.

I talked with Laguiche and his staff, with Boisveedy's staff, with infantry officers, with civilians — always the same story. Also Duncannon talking to everyone, finds the same thing.

Back to Wesserling to lunch with General Boyer. I had a long talk with him again, and with his Chief of Staff, and again I got exactly the same impressions. Some success must be obtained to keep the French in.

During these last few days spent in France Wilson had in fact noticed signs of depression on all sides, and he became more and more convinced that the country needed careful watching and that it required to be handled tactfully. He had an interview with Foch in Paris, who insisted that the B.E.F. must take over much more of

---

* King Constantine had abdicated on June 11 as a consequence o£ pressure brought by Sarrail.

the line as soon as its offensive should come to an end, so as to rest French troops. Sir Henry also went to see Joffre, whom he found likewise anxious with regard to the future, but hopeful that arrangements might prove practicable for accelerating the arrival of the Americans, and he wrote in his diary:

> And so I said good-bye to the old Marshal. I have been working now with him for 7 years and never had a cross word from him. Then I went to say good-bye to Painlevé by appointment at 5 o'clock, but as he did not send for me by 25 to 6, and as no orderly officer came to see me, or apologue, I walked out and told the messenger I could not wait any longer.

He wrote later in the evening:

> I dined alone with Foch and Madame Foch at their new flat, and after dinner had a long talk with Foch. He is desperately sorry that I am going. He is as anxious as I am about the outlook, and said again that we must relieve down to the Oise or even to Soissons, and that we must do it without bargaining if we don't want to create real trouble. He said that, if we did not do this, the present Government would treat with the Boches for a peace, as both the Army and France are tired out.
>
> In short, he is as clear as I am that France must be helped in every possible way, or she will not go through this next winter. He likes and admires Milner and thinks Lloyd George very quick. He is entirely opposed to a force going down to Italy to help the Italians to crush the Austrians, which he says Lloyd George wants to do.

Next day there is the note:

> I wrote to Painlevé saying I was sorry to have missed him yesterday, because I wanted to tell him that the stories he had circulated of my interference about Nivelle and Pétain were not true, as he would remember by my conversations with him on April 25 and May 3.

Before leaving Paris Sir Henry also saw Clemenceau, who expressed the opinion that there was nothing for it but to wait for the Americans and meanwhile not to lose men; he moreover added that he liked Pétain, just because he would not attack. "Wonderful for the old *Tigre* to say that," Wilson remarked in the diary.

Next day, June 26, brought the period of Wilson's service as Chief Liaison Officer at French G.Q.G. to an end, after it had lasted a little more than three months, and he bid Pétain good-bye. Pétain admitted to him at their -final interview that there had been great difficulties in the French Army, but added that the situation was improving and that it was only the politicians who were really dangerous.

About the Author

Charles Edward Callwell (1859-1928) was a renowned writer on military affairs, as well as a staff officer. Serving as the Director of Military Intelligence for the War Office for most of the Great War, he rose to the rank of Major-General before returning to journalism and writing in October 1918.

www.ingramcontent.com/pod-product-compliance
Lightning Source LLC
LaVergne TN
LVHW020039110826
845155LV00029B/560